# How to Grow Your Business on the Internet

"At last, a book about doing business on the Internet I can endorse wholeheartedly. If you're serious about putting your business or organization on the Internet, Emery's book **will cut months off your learning curve and steer you away from some expensive, easy-to-make mistakes.** Written in a clear style for the non-technical reader and full of practical advice, this is **a breakthrough book, easily worth ten times its cover price.**"
    Ken McCarthy, *Internet Gazette*/E-Media; ken@e-media.com

"Because of this show, I get sent literally every single book that's ever published about online computing, and I consider it part of my job to go through and evaluate each one. . . (This is) **by far the best book I've ever read about business on the Internet.**"
    Jaclyn Easton, Host, *Log On USA*

"Invest a couple of dollars in the **sound advice** which abounds in Vince Emery's *How to Grow Your Business on the Internet.* . . **an outstanding, no-nonsense guide** to help you determine which Internet services make sense for your business."
    Steve Kelley, *Online*

"Vince Emery's *How to Grow Your Business on the Internet* gives **tested, practical answers to business questions about the Internet**, from assessing the system's potentials for a particular business pursuit to using digital cash on the information superhighway. There are plenty of theories out there on how to use Internet services to advance business pursuits; **this is one of the few to provide practical applications.**"
    *Bookwatch*

"I had to write to tell you how fantastic your book is. I am in the startup phase of a new business, specializing in Web site design and programming, and Internet marketing and public relations. A personal copy of this book will be issued to each of my sales people on their first day on the job. They will then be tested on its contents during training. I consider it **the 'Bible' of real business facts relating to the Internet.** Thank you, thank you, thank you for writing **a book for business people rather than techies.**"
    Shari Peterson, The WEBster Group, St. Louis, Missouri

"You're the only one (out of the 12 other marketing Internet books I've read) that shows **a genuine expertise. Definitely the best book out there:** In my bibliography I rate it a 96."
Dan Dunne, Ph.D., Torrance, California

"Many congratulations on *How to Grow Your Business on the Internet.*"
Prof. Bob O'Keefe (creator of *Interesting Business Sites on the Web*)

"An excellent book! I especially appreciate your **coverage of secure transactions and digital cash**, a seemingly obvious subject that has been overlooked by every other Internet business book I have seen."
Mike Payson

"I have not yet finished your book but it has been **of immense value to me.** I cannot thank you enough! I am attempting to set up a Web server and it has been extremely useful. I really appreciated the Internet site references you included. Thanks again. Your book is OUTSTANDING!"
Tom Hartman

"What a delightful piece of work . . . I have reviewed a number of books on the Internet over the past few months. Your book is **by far one of the most resourceful publications that I have reviewed.**"
Ken Fews, Jr., Ken Fews World Enterprises, Costa Mesa, California

"I thought your new book was absolutely fabulous. I've read about ten books on the Internet and must say yours is **by far the most informative** to startup organizations like mine. As a business person, I really appreciated the case studies and marketing tips. **Thanks for jumpstarting my brain!**"
Jay Sharpe

```
Subject: Complaint Department
To: vince@emery.com
RE: HOW TO GROW YOUR BUSINESS ON THE INTERNET
Dear Mr. Emery:
I am very sorry to have to register this complaint about your book.  I was halfway through reading
it when I suddenly realized the book was such a valuable asset that I could no longer keep it in my
house.
I now keep the book at my bank in a safe deposit box.  Unfortunately, this means I can only access
the book during banking hours.  This is really frustrating because your book is the most fact-filled
and comprehensive source of doing business on the Internet I have been able to find (and believe me
I've been looking!)
Please do not write any more books as I only have a very small safe deposit box (besides the people
in my bank are starting to look at me suspiciously because of my frequent visits to the vault).

Yours in humor,
Dan Hayner

hayner@computek.net
```

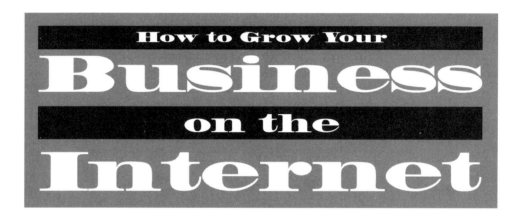

# How to Grow Your
# Business
# on the
# Internet

# Vince
# Emery

CORIOLIS GROUP BOOKS

*To my grandmother, Alice Emery, who I am always glad to see.*

*And to the memory of my late grandfather, Emmett Emery, who once observed that I love to read so much that if I were running out of a burning house and saw a newspaper, I'd stop to read it.*

*He was right.*

| | |
|---|---|
| **Publisher** | Keith Weiskamp |
| **Editor** | Ron Pronk |
| **Proofreader** | Diane Cook |
| **Interior Design** | Michelle Stroup |
| **Layout Production** | Michelle Stroup and Jenni Aloi |
| **Cover Photo** | The PhotoFile/Ed Cooper |

Library of Congress Cataloging-in-Publication Data

Emery, Vince
    How to Grow Your Business on the Internet/Vince Emery
        p.  cm.
    Includes Index
    ISBN 1-883577-29-2 : $24.99
Printed in the United States of America
10 9 8 7 6 5 4 3

# For All-in-One Internet Business Success Pack Users

If you obtained this book by purchasing the *All-in-One Internet Business Success Pack*, you'll find the Internet Business Success CD-ROM provided with this book. Included are many software programs and resources to help you set up and run your business on the Internet:

• Internet Business Test Drive—Lets you set up your own powerful virtual Web server

• Internet Phone software

• WebFX VRML plug-in for Netscape 2.0

• NetSeeker Internet Agent

• Web page design and creation tools

## Internet Business Test Drive

With this software you can set up your own business Web server for free for 60 days—a $300 value. All you need is a computer to access the Internet. No complicated software or expensive hardware is required! This is a great way to test out your Internet business without even glancing at your wallet.

Here's all you need to do to get up and running with your own Web site:

1.  Log on to the Internet.

2.  Start your Web browser and go to **http://www.coriolis.com/testdrive/**.

3.  Follow the step-by-step instructions.

Once you have set up your Test Drive site, you will be able to author your own Web pages, send and receive email, and manage an FTP site. Your Test Drive site will remain functional for 60 days, at which time, you will be given the opportunity to purchase a full I-Site Web presence package and have your Test Drive site transferred to a new site with your choice of domain names (www.yourcompany.com).

After you have set up your test drive site, you will also be able to use the EZ-Admin software provided on the CD-ROM to help you keep your site up to date. Essentially, this software allows you to maintain your site on your home computer, including Web, FTP, and email information, and the software will automatically keep all your files current.

## Internet Phone

Internet Phone is one of a new breed of software package that is revolutionizing the way we use computers and the Internet. Internet Phone allows you to place "telephone" calls to anyone else on the Web that has the same software. Even with a 14.4 Kbps modem you can have live, two-way conversations.

To use the software, all you need is a connection to the Internet, a sound card, and a microphone. Simply run the SETUP.EXE program in the \I_PHONE directory on the CD-ROM to get started.

## WebFX VRML Plug-In

You have probably heard about VRML and 3D Web pages for some time, but unless you have a T 1 connection and a powerful computer, you have probably never seen it for yourself. The WebFX plug-in from Paper Software inexpensively brings VRML technology to the masses by offering a reasonable trade-off between performance and speed that allows everyone to see what VRML is like.

The WebFX plug-in requires that you have the latest version of Netscape Navigator (currently 2.0). To install the plug-in, run the SETUP.EXE program in the \TOOLS\INTERNET\VRML\WEBFX directory. You may want to check the manufacturer's Web site to see if you have the latest version, or use NetSeeker to download it.

## NetSeeker

NetSeeker is an Internet agent that automates the process of downloading and upgrading software from the Internet. If you have ever gone searching for a certain file you need off of the Internet, you know that all the extra noise on the Net makes it difficult to find what you really need. NetSeeker solves this problem by giving you a list of the latest and greatest software available on the Web. NetSeeker will then download the files you want and begin the setup program for you automatically. To learn more about NetSeeker, read NETSEEK.DOC (MS Word) or NETSEEK.PDF (Adobe Acrobat) located in in the \NETSEEK directory.

## Web Page Publishing and Design Tools

You'll find numerous tools and resources to help you design professional-quality Web pages for your business, including the latest HTML editors, artwork, templates, and much, much more. All of this software was hand-picked by The Coriolis Group staff to give you the very best the Internet has to offer for your business.

## For More Information

Detailed information about the contents of the CD-ROM are located in the CONTENTS.DOC file (MS Word) or the CONTENT.PDF file (Adobe Acrobat). If you want to install Acrobat, run ACROREAD.EXE, which is located in the \HELPERS\ACROREAD directory on the CD-ROM.

You can also get more information about the *All-in-One Internet Business Success Pack* by pointing your Web browser to: **http://www.coriolis.com/bizkit/**.

# Table of Contents

# Chapter 4
# How to Get Up to Speed Quickly        71

# Chapter 5
# Twelve Reasons Internet Projects Fail—
# and How to Make Sure Yours Don't  111

# Chapter 6
# How to Avoid Break-Ins and Fraud:
## The Basics                                     143

# Chapter 7
# Firewalls, Encryption, Credit Cards, and Digital Cash 161

# Chapter 8
# Email: Quickest Bang for Your Buck 199

# Chapter 9
# Watch out! Internet Marketing is a Different Animal! 243

# Chapter 10
# How to Generate Internet Publicity
## that Works

**267**

# Chapter 11
# How to Advertise on the Internet

**301**

## Chapter 12

## How to Generate Vital Strategic Information With Internet Marketing Research    337

## Chapter 13

## 140 Cheap or Free Business Resources on the Internet    357

# Chapter 14
# Eleven Money-Making Businesses
# You Can Start Today                                    391

# Chapter 15
# The Internet, Logistics,
# and EDI                                                       405

# Introduction

"*The Internet is like the gold rush. Most people are picking up nuggets. We're looking for a vein.*"
Byron Abels-Smit, Aspen Media

Thousands of businesses have failed at doing business on the Internet, but thousands of others succeeded. This book provides immediately usable information, techniques, and tools for your business to exploit Internet opportunities so your business can be one of the winners. It explains what works on the Internet, what doesn't work, and why. Its goal is to provide realistic advice you can use right now.

First and foremost, this book is for *businesspeople*. It focuses on business insights, and gives true stories of the successes and mistakes of actual companies. These examples were chosen to help you put ideas into practice in your own business.

You will get more out of the guidelines laid out here if you have at least a little hands-on experience on the Internet yourself. However, if you haven't, not to worry—most topics have brief descriptions to clue you in. There is some technical material in this book, but only what you might need when making a *business* decision.

Opportunities for businesses on the Internet are very different from those faced by individual people. Most people want to *take* information from the Internet. Businesses must *provide* information as well. The actions of a private individual on the Net have consequences mostly for that individual. The actions of a businessperson impact many others: co-workers, employees, stockholders, suppliers, and customers.

## How to put this expandable book to work

Expandable book? Yes, the book you hold in your hand is only part of *How to Grow Your Business on the Internet*. There are dozens more pages of information, case histories, interviews and resources than what is on these printed pages. Point your World Wide Web browser to **http://www.emery.com** for a free information resource for readers of this book. This Internet site gives you 24-hour access to additional techniques, late-breaking news, and (sigh) corrections.

This book itself has a lot of information and covers a lot of topics. If you're like most Internet businesspeople, you'll be more interested in some subjects than others. You probably don't need to read everything here. The first chapter is written for everyone. It will give you ideas of what you can do on the Net, and answers an important question for all Internet businesses: What kinds of businesses are most successful on the Internet—and why?

For the rest of the book, read the chapters and sections that most appeal to you. The chapters are structured so you can read them all in order or skip to the topics that you most need. Don't miss Chapter 4, "How to Get up to Speed Quickly," even if you're an Internet vet. You'll find resources in this chapter that are useful for any businessperson connected to the Net.

## Short on time?

Few businesspeople can spare enough time to read this whole book. If that's you, don't despair. Most chapters in this book can stand on their own to a certain degree. In fact, if you do read this book from cover to cover, you'll notice a few redundancies when subjects are covered more than once from different angles.

What chapter should you read if you have time for only one? Jump directly to Chapter 5, "Twelve Reasons Internet Projects Fail—and How to Make Sure Yours Don't." This chapter is drawn from the experiences—good and bad—of dozens of companies on the Net. It busts common myths about Internet business, and concludes with a tested set of ten steps every successful project should take. If you're really in a hurry, skip over the subsection on legal matters.

The second most essential chapter will depend on your needs, but look at Chapter 6 if you get a chance: "How to Prevent Break-Ins and Fraud."

## Question: What *is* this Internet thing, anyhow?

If you ask a technical person what the Internet actually is, he'll rattle off a barrage of acronyms and computer arcana until your eyeballs glaze and you enter a deep trance. Then he'll ask you for a raise.

For a less mind-numbing experience, the *Wall Street Journal* described the Internet in a Nov. 14, 1994 story as "...the chain of networks that is generally the easiest and cheapest way for businesses to communicate electronically with the outside world."

The *Journal* definition describes the Internet from a *corporation's* point of view. I prefer to look at the Internet from the point of view of a nontechnical *user*.

### Answer: The Internet lets you scoop up anything in the world and bring it back to your desktop.

From a user's point of view, that's what the Internet is. You can reach anywhere without paying extra for distance. You can search for and find an incredible variety of things. ("Anything" is a slight exaggeration. But not much of one.) And you can bring what you find back to your desktop, whether your desk is at work or at home.

Note that this definition does not even *mention* computers or technology. The computers aren't important. They are only the tools. What's important is the end result: the power to reach and deliver stuff from all over the world.

## How to read Internet addresses

All through this book you are going to see boldface strands of type like this one from a few paragraphs back: **http://www.emery.com**. These are Internet addresses, and here's a quick explanation, in case you're new to the Internet.

You need a phone number when you call somebody. To send a letter, you need a street address. To reach a person or a place on the Internet, you need an Internet address. Internet addresses look like meaningless nonsense at first, but there is actually a simple logic to them.

First, any address with an "@" sign in it is an Internet email address. My address is **vince@emery.com**. When I give my email address over the phone, I pronounce it as "vince at emery dot com." Periods in email addresses are always called "dot."

The **vince** part of an email address is called a *user name*. It is always on the left, before the "@" symbol. After the "@" can come several words or abbreviations, each separated by a dot. The user name is the "who" of an email address, and the rest of the address is the "where." For instance, a message to **fred@marketing.emery.com** goes to someone in the marketing department of a company or organization called "emery," which is a "commercial" organization, or **.com**. This last term is called a *top-level domain*, and the company name part of the address is called a *domain name*, or just *domain*. Instead of a **.com** domain, my business could chose an address ending in **.us** to indicate that it is an American company; other domain names, like **.uk** or **.jp**, indicate the addresses are from other countries (the United Kingdom and Japan, in this case).

That address **http://www.emery.com**, you may notice, has no "@" symbol. It is a different kind of Internet address. It is formatted in a standard way called a *URL*, which stands for Uniform Resource Locator, a fancy name for Internet address. In the URL format, the first part of the address tells what Internet tool you use to reach the address.

To reach an Internet FTP site, the address would be something like **ftp://emery.com/main**, which tells you to use FTP to go to the address **emery.com** and look in a file or directory called **main**. Anything separated from the end of an Internet address with slashes is either a file or a directory.

In the same way, **telnet://emery.com** would take you to my Telnet site, if I had one. And, illogically, any URL starting with **http://** will take you to a World Wide Web site.

## Thanks for the memories

Fortunately for you, dear reader, as you read this book you will be able to pick up tips and tricks without the grief that other people paid to learn them. Businesspeople from dozens of companies made room in their overcrowded Daytimers for talks with me. They shared what they learned from doing business on the Net. This book would be much thinner if you only had my brain to pick.

Their memories provide some of the most valuable techniques in this book, and I'm grateful. This book also received good input from Deanna McHugh of the University of California at San Francisco and Prof. William Murray of the University of San Francisco. Keith "Free Stuff" Weiskamp and Ron Pronk of Coriolis Group Books both contributed more than their share.

The core of Internet background around which everything else in this book is wrapped comes from a group of hardworking people in Silicon Valley at Computer Literacy Bookshops. Very few companies can say that they have used the Internet at the heart of their business for years, but Computer Literacy has been a pioneer in commerce on the Internet. The practical know-how of CLBers certainly helped me during my time working with the company, and tips from many of them made their way into this book, especially from Penny Wendland, webmaster Robert Mudry (who has his own book out now), Kathleen Pearl, emailing list sage and gourmet Cherrie Chiu, and Tracy Russ, who writes email like poetry.

But most of all, I have to say that this book wouldn't be here if not for Dan Doernberg and Rachel Unkefer, the two Internet-savvy businesspeople who brought me into Computer Literacy in the first place. Thank you both very much.

# Business at the Speed of Light

*"If you don't know where you're goin', you sure won't get there."*
Satchel Paige

Across America and around the world, companies great and small are making money on the Internet:

- Last year, Digital Equipment Corporation sold $20 million of products and services over the Internet.

- Sun Microsystems sells more than $1 million over the Internet each month. In addition, Sun used the Internet to cut customer support costs by more than $1 million per year while *increasing* customer satisfaction.

- Retailer The Corner Store saw that its online sales grew faster and were more profitable than sales in its physical store. At the end of 1992, it closed the "physical" store so it could focus only on sales via the Internet and CompuServe. Its 1993 sales grew to $1 million, and in 1994 The Corner Store rang up more than $2 million in sales, all online.

- In 1992, J.P. Morgan & Co. linked to the Internet to more quickly solve computer and software problems. Technical difficulties that took days to repair are now fixed in hours or just minutes. Next, a few Morgan business strategists tapped the Internet to get economic predictions and financial research from around the world. Soon, thousands of employees used the Internet for research. Now Morgan itself provides economic and investment data over the Internet. And it even recruits new hires on the Net.

## Fast payback

For many businesses, the Internet provides the fastest payback (and highest net present value) of any investment they can make. Companies have used the Internet to *make* and *save* millions. Through the Internet, companies are able to get their hands on a staggering array of up-to-the-minute information, at speeds not possible only two years ago.

Maybe your business is just thinking about the Internet. Or maybe your business is already on the Internet and wants new ways to use it. Either way, you're joining tens of thousands of companies all over the world. Every kind of business is moving onto the Internet, from information giants Dow Jones and Encyclopedia Britannica to one-person startups running a used PC on a kitchen table.

## Avoiding booby traps

Some companies have made careful, cost-effective steps onto the Internet and earned surprisingly large and fast rewards. Other companies were ripped off by con artists, bought technology that didn't work, were invaded by hackers, or built Internet sites that yielded few results.

I wrote this book to help you avoid those booby traps and cultivate procedures that succeed. This book is not for computer wizards. It is for businesspeople.

You'll find hundreds of sales-building, cost-cutting techniques here, and you can put them to work right now. They were tested the hard way—by the real-world Internet experiences of other businesspeople and myself. You can profit from the lessons we learned. As Mark Twain said, "Learn from the mistakes of others. You can never live long enough to make them all yourself."

I have stuck my finger in the Internet fire and been burned, and I have played a hand in Internet projects that triumphed. I had the great fortune to be marketing manager of Computer Literacy Bookshops Inc., which pioneered in Internet business a year and a half before I came aboard. I have learned from my own mistakes with Computer Literacy and additional companies, from the advice of other businesspeople on the Internet, and from technical specialists. Now I want to share with you what I know about growing a business on the Internet.

## A little background

Working at Computer Literacy Bookshops exposed me to all the literature on the Internet. There are more than 300 books on the subject. Reviewing them, I saw a need for a book different from those that came before.

There were hundreds of Internet books, but only seven Internet *business* books at that time. Some were useless. Some had merit. They were written by technical authors, by academics, or by lawyers. What I wanted was an Internet business book written by a *businessperson*. When I complained about this situation to publisher Keith Weiskamp, he responded by persuading me to write such a book.

This is the first book written by a manager who worked for a company that successfully engaged in business on the Internet. My goal is to present a business view: speak your language, share similar problems, and explain what works and what doesn't work.

Here, you won't find page after page of Unix commands (valueless for an executive using Windows, Mac, or OS/2). Instead of technical tips on how to *use* Internet tools, this book shows you how to *apply* them. Rather than memorize commands, I want to show you how to make and save money. (If you need "how to use" information, Chapter 4 tells you where to find it.)

 I've tried to warn you about what can go wrong. If you manage an Internet project and want to end up with a pat on your back instead of egg on your face, keep your eye out for the bony fellow on the left. Throughout this book, he warns you of serious hazards—show-stoppers—that can kill your Internet business. He's named Mr. Doom.

I won't claim that this book is the last word on this subject. Internet business is still in diapers. Considering what it has accomplished while teething, you can imagine what marvels it will do in the strength of maturity. I hope you use this book as a starting point and improve on the principles I lay out.

For your own Internet efforts, the first thing to do is to take a look at what other businesses have done. By reviewing others' activities, you can generate ideas for your own company.

## The Internet can help you market and sell

Marketing and sales on the Internet have received more press coverage than any other networked business activities. There are two reasons for this. First, reporters find it easier to write about marketing topics than to investigate the operational aspects of business, which are more complex. Secondly, businesses love to publicize sales success stories, and there have been many.

In 1994, several companies made sales over the Internet in excess of one million dollars. Hundreds of companies generated lesser, but significant, amounts. Most sales were made to businesses, educational institutions, and government agencies.

Sales to individual consumers were healthy mostly in seven categories. In order of importance, they were: computer-related products and services, books, music, home electronics, videos, travel, and event tickets. Other niches yielded profits for individual companies, such as Hot Hot Hot, which sells only bottled hot sauce.

In 1995, the main barrier to increased consumer sales was shattered. Several companies released software to securely process credit card transactions over the Internet. At the same time, new software for Electronic Data Interchange made it easier and less expensive to use the Internet to sell to businesses.

Marketing departments pull many companies onto the Internet. This has been especially true since 1992, when something called the *World Wide Web* first appeared. The Internet used to be just walls of type and boring file lists. The World Wide Web adds color pictures and point-and-click navigation, which made it easier and faster to get around. Now there are more than 60,000 World Wide Web "pages" on the Internet.

More than 10,000 companies have opened virtual storefronts using the World Wide Web (see Figure 1.1). They range from wildly successful to so-so to flops that closed and left the Internet. Other companies use the Web as a promotional tool, providing information and advertising material on the company and its offerings. Some are dry and serious. Others are entertaining and humorous, especially Web offerings by CBS (David Letterman's lists), the Fox Network (*The Simpsons*), and Paramount Pictures (*Star Trek*).

The Internet is marketing heaven. It's dirt cheap compared with other media—a lower cost-per-impression than flyers. Response is instant. Reach is world-wide. Visitors to Internet sites leave a trail of statistics that marketers

**Figure 1.1** *The World Wide Web adds color pictures and graphics to the Internet. This is the virtual storefront of the Internet Shopping Network, a subsidiary of the Home Shopping Network. Because its overhead is lower than a physical storefront or a printed catalog, the Internet Shopping Network sells at lower prices than traditional consumer venues.*

can apply to increase response. Many businesses on the Internet use it mostly for marketing activities.

Companies use the Internet to distribute electronic mass mailings to customers and prospects. The expense for an electronic mailing list is small, the amount of work is minimal, and 1,000 or more of your best prospects can receive a personal electronic mail message from you in a few hours. You can write an electronic mail press release and send it to a list of reporters. Most large printed publications are on the Internet, so email is the fastest way to reach them.

The Internet itself is host to hundreds of electronic publications. They provide more publicity opportunities for your business. These electronic newsletters and magazines attract large readerships without print versions. The NCSA "What's New Page" attracts 3,200,000 accesses per month. Several special-interest electronic publications have readerships of more than 100,000. Electronic publications that your customers and prospects read make excellent targets for your publicity. And you can start a publication of your own.

Many companies, especially high-tech firms, use the Internet for customer support, customer service, and customer retention programs. The programs that succeed all have one ingredient in common: customers who are *already* on the Internet in large numbers.

The Internet is a useful tool for marketing research. Usage statistics from your company's site can generate valuable information. Vast quantities of private and government business and demographic data are available on the Net. Companies research prospects, customers, and potential new markets. Because the Internet is such a fast delivery medium, and because it is inexpensive, it is an ideal way to conduct marketing surveys, and specialized software products make this easier.

## The Internet as a management tool

Management has been defined as consisting of five actions: planning, directing (leadership), staffing, organizing, and controlling. All management tasks require gathering, evaluating, and distributing information.

The Internet is most helpful in gathering and distributing management information. Managers dragged kicking and screaming onto the Net never leave once they discover how well it helps them keep tabs on their business, and how it empowers them to spread their views.

This flow of information occurs both within a networked organization, and between the company and the outside world. Companies that make extensive use of the Internet see their world expand. It is easy to cross countries' borders, and there are no "long-distance charges" on the Internet. Companies with international aspirations move quickly. Companies without international plans soon make them.

When interviewing companies for this book, again and again I heard from companies that didn't expect international customers or suppliers but now find overseas activities to be a big part of their business. They type locally, act globally.

The tool that makes this possible is electronic mail, called email for short. Even in businesses where senior managers don't use email themselves, the closer contact with customers, suppliers, and employees generates valuable feedback not possible in other ways.

Additional benefits are yielded when your company has remote locations (which the Internet can link) or staff members who spend time on the road. With email and other Internet tools, anything you can do at the computer on your desk, you can do on the road.

It is even more important to closely link employees who telecommute. They risk becoming isolated and "out of the loop." Wire your telecommuters to your company via the Internet to keep in touch with them and to keep them in touch with you.

Special note must be given to the resources on the Net for financial and accounting managers. Accounting associations worldwide have built resources to rapidly spread new changes in accounting regulations and government tax policies. Some governments accept filing of tax forms electronically. If your company is larger than a "mom & pop" firm, your controller and CFO will appreciate entry to the large and rapidly-growing body of Internet financial and accounting resources.

## The Internet can help you with logistics

I already mentioned J.P. Morgan & Co.'s success in dramatically improving support from its computer and software vendors. Better support is one of the most common benefits of linking to the Internet. Every high-tech company from IBM on down offers support, bug fixes, and software upgrades on the Internet. There are tens of thousands of free computer programs on the Internet, for every brand of computer. Several companies claim that free software from the Internet has by itself paid for their Internet connection.

In addition, more than 800 computer-related discussion groups on the Internet let users ask each other questions. They are wonderful places to evaluate technical products before you buy them. Purchasers can question people who actually use the products under consideration—and receive uncensored answers. This is a much more straightforward way to find the good and bad points of, say, an accounting software program, than asking a sales representative who is paid to tell you only the sunny side. "Bugs? No! Our software never has bugs." Sure, buddy.

Advice from Internet discussion groups holds for other purchases as well, and can be a help to your purchasing department. There are discussions of security devices (**alt.locksmithing**), trucks, and autos. The quantity of discussion groups for products that aren't computer-related is not large—about four dozen—but it is growing.

Your purchasers, however, will be more interested in the National Association for Purchasing Management resources. They'll also like sending RFQs and purchase orders electronically through the Internet, without having to pay through the nose to join a proprietary network.

Until recently, the expense of using a proprietary network kept all but the largest companies from using Electronic Data Interchange, called EDI for short. EDI lets companies electronically exchange inventory, purchasing, billing, and shipping information. EDI used to require a mainframe or a minicomputer and 8 to 18 months of work by a dedicated project team. Efforts by an organization called CommerceNet and new software products let companies do EDI on a PC now, linked to the Internet.

The ultimate logistics boon, though, is for companies that not only sell their products online, but actually *deliver* their products over the Internet. I have had books, graphic art, games, and newsletters delivered directly to my computer. More than 200 software companies actually deliver their software programs over the Internet, including documentation. Not every company can do this, but it's great for those that can.

## The Internet can help your R&D

The Internet was originally a network for research. Today, it still excels at its original purpose. The Net delivers thousands of databases and archives of research data on everything: plastics, explosives, geology, medicine, vehicles, food preparation, electric power, chemistry, manufacturing techniques, even specifications for the ideal baby diaper.

Specialist discussion groups cover more than 200 areas of R&D, and electronic mailing lists are devoted to hundreds more. More than 2,000 research journals maintain back issues on the Internet. Researchers perform automated searches of articles and abstracts, finding information in minutes that would otherwise take days of digging in a library. Software archives provide tens of thousands of usable programs.

# Is the Internet right for your company?

The Internet brings many benefits to businesses, but it is not every company's cup of tea. Here are some questions to help you decide if you should hook up your company to the Net.

The Internet has been oversold. Many businesses opened elaborate Internet sites when they would have been better off just sticking to email or not even getting on the Internet in the first place. Many have left the Net, poorer but wiser. Some want to leave but are trapped because shyster cybermall operators conned them into one-year contracts. Take a careful look before you plunge into a full-blown Internet operation. You can reduce your risks and start small by sticking to "Netlurking and publicity," the first stage of the five-level plan in chapter 9 on page 258.

## 1. Who and where are your customers and prospects?

Who on the Internet would use your product or service, and in what ways? If your customers are on the Internet, then your company should be there.

*Do you sell to colleges and universities?* Almost all North American, European, and Australian institutes of higher education are on the Internet, as well as many in Asia, some in South America, and a few hundred in Africa. Whether you want students, professors, administrators, or maintenance supervisors, if they are at college they probably have an Internet address.

*Do you sell to government agencies?* In many countries (especially English-speaking ones), the Internet is a fast and economical way to reach government buyers.

*Do you sell to other businesses?* Your chances of finding business customers and prospects depend on what *kind* of businesses buy your products. You won't reach a heck of a lot of vegetarian restaurants on the Net. On the other hand, if you sell to technical companies, Internet avoidance is sure death. Besides high tech, other industries with high and growing Net participation are: the entertainment industry, publishing (books, magazines, and newspapers), booksellers, accounting firms, investment firms, petroleum-related industries, utility companies, and travel-related businesses.

If you sell to businesses, it matters *who* buys your products. For instance, more publicists are on the Net than janitors. People in technical positions are most likely to be on the Internet, which is why software and computer items are the best-selling products on the Net. Recruitment and personnel managers are often on the Internet due to the large number of job banks and recruiting resources. Accounting, financial, and investment people are a fast-growing Internet group, as are purchasing managers and buyers. You are also likely to meet sales reps, and marketing, customer service, advertising, and publicity types. An increasing number of Internet resources deal with cargo, transportation, and freight, so look for growth among shipping managers.

*Do you sell directly to consumers?* Several surveys show that most Internet users are young, well-educated males with above-average incomes. North American users are as likely to be married as single, but Europeans are mostly single. The fastest-growing demographic group on the Internet is women—also young, affluent, and well-educated. The mechanisms for advertising and publicity to Internet consumers are well-established, but the mechanisms for actually *making a sale* over the Internet have just fallen into place. It is cheap and easy to *promote* your product on the Net, but be aware that it takes a larger investment of time to *sell* online.

*Where are your prospects geographically?* For Internet marketing, two seemingly opposite trends show growth: geographic dispersement and local specialization. From the beginning, businesses on the Internet have attracted customers from remote places. If your customers are spread over a wide geographic area, it makes sense for you to apply the Internet to extend your current base and to serve distant clients inexpensively. On the other hand, an increasing number of Internet businesses succeed at focusing on a specific geographic area. Online sales of groceries have been profitable in several cities. Printers receive graphics files over the Internet and deliver finished printing. The common thread among these trends is customers who are geographically *fixed,* and who do *repeat business.*

*How do your customers buy?* There is a high correlation between customers who buy via postal mail and respond to printed advertisements, and those who buy or search for product information on the Internet. This holds true for both consumers and business customers. If you have customers who buy by mail, look more closely at the Net. This match does not carry over to other media. Those who buy via direct response television are unlikely Internet prospects. Payment method is another indicator. If your business does mostly-cash sales, the Internet may not be to your liking. Credit cards and billed accounts are the most popular collection methods on the Net.

## 2. *What kinds of products and services do you offer?*

My list of the types of organizations on the Internet and the description of Internet consumers gives you an idea of the types of offerings you can profitably market online. There have been successes—and failures—in many different product lines, but little research exists on Internet buying habits. Projecting how well your company will do on the Net is still a judgment call. You can make an informed judgment, but there are few clear-cut indicators.

The first detailed survey of Internet consumer buying habits was conducted in October and November of 1994. The University of Michigan Business School surveyed 3,522 World Wide Web users, predominantly in North America and Europe. Respondents were both men and women. They were asked what they had purchased on the Internet within the past six months.

Respondents used the Internet to *find information* about prospective purchases more often than they actually *purchased* online. The top category purchased was computer software, which 16 percent actually purchased on the Net. But two-thirds used the Internet to look up information before they purchased computer software.

The second-highest category was books: 14 percent of the respondents bought books over the Internet within the past six months. Another 46 percent used the Net to find information on books before purchasing.

The third-highest category was computer hardware, bought online by 13 percent of the respondents. An astonishing 70 percent of respondents looked for information about computer hardware.

*Other categories:*
- 11% bought music on the Net, and 35% looked for information about potential music purchases.
- 7% bought home electronics products on the Internet, and 36% looked for information.
- 5% bought videos, and 42% looked for information.
- 5% bought travel services, and 31% looked for travel information.
- 4% bought tickets to entertainment events (plays, concerts), and 20% looked for information on events.
- 3% bought casual clothing on the Net, and 5% looked for information. This is impressive, because very few places to buy clothing exist on the Internet.
- 2% bought other apparel, and 9% looked for information.
- 1% bought legal services, and 7% looked for information on legal services.
- 1% bought jewelry, and 4% looked for information. These were mostly women.
- 1% bought sunglasses, and 1% bought shoes.

If you'd like to look at detailed survey results, you'll find them at **http://www.umich.edu/~sgupta/survey3**.

People on the Internet are passionate about information. This is evident from the high percentage of people who purchased *information products* within the past six months (software, books, music, videos). If your business deals in information products or computer-related products, take a closer look at marketing on the Internet.

## 3. Can you apply the Internet to improve your operations or to cut costs?

I spoke with a manufacturer of custom-built robot submersibles, who was considering an Internet connection. The company is located in northern California, and at the time was working on a remote-controlled craft with a video camera, searchlight, and robot arm that would swim against the current up a 4 1/2-mile water pipeline in the Middle East. The company has customers all over world, and a sales agent in Brazil. The week before, an engineer had to come to the office in the middle of the night to send an emergency software fix to a customer in Sweden via modem. Normally it sends software bug fixes by Federal Express.

On the Internet, this company could store software fixes on an FTP site. Customers could download software whenever they wished, and the company would pay no long-distance phone charges for modem calls—and no Federal Express charges. It could save on phone and fax costs by sending email to its sales agent and its customers. Instead of sending bids, proposals, and specifications via fax or courier, it could email them. Its design staff could save money and time by using the Net for research. (One engineer was already using the Internet for research at home after work.)

These are the kind of savings opportunities to find in your own business. Email is cheaper than postal mail, faxes, or phone calls, and is faster than a courier service. How much would you save if you cut fax, phone, and courier bills by 20 percent? The Internet can reduce fax costs another way: You can email your outgoing faxes from your computer to a fax machine closer to your destination, reducing phone toll charges.

Ask your technical staff how much you would save if you could use the Internet to receive customer support from software and computer vendors. How much would you save downloading free software programs? Ask your marketing people how much you could save by sending and receiving graphics files over the Net, by using email for publicity mailings, and by using the Internet for marketing research. See if online forms and Internet customer support would reduce your 800 number costs. If your company sends out standardized marketing materials to customers, see if you would save printing and postage costs by making electronic versions available. Ask your purchasing staff if sending electronic RFQs and purchase orders would generate any savings. Check with your controller to see if there is any advantage to filing government forms electronically.

Sometimes cost savings pay for a company's Internet connection. Most often not. But cost and work savings do contribute, and are worth considering when you decide whether to connect to the Internet.

## 4. Will your competitors beat you if you don't?

Who are your competitors on the Internet? How do your competitors sell offerings that are similar to yours? What are their strengths and weaknesses?

If you see one of your competitors on the Internet, monitor its site every week or two. If a competitor adds new features, it may be on to a good thing. You won't want to be left out.

## 5. Can you afford the expense and the work?

I've read a lot of baloney about how it costs companies at least $15,000 or even $20,000 to get on the Internet. Rubbish! Sure, giant corporations spend hundreds of thousands of dollars on their Internet sites, but I've known many companies that spent $1,000 or even $500. I even know of one company with a sophisticated Internet site that put it up for free.

What will it cost your business? It depends. That subject is so big it would need an entire chapter to explain. In fact, that's what the next chapter does.

# Who runs the Internet?

Some people glibly say that no one runs the Internet, but that is not true. No one *owns* the Internet. Each company on the Internet owns its network, and the links between the company and the Internet are owned by the phone companies and access providers.

But to find who *governs* the Internet, you need to look in different places, because different functions are coordinated by different international organizations.

The most prominent organization is the Internet Society. Vinton Cerf, former president of the Internet Society, described its role: "The Internet Society does not operate any of the thousands of networks that make up the Internet, but it assists service providers by providing information to prospective users and involves product developers and research in the evolution of Internet standards. Corporate and individual, professional support for this organization is widespread and international."

An important part of the Internet Society, the Internet Architecture Board, is a beehive of research groups, working groups, and task forces. The Architecture Board organizes management, engineering, and design issues, paying close attention to TCP/IP and other protocols. Two of its subsidiary task forces are IRTF (Internet Research Task Force), dealing with R&D for future growth, and IETF (Internet Engineering Task Force), which handles technical issues and everyday operational aspects.

Other organizations have responsibilities within individual countries or for groups of countries, such as RIPE (Réseaux IP Européens), which coordinates internetworking in Europe.

# What Do I Need and How Much Will It Cost?

*"A computer does not substitute for judgment any more than a pencil substitutes for literacy. But writing without a pencil is no particular advantage."*

Robert McNamara

Imagine Jill the business manager asking Joe the Internet consultant how much it will cost to get her business up and running. Their conversation might sound something like this:

**Jill Business:** "So, I saw those nuns on TV surf the Net. What would it cost to get my company on the Internet?"
**Joe Internet:** "That depends. What does your company want to do on the Net?"
**Jill Business:** "I'm not really sure. What kinds of things can we do?"
**Joe Internet:** "That depends. How much do you want to spend?"

This circular conversation could last for hours, and at the end would leave Jill Business frustrated and pretty much at the mercy of Joe Internet. The Internet is complex enough, new enough, and changing so fast that it is hard to make firm statements about costs and returns. Not impossible, just hard.

I'll try to break down your options and give you lists of choices so you can generate some figures for budgeting and estimating profits and losses. To make projections and to manage your Internet project, you will have to learn a little bit about the Internet's technical issues.

David Angell and Brent Heslop, in their book *The Internet Business Companion*, clearly explain the dangers of technical ignorance: "As a business decision-maker, you need to understand the issues, even if you plan to have others do the work for you. If you don't understand the tools and options of the Internet, then technical people (consultants, server services, service providers) will decide your business objectives, which can be costly. Keep the technical people where they belong—advising and applying your Internet business strategy, not deciding it."

## Building blocks

To understand the potential gains the Internet can bring to your business and the associated costs, you need to know the major tools of the Internet: email, the World Wide Web, Gopher, FTP, mailing lists, and newsgroups.

You probably already know about *email*, which is short for electronic mail. It's easier, faster, and cheaper to send someone an email message than it is to phone, fax, or send a postcard. Email is becoming the dominant way businesses communicate, and is the most-often-used facility of the Internet. The simplest form of Internet access is email only.

The *World Wide Web* is multimedia for the Internet. It provides an easy point-and-click way to find information from the tens of thousands of information sources on the Net. The Web displays information on computer screens in the form of pages of text and pictures, and can also include sound and even moving images. Businesses also use the World Wide Web to *collect* information. Web software can provide electronic forms into which a person can enter data, such as credit card information to make a purchase. To find information on the Web, a person needs software called a *Web browser*. You may have heard of the popular browsers Mosaic and Netscape. To provide information to the millions of people who use Web browsers, your business will need software called a *Web server*. The runaway successes of Web servers for some businesses are responsible for a good deal of the wild-eyed media coverage about the Internet.

---

*Important note: This concept of two kinds of software—a* server *to provide information and a* client *to read it—is at the center of all Internet services. It is important to understand this* client/server *concept, because every Internet management decision will revolve around clients and servers. Any Internet transaction has three parts: the client, which asks for information; the server, which provides the information; and the Internet itself, which passes the client's request to the server and carries the requested information back to the client.*

Client *means the client software, the actual program that an individual Internet user runs to use services on the Net. The client is what asks for data and reads it. To read an email message, for example, you must have email client software.*

Server *can have different meanings. It can be the server software program that provides data, the computer hardware where the server software lives, or it can refer to both the computer and its software program together.*

---

*There are dozens of different kinds of Internet clients and servers.*

- *FTP servers* can store and provide documents, graphics, software programs—anything that you can turn into a computer file. These servers are cheap to run, easy to set up, and provide a cost-effective way to make large amounts of information available. FTP, which stands for *File Transfer Protocol*, is not quite as easy to use as Web software, and lacks the glamor of graphical design on the Web.

- *Gopher servers* are almost as easy to set up as FTP servers, and can provide anything that an FTP server can, with two additional advantages: Gopher software presents a clear menu of choices, making it easier for non-technical people to use, and Gopher files are easier to find because they are searchable by subject and can be linked to World Wide Web pages and to other Gopher servers.
  Gopher is very efficient. You can run a Gopher server on an old 386 PC or a 68030 Macintosh and handle hundreds of simultaneous requests. Your Gopher server would present an inquirer with menus of as many items as you wish. Gopher servers present four kinds of items: 1) Text files; 2) So-called *binary files*, such as graphics, sound files, and software programs; 3) Links to other Internet resources; 4) Information that helps you find particular files. Businesses have created Gopher product catalogs.

- *Mailing list servers* are extremely valuable tools for businesses on the Net. There are obvious uses, such as sending many copies of one message to your customers or to your employees. But you can also use a mailing list server to create discussion lists, in which every message from one member of the list is copied and sent to all other members. And you can use a mailing list server to send out information in response to inquiries from people.

- *Newsgroups* conduct a different sort of discussion. A newsgroup is a series of messages covering the topic of that particular group. You can just read the messages, you can reply to any of them, or you can ask a question. Your reply or question will be seen and may be commented upon by all the readers of that particular group. Newsgroups are extremely valuable sources of information, and can also be effective as a means of communication. There are about thirteen thousand public newsgroups, called *Usenet*. Some individual groups have more than a hundred thousand regular subscribers. You can also create your own private newsgroups. Some people call newsgroups by another name, *netnews*. It means the same thing. You need *newsreader* software to read newsgroups.

There are dozens of additional Internet services your company can use or provide, everything from videoconferencing to network management tools. The six we have already described—email, the World Wide Web, FTP, Gopher, mailing lists and newsgroups—are the most useful for most businesses.

## Obvious costs and hidden reefs

Any time you're involved in a high-tech project, you know you must budget for hardware (like computers and cables) and software. For Internet projects, you must also add two more certain costs: payment for a telephone line or lines to connect with the Internet, and payment for your Internet access itself.

You may purchase both your line and your Internet access from your local telephone company. Or you may purchase the line from your phone company, but your Internet access from another company. This second company is called an *Internet access provider* or Internet service provider. The word "service" takes on many meanings when discussing the Internet, so to avoid confusion this book uses the term *Internet access provider* throughout. Keep in mind that an access provider and a service provider are the same thing.

The charges from your phone company and your access provider involve many factors: the speed of your connection, your distance from the telephone switching station, the types of services you use, and many more considerations. The subjects of your connection and your access provider are important enough for them to be discussed in detail in the next chapter. We will only touch on them here. When you calculate these expenses, be ready to do some number-crunching. Most of the Internet services you need are priced separately, so you will have to work out several alternative sets of costs.

In addition to those obvious costs—hardware, software, phone lines, access provider—there are other expenses that may not come to mind as quickly. Training, for instance, often costs more than hardware and software put together. Your technical people will need education in their new environment, and your end-users will need training as well.

The firm of Ernst & Young estimates that for networked systems, 20 percent of your cost will be buying hardware and software, and 80 percent of your cost will be maintenance and additional expenses. The biggest expenses in doing business on the Internet may not be your costs to deliver and present information, but the labor costs of interacting with your customers and updating your information. Don't forget to allow for end-user support and lost productivity during the ramp-up and learning stages. *Training and personnel costs will be more than half of your expenses.*

Since the Internet is a public network, you will need to invest more in security than you would for a standalone computer or a project restricted to your own internal network. Budget for sufficient security, including purchases, installation, and maintenance. If you can't afford security, don't implement your project until your next budget cycle. Or change the design of your Internet project to eliminate the dangers. *Security is extremely important on the Internet.* Failure to understand the significance of this statement can damage your business. For more information on security issues, see Chapters 6 and 7.

For many businesses, five factors have the biggest influences on Internet project costs:

1.  How many people within your company will use the Internet? You will need to buy client software for each of these people. You will need to train them. You may need to buy networking cards for all their computers. You may need to run cabling to their desks.

2.  How many Internet services (email, Web, Gopher, etc.) will you offer? The more services you offer, the more hardware you will have to buy, the more training your staff will need, the more time it will take

to update your information, and the more promotion you will need to tell your customers about these services. Whew!

3. What type of computer and operating system will you use? On a mainframe or midrange computer, your email software will cost less per user. If you use Unix, most of the software you need will be free, but you will invest more in system setup and ongoing system maintenance. If you use Windows 95, you may need more custom programming to meet your needs. Be aware of the tradeoffs between one platform and another.

4. What speed of connection will you buy? A faster connection means higher phone company charges, higher access provider fees, and more expensive hardware and maintenance. A 28.8 Kbps connection can cost less than $10 per month, but a 155 megabits-per-second ATM OC3 connection can cost more than $10,000 per month.

5. How much work will you do in-house and how much will you farm out? Your project will go faster with less bumps in the road if you buy instead of build whenever you can. This also makes costs much more predictable; you can hold an outside vendor to a fixed price agreement, but if your own programmers go way over budget, you have no recourse but to pay. Use the services offered by your Internet access provider as much as possible, and whenever possible hire consultants to reduce your own staff's workload.

To reduce the impact of uncertainties on your own staff, before you sign a purchase order with a vendor, you need to predict the quality of support you will receive. Make sure you understand the vendor's pricing structure, especially for licensing, upgrades, and support. Compatibility often affects support. Find out if the vendor's product will interoperate with other software, both software that you use in-house as well as the software your access provider uses. Find out how much training and implementation will cost.

Does your prospective vendor provide estimated or guaranteed turnaround times and response times for support? How does a tech support question escalate through the vendor's chain of command? How many support technicians does your vendor have? An extremely important issue with Internet support is that your vendor offers 24-hour support. The Internet runs 24 hours every day, and it is impossible to predict when you will need emergency support. If your Internet vendor agreements cover support issues adequately, it will do a great deal towards helping you meet your budget predictions.

When gathering information for an Internet project's budget, be on the lookout for four kinds of expenses: fixed, period, project, and transaction-based.

Assuming that all costs will be fixed will cause you grief. Some costs are fixed. You buy a cable, it costs a set amount. Other costs will be period-based, such as a monthly charge or annual software support agreement. Some will be project-based. Hire a consultant to do a project. When it's done, your expenses stop. The costs to watch out for will be transaction-based.

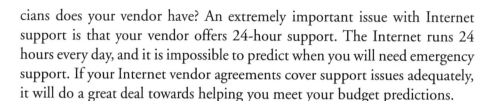 Transaction-based costs on an Internet project are less predictable than other types of costs. For example, if you pay a nine-cent fee for every credit card transaction you process, a surge in credit card orders will cause more nine-cent fees. This can get you into trouble if you pay your Internet access provider a transaction-based fee tied to the number of email messages that you send or receive, or to the number of hits your World Wide Web page generates. Mind you, some types of transaction-based fees are reasonable. But per-message charges for email penalize you when you succeed, and they discourage you from using mailing lists. Besides, per-message charges for email are a scam. It costs your access provider no more to send out 100 email messages than one. This practice not only cripples your ability to make accurate cost projections, it should be a red flag when you evaluate a possible provider.

The worst offender is emailMCI, which actually charges you *more* for each message as your volume goes up. Email is supposed to be cheaper than snail mail, but with emailMCI you can pay over $1.00 for each message! Super-highway robbery.

The same holds true for a Web page. If you put your home page on your provider's computer, you already pay for your page to be on the Net. It is reasonable to pay for the disk real estate you use, and an amount for maintenance. But your provider pays a flat monthly rate for its Internet access, and it is unreasonable for you to be charged per-hit. You should smile when someone reads your Web page, not cringe at the expense. When you budget for an Internet project, watch out for these traps.

By the way, if you're looking for an Internet access provider, you can find three different lists of them at **http://www.commerce.net/directories/products/ inet.prov.dir.html**, **http://www.netusa.net/ISP**, and **http://www.clarinet/iap**. The last two cover providers all over the world. You can search by country, and in the United States by telephone area code to find a provider in your area. To find an Internet consultant to help you with the technical or marketing aspects of your project, go to **http://www.commerce.net/directories/consultants/consultants.html** or send email to **consultants@commerce.net**.

If you are a retailer, another way to get Internet access is to rent space from a cybermall. There are Gopher malls, but most Internet malls are on the World Wide Web. One mall is Downtown Anywhere (**http://www.awa.com**) where customers can visit 40 merchants at one address. Merchants pay Downtown Anywhere 8 to 15 percent of sales (depending on services provided) or flat fees of $200 to $2,000 per month. Your site on a cybermall will thrive or die based on how well the mall promotes itself to draw traffic. Mall promoters will try to tie you to a 6-month contract. Go for three or fewer until the mall proves itself.

## Internet hardware considerations

The next few sections give you a sense for some of the hardware options available to you for connecting to the Internet. I say "sense" because Chapter 3 explores these options in more depth. If you find yourself scratching your head over some of the brief hardware descriptions I provide in this chapter, don't fret. I'll explain much more in the next chapter. The material here just provides you with an overview.

If you want to fetch material from the Net but don't want to provide any, your needs are pretty simple. You just need the one computer you work on, the fastest modem you can buy, and the fastest Net connection you can afford. Even if you want a fast ISDN connection, the same principles apply.

Life gets more complex when you want to *provide* information—such as your own World Wide Web home page—or if you want your Internet connection to reach several people on a Local Area Network (LAN) or any other kind of internal company network.

To provide information, you will need a computer to act as a server. A server is where your data lives. Your server can cost less than $100 or more than $100,000. Your server can be a computer of your own, or you can use a computer managed by your Internet access provider as your server. If you are new to the Internet, or if you are a Net veteran but have never created a server before, you will save time, money, and Tylenol by borrowing expertise from your access provider. You may even be able to rent space on one of your access provider's computers. Or your provider may require you to supply a computer to keep on the provider's premises, which the provider's technical staff will manage.

If you are linking people in your business to the Internet, you will need a different kind of server, a gateway server to process your company's inflow and outflow of information. Your provider may help you with your gateway, but you will probably want to run it on your own computer. Depending on your connection speed and what kind of network you use inside your company, you may want to get a router. A *router* is a box that takes Internet signals and feeds them to your LAN, and vice versa. Most routers cost between $1,500 and $6,000. If your needs are small enough, you can add router software to your server computer to avoid buying a separate hardware router.

If you have a high-speed line, you may need another $750 box called a *CSU/DSU*. It takes the signal from your leased phone line and coverts it so the router can read the signal. These will be the central parts of your Internet connection. You may need other hardware as well. Cables, perhaps, and a firewall to keep out hackers. You might need a costly box called a *switch* to translate between software formats. There are many Internet gadgets you can add—even beepers that bring email messages to you when you're away from your computer.

## Server computers

There's a lot of talk about how fast and big your server computer has to be to offer services on the Net. In real life, you don't neccesarily need a $6,000 high-powered Unix workstation. You might, but the computer is not what slows most sites down. The slowest thing in most Internet sites is the *connection* between a company and its Internet access provider. Even an old 386-based computer is faster than a 28.8 Kbps connection. (Kbps stands for kilobits-per-second, a measurement of network speed or *bandwidth*. A kilobit is 1,000 bits of data.)

Does your server need to support ten users concurrently? Two hundred? A thousand? Are your computers linked on a single LAN, or are they dispersed over many buildings, or even throughout different countries? Are visitors to your Internet site downloading huge files of graphics, or just text? Part of the need for speed depends on what Internet services your server supports. A World Wide Web server must be fast. An email server can be slow. For a Gopher server, you can get an old PC with a 14.4 Kbps modem and a PPP connection. In this last case, your costs are less than $1,000 plus labor.

To get an idea of how much computer power you need, take a look at what other businesses use:

- *Boardwatch* magazine runs its Web server on a 386SX 20 MHz PC "machine that lays on its side and we can't find the cover or most of the pieces for it." On *Boardwatch*'s 56 Kbps connection, the 386 server handles 7,000 hits/day from 1,000 visitors/day.

- Email orders come to Windows NT and OS/2 software seller The Corner Store on two 486/66 PCs, each with 530 Megabytes to 1.2 gigabytes of disk space and 16 megabytes of memory running Windows NT. The two PCs alternate on receiving email. "We have two SMTP servers. One picks up (the modem line) after three rings and one after four rings."

- Aspen Media uses a high-speed T1 line to provide a place for designers to display hundreds of huge graphics files. For its server,

> Aspen uses a $24,000 Silicon Graphics Indy 128 computer with 128 megabytes of memory and 1 gigabytes of disk with space to add 2 gigabytes more.

There is no one answer to the question of what kind of computer you need. The computer that handles your World Wide Web site will have a need for *multitasking*, to do several things at once. For example, a Web computer may need to track a person who makes several visits over a period of time, to build an itemized invoice for a purchase. The Web server sees the person as a series of unrelated requests that the server ties together. It does this with something called CGI (Common Gateway Interface). To store the information from these CGI transactions, you'd need at least 8 megabytes of memory—16 megabytes would be better. If you plan on 2,500 hits per day on a Unix machine, you'll need that memory to run two to four Unix processes at once. Of course, your Web server could also run under OS/2, Windows NT, Macintosh, AS/400, and many other operating systems.

## Modems and their ilk

To connect to the Internet, you will need either a fast modem, an ISDN connection and its required hardware, or a leased phone line, such as T1. I'll cover these options in depth in the next chapter. For now, I'd just like to make a few basic points.

First, you really don't want to do business on the Internet with anything slower than 28.8 Kbps speed. A 14.4 Kbps connection may be acceptable if you call into a Web site, or if you just want to provide email and/or FTP service, but it's unacceptable if your system is being accessed heavily by customers—especially if you provide a Web site. Even a 28.8 Kbps modem can support only a bare-bones, no-frills low-use Web site without clogging. (By the way, if you have a 28.8 Kbps modem on a PC, your system must have a serial card with a UART chip N16550AF to support this data transfer rate.)

If you provide a World Wide Web site on your own computer, you'll need at least an ISDN level. (ISDN stands for Integrated Services Digital Network; its basic level of service, called BRI, provides data transfer rates from 56 Kbps to 128 Kbps.) If you want ISDN speed, you'll need special hardware, and you'll find that different vendors offer widely different prices and services. For instance, Adtran, Inc. (404-945-3887) provides two ISDN "modems." Its ISU Express ISDN box handles both voice and data over one ISDN phone line— voice and data at 64 Kbps and data at 128 Kbps. It supports multiple connections, so you need only one phone line to handle voice, fax, and Internet. The ISU Express costs $900 for voice and data and $700 for data only. Adtran's ISU 2x64 model can cost more than $1,000 and supports up to two computers.

When shopping for other ISDN communication (essentially a modem, but technically not the same) products, look for one that has a built-in NT1 adapter (this device, as I'll explain in more depth in Chapter 3, provides the communication interface between your telephone line and your computer). You can purchase ISDN cards and modems from AccessWorks, Hayes, ISDN-Tek, Motorola and ZyXel as for as little as $300. Get one that doesn't take an external NT1, unless you want to connect other ISDN phones and gadgets to the same device.

Ascend Communications makes solid ISDN routers for home and small office use. IBM WaveRunner Digital Modem for ISDN is highly rated. This model includes built-in Windows and OS/2 support, and will only cost you about $850.

## *Connecting to your LAN*

Not too long ago, to connect your LAN to the Internet you would have had to set up your network so your users could run DOS/Windows for everyday tasks and switch over to unfamiliar Unix to use Internet applications.

Things are much easier now. The main personal computer and workstation operating systems—NetWare, OS/2, Mac's System 7.5, and the latest Microsoft Windows variations—come with built-in (or in the case of Windows for Workgroups, fairly easy to install) TCP/IP software. With TCP/IP already included, your computers can speak the *lingua franca* of the Internet.

There are also Internet client software packages available for every operating system, so there is no need for your users to switch back-and-forth between Unix and whatever your people normally use.

That's the good news. The bad news is that you will still need a way to move data between your LAN and the Internet. Even worse, it is extremely difficult to make some popular LAN software packages work well with the Internet, especially Microsoft Mail, Lotus Notes, and cc:Mail.

First, to direct incoming Internet traffic to your LAN computers, you will need either a gateway computer, a router, or a switch. If you have a small-bandwidth Internet connection (56 Kbps at the most), you can buy router software and install it on your LAN server computer. (This discussion pertains to performance issues only. At your own business, security concerns may rule out running router software on your computer.)

If your connection speed is ISDN (56 Kbps or higher), you will need to buy a small box called a *router*. This will set you back $1,200 to $7,000, depending on your Internet connection speed and the number of computers in your LAN.

If you have an ISDN Internet connection, there is a silver lining. Several companies make ISDN routers for LANs that cost less and are easier to run than a conventional router. Ascend Communications, for example, makes a well-regarded ISDN router for up to eight computers; it sells for $1,800.

## *Internet email considerations*

Setting up an Internet email server can be complicated because you have several decisions to make. Will you use Internet email software to connect to your company's computers, or will you link your existing email software to the Internet?

In other words, will you use mainframe or LAN email client software (Lotus cc:Mail, Microsoft Mail, Lotus Notes, QuickMail, OfficeVision, All-in-1, etc.), or do you want to go for "pure" Internet mail all the way to the desktop?

This is not a seat-of-your-pants decision. There is a lot involved here, so you may want to investigate your options thoroughly.

Because email on the Internet is such an important topic, I've devoted Chapters 8 to the subject. Here, I'd just like to get you started thinking about your options. Table 2.1 shows the pros and cons of the various email approaches available to you.

***Table 2.1*** *Your email options and how they compare.*

## Mainframe or LAN email software clients

**Pro**
- Many products available for most operating systems
- Use same operating system as other business applications
- Integrate with mail-enabled applications
- Feature-rich

**Con**
- Require application gateways or switches
  - –Expensive—gateways cost $2K to $5K apiece, and you need one for each brand of client; switches are hardware that handle many brands, but cost $20K to $300K
  - –Difficult to install
  - –Time-consuming to maintain
  - –Buggy (more on this in a bit)
- Users on the Net must have two addresses, one for the email client and one for the Internet
- Mainframe and LAN mail clients usually cost more than Internet email software

## Internet email software clients

**Pro**
- Many available for most operating systems
- Use same operating system as other business applications
- Integrate with Internet services
- Good software is available free or inexpensively
- Users need to learn only one email address
- No application gateways or switches required

**Con**
- Not integrated with mail-enabled applications
- Require user retraining if replacing existing email client

*Exceptions*

If you use Unix, Internet email is already integrated, so you don't need a gateway unless you use Lotus Notes.

If you use Macs, you have a much easier and cheaper gateway than other platforms: Mail*Link Remote, described below.

If you use OS/2 Warp, you need to know that the Internet Access Kit included provides email for one user, but can have problems when used on your LAN.

If you use Windows 95, its Universal In-Box simplifies the situation.

Table 2.1 provides you overall criteria for choosing which kind of mail client software you want your users to use to send and read email. If you are a one- or two-person business, your decision is easy: use an Internet email client. It's the simplest, easiest, and most functional solution. You can get good standalone Internet email client software for Windows, Unix, OS/2, Macs, and all other platforms.

With a larger business, you have more factors to consider. The resources of the Internet itself add significant value to Internet email clients, so you may want to replace LAN email software with Internet email software, unless it is cost-prohibitive or you are using Lotus Notes. Notes adds so many capabilities that removing it would be counterproductive—even though Notes' own email client is primitive. If you use a mainframe computer, email tradeoffs have other implications, as I'll explore in more depth in Chapter 8.

In addition to client software, a company larger than a couple of people will need one more software program to use Internet email. Whether you use LAN client software or not, you will need software to pass email back and forth between your clients and the Internet. You must choose between either a UUCP server or an SMTP server.

Each of these alternatives creates a different set of email standards for your network administrator, but your users won't be affected.

## UUCP is simpler

UUCP is the simpler of the two. It stands for Unix-to-Unix Copy Protocol, but don't bother to remember that since nobody ever uses its full name. The magic of UUCP is that you can use Internet email, but you don't need to have your computer permanently connected to the Net 24 hours a day.

Instead, your computer uses a modem to periodically call your Internet access provider's computer, which *is* permanently connected to the Net. Your computer sends your outgoing email messages to the access provider's computer, receives any incoming email that has accumulated, and then hangs up. It is simple to completely automate this process of calling and passing messages so your computer sends and receives your messages every fifteen minutes, or for any time interval you specify. This does add a delay time to your email correspondence, which is the main drawback of using a UUCP connection for your email.

The advantages of UUCP are low cost and high security. UUCP is much cheaper than a direct connection and easier to maintain, and it is harder for a hacker to break into your computer since it is infrequently connected to the Internet.

For costs of UUCP, just ask your access provider the fees for a UUCP account.

## *SMTP is bigger*

As Computer Literacy Bookshops' Webmaster Robert Mudry puts it, "SMTP is 24-hour instant gratification compared to UUCP."

SMTP (short for Simple Mail Transfer Protocol) requires that your mail computer to be up, running, and connected to the Internet all the time. If you are going to turn off and on the computer that is your email server, use UUCP. With SMTP, if you are not connected at the instant an incoming message arrives, the message goes away and comes back later for another try. If you have a leased line to your access provider or a 24-hour SLIP or PPP connection, you might want to use SMTP.

The way SMTP delivers mail makes little sense to the average non-technical person. SMTP doesn't actually deliver mail itself. It passes mail to another program. To use SMTP, you need two or more pieces of software: an MUA (Mail User Agent)/email client and an MTA (Mail Transport Agent) program, such as Sendmail. The user needs the email client to read and send mail and the MTA program to deliver incoming messages to client programs or to a POP (Post Office Protocol) program or an IMAP (Internet Mail Access Protocol) program. The receiving program then delivers the message to the final client program on the addressee's PC. To send or receive mail, Sendmail (or the other SMTP program you use) must run continuously as a server. Your internal SMTP server will be complicated to set up and maintain.

Sendmail comes in many versions. If you use a commercial version of Unix, throw away the version of Sendmail that comes with it and replace it with the free version. The free one probably has better documentation and more recent bug fixes. Sendmail is included with OS/2 and Windows 95. There are also other MTA programs you can use instead of Sendmail. Smail 3.1x by

Ron Karr is a drop-in replacement for Sendmail that is easier to set up; it handles both UUCP and SMTP. One called MMDF (Multichannel Memorandum Distribution Facility) is older than Sendmail and still in use.

As I mentioned earlier, with a small business, your choice is easy—Internet email. If, however, you have a medium- to large-sized business with a number of computers, your work is cut out for you. You will want to send and receive email into a gateway computer system that will feed it through a router through a LAN into the email software on everybody's computers. Many LAN gateways for DOS and Windows are expensive, hard to manage, and notoriously buggy. For example, the gateways from both Microsoft and Lotus for their Windows email packages are DOS programs that cost more than $3,000 and drop file attachments. John Dvorak pointed out that Lotus Notes has difficulty when it leaves "its own little world," and the $2,500 Notes gateway is part of the reason why. Windows 95 makes intercommunication easier because it features a Universal In-Box for email, voicemail, and faxes. The In-Box was designed from the start to be able to communicate with Internet email.

For the Macintosh platform, on the other hand, you can buy gateways for Microsoft Mail, QuickMail, PowerShare, and Lotus Notes that are not only inexpensive (under $500), but more stable.

If you work for a large company, you might need to link your existing X.400 email system with the Internet. This can be more difficult than using a LAN gateway. X.400 uses a different addressing scheme, which MCIMail and AT&T EasyLink also use. The X.435 EDI standard is a subset of X.400.

## Other Internet software

I've mentioned Internet email software and briefly described the World Wide Web, FTP, Gopher, mailing lists, and newsgroups. There are many more Internet software tools to cover. I'm only going to touch on these because they're covered well in just about every other Internet book.

If your business will have a full-time Internet connection (24-hour ISDN or faster), you will need a computer acting as a server. Your Internet server computer must at least handle email with a SMTP or UUCP server and a post office server running POP or IMAP (Internet Mail Access Protocol), and it must run DNS. Let's start our look at other software with DNS.

- **Domain Name System (DNS):** DNS is the navigation system that Internet computers use to find each other. The Unix software program BIND is the most common DNS program. It is included with most versions of Unix, but must be added to other operating systems. If you run only one computer on the Net, even if you have a fast 128 Kbps connection, you won't need your own DNS server. Your Internet access provider's server will carry DNS for you. If your network has a firewall, you may want to run DNS on your firewall computer. The main advantage of having your own DNS server is that you can add and change user names and subdomain names without paying a fortune to your access provider. You won't need DNS until you have multiple users on the Net with different email addresses. There is DNS server software for all operating systems.

- **Telnet:** Telnet software lets you use the Internet to remotely access another computer and run programs on it. You will find this useful for field staff or customers who need to run software programs on your computer.

- **WAIS (Wide Area Information Server):** WAIS is an extremely useful software product, available in both free and commercial versions, which makes it possible for your business to present large numbers of documents or large amounts of data so users can easily search and find just what they need. WAIS is covered in this book's chapter on advertising, although it has many non-advertising uses.

- **Network administration tools :** Your system administrator will need Ping, NSLookup, and Whois for DNS troubleshooting. The free software tools Ping, Traceroute, Ifconfig, Netstat, and Route are key software tools used to administer your system.

- **IRC (Internet Relay Chat):** IRC lets people anywhere on the Net have typed real-time conversations.

- **DHCP (Dynamic Host Configuration Protocol):** DHCP gives computers on a LAN temporary Internet addresses. If your LAN uses NetWare, you might want to take a look at Novix from Firefox, Inc. This money-saver for NetWare users operates as a NetWare NLM (Network Loadable Module) and dynamically assigns IP addresses to computers. This means you don't need to load TCP/IP software on each computer—you only have to load it once on your NetWare Server as an NLM. Novix increases security, saves work in configuring PCs, and uses less memory than TCP/IP would use if stored locally on each system. It is also easy to install and fairly easy to maintain. Keep in mind, however, that DHCP servers need the protection of a firewall.

  A 5-user starter kit is available for $1,400 from Firefox, Inc., 2841 Junction Ave. #103, San Jose, CA 95134, (800) 230-6090.

- **Games:** Internet games include MUDs (Multi-User Dungeons, or in businessspeak, Multi-User Dimensions) and MUSHs (Multi-User Shared Hallucinations), among others. As a player, you meet other characters and battle monsters in a virtual world. Some businesses use Internet games for online conferencing to let a group of people conduct an ongoing discussion.

- **CU-SeeMe:** This free software lets PCs and Macs run multiple windows to transmit video, text, and sound. It makes a primitive kind of videoconferencing possible. To get the software, anonymous FTP to **fated.cornell.edu** and look in the **pub/video** directory.

- **Internet Voice Chat:** Would you like to make free phone calls anywhere in the world? This software lets you conduct live voice conversations through your computer over the Internet. It's like a low-quality phone but without long-distance charges. To get the software, go to **ftp://b61503.student.cwru.edu,www.unb.ca** or to **ftp://ftp.demon.co.uk**. There are other Internet voice communication software products called Internet Phone and PICK.

When choosing software, in addition to your up-front costs, find out about the annual support costs and software upgrade fees. Estimate what the training costs will be on a per-user basis (or per developer, if this is a development tool). Too many companies purchase multiple-user site licenses for software packages, then ignore the need to train people in the use of the software. The result? The software is ignored or misused by employees, and money and time are wasted.

You'll need to determine if a particular software package is designed for programmers, power users, or regular end-users. (Don't believe the brochure.) What operating system(s) does it support? (The more, the merrier.) Does it run on multiple brands of hardware? Look closely at its hardware requirements (disk space, memory, CPU speed). This is an area where software companies often understate true needs, especially for memory. If a software program forces you to add new hardware such as memory chips, the hardware additions can cost more than the software. Pay attention to the vendor's reputation and to the market momentum for this product. Don't get stuck with dying products.

A very important question to ask: *Does the vendor provide online support via the Internet?* Online Internet-based support reduces the time your own technical people will need to spend.

## *An Internet software checklist*

Here are the major kinds of software used on the Internet. You won't need all of these. Some (like TCP/IP) are required but are probably built into your computer's operating system. Others are optional; you may need them, depending on which Internet services you want to bring into your company and which ones you want to offer to the world. Use this as a shopping list when choosing an operating system:

**Client software** (one copy for each person on the Net)

- ❏ An integrated Internet client package, or
- ❏ IRC "Talk" client
- ❏ Newsreader
- ❏ FTP client
- ❏ Telnet client
- ❏ Gopher client

- ❏ Web browser (Note that Netscape, the most popular Web browser, also handles Gopher, Telnet, FTP, newsgroups, and outgoing email)
- ❏ Finger client
- ❏ NFS client
- ❏ TIA (The Internet Adapter) software if you use a dial-up shell account
- ❏ Encryption software, if legal in your country

**Email software**

- ❏ An email client for each user (either an Internet email client or a LAN email client; could be part of an integrated client package)
- ❏ Either an SMTP or UUCP email server
- ❏ Privacy-Enhanced Mail software
- ❏ Digital signature software
- ❏ POP or IMAP to deliver email to each person's client
- ❏ An MTA program such as SendMail, Smail, or MMDF
- ❏ Gateway software if you want to link LAN email clients to the Net
- ❏ Mailing list server
- ❏ X.400 for TCP/IP software, if you use X.400
- ❏ Directory sychronization software, if you are a large company (500+ employees) and use different email clients

**Server software**

- ❏ TCP/IP server
- ❏ FTP server(s); you might want separate servers for internal and external use

❏ Web server(s); you might want separate servers for internal and external use

❏ Gopher server

❏ WAIS server

❏ Firewall software

❏ Credit card processing software, if you make sales on the Net

❏ DNS server

❏ NFS server

❏ DHCP server if you have a LAN (or Novix if you use NetWare)

❏ Telnet server

❏ NNTP server

❏ Finger server

❏ IRC server

❏ NTP (Network Time Protocol) server

**TCP/IP network administration tools** (For a catalog of TCP/IP network maintenance software tools, have your system administrator check RFC 1470)

❏ Ping

❏ Traceroute

❏ A packet monitor, either Sniffer, from Network General; LANWatch from FTP Software; or the free package Tcpdump

❏ A DNS tool, either NSLookup, Dig, or Host (all free Unix tools), or for non-Unix systems, OC/TCP or OnNet (from FTP Software)

❏ An SNMP Management Information Base (MIB) browser. (You don't need a full SNMP management station unless you have a huge network.)

**Special-purpose software**

❏ Videoconferencing software (CU-SeeMe, Voice/View)

❏ Voice communication software

❏ Site-licensed software distribution managers

❏ EDI software

❏ Interfaces from Internet sales order systems to accounting systems

❏ Remote access software for telecommuters

❏ World Wide Web page editing software

❏ Other Web site enhancements and tools (Harvest, WebChat, etc.)

# How to get your own domain name

To join the major leagues as an Internet business, you'll want to register your company's own domain name, like **ibm.com** or **microsoft.com**. It costs nothing or very little, and adds weight to your online image.

Your Internet access provider will do this for you. If you have an ISDN connection or anything faster, your provider should do it for free. With a slower connection, expect to pay your provider or a service bureau to register your domain name. Prices for registration range from $20 to $245. The average is $25 to $50. If you pay $100 or more, expect special services in addition to vanilla registration. Otherwise, you're being overcharged.

Your name cannot duplicate any existing domain name. To see if your idea has been taken by someone else, look up the name at InterNIC's "Whois" searcher at **http://internic.net.rs-internic.html**. (This is also a great place to search to find sites and people on the Net.) Your registration takes about three weeks to be approved or rejected.

Most businesses in the U.S. (as well as many in Canada, Europe and Japan) choose a **.com** top-level domain (such as **emery.com**) for "commercial," although there are other alternatives. You may use **.org** for an organization. You could instead choose to end your name with a country code, such as **.us** for the United States (**emery.us**). Businesses in many countries, especially outside the U.S., use **.co** for "commercial" plus a country code, such as **barclays.co.uk**.

There are naming conventions for Internet servers, like **www.yourco.com** for World Wide Web sites. If a name starts with **www**, some software automatically knows that it is a Web site. For the same reason, name your gopher server **gopher.yourco.com** and your FTP site **ftp.yourco.com**.

# How to Get Started without Getting Ripped Off

*"Spend at least 10 percent of your budget on the best professional advice available before you spend a nickel on anything else."*

Harvey Mackay,
*Beware the Naked Man Who Offers You His Shirt*

There is no single "right" way to get connected to the Internet, but there are plenty of "wrong" ways. That's because there are so many variables involved in getting connected, and each variable means you have to answer one or more questions:

- Who do you go to if you want to get connected?
- What level of service do you need?
- How much should you pay in startup fees?
- How much should you pay for ongoing access?
- Are there any hidden costs involved in getting connected, and if so, what are they?
- What hardware will you need?
- What software will you need?
- How fast should your connection be?
- Do you even *need* to be on the Internet to do business online?

And perhaps the most important question:

- How do you know you're not getting ripped off?

You *won't* know, unless you first examine which services are "out there" waiting to take your money and without finding out what, specifically, the different "services" provide. Unfortunately, getting a business connection to the Internet is rarely instant and easy. The truth is, the more knowledge you have about the Internet—including your available hardware and software options— the more likely it will be to find a satisfactory approach to doing business online.

A good first step is to determine which services are available to help you do business online. Several options are available, so you need to choose carefully. Here are some of the approaches you can take:

- Use a traditional online service (America Online, CompuServe, etc.)
- Get a SLIP, CSLIP, or PPP connection (a modem connection)
- Get a direct ISDN connection (what many businesses use)
- Get a direct high-speed T1 or T3 connection

# Using an online service

Traditional (if you can call being in business for 10 years or less a "tradition") online services include Prodigy, Delphi, America Online, and CompuServe. But there's also an important newcomer: Microsoft Network.

## *What about CompuServe, America Online, Prodigy or Microsoft Network?*

Commercial online services such as these, Delphi, NiftyServe in Japan, Minitel in France and Cix in the U.K. offer some advantages, and for all but the smallest businesses, some disadvantages. They are easier to set up and easier to navigate. Your network connection is a direct line and more secure than the Internet. Inhabitants of the commercial services are more tolerant of advertising and blatant promotions than Internet dwellers. It's easier for you to set up a business site on the commercial services; hand-holding is provided. On the Internet, you have to pay a service provider or do it on your own.

On the other hand, commercial services cost way more, often putting per-message charges on incoming and outgoing mail. Print publications that put an ezine on a commercial service typically get only 10 to 15 percent of the connect-time income they generate. On the Internet, you can keep it all. To put up your online store in CompuServe's Electronic Mall, you'll shell out $15,000 to $20,000 plus two percent of your sales plus advertising fees. Prodigy charges $27,500 a month for its Standard Advertising Unit of five screens. America Online charges content providers (companies whose product is information delivered over AOL, such as online magazines) an outrageous 85 percent of revenues. Microsoft Network charges content providers between thirty percent and ten percent of revenues.

Some of the commercial services also restrict the kind of information you can provide. Prodigy is the worst. Prodigy employs editors who screen every message before allowing it to post to Prodigy's equivalent of newsgroups. Sometimes delivery is delayed for days. It also uses software to scan messages for what Prodigy deems "unacceptable" language. America Online does some censorship. Gary Wolff of *HotWired* says a ludicrous example happened when Penn Jillette was on *Wired*'s AOL site for a live realtime chat with AOL subscribers. AOL said he couldn't use profanity. Jillette said that was fine. (The man has been on network TV dozens of times. He knows how to play by the rules.)He used comic-book punctuation in one sentence (something like !&@#!!). AOL was monitoring his chat and pulled the plug. That level of censorship was too much for *Wired,* so it left AOL.

The main difference is the people and companies you reach and the ways in which you can reach them. The Internet has by far the largest customer base, the most global reach, the most information and the fastest growth. If your business is on the Internet, subscribers to all the commercial services except Minitel can reach you via the World Wide Web. If your business is on one of the commercial services, your visitors are restricted to only subscribers of that particular service. There are companies doing business successfully on all the commercial services as well as on the Internet. There is no one best way for all businesses. You have multiple choices.

## Internet via your modem

By far, the most popular approach among small businesspeople who want to connect their businesses to the Internet is to set up a SLIP, CSLIP, or PPP account. This is also where many businesses get ripped off.

 I wish I didn't have to say this, but too many Internet access providers charge premiums for services that you can get for free or for minimal cost—only because they know their potential subscribers have no idea how to go about getting set up on the Internet nor how to conduct their business on the Net.

Always get *at least three* price quotes from three different access providers before making any choices.

### Shell accounts

The simplest kind of Internet account is a basic dialup (shell) connection between your computer and your service provider's system. With only a dialup connection, your computer functions as a terminal. Your system isn't really on the Internet, but your service provider's system is and simply passes data between your computer and the Internet server to which it is connected.

Under this simple approach, you can only run one network program at a time, and, without adding software, you can only send and receive text (no graphics, sound, or other multimedia data). One software program you can add is TIA (The Internet Adapter). It fools your shell connection into thinking it is a SLIP connection, so you can run most SLIP software. A simple dialup connection isn't a viable option for most companies serious about doing business on the Internet.

## *SLIP, CSLIP, and PPP*

The first, and most important, question that you're going to want me to answer is probably: "What's the difference between SLIP and PPP?"

SLIP stands for Serial Line Internet Protocol, and is a standard method for connecting to a service provider via telephone lines.

SLIP was one of the first communications packages to provide home or office PCs with a connection to the Internet, but it's not the best or even the fastest. However, a modified version of SLIP, called CSLIP (Compressed SLIP) does offer slight speed advantages.

PPP (Point to Point Protocol) serves an almost identical function as SLIP, except PPP is a more robust set of protocols—especially in the area of error detection and error handling. For this reason, PPP access providers boast that Internet connections are 5 to 10 percent faster than with SLIP, and transmission errors are far fewer.

With any kind of modem connection to the Internet, you are limited to a speed of 28.8 Kbps. That speed is useful for tranferring email via UUCP, and for one person to surf the Web with Netscape, but it will not support many services that your business can provide over the Net. For instance, you could run a World Wide Web server to provide your own home page even on a slow 9.6 Kbps modem, but it would run at a crawl, so slowly that some visitors would be unable to get in. Most Web page servers need at least a 56 Kbps connection.

Measuring the performance differences among SLIP, CSLIP, and PPP is splitting hairs. A more important consideration is the speed and capability of your *provider's* host system. Regardless of your line speed and connection method, at any given time your Internet connection speed will be limited by the slowest point between links.

You don't want that slowest link to be your service provider's lines. Before you set up an account with a provider, find out how *its* system connects to the Internet. If it's anything less than a T1 or T3 connection (which I'll explain later), you will notice slowness.

So how important is it to get a PPP connection rather than a SLIP or CSLIP connection? If you find a local access provider who offers PPP connectivity, and the price is right, take advantage of it. If your local provider of choice only offers SLIP or CSLIP connectivity, you're still in good shape, but you might need to monitor your system's network connection more closely. Customers become frustrated when they attempt to connect to your Internet site repeatedly, only to find that the site's often not available.

And that brings up an important problem with SLIP, CSLIP, and PPP connections: They often are not up 24 hours per day. When you purchase a SLIP, CSLIP, or PPP connection, you'll be offered various options for paying connect-time charges. The more time you want your system to be connected to the Internet, the more you can expect to pay. A 24-hour account via a SLIP, CSLIP, or PPP might not be cost effective. That will depend on your provider's rates.

## *Locate your home page on your access provider's system*

A good option with a SLIP, CSLIP, or PPP connection is to use your local system for outbound access only, and put your Web site on your provider's computer. You'll pay more for this approach because you'll be leasing hard disk space from your provider. But customers will also be able to access your business 24 hours per day, 7 days per week.

Locating your Web site on your provider's server also typically offers faster connections for your customers, since your provider's connection to the Internet will almost certainly be faster than your connection to your service provider.

If you use a modem to make your connection to the Internet with standard telephone lines (ISDN is an exception), make sure your phone company has not put you on a Digital Added Main Line (DAML, pronounced "dam-el" to rhyme with "camel"). A DAML is used by local phone companies when they run out of lines in a neighborhood. DAMLs jam two phone lines into the wires of one.

This is normally not a problem for regular telephone voice transmission. But if you have a DAML and use a modem, it will run only half as fast as normal. Usually, DAMLs are temporary, and remain in place only until your phone company can add more physical lines in your neighbood. This happened to me. If you find out that you are on a DAML, badger your phone company frequently to add a "real" line.

## The next step up: An ISDN connection

Normally, a modem connection made through standard telephone lines and switching equipment is limited to 28.8 Kbps because phone line noise limits reliable transmissions to 31 Kbps or less. There is a kind of 56 Kbps connection called switched 56, but other connections using newer technology are usually more cost-effective than switched 56. If you want or need more speed than a modem connection offers, the next step up is an ISDN connection.

ISDN stands for Integrated Services Digital Network, and it's only slightly less complicated than the federal budget. The basic ISDN connection provides up to 64 Kbps in bandwidth. Standard SLIP and PPP connections require a modem at your end, and an ISDN connection requires special hardware at your end. Your Internet access provider must also support ISDN (most medium to large providers do). ISDN is becoming the most common choice of businesses, whether located in homes, factories, or offices.

### *How ISDN technology works*

An ISDN connection uses standard telephone lines but provides digital transmission via improved line-switching equipment. That means you can set up an ISDN connection only if your phone company has converted to ISDN switching facilities. (Even then, you might not be able to use ISDN, as I'll explain shortly.) A benefit of ISDN, in addition to the increased speed, is its ability to send or receive data and voice transmission simultaneously.

There are actually two main flavors of ISDN, but the least expensive and most widely used is called the Basic Rate Interface (BRI). In fact, before I can explain more about the benefits, problems, and expenses involved with ISDN, I need to explain ISDN itself.

A standard telephone connection consists of two copper wires. An ISDN BRI connection only requires one of these wires and divides it into three "channels." Two channels are called bearer channels (B channels for short). Each B channel has a speed of 64 Kbps. A BRI connection also uses a third, D channel.

Assuming that your phone company supports ISDN, there are still some other requirements that your equipment must satisfy. First, your external phone line must go straight from your ISDN equipment to the phone company's junction box where the line comes into your building from outside. A telephone technician can tell you whether your line meets this requirement.

Also, the external line from the junction box to the phone company's ISDN switching facility should be 18,000 feet or *less*. If your home or office is located 3 miles or more from this switch, ISDN is literally out of reach—unless the phone company can boost your signal with a repeater (at an additional cost to you, of course).

If you and your phone company meet all the ISDN requirements I've explained so far, you'll then need to purchase a device called an NT1 or NTU1 (NT stands for Network Terminator), which supplies power to your ISDN line. Some ISDN modems have an NT1 built in. If you connect your ISDN line to your PC or Mac, you can purchase a controller card that comes with a built-in NT1.

In the U.S., ISDN actually has two 56 Kbps channels bonded together, so you can make two 56 Kbps connections at once, giving you an effective speed, with most computers, of 115 Kbps. If you want to do this, you'll need a router, a box that handles the connections from your PC to the phone lines.

You can buy ISDN routers as standalone boxes or as add-in cards that plug into PCs and Macintoshes.

That's the easy stuff. Before you decide to purchase ISDN, you should consider these additional questions:

- How many devices do you want to attach to ISDN? A device can be a computer, fax, telephone, or any similar device. The ISDN router you buy can only support a limited number of devices, or "terminals" as they are referred to in the communications industry, no doubt to confuse the rest of us. ("But that's not a terminal, it's a Princess phone!") ISDN routers can connect from one to dozens of devices. The fewer the devices supported, the lower priced your router. You can get routers that convert between ISDN and Ethernet, Appletalk, and other network protocols.

- Do you want to use one B channel as a phone line? You have two 64 Kbps B channels available. You can use one for voice and one for data. Be warned, though, that using a B channel for voice means you will have to buy a special ISDN phone ($150 and up) or a converter gadget called a TE1 that lets you plug a regular phone into your ISDN B line.

- Do you want to bond both B channels? Bonding gives you a data speed of 128 Kbps, twice as fast as a single B channel. Depending on the type of ISDN router you buy, bonding may require a terminal adapter. The formal high-tech term for bonding is "inverse multiplexing."

- Do you need X.25 packet networking? Probably not. X.25 is slow (2.4 to 9.6 Kbps) and obsolete. If for some odd reason you want to do X.25 networking, you need to buy a separate terminal adapter for X.25.

- Do you need a repeater? If your home is too far away from your phone company's switching office, your phone company will sock you with an extra monthly charge for a repeater, a device that boosts the signal strength so that it will reach the extra distance.

- Have you had a Loop Quality test performed? This is a test your phone company can make to determine whether your phone lines can actually carry ISDN. Ask for this to be done first. You don't want to find out after your ISDN installation that your line doesn't support it.

- What kind of ISDN switch is used by your phone company's switching office? Your equipment must be compatible with that switch. Some switches have a reputation for being easier to connect with than others. For example, Pacific Bell uses both AT&T and Northern Telecom switches. If you are in a neighborhood served by the AT&T switches, ISDN will be easier to install and will be less troublesome to use than if you were in a neighborhood serviced by the Northern Telecom switches.

## *How much does ISDN cost?*

If you decide you want the benefits that an ISDN connection brings, your next order of business is to tally up the potential costs—before you actually make any purchases. In an illuminating article in the February, 1995 issue of *LAN Magazine*, Internet veteran Karl Auerbach gave a detailed account of his tasks in setting up an ISDN connection for his home-based business. He listed these one-time setup costs:

| | |
|---|---|
| Internet access provider fee | $500 |
| Phone company line installation | $140 |
| Two ISDN Ethernet bridges | $1,850 |
| Router | $1,500 |
| 10BaseT hub | $200 |
| Network software for each PC | $400 |
| Telephone company ISDN charge | $72 |

Auerbach used a recycled 386 PC as his router to direct Internet traffic to the other computers his business uses. These costs don't include computer maintenance, which Auerbach, a technical expert, says took a few hours per week.

Of course, you won't incur the same charges as Auerbach—you might spend more or you might spend less, depending on your requirements. In general, an ISDN connection, including installation and equipment (not counting your computer) can run from $300 to $2,500.

Your phone company will also charge you a monthly charge for your ISDN line, typically between $15 to $25 per month, plus a metered usage charge. Most will charge $80 or so extra for installation if you need to add inside wiring and a jack, which is the same as a regular telephone jack.

Internet access provider fees for ISDN service range from about $25 to $400 per month, and more in some areas. If you use an Internet access provider that provides a kind of access called ISDN Centrex, your monthly phone company cost is $23 with no usage fees, and you pay about $400 per month to the Internet access provider. Obviously, flat rates are better than fluctuating fees because you can more easily plan your business expenses.

It is definitely worth hunting for an Internet access provider that can provide ISDN Centrex.

Access provider GeoNet (**http://www.geo.net**) has 21 switches in California that offer ISDN Centrex. GeoNet also has a $70 try-out offer. It lends you the necessary equipment until you decide whether to keep its service.

At present, telephone companies in North America, Europe, and Japan are pushing to make ISDN as accessible and as popular as possible. The greatest penetration is in Germany, where Deutsche Telekom put in place blanket coverage of Western Germany in early 1994, and will achieve blanket coverage in Eastern Germany sometime during 1995.

Deutsche Telecom plans to equip all of its exchanges with digital ISDN equipment by the year 2000. It's probably no surprise, then, to hear that Germany currently has more businesses using ISDN than any other country. Base rates for a 64 Kbps ISDN line in Germany start at 450 Deutschmarks per month.

# What one company really paid

Circle International is a shipping and logistics company headquartered in San Francisco with operations in 306 cities around the world and annual revenues of over $180 million. Circle is a sophisticated network user, employing EDI and running an email network for its customers. To link to the Internet, Circle was given cost estimates of more than $25,000 to install a Unix computer to act as a server, set up access from an Internet access provider and provide technical support.

After investigating different possibilities, Circle instead spent about $6,000. It hired local Internet consultant and access provider Liberty Hill Cyberwerks (**http://cyberwerks.com**), which "specializes in companies with a lot of information, not just a home page," according to a Liberty Hill spokesman.

For about $300, Circle bought a 386 PC clone that is located at Liberty Hill's facility. All of Circle's software runs on the 386: a World Wide Web server (**http://circleintl.com**), a Gopher server, a mailing list server, a UUCP server for receiving and forwarding email, and Telnet. The software runs on the BSD OS, a version of Unix that runs on PCs. Eric Thiese, who managed the Liberty Hill side of the project, says BSD OS is "a great package. It's much, much, much easier to get up than Linux, and the support people are very helpful." Thiese said BSD is preconfigured to run Internet software, and so takes only a short time to set up "if you buy the hardware that's on BSD's list of supported products. If you deviate from that, you're dead meat." Circle's PC shares a T1 speed connection on a sort of party line arrangement with other Liberty Hill clients.

First, Liberty Hill built Circle's Gopher server and Web pages. That took about one worker-week, including the translation of Circle's marketing materials from Microsoft Word to HTML for the Web. Liberty Hill set up a dial-up UUCP connection between Liberty Hill and Circle for email. Liberty Hill receives and stores Circle's Internet email. Several times a day, Circle's computer automatically connects to the 386, retrieves incoming email, and disconnects. This isolates Circle's computer network from the Internet and keeps it secure. For the same reason, Circle employees who want to send Internet email or read newsgroups must use Telnet to reach the 386 PC and use the Internet software there.

Updates for information and software and user training are provided under contract from Liberty Hill, and add up to eight hours or less per month. Circle tracks additions to its print mailing list by source, and calls to its 800 number by source, so Circle's marketers know what results their Internet prospecting generates. Its customer order software tracks the origin of customers. Without being specific, Jon Himoff, Circle's director of global marketing is pleased with the contacts generated from the Net.

In the U.S., Pacific Bell seems to be following suit by aggressively installing ISDN equipment throughout California and encouraging its use. In fact, Pacific Bell provides a very well-written document that explains ISDN on its World Wide Web site at: **http://www.pacbell.com**.

Except for Pacific Bell, most U.S. phone companies seem to be in the dark about ISDN—even if they offer the service. Phone company sales reps will describe services that are not available and they'll often give you inaccurate price quotes, and the technicians will often screw up your installation.

But for high speed and reliability, ISDN is worth a close look. Here's a rundown of ISDN offering by the Baby Bell phone companies:

*In California* (not yet in Nevada, which the company also serves), Pacific Bell offers home ISDN for $24.50 per month, which actually works out to $26.00 per month when taxes and surcharges are included. Installation is $150, but Pac Bell will cut that to $70 if you sign a contract to keep the service for two years.

*U.S. West* serves 14 Western states and charges $70.00 per month for usage and $70 for ISDN installation—a good deal if you can get it. U.S. West only offers ISDN in larger cities within its service region. Call 800-898-WORK for more information.

*Ameritech* serves Illinois, Wisconsin, Michigan, Indiana, and Ohio, but provides ISDN only in scattered areas. Ameritech has a patchwork quilt pricing structure, which includes a $150 installation fee plus monthly charges that range from $33 to $106, plus usage charges ranging from dirt cheap to outrageously high. Ameritech's Web site, **http://www.aads.net**, neglects to mention ISDN. Maybe it'll correct this oversight soon.

*Southwestern Bell* serves Texas, Oklahoma, Kansas, Arkansas, and Missouri with a version of ISDN that they call DigiLine. It's only available in some parts of major cities. DigiLine has a painful installation fee of nearly $600, plus a monthly usage charge of $58 (a flat rate). You can find information at its Web site: **http://www.sbc.com**.

*NYNEX* services New York state and parts of New England. The company seems to understand little about ISDN, but says it "may" offer ISDN in the future for a $450 installation fee and a $35 per month flat usage charge. You can hear NYNEX's promises by calling 800-GET-ISDN.

*Bell Atlantic* serves Pennsylvania, New Jersey, West Virginia, Virginia, Maryland, Delaware, and Washington, D.C. Its home installation fee is only $80 or less, and charges are $19.50 per month. However, Bell Atlantic does charge between 1 and 5 cents per minute as an additional usage fee. You can get more information either at **http://www.ba.com** or by calling 800-570-ISDN.

*Bell South* serves nine Southern states with a home ISDN service that it calls Individual Line Service. It charges a $250 installation fee, plus $95 (flat rate) per month. However, the service is only available within a few large cities. For more information, call 404-496-2700.

## Other digital connections

If you've grown accustomed to a 14.4 Kbps or 28.8 Kbps modem connection, the 56 Kbps to 128 Kbps potential of ISDN might seem like dream speed. But Internet connections can be much, much faster. The only problem: Increased speeds can't be achieved through standard phone lines. Dedicated lines are required.

For extremely high speed, these four are the most widely used Internet connections:

- Frame Relay
- PRI ISDN
- T1
- T3

## Frame Relay

In some places, frame relay offers a more cost-effective Internet connection than ISDN.

Frame relay gives you a sort of "party line" connection. It links several businesses to the Internet on one high-speed line, usually a T1 line, but sometimes an even faster line. This sharing keeps the price down. Each business is guaranteed a minimum speed, for instance 56 Kbps (usually the slowest frame relay speed available) or 128 Kbps.

Some ISDN connections charge you more based on distance, but frame relay rates usually use distance-insensitive pricing. Depending on the speed you want, your phone company's pricing, and your Internet access provider's rates, frame relay can cost between $500 and $2,000 to install and $100 to $500 per month. In addition, you will need hardware. You can use a frame relay access device, called FRAD for short, as your Frame relay "modem," or the kind of CSU/DSU gadgets that more expensive leased-line Internet connections require.

## PRI ISDN

PRI stands for Primary Rate Interface. I'm only going to touch on PRI ISDN connectivity briefly because it's physically identical to T1 connectivity (which I'll discuss next).

The major difference between PRI ISDN and T1 connections is the type of provider you have to deal with. PRI ISDN is offered by local phone companies, while T1 is offered by leased-line providers, such as Sprint and Tymnet.

A PRI connection offers a bandwidth of 1.544 megabits per second. For the arithmetically challenged, that's 27.5 times faster than a 56 Kbps connection. In Europe, PRI ISDN operates at 2.048 megabits per second.

PRI uses 23 B connections and one data connection, and can support up to 64 "terminal" devices at one time, and up to eight separate phone numbers. PRI ISDN connections cost thousands of dollars per month, plus you'll pay several thousand dollars in installation fees alone.

## Getting a T1 connection: is it worth the cost?

T1 is an abbreviated reference to a North American T1 Trunk cable, a dedicated physical copper-wire cabling system that has much greater speed than standard phone cables. As I mentioned in the previous section, if you lease a T1 connection from your local phone company, you'll be getting PRI ISDN connectivity.

Like PRI ISDN, T1 service operates at 1.544 megabits per second, and you can get a T1 connection from almost anywhere in the U.S. and in many other countries—especially in Europe and the Pacific Rim. Regardless of whether you purchase T1 service from a phone company or from another provider, your outlay in both startup and ongoing costs will be substantial.

Instead of a modem, for T1 you will need a box called a CSU/DSU, which will move Internet traffic to and from your router. Your phone company charges for T1 depending on how close you are to your access provider's nearest location (called Point of Presence or POP for short), so it pays to be close.

For a full-speed T1 Internet connection, expect to pay your Internet access provider between $250 and $1,000 for startup costs and $1,000 to $2,800 per month. Add to this the communications line costs from your phone company, which will fluctuate due to the distance factor, with setup between $1,000 and $4,000 and monthly fees of $200-$900. You'll also need a CSU/DSU and router for $4,000 to $9,000.

You can also get slower-speed, less expensive fractional T1, discussed later in this book. Expect Internet access provider charges of more than $500 for startup and monthly fees of $250 and up, plus phone company fees of $1,000 and up for startup and monthly fees of $125 and up for fractional T1.

## *Do you need T1?*

It's a generally recognized axiom that in planning a business, you should plan for growth. That statement suggests that you consider purchasing an Internet connection that's larger than you currently need. But for most businesses, T1 connectivity is excessive.

Today most T1 users are small- and medium-sized Internet access providers who need to provide bandwidth for their customers. Other T1 customers are major businesses running LANs or WANS that support hundreds, or even thousands of terminals. For these customers, T1 is not so much an Internet solution as it is part of a broader networking solution. Some T1 customers are corporate Web sites (cybermalls) that also lease Web space to other businesses.

If your business is small- to medium-sized, and you want to conduct all or part of your business on the Internet, you will probably find that 56 Kbps or 128 Kbps provides plenty of speed to support incoming and outgoing Internet traffic. If you locate your Web server on your access provider's server, even that level of performance may be excessive.

If your business is looking for a total networking solution that includes but isn't limited to the Internet (for instance, you want to set up a LAN for all local offices and you plan on conducting business on the Internet), you might very well require the kind of bandwidth that T1 can provide.

Videoconferencing and heavy graphics transfer are areas where T1 can be an important consideration. Videoconferencing quality on a 128 Kbps ISDN connection is possible, but graphics and video resolutions will be less than ideal, and video transfer times might be slow.

In fact, any business that regularly transfers video, large audio files, large graphics files, or other extremely load-intensive images should consider T1 as a connection option. For instance, if you run a medical facility and you want to regularly receive medical x-ray images across the Internet, T1 might be your connection of choice. For video and graphics companies, Sprint offers a special T1 solution called Drums (**http://www.sprint.com/drums**).

Some businesses now shop for office space specifically with an eye toward buildings that have T1 connectivity (the cabling and switch) built in. Commercial developers often use T1 as an incentive to attract companies with heavy networking needs. However, T1 connections can be complex and require dedicated administrative support. Most companies that use T1 have at least one full-time network support employee.

### *Fractional T1*

If you feel that your business might grow beyond the 128 Kbps ceiling, you can still have some of the speed of T1 for only part of the cost. Many T1 providers offer a service called "fractional T1," where customers purchase portions of a T1 line in 56 Kbps or 64 Kbps increments.

This is possible because a T1 line is actually 23 smaller channels put together. Under this approach, you pay only for the portion of the total bandwidth you use. If you only need 256 Kbps, that's all you pay for.

## T3 connections

T3 cables provide some of the fastest communication available over the Internet, operating as high as 45 megabits per second. T3 connections use fiber optic cables rather than the copper wire cables used by ISDN and T1 lines. I mention T3 chiefly to make you aware of its presence; your business is unlikely to need T3 performance any time in the near future. At present, T3 is used mostly by national Internet access providers and large networks.

## Other connectivity options

There are other Internet connectivity solutions available, but the ones I've mentioned so far account for the great majority of connection options. As technology improves, though, expect to see new connectivity opportunities appear, and existing options disappear.

One of the newest connections is called Asychronous Transfer Mode (ATM), which provides up to 155 megabits per second of bandwidth. As the demand for speed increases with the increased popularity of the Internet and other online services, ATM performance levels may soon become the norm rather than the exception. In some very large corporations with extensive networking facilities, ATM has already become the standard.

## Choosing your Internet access provider

When you're ready to select an Internet access provider, the first question you might ask is: "How can I find a *local* provider?" While it's true that many national providers aggressively seek your business, they may not be right for your company.

 With some Internet providers, especially national providers, you will have to pay long-distance charges each time you use the Internet. These long distance charges can wipe out any savings you make from negotiating bargain rates for access. This is especially true of modem-based Internet accounts, but distance charges from your phone company's switching center or your Internet access provider's nearest POP (Point of Presence) can also blindside you with extra distance-based costs if you don't watch out.

If you are considering a national or worldwide Internet access provider, customer service may be hard to come by. You are not likely to be considered a preferred customer, just another notch in their sales belt. Your ability to negotiate on contractual terms will be severely limited.

However, a national provider makes sense if you or others in your company will need Internet access during frequent road travel. That's probably the major benefit of a national provider: the ability to dial in to your Internet account from anywhere in the country. A business with locations in several states or countries may also prefer a national provider.

But for most business purposes, a local or regional provider offers more benefits. A local provider is more willing (or should be) to visit your site to make presentations and to consult with you on your company's needs; dialing up to the Internet is a local call; and customer service hours will match your time zone and you will (or again, should be) given a personal account representative whom you can call directly to resolve any problems.

## Finding a local provider

So what's the first step in finding a local provider? The Yellow Pages? Possibly, but what category do you look under all—"Internet Services?" There ain't no such animal. "Communication Services?" Good luck. "Telephone Consultants?" Nope.

Perhaps you could try "Computers - Networking"? Actually, it's a good bet that one or more of your available local providers will be listed here. But for something this important, cold-calling a provider that you randomly select from the Yellow Pages does not make good business sense. You might get lucky, but more likely, you'll waste a tremendous amount of time.

There are lists of Internet providers available on the Internet itself, but if you don't yet have an Internet account, how do you access these lists? Besides, most of the lists I've seen, such as the PDIAL list, are horribly out of date and are incomplete. They might get you started in the right direction, though. (The PDIAL list is not a good place for businesses to look. It includes many nonprofit and academic provides that require their customers not to use the Internet for commercial activity.)

If you have Internet access, or have a friend who does, you can get a copy of the InterNIC list on the World Wide Web at **http://www.commerce.net/ directories/products/inet.prov.dir.html** or by sending email to **rfdesk@internic.net**. Another list, which includes more countries, is **http:// www.netusa.net/ISP**. Or try **http://www.clarinet/iap**.

Jeff Duntemann, editor-in-chief of *PC TECHNIQUES* magazine, suggests that the best way to get on the Internet is to use good old fashioned networking skills of your own. Begin by calling every business associate you know and ask for references and advice. Call your local chamber of commerce. If a local

Internet provider hasn't registered with your chamber of commerce, you already know it's less than on the ball.

Check with professional organizations and user groups in your area. You'll probably find some savvy businesspeople within these groups, several of whom will be happy to relate their own war stories on finding an Internet access provider.

This is important. Even if you do obtain a list of every Internet access provider in your area, you'll want references from their customers. You can ask the provider's sales reps for references, but you're only going to get references that the company knows will say good things about them. That's not what you want. You want the truth about a provider—warts and all. Members of local professional societies and users groups provide the best resource pool for getting "real" references about local providers.

## *Evaluating your available provider pool*

After you've uncovered all of the Internet access providers in your area and determined through references which ones *aren't* worth calling, you're on your own. At this point, you're basically conducting a series of job interviews. But unlike other job interviews, you're probably not going to be entirely sure of the skill set you should expect from your provider. But it's *critical* that you understand this skill set. Otherwise, you most certainly are either going to get ripped off or you're going to be disappointed.

The first point of order: *Never call a potential Internet access provider until you're relatively sure about the types and levels of services your business will need.* If you don't do this reality check first, you won't be prepared to ask potential providers the questions that really matter.

So begin by asking those questions of yourself first. Here's a laundry list to help get you going:

- How many of your employees will use Internet email? Email is still the largest category of use for most people who do business on the Internet, so you'll want to know how closely Internet traffic will be tied to email traffic. However, it's also true that email is not resource intensive. If *most* of your employees will use *only* email, you can have a relatively slow connection and still provide your employees with good email service.

- For email, will you use no mail server, or UUCP, or SMTP? The differences are covered elsewhere in this book. UUCP costs much less.

- Which of your employees will be resource hogs? For instance, if your company has an art department, they're likely to upload and download large graphic files routinely. They'll need more Internet access time and resources than employees who mainly use the Internet for email.

- Most companies can only reach the Usenet newsgroups supplied by their access providers. Will you use only the newsgroups provided by your Internet access provider, or do you want to install a newsgroup feed to your own computers? Will the newsgroups you want be available from your provider?

- How many people will use FTP to copy files and bring them into your company?

- How many employees will use the Internet to do research?

- Will your company need a server for FTP, Gopher, the World Wide Web, or mailing lists, and if so, will the server be located on your own computer or on your access provider's system?

- Do you intend to do videoconferencing?

- Will your company use the Internet to link local area networks at different sites into a company-wide network?

- Will you process credit card transactions on the Internet? If so, definitely tell your provider ahead of time. This can affect the way it sets up your account.

Answers to these questions will help you determine both the level of service you require and the type of connection that will be best for your business. After you have a good feel for the level of Internet service your company will require, you can begin to approach individual vendors.

## Consider the technical capabilities
## of potential providers

Much of the material I've presented in this chapter so far focuses on the potential technical requirements and issues that you'll need to deal with at your site. But equally important, if not more so, is the need to assess the technical capabilities and limitations of potential providers. Your company might have state-of-the-art equipment, but if your provider doesn't, you're going to lose patience with your provider pretty quickly.

The most important question you can ask an Internet access provider is: "How long have you been in business?" If they hem and haw, run, don't walk, in the other direction. But length of operation is not always indicative of the level of service to expect. Some providers start small, then take on an increasing number of customers to keep their cash flow growing, and eventually reach critical mass. This is what separates business-savvy providers from the fly-by-nighters. A provider that takes on every new customer without assessing its growth strategy and its existing traffic capacities is not going to be around for long.

The best way to analyze a provider's equipment is to visit its site—preferably unannounced. If the provider's system has banks upon banks of modems, you can suspect that most of its customers are using dial-up shell accounts; they're not business customers, so this provider might not be equipped to handle the level of service that your business requires.

The hardware and software that your provider shows you might be a mystery to you. But you can still tell a lot about a provider by making a tour. Does the company seem to have enough employees to handle its customer load? Talk to some of the employees. Do they seem qualified? Are they helpful?

To prevent yourself from being duped or conned, you'll want to ask questions that any provider should be able to answer instantly. Here are some essentials:

- How many connections does your potential provider have with *its* access providers? There is a food chain here. Your provider leases lines (probably T1 or T3) from Sprint, AT&T, MCI, or some other large telecommunications company, then splits that line and sells part of its capacity to you. You want your provider to have multiple connections. For example, say that MCI's line goes down and your provider has only one MCI connection; your entire Internet access goes down. If your provider has multiple connections, you are protected from the failure of a single carrier.

- Does the provider offer training and consulting services to help you get started? Many providers now offer installation packages. You can waste days, if not weeks, trying to install software. If a turnkey approach is available, take advantage of it.

- What percentage of the provider's customers are businesses?

- What percentage of customers have the same speed and connection type as the one you are considering? For instance, just because a provider offers T1 connections, you can't assume they also have extensive experience in helping customers set up and maintain T1 connections. You don't want to be one of your provider's "experiments."

- Where is the provider's closest Point of Presence (POP) to your business?

- If you need a router, who will pay for it—you or your provider? And who maintains it?

- Is there an extra charge for technical support?

- What security precautions are in place? I know of one company that accidentally gave out one customer's password to a different customer, believing that the second customer had recorded his user ID incorrectly. That's frightening.

Perhaps the single, most frequently heard problem voiced by Internet customers is that their provider cannot handle the customer load. Although there's no way to determine for certain whether a provider has sufficient resources, a site inspection can sometimes be revealing:

- Have the employees you met been with the company long? (You can expect any company to have a certain percentage of new hires; but if *everybody* you meet has just come on board, something's wrong.)

- Do the employees look overworked or unduly stressed?
- Are the phones ringing off their hooks, unanswered?

Some good old, tried-and-true detective work can sometimes reveal a company that's taken on more than it can handle. If you suspect this, get on the phone to some of the provider's other customers. Ask what kind of service they've received *lately*. If you get answers like, "Well, when we first joined with them, they bent over backwards, but now we can't get technical help," that's a very bad sign. You might try calling tech support yourself, just to see how long it takes you to reach a human.

Also suggest that a potential provider come to *your* site for a visit. By looking at your equipment and your company as a whole, a provider might be able to make helpful suggestions about the line speed, connection type, level of service, and other Internet options for your business.

## *Cost considerations and contractual terms*

I've already covered most of the costs you can expect for various Internet configurations. But published fees are not always the same as actual fees. This fact can work both in your favor and against you.

For instance, some providers offer a bargain-basement per-month charge, along with a low one-time installation charge, but then tack on numerous, "hidden" fees, including per-message charges for email or per-bit charges for FTP, Gopher, or Web downloads. Ask your provider if there is any additional charge for any of these services and if so, find out how much:

- Incoming email
- Outgoing email
- Per-hour usage charges (over the agreed-upon limit)
- Disk space use (over a specific limit)
- A corporate mailbox or node
- Additional hardware
- Installing lines

- Registering a domain name
- Training and technical support

This last item is especially important. Some providers keep costs low by leaving its customers hanging out to dry when they have technical problems—either by providing little if any technical support or by charging heavy technical support fees. Make sure your contract with your provider clearly details *all* charges that you can expect to pay.

On the other hand, you can often get a provider to lower its prices by negotiating on various terms. Your best negotiating strategy, though, is to comparison shop. If you know what a provider's competitors charge, you're in a position to negotiate.

 Some providers will slash their fees if you agree to sign a six-month or one-year contract. *Don't agree to this* the first time you do business with a provider. If its service doesn't meet your expectations, you'll be stuck for months.

In any case, if a provider offers you a contract with terms that appear fixed, and they are not satisfactory to you, negotiate to have them changed. All but the largest providers are willing to be reasonably flexible—if not about price, then perhaps about conditions. If your provider will register a custom domain name for you, make sure *you* own that domain, not your provider. If you need to cancel your account and move to a different provider, you'll want to take your domain name with you.

 Some providers will include a disclaimer in the contract saying that they do not bear the responsibility for providing a functional service. Don't put up with that. With any connection of ISDN speed or faster, your contract should specify the maximum length of turnaround time your provider has to forward any Internet traffic to or from your business. Otherwise you are left with no recourse if your email piles up for five days on your provider's system. Depending on your company's needs you might specify a maximum delay ranging from fifteen minutes to 24 hours. Also, termination terms should be as specific as possible and not vague. And don't tolerate any clause that limits you to using just one provider for access or for providing information.

Never allow your Internet provider to claim rights to any information, software, or other intellectual property that comes from your company. For instance, when you sign on as a business on America Online, you must grant AOL the "royalty-free perpetual right and license" to publish and use anything you post on AOL. That's bad for publishers, financial services, and many other information services. Don't accept this. In fact, you should insist that the contract specifically *prohibits* your provider from disclosing any financial information or trade secrets.

---

## How one business chose its provider

Bryon Abels-Smit is vice president of Aspen Media, in San Francisco. Aspen needed a high-performance, 24-hour Web site. Speed and reliability were important because the company planned to sell Web space to its clients. To meet these needs, Abels-Smit and other members of the company went in search of the best access provider available.

After some preliminary winnowing, which included gathering recommendations and critiques about local providers from customers who were already on the Internet, Aspen narrowed its choices to four providers: SlipNet, Netcom, Exodus, and an unnamed provider based in Berkeley.

The Berkeley provider was initially recommended by advertising agency Foote, Cone and Belding. But when Abels-Smit tried to look at the provider's Web site and the Web sites of its clients, "It was difficult to get through," he said, "and it was slow. And when I talked with someone about what we needed, the service just wasn't there." So the Berkeley provider was the first to be dropped from the list.

At SlipNet, "The people were interested in service," Abels-Smit noted, "but they were overwhelmed. They seemed to be running everything with just three people, and that included the staff involved in providing 24-hour, on-call service. When I went in to look at the place, I saw a whole bank of modems. I thought, 'How much of that is just for dialup lines? What kind of connections are they pushing?' "

Abels-Smit noted that the staff used several Macintoshes and seemed comfortable with them, but didn't seem as familiar with Unix, even their technical expert. "We used SlipNet temporarily for a dialup connection before getting our leased line installed, and even then they were down off and on for a week," he said.

At one point, Aspen employees received a "link dead" error message, which means the service is down. "When SlipNet's lines were up, we got lots of busy signals. One time it took nearly an hour to dial in. What really helped us make our decision was that the people didn't seem to have much *business* experience, either in running a business or in serving businesses."

Aspen also found that their next choice, Netcom, was less than satisfactory. "What turned us off to Netcom happened in December, 1994. We had the *San Jose Mercury News* come in to do a presentation." The presentation was about the *Mercury News'* new *Mercury Center*, the Internet version of the newspaper. Aspen had executives from advertising and publicity companies in several cities come in for the presentation.

The *Mercury Center* people set up a line and a screen to make their presentation. "For two-and-a-half hours," Abels-Smit recalled, "they were unable to get online and, when they did connect, they got disconnected after five minutes!" Obviously, Aspen couldn't afford for that to happen. "That's a killer in business," he said, "especially when you're dealing with professionals who don't know that much about the Web. To them, that's like a lost Federal Express shipment or missing an important phone call."

Finally, Aspen turned to access provider Exodus. "The sales representative did work for *me* instead of the other way around," Abels-Smit said. And the company seemed to "understand what you need to do to maintain a business. I could tell this from talking to the sales rep, by the questions he asked, and by his level of technical awareness."

According to Abels-Smit, the rep asked what Aspen's ultimate goals were for its Web site and asked about the kinds of servers the company had already looked at. "The rep brought in Avco [a Silicon Graphics reseller] to do a presentation on SGI. He brought in TCG [a local and long distance phone company that had laid a fiber optic grid over the entire downtown San Francisco area] to pull our T1 line. They recommended a firewall manufacturer."

A site visit to Exodus confirmed that the company served mostly businesses with non-dialup connections. Aspen had made its decision.

# How to Get Up to Speed Quickly

*"The first man gets the oyster. The second man gets the shell."*
Andrew Carnegie

At this point, you probably feel like a mosquito in a nudist colony. You know what you want to do, but you don't know where to start.

Here is help. There is one sure way to cut weeks off your Internet project time and save a lot of money, without using magic, without cheating. That one sure way is to do a little homework first.

Not as much homework as you used to have to do to get up to speed on the Net. Over the last year, Internet software has made giant strides in ease of installation and use. In most cases, you will *not* need to learn technical details like how to install a TCP/IP stack. But you still need to learn how the Internet works, what you can do in it, and how to find stuff on the Net. And you'll need to monitor a couple of newsletters or magazines to keep up with the rapid changes. There are also important technical resources that can save trouble for your technical staff.

You'll find the Internet holds key resources that can help you learn and keep you informed. In fact, using the Net to teach you about itself is one of the best and fastest ways to get up to speed. Your problem is choosing from hundreds of resources. Books about the Internet crowd the shelves—more than 350 in English, more than 100 in Japanese, 70 in German, and dozens in other languages. Dozens of journals, magazines, and newsletters cover the Internet. Hundreds more resources are available within the Internet itself. Some are duds, but many are valuable. How can you tell which is which?

Look here first. This chapter is designed to save time by steering you in the right direction, towards proven resources. You don't need to read *all* these books or visit *all* these Internet sites. No business needs all of them. And if you're in management, you can delegate Internet studies to your staff. (After all, you read *this* book. You've suffered enough.) But budget to buy at least six books.

In any case, I've tried to describe these resources so you can more easily pick and choose the ones that best fit your needs. Each item was selected for its relevance for *businesses*. To clarify which items I found the most helpful, I've used a five-star rating system. Stars indicate *usefulness* and no other factor—

---

*Your guide to the stars*

| | |
|---|---|
| ☆☆☆☆☆ | Highest rating; extremely valuable for all businesses. Rarely given. |
| ☆☆☆☆ | Very useful to most businesses. |
| ☆☆☆ | The most variable rating, ranging from barely useful to all businesses to quite useful, but only for a specific audience. |
| ☆☆ | May have some use, not as helpful as its competitors. |
| (no stars) | An Internet resource with no stars may be good or may be bad; lack of stars indicates I haven't checked it. |

---

not good design, not easiness, not cute cartoons. I looked strictly for what would most benefit a business.

Nontechnical books are presented first, followed by nontechnical periodicals. These are the tools that can help get your Internet projects started, help it run smoothly, and ensure growth. Next come printed directories to help you find stuff on the Net. Technical books and periodicals follow, not for businesspeople, but for your technical staff to build expertise.

Online resources follow, beginning with nontechnical resources to help you learn about the Internet. Next come the Internet's own online directories of itself, and its search engines to help you find things. Then the Net's own technical guides to itself.

I wanted to give a top ten list of books and periodicals, but I would have had to build a different list for every reader. I recommend *The Cuckoo's Egg* and *The Internet Letter* to everyone, but beyond those two titles I have a hard time making a blanket recommendation. Get books that meet your company's specific needs. If you sell on the Net, you need *Successful Direct Marketing Methods*. If not, you probably don't. I'd recommend *Low-Cost Email with*

*UUCP*—but only if you have or want a UUCP server. Many other books are platform-specific, useful only if you have Microsoft Windows, or only if you use a Mac, and so on. So you'll have to build your own shopping list.

If you can't find these books nearby, I have four sources to recommend. My alma mater, Computer Literacy Bookshops, carries the world's largest selection of computer books. It ships all over the world, and is your best bet for English-language books. Fax to 408-435-1823, phone 408-435-0744.
Address: **info@clbooks.com** (email)
　　　　**http://www.clbooks.com**

In the U.K, there is a close second: Computer Manuals Ltd. Phone 0121-706-6000.
Address: **order@compman.demon.co.uk** (email)

The best selection of Internet books I've found in Japanese is carried by Toshokan Ryutu Center. Fax 81-3-3943-9555 or phone 81-03-3943-9990.
Address: **wwwadmin@ns.trc.co.jp** (email)
　　　　**http://www.trc.co.jp**

For German-language Internet books, try JF-Lehmanns Fachbuchhandlung.
Address: **http://www.Germany.EU.net/shop/JFL**

## Nontechnical books

Most books covering the Internet are nontechnical books for beginners (*newbies*, in Net lingo), rehashing the same information again and again. Most are competent. Few of those are included here.

You do need a book or two to get started. I recommend buying any two introductory "how-to" books, one each from two different publishers. Because most publishers use a somewhat different approach, when you can't find what you need in one book, the other may help.

The most important thing about your introductory books is to *get books for the same operating system you use*. Until Michael Fraase wrote *The Mac Internet*

*Tour Guide* in 1993, all Internet books assumed you used Unix. If you pick up an introductory Internet book that doesn't say what operating system it covers, it's probably a Unix book—which won't meet your needs if you use something else. Instead, choose from books for the Mac, DOS, Windows, OS/2, and VAX/VMS operating systems.

When you buy a beginner's book, also check whether the book includes a disk. If your business already has its Internet client software, don't look for a book with a disk. Chances are the book will mostly discuss using its specific software, and will be of limited use when you use other software. Of course, if you haven't yet selected your Internet software, buying a book with a disk can be an inexpensive way for you to test-drive software. (Note that the *only* time to avoid a software disk is when buying a beginning Net book. With other books, software can be *great!* )

The third thing to verify is that your introductory book has a section on Mosaic or the World Wide Web. Most business users use email and the World Wide Web more than any other features of the Internet, so a book without Web coverage won't teach you what you most need to know. If it doesn't cover the Web, put it back on the shelf.

After you have your two introductory how-to books, take a look at the books presented in this chapter. All are listed in alphabetical order by title. Most of the books below are not for newbies, but deal with specific aspects of the Internet. Rather than give an overall introduction, these books cover business issues, explain particular Internet services in detail, or tell how to use the Net in a specific country. Three books are not about the Internet, but will be extremely useful to businesses on the Net. I culled through dozens to choose these. Since the Internet is worldwide, I included a few volumes in languages other than English.

---

*Access the Internet* by David Peal ☆☆☆ (1994), Sybex Inc., 230 pages and disk. ISBN 0-7821-1529-2.

After all that talk about avoiding introductory books with disks, what's this first book about? Yeah, an introductory book with a disk—but one with a difference. This is the simplest, fastest way I've found to connect to the Internet. The book itself tells clearly how to install and use the NetCruiser software, which comes with it. No big deal. What's special is on the disk: NetCruiser from Netcom. Less than five minutes after I popped the disk in my computer (I timed it), I had opened an account, selected my Internet address, and was cruising the Net. Other books claim to get you up this fast, but most require you to open an account *before* you use the software. This does it all for you. The software works only in the United States, and requires Windows, a modem, and a PC with a 386, 486, or Pentium processor. A second edition will probably be out by the time you read this.

*Canadian Internet Handbook*, by Jim Carroll and Rick Broadhead ☆☆☆☆ (1994 edition), Prentice Hall Canada, 410 pages. ISBN 0-13-304395-9.

If you do business in Canada, buy this book. It tells how to get Internet connections in Canada (focusing more on single-computer connections than ones for companies) and provides a healthy directory of Canadian Internet resources. The 1994 edition is useful, but hopefully an updated version will appear.

*Connecting to the Internet* by Susan Estrada ☆☆☆ (1993), O'Reilly and Associates, 170 pages. ISBN 1-56592-061-9.

A little out of date, this is still the only book that explains how to select an Internet access provider and choose what kind of connection is best for your business.

*The Cuckoo's Egg: Tracking a Spy through the Maze of Computer Espionage* by Cliff Stoll ☆☆☆☆☆ (1989), Pocket Books, 332 pages. ISBN 0-67172-688-9.

This terrific book spent five months on the *New York Times'* bestseller list. It's as exciting as a Tom Clancy novel, only funnier and with more romance. And it's all true! The author is sent to find the cause of a 75-cent error in an accounting program. It alerts him to an Internet intruder—an East German spy funded by the KGB—breaking into hundreds of military bases and defense corporations! The FBI and CIA get into the act. As the suspense mounts, you learn important facts about Internet security. I like this book so much I read it three times.

*Cyberspace and the Law* by Edward Cabazos and Gavino Morin ☆☆☆ (1994), MIT Press. ISBN 0-262-53123-2.

An overview of Internet law, mostly American. Includes full text of the Electronic Communications Privacy Act and related U.S. and state regulations.

*Dai 3 no Kaikoku* by Tuguchika Kaminuma ☆☆☆ (1994) Kinokuniya, 288 pages. ISBN 4-314-00692-7.

An overview book, first covering general Internet background and the Net in the U.S., then the Net in Japan and business use of the Net. Not a how-to book.

*Doing More Business on the Internet* by Mary Cronin ☆☆☆☆ (1995), Van Nostrand Reinhold. ISBN 0-442-02047-3.

Second edition of the first book in English about the Internet and businesses, this is a useful idea-stimulator. Based on interviews with more than 100 companies, this isn't a how-to book, but instead a nontechnical person's look at what businesses have done on the Net. The second edition has grown to cover the World Wide Web.

*The Elements of Email Style* by David Angell and Brent Heslop ☆☆☆ (1994), Addison-Wesley Publishing. ISBN 0-201-62709-4.

A book for people who write a lot of email, and want to make it effective. This book points out differences between email style and letter-writing style, and tells when to use each. It is useful for publicity and customer service people.

*Finding It on the Internet* by Paul Gilster ☆☆☆☆ (1994), John Wiley & Sons. ISBN 0-471-03857-1.

After people are up on the Internet and learn how to use email, the most common question is "How do I find anything?" Gilster tells how to use Internet search tools, and provides search strategies. Some of the book concentrates on Unix commands, but most of it applies to all platforms. Contains the most irritating use of boldface type I've ever seen in a book.

*From EDI to Electronic Commerce: A Business Initiative* by Phyllis Sokol ☆☆☆ (1995), McGraw-Hill, 305 pages. ISBN 0-07-059512-7.

 This is both a rewarding and a frustrating book. It gives businesspeople realistic instructions on how to cost-justify and implement EDI. The author clearly knows her subject and delivers—in a wooden writing style—much valuable information. But, having worked only with value-added networks, she is biased toward them. Even though this book was published in 1995, the word "Internet" is not mentioned once. The author assumes transactions will be processed in batch mode, and shows little understanding of online transaction processing. Most infuriating, she discusses standards, but doesn't tell where to find them. She names EDI organizations, but doesn't tell how to contact them. She mentions publications like *EDI World*, but doesn't tell where to reach them. Minor quibbles are that the book is U.S.-centric with scant international information, and is poorly indexed. On page 53, it states that bisynch protocols can go up to 9600 bits per second and asynchronous protocols handle up to 4800 bits per second. Those speeds are now considered horribly slow. In spite of its shortcomings, this is an important guidebook for any company considering EDI, and I do recommend it. Just keep its flaws in mind.

*Hayawakari Internet* by Dr. Haruhisa Ishida ☆☆☆ (1994), Kyoritsu Publishing, 128 pages. ISBN 4-320-02718-3.

Not specifically a business book, but good for Japanese executives who want a short, clear overview by a distinguished authority. Covers major issues without too much technical detail. Includes a chapter on firewalls and security.

*How to Advertise on the Internet* by Michael Strangelove with Aneurin Bosley ☆☆☆☆ (1994), Strangelove Internet Enterprises, 212 pages. ISSN 1201-0758.

A good look at Internet advertising and publicity, written for marketing people. Covers most of the bases, with lots of examples. Where it lacks specific how-to instructions, it tells you where to go on the Net to get free details. Does not cover credit cards or security issues. Needs, but lacks, an index. Recommended for all ad-pub people on the Net.

*Inside the Information Superhighway Revolution* by Nicholas Baran ☆☆☆ (1995), Coriolis Group Books, 268 pages. ISBN 1-883577-10-1.

A clear overview of all aspects of the "Information Superhighway," of which the author considers the Internet as only one part. Focuses on the United States. Stimulating foreword by Jeff Duntemann.

*Internet & Jyouhou super highway* by Toshiharu Aoki ☆☆☆ (1995), Omusya Press, 216 pages. ISBN 4-274-94531-6.

There is no English-language equivalent to this illustrated Japanese book, which provides an overview of the historical and political aspects of the Net as well as a fair amount of technical detail. It covers requirements for business connectivity, especially ISDN, and briefly touches on the Japanese PNES association and BBCC.

*The Internet Business Companion* by David Angell and Brent Heslop ☆☆☆☆ (1995), Addison-Wesley Publishing Company, 242 pages. ISBN 0-201-40850-3.

A good overview on how to implement the Internet in your business. Forgets to say that you may need an SMTP or UUCP server for email, and only mentions handling credit cards. (It recommends unencrypted card numbers— for shame!) Overall is a strategically sound book. No coverage of EDI. A short, easy read, with lots of solid information.

*Internet in Plain English* by Bryan Pfaffenberger ☆☆☆ (1994), MIS Press, 462 pages plus disk. ISBN 1-55828-385-4.

A good dictionary of Internet terms and abbreviations, clarifying them for nontechnical people. Comes with a disk of NetManage's Windows software Chameleon, which has little to do with the book.

*Internet Kakumei (Internet Revolution)* by Kenichi Omae ☆☆☆ (1995), President Books, 250 pages. ISBN 4-8334-1554-2.

Japanese-language overview of the Internet and Japan, with interesting observations about the changes made in companies by networks and products like Lotus Notes.

*Internet Secrets*, John R. Levine and Carol Baroudi, editors ☆☆☆☆ (1995) IDG Books, 990 pages and two disks. ISBN 1-56884-452-2.

Another mammoth book written by committee, but this one has more to interest businesses than the others. Includes information for both technical and nontechnical people. Although the section on business and the Net is lame, other chapters give solid coverage of setting up servers (including a Web server using Windows), encryption, and managing email in a business. Besides shareware, the disks contain a useful directory of 6,500 Internet email lists to which you can subscribe.

*The Internet Unleashed,* Phil Paxton, editor ☆☆☆ (1994) Sams Publishing, 1,387 pages and disk. ISBN 0-672-30466-X.

Written by a committee of dozens of authors, this hodge-podge is uneven, bouncing from simple to technical and from advanced to introductory. There is so much here that parts of the book will be useful to almost everyone. The disk includes NetManage's Chameleon Sampler of Windows Internet tools.

*Merriam-Webster's Guide to International Business Communications* by Toby D. Atkinson ☆☆☆☆ (1994), Merriam-Webster, 327 pages. ISBN 0-87779-028-0.

How do you write email to make it understandable by people in other countries? What export documentation do you prepare to ship products overseas? What fields does your customer database need to handle addresses, titles, and names for international customers? This is not an Internet book, but it does have a staggering amount of information for American and Canadian businesses with overseas customers. Most of the book is a country-by-country reference of address formats, phone system information, money formats, and other information needed daily when doing business internationally.

*Mosaic Explorer Pocket Companion* by Jeff Duntemann, Ron Pronk, and Patrick Vincent ☆☆☆ (1995), Coriolis Group Books, 241 pages. ISBN 1-883577-24-1.

Somewhat misnamed, this small, fast-paced book does not cover only Mosaic, but gives an entertaining introduction to the entire World Wide Web. A funny section, "Forty Questions You Can Ask Us without Getting Flamed," gives you a solid background on the Web. It's followed by an illustrated directory of Web sites, and brief but clear directions for nontechnical people on how to use HTML to design your own home page.

*Netiquette* by Virginia Shea ☆☆☆ (1994), Albion Books, 154 pages. ISBN 1-56592-063-5.

A friendly, gentle explanation of how to behave on the Internet and why. Large companies buy dozens of copies of this book to distribute to all employees who receive Net access. That's a good idea, and much cheaper than cleaning up the aftermath caused by a newbie's blunders.

*Successful Direct Marketing Methods*, fifth edition by Bob Stone ☆☆☆☆ (1994), NTC Business Books, 654 pages. ISBN 0-8442-3510-5.

This book contains absolutely no information about the Internet, but if you do direct marketing, you need this book. And *all* selling over the Net is direct marketing. Stone's tome is the bible of the direct marketing business, and tells you what kind of research, testing, customer records, and analyses you need. And it shows you quite competently how to do them.

*The Usenet Book* by Bryan Pfaffenberger ☆☆☆ (1995), Addison-Wesley Publishing, 468 pages. ISBN 0-201-40978-X.

Half of this book has the most detailed coverage of newsgroups I've found yet, including directions for starting your own. The remainder is two directories: first in-depth descriptions of the top 300 groups, then a subject directory of 3,000 groups. Covers few business-specific groups.

*Your Internet Consultant: The FAQs of Life Online* by Kevin Savetz ☆☆☆ (1994), Sams Publishing, 550 pages. ISBN 0-672-30520-8.

This question-and-answer guide to the Internet is both useful and amusing. Savetz dug up the Net's most helpful FAQ lists of Frequently Asked Questions (361 of them) and put a lot of work into editing them, bringing in specialists to add depth where needed. My favorite is how astronomers use Multi-User Dungeons (MUDs) to conduct research!

## One-of-a-kind hybrid

*Commercial User's Guide to the Internet* ☆☆☆☆☆ Published monthly by Thompson Publishing Group, 1725 K Street, 7th floor, Washington DC 20006.

This guide crosses several boundaries. It is a monthly 12-page newsletter plus a fat 600-page looseleaf book with monthly updates. It is aimed at nontechnical business readers, but also adds valuable data for technical people. It includes both overview information and how-to instructions, plus a very useful directory of Internet resources. The best part is not how much it includes, but the high quality, and the fact that all information is carefully tied into business operations. It is not perfect; there are a couple of surprising omissions and a few errors. The major drawback is its steep $400 a year price tag.

## Nontechnical periodicals

There are scads of magazines about the Internet, with more on their way. This is not a complete list. It does not include several magazines, journals, and newsletters that I did not review. It does not include specialized nonbusiness publications, such as those covering the Internet for librarians or genealogists.

It does, however, include most magazines, journals, and newsletters about the Internet with useful information for businesses. You won't need all of these, but you should subscribe to two or three that you think would be most helpful.

---

*Boardwatch* ☆☆☆☆ Published monthly by Boardwatch Magazine, ISSN 1054-2760.
Address: **subscriptions@boardwatch.com** (email)

This is a magazine specifically for people who *provide* online information. Its design is not elegant, but don't let looks deceive you. If you are interested in business, legal, and technical developments of the Internet, you will read important news here that you won't find anywhere else. For instance, *Boardwatch* was one of only two publications that covered one of the biggest Internet stories of 1994, the furious infighting among the members of the Commercial Internet Exchange that ended when Rick Adams reduced the organization to a personal dictatorship and others broke away to compete. Most of the magazine's lively in-depth writing covers bulletin board systems and commercial services (such as CompuServe and AOL), with 50 percent on the Internet. Big tip: Always read the opinionated "Letters to the Editor" pages.

*Cook Report on the Internet* ☆☆☆ Published monthly by Gordon Cook, ISSN 1071-6327.
Address: **cook@cookreport.com** (email)

This newsletter covers policy and political issues relating to commercial use of the Internet. It breaks scoops, and provides good old-fashioned muckraking, as when it broke a scandal in Indiana about the state government's "Access Indiana" Internet program channeling funds to Ameritech. Good coverage of international developments, especially in Russia. Not a "how-to" source.

*Database: the Magazine of Electronic Database Reviews* ☆☆☆☆ Published bimonthly by Online Inc., 462 Danbury Road, Wilton, CT 06897 USA. ISSN 0162-4105.

Pricey but very useful publication for online researchers. Covers CD-ROMs as well as the Internet and other online services. About half of the articles are Internet-related. Reports on new resources, evaluates research sources in depth, and gives tips on finding information. Provides a few stories for database providers.

*DM News* ☆☆☆ Published weekly by Mill Hollow Corporation, 19 W. 21st Street, New York, NY 10010 USA.

This direct marketing newspaper does a very good job of covering marketing-related Internet news all over the world. It's valuable for marketing, order desk, and fulfillment managers. Subscriptions are free to qualified U.S. subscribers, fee-based to those in other countries.

*EDI World* ☆☆☆ Published monthly by EDI World, Inc.,. ISSN 1055-0399.
Address: **ediworld@aol.com** (email)

The only monthly publication covering EDI from a businessperson's point of view, this magazine concentrates on the information you need to get started with electronic business transactions, especially financial, purchasing, shipping, and manufacturing transactions. Covers both Internet and non-Internet EDI.

*Inside the Internet* ☆☆☆ Published monthly by The Cobb Group, 9420 Bunsen Parkway, Louisville, KY 40220 USA. ISSN 1075-7902.

12-page newsletter covering Internet resources and basic techniques for non-technical users. Covers all operating systems. Skillfully written, with well-chosen topics. Distributing this is a good way to get employees comfortable with the Net.

*Internet Bulletin for CPAs* ☆☆☆☆ Published monthly by Kent Information Services, ISSN 1078-2176.
Address: **mail@kentis.kent.oh.us** (email)

This slickly designed 12-page newsletter covers AICPA's online activities, how to use Internet tools, security issues, online resources for accountants, and where to go to get updated tax information online. Covers all operating systems, and how to access the Net from CompuServe, America Online, and Delphi. Emphasizes real hands-on issues, not pie in the sky. ("Because of comments from several California users on constant busy signals, we are no longer recommending NetCruiser for California users until this problem is resolved.") Focuses on the U.S.; could use more on international issues. Subscribers receive a booklet on inexpensive ways to connect to the Internet, a *Getting Started on the Internet* booklet, the book *Big Dummy's Guide to the Internet* by Adam Gaffin on disk, and the materials to earn CPE credits for learning to use the Internet. A good value for accountants.

*Internet Business Advantage* ☆☆☆ Published monthly by Wentworth World-wide Communications.
Address: **info@wentworth.com** (email)
       **http://www.wentworth.com/webworld/IBA.htm**

Simple and sometimes overly optimistic newsletter with nontechnical how-to information for confused people in small U.S. businesses. Good for some people, although I am not enthusiastic about it myself. Check out its home page to see if you like it.

*Internet Business Report* ☆☆☆ Published monthly by CMP Publications.
Address: **ibrsub@cmp.com** (email)

Good coverage of Internet industry issues (company profiles and executive interviews with major players). No how-to information. CMP offers a free trial issue, but getting one is outrageously difficult. Between my editor and me, it took nine tries to get one sample copy.

*The Internet Connection: Your Guide to Government Resources* ☆☆☆ Published ten times per year.
Address: **connect@kraus.com** (email)

Newsletter written by librarians pointing out new government sites on the Net. Not as much coverage of business sites as there could be.

*The Internet Letter* ☆☆☆☆ Published monthly by NetWeek Inc., ISSN 1070-9851.
Address: **info@netweek.com** (email)

Subtitled *On Corporate Users, Internetworking & Information Services*, this 12-page newsletter covers the Net from a businessperson's point of view. It covers Net stories important for businesses, often months before other publications. Out of all the Internet publications I read, this is the one I grab first.

*Internet Magazine* ☆☆☆ Published monthly by Impress Corporation.
Address: **http://www.impress.co.jp/magazine/inetmag/index-jp.sjis.html**

A good Japanese magazine, written for individual users but giving good listings of Net resources, some of which will be useful to businesses, and extremely clear how-to articles. Each issue reviews and compares Japan's Internet access providers, including their prices, and most issues include a CD-ROM.

*Internet Report* ☆☆☆ Published monthly by IWT Magazin Verlag GmbH.
Address: **http://www.iwtnet.de/inet_report**

German "how-to" newsletter with simple tips for small and medium-sized businesses.

*Internet Research* ☆☆☆ Published quarterly by Mecklermedia, ISSN 1066-2243.
Address: **info@mecklermedia.com** (email)

This is an expensive academic journal covering Internet applications and policy. No how-to instructions here, but it provides strategy and background information. It attracts top names. For instance, its article announcing Mosaic was co-written by Marc Andreessen, co-author of both Mosaic and Netscape.

*Internet User* ☆☆☆ Published monthly by Softbank.
Address: **unixuser@softbank.co.jp**

Japanese magazine for beginning Net users, covering the basics. Each issue reviews Net access providers in Japan and includes a CD-ROM.

*Internet World* ☆☆☆☆ Published monthly by Mecklermedia, ISSN 1064-3923.
Address: **info@mecklermedia.com** (email)

Most issues of this glossy magazine provide something relevant for Internet businesses and some have very valuable articles. Topics range from introductory stuff for newbies to sharp analyses of key issues.

*.net* ☆☆☆Published monthly by Future Publishing.
Address: **netmag@futurenet.co.uk** (email)
         **http://www.futurenet.co.uk/home.html**

I love this British mag. It's a Eurohip *Wired*, with a different attitude, and more useful how-to stuff. Only a tiny amount of business coverage, but highly recommended if you want to keep tabs on the Brit Net blast. Way fresh.

*NetGuide* ☆☆☆ Published monthly by CMP Media,
Address: **netmail@netguide.cmp.com** (email)
         **http://techweb.cmp.com/net**.

The first issue of this magazine was a wonder, with thought-provoking articles by top-name writers. Then it slid downhill. Now it's the *People* magazine of the Internet, but still useful for newbies. About two-thirds of its writing covers the Internet, one-third covers other online services.

*New Book Bulletin* ☆☆☆ Published quarterly by Computer Literacy Bookshops.
Address: **info@clbooks.com** (email)

Free 12-page newsletter/catalog providing short reviews of about 100 new and important computer books, including all important new Internet books in English. A good way to keep up with hot topics as they emerge.

*Online: the Magazine of Online Information Systems* ☆☆☆ Published bi-monthly by Online Inc., 462 Danbury Road, Wilton, CT 06897 USA. ISSN 0146-5422.

Only about 35 percent of this pricey magazine for researchers and information providers deals with the Internet. A sister publication of *Database*, this one covers non-database sources as well.

*West Coast Online* ☆☆☆ Published monthly by WCO.
Address: **info@wco.com** (email)

Monthly newspaper covers online life in Northern California. Each issue is a grab-bag of business, nonbusiness, technical, and nontechnical stories.

*Wired* ☆☆☆ Published monthly by Wired Ventures Ltd., ISSN 1059-1028.
Address: **http://www.wired.com**

Famous for eyeball-searing graphics and top-notch writing with an attitude, *Wired* covers high tech as a *lifestyle*. Not all stories are Internet-related, and there are few articles specifically about Internet business, but those few are choice.

## Printed Internet directories

There is no such animal, in print or online, as a complete directory to the Internet. It grows so fast that no one can keep up with it. This makes printed directories out-of-date almost instantly. When buying a printed Internet directory, always double-check that you have the latest edition. A year-old Net directory is less useful than a two-year-old phone book.

People who actively use the Internet for several months favor searching online before turning to a printed directory, but newbies use directories more often than any other type of book. Buying a directory or two is actually a good trick to cultivate your employees' eagerness to use the Net. When they leaf through a *Yellow Pages* or *Free $tuff* book and see all the great goodies they can scoop up online, your staff will rank Internet access equal to a visit from Santa Claus.

Even experienced Netheads will find some of these useful, because they contain specialized information difficult to find online. *Directory of Electronic Journals, What's on the Internet,* and *!%@:* (Say that out loud!) all fall into this category.

---

*!%@:: a Directory of Electronic Mail Addressing & Networks,* fourth edition by Donnalyn Frey and Rick Adams ☆☆☆ (1994), O'Reilly & Associates, 641 pages. ISBN 1-56592-046-5.

This is the directory with the hardest name to pronounce, and the only one listing the many networks that make up the Internet, with contact names and information for almost 200 of the largest ones. Also provides Internet domain addresses for thousands of companies. Useful for marketing people to find addresses outside your company, especially if your company is thinking of doing joint promotions with Internet access providers.

*Directory of Electronic Journals, Newsletters and Academic Discussion Lists,* fourth edition by Lisabeth King and Diane Kovacs ☆☆☆☆ (1994), Association of Research Libraries, 588 pages. ISSN 1057-1337.

Lists 1,800 academic mailing lists on every topic imaginable—including business-related subjects—and 440 electronic newsletters, with instructions on how to contact them. Many good sources of information not listed elsewhere.

*The Federal Internet Source,* Jayne Levin, editor ☆☆☆ (1994), National Journal Inc., 50 pages. ISBN 0-89234-062-2.

A quick but good introduction to Internet tools, followed by hundreds of U.S. government Gopher, FTP, Telnet, and World Wide Web sites. Each site has a description and notes on its links to other sites.

## Battle of the *Internet Yellow Pages*

There are two books titled *Internet Yellow Pages*, printed by different publishers and written by different authors.

The Hahn & Stout version has fewer entries, but more description of each entry. It reads as though each site was inspected personally by the authors, and its tone is more light-hearted. The Maxwell & Crycz version has more entries but less description. It also claims to be less sexist, and features no erotic sites. The Hahn & Stout book does list a few sexy sites.

Each directory has its proponents. Both are useful books. I have noticed that when browsers compare the two side-by-side, about three-fourths of them buy the Hahn & Stout book. Its second edition is also more recent. In my opinion, its recency gives it an edge over its rival.

*Internet Yellow Pages*, second edition by Harley Hahn and Rick Stout ☆☆☆☆ (1995), Osbourne McGraw-Hill, 812 pages. ISBN 0-07-882098-7. (Due to trademark restrictions, in some countries this is called *Internet Golden Directory*, but has the same ISBN number.)

*New Riders Official Internet Yellow Pages* by Christine Maxwell and Czeslaw Jan Grycz ☆☆☆ (1994) New Riders Publishing, 802 pages. ISBN 1-56205-408-2.

*Free $tuff from the Internet* by Patrick Vincent ☆☆☆ (1994), Coriolis Group Books, 459 pages. ISBN 1-883577-11-X.

This directory is a good one to give to new people on the Net, because they will immediately see dozens of things (software, graphics, books, reports, coffee samples) they just *have* to have. Greed is one of the strongest motivations to acquire Internet proficiency. Most directories have only listings, but this one describes every site *in detail*. It's fun to read, and lists many good business resources.

*Fulltext Sources Online* by BiblioData ☆☆☆ (1995) BiblioData, Box 61, Dept. GB, Needham Heights, MA 02194 USA, 390 pages. ISSN 1040-8258.

A directory of more than 5,000 printed journals, newspapers, newsletters, newswires, and TV/radio transcripts that make complete text available online. It covers Internet and non-Internet sources in several languages. Researchers will love this valuable, well-indexed tool. Updated twice a year.

*Newspapers Online* by BiblioData ☆☆☆ (1995) BiblioData, Box 61, Dept. GB, Needham Heights, MA 02194 USA, 540 pages. ISBN 1-879258-12-9.

A directory of online versions of printed newspapers. Each paper receives a detailed one to two-page description of what it makes available online, what is in its online archives, and site-specific tips on how to search and find what you want.

*What's on the Internet* by Eric Gagnon ☆☆☆☆ (1994) Peachpit Press, 255 pages. ISBN 1-56609-162-4.

Well-designed directory of Usenet newsgroups. Gives descriptions, sample subjects, traffic volume, and sometimes FAQ locations for more than 1,000 groups, but covers only a few business-specific groups. Lists 7,900 newsgroups alphabetically, and indexes major groups by subject. Useful for marketers and researchers.

## Technical books

There are many technical books about different aspects of the Internet, especially about TCP/IP. Most are quite good. I have listed only a select group, valuable either because they do an exceptional job of presenting essential technical lore, or because they include information that's hard to find elsewhere.

*DNS and BIND* by Paul Albitz and Cricket Liu ☆☆☆ (1992), O'Reilly & Associates, 280 pages. ISBN 1-56592-010-4.

The definitive book on the Domain Name System, but your company needs it only if you run a DNS server.

*E-Mail Essentials* by Ed Tittel and Margaret Robbins ✫✫✫ (1994) Academic Press, 298 pages. ISBN 0-12-691397-8.

A very clear (if sometimes too simple) how-to guide for new network administrators or advanced users who need to set up and manage email. Covers Internet email as well as NetWare, Banyan VINES, X.400, and Microsoft Mail. Touches on Lotus Notes. A good starter book.

*The Email Frontier: Emerging Markets and Evolving Technologies* by Daniel Blum and David Litwack ✫✫✫ (1994) Addison-Wesley Publishing, 476 pages. ISBN 0-201-56860-8.

Not a how-to guide, but a detailed survey of *all* types of email, not just the Internet, in a dry writing style. The only book I found that covers using email for EDI, a growing trend.

*E-Mail Security* by Bruce Schneier ✫✫✫✫ (1995) John Wiley & Sons, 365 pages. ISBN 0-471-05318-X.

Very clear step-by-step coverage of how to implement Pretty Good Privacy and Privacy Enhanced Mail software.

*Firewalls and Internet Security: Repelling the Wily Hacker* by William Cheswick and Steven Bellovin ✫✫✫✫✫ (1994), Addison-Wesley, 306 pages. ISBN 0-201-63357-4.

This book should be read by every manager of an Internet site, even nontechnical managers. It is the most important work on Internet security, and it is well-written and well-edited. The authors point out that when Internet hackers break into most companies, the companies don't even know the break-in happened. They show how to prevent break-ins and detect break-in attempts. German, French, and Japanese translations are available. Some parts of this book are extremely technical, but the rest of it has value even for nontechnical managers. Here's my reading plan for nontechies: the Preface, Chapter 1: Introduction, the first two pages of Chapter 2, all paragraphs with pictures of little bombs in all chapters, the first six pages of Chapter 3 and its last section "3.9 What Firewalls Can't Do," all of the short Chapter 9, Chapter 12: Legal Considerations, and the short concluding Chapter 14. This quick method packs extremely valuable information into three hours reading, tops.

*Low-Cost E-Mail with UUCP* by Thomas Madron ☆☆☆☆ (1995), Van Nostrand Reinhold, 411 pages plus 2 disks. ISBN 0-442-01849-5.

Supplies a step-by-step explanation of how to use UUCP to set up Internet email in your company. If your business decides not to have an SMTP email server and goes with UUCP instead, get this book. It makes adding email much easier. The book covers UUCP for Unix, DOS, Windows, Macs, and OS/2, but the software on the two disks is for DOS and Windows only. For other operating systems, the book tells where to find software on the Net.

*Managing Internet Information Services* by Cricket Liu, et al. ☆☆☆☆ (1994), O'Reilly & Associates, 630 pages. ISBN 1-56592-062-7.

How to run Internet servers for mailing lists, FTP, Telnet, Finger, Gopher, WAIS, and the World Wide Web. Written for Unix system administrators, but some of the information is so valuable and hard to find elsewhere that I recommend this book for non-Unix administrators as well. It does not cover SMTP or UUCP mail servers.

*Newton's Telecom Dictionary* by Harry Newton ☆☆☆ (1994), Flatiron Publishing, 1,173 pages. ISBN 0-936648-60-0.

I wasn't sure whether to list this as a technical book or a nontechnical book— it fits both categories. It clearly explains many technical and nontechnical Internet terms, making few errors. (Although I caught a couple. The talking computer HAL was in the movie *2001: A Space Odyssey*, not *2000* as listed, and his name stands for Heuristic Analog, not the meaning given. I found definitions for neither Digital Added Main Line nor its acronym DAML. But these are exceptions.)

*PGP: Pretty Good Privacy* by Simson Garfinkel ☆☆☆ (1995), O'Reilly & Associates, 393 pages. ISBN 1-56592-098-8.

How to use PGP for encrypted email and digital signatures. Covers Unix, Mac, and DOS/Windows.

*Sendmail* by Bryan Costales with Eric Allman and Neil Rickert ☆☆☆ (1993), O'Reilly & Associates, 792 pages. ISBN 1-56592-056-2.

If your company uses Sendmail, you need this, the definitive book on how to configure and run the notoriously complex program. Covers the Unix version, but many points apply to other platforms as well.

*TCP/IP Illustrated, Volume 1: the Protocols* by W. Richard Stevens ☆☆☆☆ (1994), Addison-Wesley Publishing, 576 pages. ISBN 0-201-63346-9.

Shows how the protocols work by examining real examples in several flavors of Unix. This has become the standard reference for TCP/IP protocols. For experienced programmers and advanced network administrators, it gives good coverage of technical issues that affect performance and contention.

*TCP/IP Illustrated, Volume 2: the Implementation* by Gary R. Wright and W. Richard Stevens ☆☆☆☆ (1995), Addison-Wesley Publishing, 1,174 pages. ISBN 0-201-63354-X.

I am over my head with the technical depth of this book but still can appreciate its worth. For network programmers and *advanced* TCP/IP network administrators, the authors clearly and thoroughly explain all 15,000 lines of code that make up BSD Unix's version of TCP/IP. The book defines every API function and data structure. It's most valuable for companies using Unix, but the mindboggling yet well-organized detail (no theory here, just the real world) make this useful for TCP/IP programmers in other operating systems as well. Not for beginners.

*TCP/IP Network Administrations* by Craig Hunt ☆☆☆ (1992) O'Reilly & Associates, 472 pages. ISBN 0-937175-82-X.

How to set up and administer TCP/IP in a Unix shop.

*Videoconferencing: the Whole Picture* by Toby Trowt-Bayard ☆☆☆ (1994) Flat-iron Publishing, 458 pages. ISBN 0-936648-48-1.

The first book on videoconferencing. It is helpful, but provides little information specific to the Internet. Useful purchasing checklist in Appendix B.

## Technical periodicals

I wasn't able to find much in the way of magazines or journals providing solid technical information about the Internet. If you find something valuable in this category—in any language—I'd appreciate hearing about it: **vince@emery.com**. Look for updates at **http://www.emery.com**

---

*ConneXions* ☆☆☆☆ Published monthly by Interop Company,
ISSN 0894-5926.
Address: **connexions@interop.com** (email)
> **http://www.interop.com/sbexpos/interop/connexions/cnx_info.html**

This well-edited newsletter provides tutorial-style articles on TCP/IP and re-lated protocols and network technologies by top technical authors, plus case histories and profiles of new technical developments. Internet Society members and Networld+Interop attendees receive a 20 percent discount.

*IAJ News* ☆☆☆ Published quarterly by the Internet Association of Japan,
Address: **iaj-sales@impress.co.jp** (email)

Newsletter covering new technical and nontechnical Internet developments in Japanese.

*Proceedings of the Internet Engineering Task Force* ☆☆☆ Published monthly by Corporation for National Research Initiatives.
Address: **ietf-info@cnri.reston.va.us** (email)

The IETF is one of the organizations determining the technical future of the Net and its protocols. The proceedings include minutes from working group meetings, participant lists, and materials from presentations. There is no how-to information here. This publication is useful mostly for large corporations concerned about the effects that future technical changes will have on them.

*Sys Admin: the Journal for Unix Systems Administrators* ☆☆☆ Published bi-monthly by R&D Publications, ISSN 1061-2688.
Address: **postmaster@rdpub.com** (email)

More practical tips on how to manage Unix Internet software than you can shake a script at.

## Find out about the Internet from the Internet

The Internet is a huge storehouse of all kinds of information, so it's no surprises that the Net has lots of information on how to use itself. Best of all, it's free. One thing to keep in mind is that the Internet is always changing. Don't be surprised if some of these resources shut down or get up and walk away to a new address.

This section lists Internet resources that tell you *how to* use the Net. *Where to* resources are listed in the next section.

*Accessing the Internet by Email* ☆☆☆ Very good how-to guide by Bob Rankin telling how to use different Internet tools (like Gopher and FTP) if you have only email access to the Net. Email to: **listserv@ubvm.cc.buffalo.edu** and leave the Subject line of your message blank. In the body of your message, type: **GET INTERNET BY-EMAIL NETTRAIN F=MAIL** and nothing else. Note that the dash in "EMAIL" goes *before* the "E", not after it.

*All the FAQs* ☆☆☆☆ The name is a slight exaggeration. FAQs are lists of answers to Frequently Asked Questions about a topic. This site has hypertext versions of the FAQs from the most popular newsgroups. The FAQs tell about the newsgroups themselves, and in many cases provide a good introduction to the topic that a newsgroup discusses. Many newsgroups discuss the Internet, so you'll find a lot of information here about the Net.
Address: **http://www.cis.ohio-state.edu:80/hypertext/faq/usenet**

*A Cruise of the Internet* ☆☆☆☆☆ Excellent free software from Merit Network that gives you a hands-on look at Internet tools and then gives you a tour of the resources of the Net. For the Microsoft Windows version, **ftp:// nic.merit.edu**, then go to **internet/resources/cruise.dos/meritcrz.zip**. This is a zipped file. You will need PKunzip (available as shareware or as a commerical product) to unpack the file. For the Macintosh version, FTP to the same site, but go to **internet/resources/cruise.mac/merit.cruise2.mac.hqx**. You can use either StuffIt or BinHex to decode the file.

*Digital Highway Report* ☆☆☆ An online newsletter in Japanese covering U.S. computer, telecomm, and digital culture.
Address: **http://www.webcom.com/~dhrpt**

*Elements of E-Text Style* ☆☆☆ A guide for formatting electronic documents, including email, and outlining how electronic writing style differs from tradi-tional media. Useful for marketing and customer service people who will send a lot of email.
Address: **gopher://palimpsest.stanford.edu:70/00/wais/Net/estyle.10.txt**

*EFF's Guide to the Internet* ☆☆☆ From the Electronic Freedom Foundation, this good how-to guide for new users is also known as *Everybody's Guide to the Internet*.
Address: **http://www.eff.org/pub/Net_info/EFF_Net_Guide/neguide.faq**

*FAQs about newsgroups* ☆☆☆ An archive of frequently-asked questions about newsgroups.
Address: **mail-server@rtfm.mit.edu** (email)
        *type* **help** *in the body of your message*
*or*       **ftp://pit-manager.mit.edu/pub**

*FAQs from newsgroups* ☆☆☆ A newsgroup that posts FAQ lists from many of Usenet's most popular newsgroups, including Internet topics and business topics such as copyright law and investments. This is a good way to find out about new groups, which appear all the time. Don't post questions here; this is a read-only newsgroup.
Address: **news.answers**

*Finding addresses FAQ* ☆☆☆ Answers to common questions about how to find someone's Internet address.
Address: **gopher://english.hss.cmu.edu/Internet/Finding%20Addresses**

*The Free Online Dictionary of Computing* ☆☆☆ by Denis Howe. Its name describes it.
Address: **http://wombat.doc.ic.ac.uk**

*Global Network Navigator* ☆☆☆☆☆ An online magazine with clear instructions on many aspects of the Internet. One of the most fun and most useful spots on the Net.
Address: **http://gnn.com/gnn/GNNhome.html**

*GNET Archive* ☆☆☆ An archive of papers covering technical, business, and political issues about the Internet in less-developed countries. Includes directories of people and resources in those countries. Archived documents are available in summary and full-text versions.
Address: **gopher://gopherr.igc.apc.org:70/1ftp:dhvx20.csuch.edu@/global_net**

*Gopher-News* ☆☆☆ A mailing list about Gopher and Gopher servers, including announcements of new servers. To subscribe, email to: **gopher-news-request@boombox.micro.umn.edu** and ask to be added.

*How to Find an Interesting Mailing List* ☆☆☆ An instructive guide and list by Arno Wouters. Email to: **listserv@vm1.nodak.edu**. In the body of your message, type **get new list wouters** and nothing else.

*How to send email in Russian* ☆☆☆ A list of frequently-asked questions.
Address: **ftp://cs.umd.edu/pub/Cyrillic**

*In acht Sekunden um die Welt* ☆☆☆ Three chapers from the German book by Gunther Maier and Andreas Wildberger.
Address: **http://www.wu-wien.ac.at/netzbuch/netzbuch.html**

*The Internet Hunt* ☆☆☆ A training game for experienced Internet researchers, the Internet Hunt posts ten or eleven questions every month and challenges you to find the answers. All answers are available somewhere on the Net. Winners' names are posted on a list of victors. A fun way to familiarize yourself with some often surprising corners of the Net. *Bon chance!*
Address: **gopher://gopher.cic.net:2000/00/hunt/release**

*Internet user guides* ☆☆☆ Several user guides are available from the Merit Network Information Center. Gopher to **nic.merit.edu**, go to **Introducing the Internet**, and take your pick.

*Internet: Werkzeuge und Dienste-von Archie bis World Wide Web* ☆☆☆☆ A condensed World Wide Web version of the book by M. Scheller, K.P. Boden, A Geenen, and J. Kamperman. Lots of how-to info in German. Includes a brief list of resources, with few business resources.
Address: **http://www.ask.uni-karlsruhe.de/books/inetwd.html**

*Internetwork Mail Guide* ☆☆☆ How to send email between the Internet and CompuServe, America Online, Prodigy, MCIMail, and most other non-Internet online places.
Address: **http://alpha.acast.nova.edu/cgi-bin/inmgq.pl**

*Japan Network Information Center (JPNIC)* ☆☆☆☆☆ Best source I've found for information in Japanese regarding the Internet. Allocates Japanese domain names and acts as international and domestic liason to the Internet.
Address: **http://www.nic.ad.jp/index.html**

*Matrix News* ☆☆☆ A monthly journal about the Internet. This is a read-only newsgroup.
Address: **clari.matrix_news**

*Media coverage of the Internet* ☆☆☆ A newsgroup that reports media stories about the Internet and comments on them. Useful to find what's hot on the Net according to misinformed journalists and what the real story is according to Internet people with first-hand knowledge of the subject.
Address: **alt.internet.media-coverage**

*National Information Infrastructure* ☆☆☆ Full report by the Clinton administration telling how Uncle Sam should incent the private sector to build up telecommunications and the information highway. No how-to instructions here, but offers background for policy wonks.
Address: **gopher://ace.esusda.gov**
*select*      **Americans Communicating Electronically**
*then*        **National Policy Issues**

*Network/Compter Technology Security Index* ☆☆☆☆☆ This site provides *everything* about security on the Net: FTP, Web and Gopher sites, discussion lists, electronic publications, and security incident bulletins from seven organizations.
Address: **http://www.tezcat.com/web/security/security_top_level.html**

*Net-Happenings* ☆☆☆☆ Weekly newsletter of what's new on the Net from InterNIC (The Internet Network Information Center). Describes news, publications, newsletters, conferences, new resources, and software tool updates for the Internet community. Email to **majordomo@is.internic.net** with nothing in your message but **subscribe net-happenings youremailaddress**. A Web version is at **http://www.mid.net/NET**. Also available as a newsgroup. Address: **comp.internet.net-happenings**

*Netiquette questions and answers* ☆☆☆ A newsgroup where newbies can ask questions and have them answered by old pros. Look through this group when you first get aboard the Net; chances are you'll find answers to the same questions you have. One warning: This newsgroup generates 50-80 postings each day.
Address: **news.newusers.questions**

*Nettools* ☆☆☆ A guide to Internet tools (FTP, Gopher, Web, WAIS). Email to: **listserv@earncc.bitnet** and in the body of your message type GET NETTOOLS TXT to receive the plain vanilla text version. If you'd prefer a PostScript version, in the body of your message type GET NETTOOLS PS and nothing else. This guide is also available by FTP: **ftp://naic.nasa.gov/files/general_info** and get the file **earn-resource-tool-guide.txt** for the plain text version, or **earn-resource-tool-guide.ps** for the PostScript version. You can find this guide on the Web at **http://naic.nasa.gov/naic/guide/tools/index.html**.

*Newbie newsgroup* ☆☆☆ Help for new Internet users is the special topic of the newsgroup.
Address: **alt.newbie**

*Saturn: a Beginner's Guide to Using the Internet* ☆☆☆ Instructions on how to use the Internet for VAX/VMS users by Kyle Cassidy.
Address: **ftp://gboro.rowan.edu/pub/Saturn-Guide**

*The Scout Report* ☆☆☆☆ Weekly newsletter every Friday from InterNIC with what's new and cool on the Net. Not as lengthy as *Net-Happenings*.
Address: **majordomo@dstest.internic.net** (email)
*enter*     **subscribe scout-report youremailaddress** in message (nothing else)
*or*     **http://rs.internic.net/scout_report-index.html**

*Tcl and Tk information* ☆☆☆☆ Tons of links to all kinds of technical information about the "tickle" language and the "tee-kay" toolkit, useful for Internet server programming. Windows and Windows NT versions are available. Address: **http://cuiwww.unige.ch/eao/www/TclTk.html**

*Usenet newsgroup announcements* ☆☆☆☆ A newsgroup that provides how-to instructions about Usenet newsgroups. You can't post your own questions here; this is a read-only newsgroup. This newsgroup is low volume, but provides very helpful information, especially for marketing via newsgroups. Address: **news.announce.newusers**

*Wired Japan mailing list* ☆☆☆ A Japanese-language mailing list for *Wired Japan*. Not much on business, but keeps you in touch with efforts to reach Japan's screenagers. Email to **listproc@ecosys.com** and in the body of your message type **subscribe NETSURF yourfirstname yourlastname**.

# Where to find stuff on the Net

You will probably use this section more than anything else in the entire book, so color the edges of the pages with a day-glo highlighter and leave a big bookmark here.

This section contains only two types of resources: places that give you search engines to find topics or addresses and places that provide directories or lists. Some sites provide both. The most valuable sites are the search sites. If you use the Internet to gather information, you will return to these search sites again and again. As an easy flag, look for the word "search" in the first three words of my descriptions of all sites offering searches.

The three search engines I use most often are Yahoo (easiest, fastest and with useful directories as a bonus), Lycos (searches more sites and presents findings with explanations), and EINet Galaxy. I also use the Internet Sleuth (listed under *Catalog of Searchable Databases*), which searches 450 places at one time.

Directories online are useful, too, especially because they are inevitably more up-to-date than their printed counterparts. You can update an online directory several times a day, a convenience impossible with a printed book. There is another great advantage of directories carried on the World Wide Web: When you read something you like, click on it and the Web takes you there. It is impossible to exaggerate how much easier this makes information-hunting.

When your business first connects to the Internet, of course your staff will need training, some more than others. People who are already on the Net at home may need no training. But in addition to classes, plan time for your newbies to just browse the Net to familiarize themselves with its resources and tools. The amount of time you should allow depends on which Internet tools (Gopher, Web, FTP, etc.) your people use, and their positions. Someone in marketing, for instance, should spend from five to ten hours a week for the first four weeks just poking around and finding surprises.

Time invested in early exploration will pay ongoing dividends later, because those explorers will know how to find resources on the Net and how to use them. Encourage your people to try as many of the resources described here as they possibly can. Net users familiar with many alternatives are less likely to ossify into a few rigid use patterns that give them access only to limited information.

Pass this chapter to your newbies. The directories and lists in this section are not *business-specific* directories, although they list businesses and sometimes list valuable resources for businesses. The directories here are general lists. (You'll find a catalog of business-specific resources in Chapter 13.) The general nature of these lists makes them especially valuable for exploration by new Net users. The treasures that users find while probing will build their sense of control over the Net, instead of letting them be overwhelmed by its immensity.

Along with the resources, here's a handy trick that doesn't quite fit anyplace else: how to find a person's email address when you know only his/her company address. Just send email to **postmaster@address**—insert the company's address in place of "address". For example, if you knew Effie Perine worked for Spade & Archer where her company address was **detect.com**, to find Effie's address you'd send a message to **postmaster@detect.com**. Most sites have someone in charge of mail. In your message, ask for the email address of the person you are trying to reach.

---

*Aliweb* ☆☆☆ British search engine.
Address: **http://web.nexor.co.uk/public/aliweb/search/doc/form.html**

*Apollo Directory* ☆☆☆☆ Search for businesses on the Net by geographic location, by category, and by key words.
Address: **http://apollo.co.uk**

*Catalog of Searchable Databases* ☆☆☆☆ The Internet Sleuth links with more than 450 searchable indexes and databases on a variety of topics.
Address: **http://www.intbc.com/sleuth/index.html**

*EINet Galaxy* ☆☆☆☆☆ A very good search engine makes this one of the first places to look to find something on the Net. Good options and fast. Gives you a custom-built Web page of hotlinked findings. For each link, a score tells how closely it fits your search parameters and the size of the file, so you don't waste time on a huge, slow file that barely has what you are looking for.
Address: **http://galaxy.einet.net/galaxy.html**

*Email address database searcher* ☆☆☆ If someone has posted a message to a Usenet newsgroup, his or her name and address is added to the Usenet address database. Send email to: **mail-server@pit-manager.mit.edu** with this message: **send Usenet-addresses/name**. Replace "name" with the actual name of the person you're hunting for.

*European home page* ☆☆ Slow as molasses, this site gives you a GIF map of Europe that you can click on to find home pages of European nations. To save you time, I've listed them below. Also provides a tiny amount of useless EC information.
Address: **http://s700.uminho.pt/ec.html**
    *Austria*    **http://www.ifs.univie.ac.at/austria.html**
    *Belgium*    **http://pespmc1.vub.ac.be/BelgCul.html**

*Bulgaria* **http://asudesign.eas.asu.edu/places/Bulgaria/map.html**
*Croatia* **http://tjev.tel.etf.hr/hrvatska/HR.html**
*Czech Republic* **http://www.cesnet.cz/html/cesnet/map.html**
*Denmark* **http://info.denet.dk/dkmap.html**
*Estonia* **http://www.eenet.ee**
*Finland* **http://www.funet.fi/resources/map.html**

*France* ☆☆☆☆ Key word search for French sites, a clickable map of France, a clickable map of the World, and a list of French Web servers. Few servers provide business resources, but there are one heck of a lot of Internet service providers in France. In English and French.
Address: **http://web.urec.fr/france/france.html**

*Germany* ☆☆☆ Clickable map of Germany in English and German, plus a list of Web servers in German only.
Address: **http://www.informatik.tu-muenchen.de/isar/WWWother/ demap.html**

*Greece* **http://www.forthnet.gr/hellas/hellas.html**
*Hungary* **http://www.fsz.bme.hu/hungary/homepage.html**
*Iceland* **http://www.rfisk.is/english/sites.html**

*Ireland* ☆☆☆ Points to multiple national Irish home pages. Few sites.
Address: **http://www.ul.ie/World/Ireland.html**

*Italy* ☆☆☆☆ Multiple search methods, in English and Italian. Find sites by geographic location, by subject, or by type of sponsoring organization. Also has Whois search for Italy, daily news and other info.
Address: **http://www.mi.cnr.it/NIR-IT/NIR-map.html**

*Latvia* **http://www.riga.lv**
*Lithuania* **http://neris.mii.lt**
*Luxembourg* **http://www.restena.lu/luxembourg/lux_welcome.html**
*Monaco* **http://www.monaco.mc**
*Netherlands* **http://www.eeb.ele.tue.nl/map/netherlands.html**
*Norway* **http://www.service.uit.no/homepage-no**
*Poland* **http://info.fuw.edu.pl/pl/PolandResourceMap.html**

*Portugal* ☆☆☆ Slow site in English and Portuguese lets you search by town or name. Few sites.
Address:  **http://s700.uminho.pt/homepage-pt.html**

*Romania*  **http://www.info.polymtl.ca/zuse/tavi/www/Romania.html**

*Russia* ☆☆☆ List of Russian servers in English and Russian. Few sites.
Address:  **http://www.RAS.ru/map_list.html**
An alternate Russian site provides a clickable map and more sites.
Address:  **http://www.ac.msk.su/map.html**

*Slovakia*  **http://www.tuzvo.sk/uvt.html**
*Slovenia*  **http://www.ijs.si/slo/resources.html**

*Spain* ☆☆☆ Searchable database of Spain's email addresses, a clickable map of the world, and a list of Net sites. The sites list includes businesses. In Spanish with some English.
Address:  **http://www.uji.es/spain_www.html**

*Sweden*       **http://www.sunet.se/map/sweden.html**
*Switzerland*  **http://heiwww.unige.ch/switzerland**
*Turkey*       **http://www.metu.edu.tr/Turkey**

*United Kingdom* ☆☆☆☆ Searchable database of sites, clickable map of university servers, subject list of Web servers, list of commercial sites.
Address:  **http://scitsc.wlv.ac.uk/ukinfo/uk.map.html**

*Four11 Online User Directory* ☆☆☆☆ This search site for email addresses contains only a half-million listings, but is still extremely useful. Gives you data contained in no other site. You can search for someone's current email address by any combination of a person's first name, last name, city, country, company, and—get this—old email address. The basic service is free. The company charges for expanded services, including Pretty Good Privacy encrypted key service.
Address: **http://www.four11.com**

*Global Online Directory*  ☆☆☆ Searchable online Yellow Pages, not as useful as some others. Search by type of organization, topic, geographic location,

keyword. Also provides a "New Listings" section.
Address: **http://www.cityscape.co.uk/gold/indexdir.html**

*Gopher Jewels* ☆☆☆☆☆ A list of good Gopher sites. Check out these sublists: Books & Journals, Economics & Business, Federal Agency and Related Gopher Sites, General Reference Resources, List of Lists, Patents, and Copyrights.
Address: **gopher://cwis.usc.edu**
*look in* **other_Gophers_and_Information_Resources**
*or Web browse to* **http://galaxy.einet.net/GJ/index.html**

*Harvest* ☆☆☆☆ Searchable database of Web sites built as a demo of the Harvest search engine. All search engines can look for key words, but Harvest can find topics. A crowded site, but the fast search speed makes it worthwhile.
Address: **http://rd.cs.colorado.edu**

*Hytelnet* ☆☆☆ Database of Telnet sites. In the United States, **telnet://lawnet.law.columbia.edu** Log in as: **lawnet**
In Europe, **telnet://info.mcc.ac.uk** Log in as: **hytelnet**
From the World Wide Web:
Address: **http://moondog.usask.ca/hytelnet/start.txt.html**

*Internet Mall* ☆☆☆ Directory lists one-paragraph descriptions of Internet merchants.
Address: **http://www.mecklerweb.com/imall/imall.htm**

*Japan Network Information Center (JPNIC)* ☆☆☆☆☆ Japanese Whois searches to find who Internet domains belong to, JPNIC database of information.
Address: **http://www.nic.ad.jp/index.html**

*JumpStation II* ☆☆☆☆ Searches for key words in World Wide Web document titles and section headings in Web documents. It also does subject searches of Web pages, and URL searches. The URL searches can use wildcards, so if you remember part of a URL, JumpStation II can rediscover the entire address.
Address: **http://www.stir.ac.uk/jsbin/jsii**

*Lycos* ✰✰✰✰ Searches more than two million unique URLs as of February 1995, and has since added 50,000 or more new URLs each week. You can query Lycos using any words, and Lycos looks through its huge database of Web, Gopher, and FTP sites. The database is built by a software robot that cruises the Net looking for documents. For each document it finds, Lycos stores the document's title, headings, subheadings, links, the 100 highest-weighted words, and the first 20 lines. Lycos does not search any servers that exclude robots. Due to its intense popularity, this site is often slow.
Address: **http://www.lycos.com**

*Netfind* ✰✰✰ Searches for anyone's email address any place in the world, given a person's name and a rough description of where the person works. Requires you to download software.
Address: **gopher://gopher.micro.umn.edu:70/11/Phone%20Books/other**

*Netscape Web site* ✰✰✰✰ News and announcements from the hottest company on the Net. Lots to see here, and it changes all the time. Look for the electronic newsletter *Off the Net*, Netscape's own What's New directory. Lots of technical info as well as nontechnical.
Address: **http://www.netscape.com**

*NCSA What's New page* ✰✰✰✰✰ The most heavily-visited site on the Net, and one of the most rewarding businesspeople can visit. Lists new Web sites with one-paragraph descriptions, posting dozens of new ones every couple of days. Impossible to visit without finding valuable new sites. Reading the entire list and exploring the several good new sites can easily take three to five hours per week, but even short visits are profitable.
Address: **http://www.ncsa.uiuc.edu/SDG/Software/Mosaic/Docs/whats-new.html**

*Open Market's Commercial Sites Index* ✰✰✰✰ Mammoth, searchable list of company sites. Also provides its own What's New list of business sites.
Address: **http://www.directory.net**

*Publicly Accessible Mailing Lists* ✰✰✰✰ Searchable database of email lists and their topics.
Address: **http://www.neosoft.com:80/internet/paml**

*Russian email address database* ☆☆☆ This search site for finding Russian email addresses includes the Relcom directory of business addresses and the Russian Electronic Academic Research Network directory of academic addresses.
Address: **telnet://ukanaix.cc.ukans.edu**
*log in as* **ex-ussr**
*or* **ftp://cs.umd.edu/pub/cyrillic**
*Once in the Cyrillic subdirectory, select* **relcom_and_internet**

*Veronica* ☆☆☆ Here you can search Gopher menus worldwide.
Address: **gopher://veronica.scs.unr.edu**

*W3 Catalog* ☆☆☆ Searchable list of Web sites plus a What's New list.
Address: **http://cuiwww.unige.ch/w3catalog**

*Web Crawler* ☆☆☆☆ Searchable database of the *contents* of Web sites (not just titles and URLs), searchable by key words.
Address: **http://webcrawler.cs.washington.edu/WebCrawler/WebQuery.html**

*What's New in Japan* ☆☆☆☆ English and Japanese lists of new Web sites in Japan, and sites in other countries operated by Japanese organizations.
Address: **http://www.ntt.jp/WHATSNEW/index.html**

*WWPing* ☆☆☆ Regular Ping searches domain names. WWPing does that and searches Web HTTPs as well.
Address: **http://www.stir.ac.uk/jsbin/wwping**

*WWW Servers in Japan* ☆☆☆☆☆ Lengthy list of servers in Japan (classified by originating city) and Kansai earthquake relief servers. *The* jumping-off place for Japanese Web browsing, although some good servers are not listed. The servers it links to are in Japanese, English, and/or German. Available in English and Japanese language versions. This is a large (60 k) text file. This is a case-sensitive server. You must use upper and lower case exactly as listed here.
Address: **http://www.ntt.jp/SQUARE/www-in-JP.html**

*WWW Virtual Library* ☆☆☆☆ Lists of Web sites by topic. Different people contribute to each topic list; quality differs. Some topics have awe-inspiring lists; some have little. Good sections on Web development, finance sites, German resources, electronic journals, and newspapers. Usable list of standards bodies. Lame list of commercial services.
Address: **http://www.w3.org/hypertext/DataSources/bySubject/Overview.html**

*WWW Worm* ☆☆☆☆ Good and fast search engine combs through titles, names, and contents of Web sites.
Address: **http://www.cs.colorado.edu/home/mcbryan/WWWW.html**

*X.500 email address searcher* ☆☆☆☆ Choose to search Texas, the U.S. or worldwide for email addresses of faculty, students and staff at universities.
Address: **http://x500.utexas.edu**

*Yahoo Server* ☆☆☆☆☆ This great searcher is fast and flexible, and contains a valuable hidden bonus. Click on the word "More" at the bottom of the page and you'll see a terrific list of other places where other stuff can be found. Yahoo searches a subject-oriented database of Web sites.
Address: **http://www.yahoo.com**

# Twelve Reasons Internet Projects Fail—and How to Make Sure Yours Don't

*"Don't assume compatibility. This is how most systems integrators get rich."*
Karen Watterson, *Client/Server Technology for Managers*

Businesses and the Internet are like teenagers and sex. Everyone's obsessed with it. Everyone thinks everyone else does it. Everyone wants everyone else to think they do it, too. But hardly anyone *really* does it, and most of them do it badly.

The Internet flops I've seen often stumbled into one or more of twelve pits. Internet successes usually avoid them. Here are the chasms and tips to avoid falling into them.

## 1. The compatibility fallacy

Always verify that new hardware or software will work with the rest of your system—never assume. It's also a good idea to check with your Internet access provider to see if your provider has other clients using the product you're considering buying.

 I have heard sad stories about projects derailed or delayed because software worked with Unix, but not *that* kind of Unix, or ran on Windows NT but not Windows 3.1, or wouldn't work with NetWare, or wasn't supported by an Internet access provider. Hardware problems abound, too, from unlinkable cables to networking cards that don't fit in PC slots.

And whenever you're told "Yes, those will work together" by someone who wants to sell you something, get a second opinion from someone who has no financial interest in the answer. Also, when determining compatibility, make sure you can connect your hardware and software to any planned expansions and changes, as well as to your existing systems. I know of one project that worked fine under Unix, but was scrapped when the IS department changed to Windows NT systems.

## 2. No management support

You'll need to justify pursuit of your project to managers by using *business* terms and reasons, not technical reasons. Build your case with striking, easy-to-remember words and images. It never hurts to mention specific examples from your competitors.

 Projects without management support risk the perils of reallocated resources, cancellation, postponement, and budget reductions. New Net projects have been killed or have been chopped back to the point where they were no longer effective, all due to lack of support from senior managers. If you want your project to prosper—and you want credit for its success—you need a visible and vocal champion among higher management.

Most senior managers will want answers to questions like these:

- What is the Internet, anyhow?
- Wouldn't CompuServe/America Online/Microsoft Network:
  - Cost less?
  - Be easier?
  - Reach more people?
  - Do all the same things?
- How much will starting this project cost? How much per month to run?
- How long will it take to get this project up and running?
- How much in *savings* will this project generate? Where did you get your figures?
- How much in *revenue* will this project generate? How did you arrive at those figures?
- Will this project slow down any urgent MIS projects?
- Can hackers break into our computers through the Internet?
- How do you know our customers use the Internet?
- Won't that give our staff erotica and videogames? (I'm not sure which category managers find worse.)
- How can we measure whether this works or not?

And, for sales-related Internet projects:

- What's the minimum monthly sales volume for your Internet project to break even?
- Will this *increase* revenue or only *shift* it from one channel to another?
- How will you sustain unit margins over time if competitors come in with lower prices?
- Can we offer lower prices on the Internet and higher prices elsewhere?
- How will you manage pricing conflicts with your other sales channels?
- How can you measure the impact of your Net projects on your existing distributors or resellers?

This book gives you much of the ammo you will need to answer those questions. Make sure your projections are realistic and on the conservative side. Remember: it is always better to underpromise and overdeliver, than the other way around.

Besides pointing out what your competitors do on the Net, it can be helpful to enlist support from equal-level managers with other companies. If you know a peer of your managers who has profited by the Internet, ask the peer manager to call your managers and talk with them.

It helps to know what your management's hot buttons are. For instance, David Spector, vice president for technology services at J.P. Morgan in New York, convinced his top management to connect to the Internet. The deciding factor he presented was that Morgan would be able to increase the quality of support it received from vendors.

Internet traffic (especially the World Wide Web) can produce a great deal of statistics for analyses and reports. This can be valuable to top management. Instead of depending on producing warm fuzzy feelings, you can actually show how many messages, file downloads, and sales leads the Internet has generated.

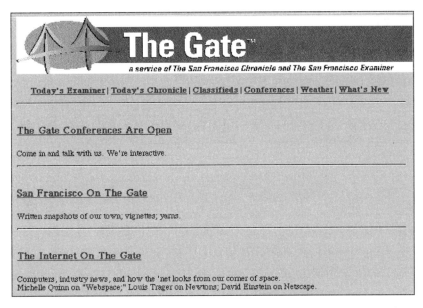

**Figure 5.1** *The* Electric Examiner *tracked the number of accesses to its Web page, along with points of origin for its cyberspace readers. The results surprised its managers.*

The reporting capabilities the Net supplies can also show managers exactly why you've done things and who your Internet readers are. Chris Gulker found this helpful when his editors at the *Electric Examiner* (**http://www.sfgate.com**) questioned his choice of Web page material. (See Figure 5.1.)

"Editors said, 'You don't have enough stories about city council meetings,'" reported Gulker. "I told them, 'We tried running city council meetings. No one looked at them,' and showed them exactly how many readers read other stories and how few read city council stories." He also showed them *where* readers of *Electric Examiner* are. Based in San Francisco, the *Electric Examiner* has more readers in the U.K. than in nearby Berkeley.

This level of accountability is hard to beat. You can use it to produce reports and especially to track sales sources. For many senior managers, reports equal results. Producing detailed, informative reports assures continuing support for your Internet project.

## 3. Trying to build Rome in a day

In some ways, this is the most important advice I can give you: *Start simple!*

A team at a major company has been building a too-complex Internet site for more than a year. It still has nothing to show for it. This is ridiculous. For your first Internet project, or your first World Wide Web site, plan the most basic, stripped-down, bare bones minimum possible. Then simplify *that,* and put it online. Start small and grow.

 Don't aim for perfection—your Net site will evolve constantly, and will never be perfect. Don't wait until you get things finished—they never will be. Just get something 80 percent done and launch it. Write EXPERIMENTAL and UNDER CONSTRUCTION all over it if you like, but put it out there. No matter how rough and crude your first effort may be, get it up quickly.

Why? First of all, when you have a nasty surprise, you're a damn sight better off if you find it with a three-page Web site instead of a thirty-page one, or with a handful of FTP files instead of 600. "What? You mean we have to re-input all 600 files?" You don't want that. Second, the more complex you make your Internet site, the more likely you are to have bugs, *and the longer it will take you to find them.* There is mathematical proof of that.

Put a small piece of your Internet site up first. Tweak it and polish it, and you will always have that functional core in place. If problems develop while adding to your site, you'll know any problems come from the new stuff.

When you have one small piece up and running, you have a visible sign that your entire project may work. It creates a feeling of momentum, and it boosts morale for your project team.

## 4. The "not invented here" syndrome

You don't need to write your own Internet software any more than you would build your own delivery trucks. Trying to do everything in-house increases the odds that your Internet project will be an unusable dud.

Farm it out. Buy canned software. Hire temporary programmers and consultants to build your Internet presence. In most cases, you can even put your FTP server, mailing list server, Web pages, and Gopher server on your access provider's computer instead of your own.

When you compare the price of "store-bought" with homemade, the roll-your-own version may *seem* cheaper. The purchase price of the software looks large at first, but it's trivial when you compare it to training, human resource, and maintenance costs. You'll save money on the back end. Purchased products have less impact on your company's other computer-related projects. They save time, so your project comes to life more quickly. And you'll probably gain a more polished, professional Internet presence than you could build on your own.

## 5. Getting ripped off by providers and consultants

When the Coriolis Group (the publisher of this book) first linked up to the Internet, its access provider wanted to charge $200 for each user name added to its Net address! The Coriolis Group quickly found another provider.

 I've seen more companies get ripped off by access providers and consultants than damage by hackers, industrial spies, and credit card scams combined. Some access providers have pulled off amazing swindles and charged outrageous prices for negligible services.

Chapters 2 and 3 covered this topic in detail, but it's worth bringing up again. The most important thing to remember is: Always, always, *always* get three price quotes before making a commitment. Don't be surprised if you get a 10-to-1 difference between your highest quote and the lowest. Also, the cheapest price may not be your safest bet—the quality of work may be shoddy. You may want to choose a price in the middle. If you have three or more quotes, at least you'll have an idea of the going rate.

# 6. Corporate culture shock

Paul Saffo, a fellow at the Institute for the Future (Menlo Park, CA), says that when a company gets on the Internet, traditional corporate hierarchy evolves into a more flexible organization. Company decision making evolves from top-down to distributed decision making. Teamwork grows among employees, and collaboration increases with suppliers and customers. These processes involve active participation by motivated employees at all levels in a company.

 A networked environment transcends the traditional barriers raised by departments and management levels. It even crosses company lines. The Internet—especially email—disperses knowledge throughout a company, which may cause power shifts. If managers resist change, hoard information, or try to exclude others from Net access, problems are inevitable. You can minimize the impact of these changes by preparing your organization for what will happen.

Some changes are subtle and will not happen overnight. Exaggerating them affects your credibility within your organization. But you can explain to employees how their duties will change and what changes the decision-making process will undergo.

Before your project is launched, keep predictions to a minimum. If they involve numbers, be conservative. Sure, other companies' Web pages may receive 10,000 "hits" per week, but you have no guarantee that your site will do as well. If people within your organization expect 1,000 hits in a day and receive 150, they will see your Web site as a failure. If they expect 50 hits in a day and receive 150, they will be elated.

Choose your predictions carefully. Keep them to a minimum. Make them realistic.

You will need to spend time managing people's *expectations*. Your project will not change the world, nor save your company. The Internet will not make up for bad management nor make you rich quickly. Treat your first Net project as an experiment, and make sure that people know that it is not the Holy Grail. Allow for time in your plan to deal with your staff's expectations. It's easier to prevent misunderstandings than to clean up the consequences later.

Depending on what your company does on the Internet, people's tasks will change. New responsibilities will be added to some people's jobs. Although many existing chores will remain, some employees will have new ways of completing the same tasks.

 Expect resistance from staff members. When confronted with a new way of doing things, people often naturally resent and complain about it. Know that changes in employee behavior will take time. This is as true for big changes—like learning a new email system—as it is for small ones—like convincing employees to email reports instead of sending them via more costly fax or Fed Ex.

Someone will need to tell employees *how* to do new activities. Someone will need to explain *why*. And someone will need to check up to make sure that the new behaviors have taken place. If not, someone will need to find how to make the new procedures more do-able.

You make success more probable for your Internet project if you initially have personnel and resources working to ease staff resistance, and make sure to follow up later.

## 7. The "Internet rules are made to be broken" fallacy

You might feel you're doing fine on the Net, but your company president will feel otherwise the morning he checks his email and finds 200 pieces of hate mail.

 The Internet has been around long enough—nearly 25 years—and has enough millions of people onboard, to have developed its own rules. No matter how large your company may be, the Net is a redwood to your sapling. You must bend to its rules rather than the other way around.

> This doesn't mean that every raving flamer can tell you how to run your business. But if you hear the same accusation from three or four—or twenty—people, you know that you have done something that violates Internet rules in *principle*, even if you feel you didn't. As in any court of law, your perception of whether you obeyed the law is irrelevant; it is the judge and jury that make the decision. You have broken a rule when *other people* decide you have broken it.

A manager with the publisher of the *NetGuide* series of books has carried on a valiant but hopeless discourse on the newsgroups for months. The company promoted a new book by posting announcements in dozens of newsgroups. The newsgroups regarded the announcements as spamming, and banned any postings bearing the publisher's Internet address. The manager, apparently writing from his home email address, argued that since each announcement was slightly different, it was not spamming. The rebuttal was that it was *too* spamming. This manager missed the point. It doesn't matter whether his announcement was *technically* a spam, nor does it matter whether his company *intended* it to be a spam. If it is *perceived* as a spam, he should beat his breast in repentence, say *mea culpa,* and promise never to do it again.

Pay attention to the code of the Internet. You can break some rules in the short term and make a profit, but if you want to build an ongoing business with a repeat clientele (and avoid the Net's own frontier justice), you have to play by the rules.

## 8. The "If you build it, they will come" fallacy

Suppose you built a Web page and nobody came?

Author Jaclyn Easton interviewed merchants on the Internet while researching her book *Shopping on the Internet and Beyond.* She found dozens of disappointed companies with rarely-visited Gopher servers and Web sites. These merchants complained of too few Internet orders. Easton noticed the complainers had one oversight in common: little or no promotion for their sites.

Advertising by mental telepathy doesn't work. I estimate that at least 80 percent of the businesses on the Net that I have spoken with are disappointed by their response. This is especially true of consumer retailers on the Internet. People won't magically show up at your Internet site. You need to promote your Internet offerings as vigorously as your toll-free 800 number or your mail order catalog.

In your budget, allow for trade advertising and PR costs in order to create awareness of your Internet services. I'll go into this in depth in the marketing chapters of this book. For now, keep in mind two separate goals:

1. Draw first-time visitors.

2. Gratify visitors so they return.

To generate repeat visits, plan for the editorial investment needed to sustain interest in returning. You have the classic retail display window challenge: Put something new and exciting in your front window to get people to come back. It will take staff time to create a steady stream of updated and new information and to promote your site.

"If you build it, they will come" is overly optimistic. But if you promote it, they will notice...and they may come.

## 9. The "Walt Disney was wrong" fallacy

Disneyland opened before it was ready. The first day, while crowds surged through the gates, frantic workers still poured cement and built scaffolds. You will probably feel like those busy workers the first day you open your Internet servers. Nothing's finished, but visitors stream in.

You can draw comfort from a line in Walt Disney's opening speech that day: "As long as there is imagination left in the world, Disneyland will never be completed." Neither will your Internet presence.

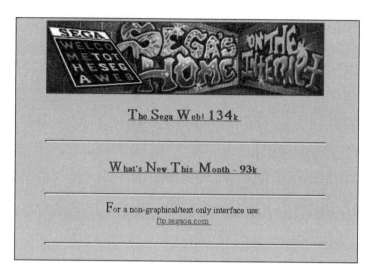

*The Sega page is an example of a Web site designed to invite both new and repeat customers. The interface is simple yet friendly, and a "What's New" link near the top of the page encourages customers to return to the page occasionally.*

 Some companies assume the opposite. They imagine that once they get their servers up, that's it. They can leave it as is. One of two calamities happens to these companies. Some panic ("When will it be done?" thundered an angry V.P.) and believe that they did something wrong because they can't get finished. Others never add anything to their sites, and watch them wither and die.

Your Net sites will require *active* management. It's like a garden. You invest a huge effort in soil cultivation and planting. But unless you take care of bugs, prune dead wood, and plant new growth, you won't harvest much. For your Internet sites, you'll also need to take care of bugs, prune dead wood, and especially plant new growth. Your staff will need to add new files, update information and add new Internet services as they emerge. This becomes an even more urgent priority when any part of your Internet efforts touches your customers.

Ongoing costs—*especially customer support,* if you sell on the Net—will be your largest expense. You'll get a good payback if you invest extra time and money designing your system to be as easy to use and easy to update as possible.

*The Apple home page is visually complex, but it still invites customers through a graphically appealing interface and messages that tell customers what's new at this site.*

Here are some rough estimates. For a small company, answering email from customers and prospects can take from 5 to 30 hours a week if you don't take sales online, from 20 to 80 hours if you do. Large companies have from dozens to a couple of hundred full-time employees handling email customer support and email sales.

Email press releases and mailing list announcements can take one nontechnical employee from 4 to 6 hours each to do. Email newsletters range from 8 hours per issue to 80, depending on the length and complexity of your newsletter, and how many people contribute articles.

Since the uproar over its Pentium chip, Intel reportedly has four full time employees who monitor Internet newsgroups (these are discussion groups arranged by topic) and post carefully composed responses to Intel-related items. For smaller companies, newsgroups (valuable resources for both research and publicity) can occupy between 5 and 30 hours of netlurking. In addition to this, employees throughout the company will spend time on newsgroups related to their specific jobs, such as accounting and taxation newsgroups for accountants. This normally takes less than an hour per person per week.

A Gopher server or an FTP server will need 4 to 8 hours per week to maintain, depending on how many changes you add each week to your server. This includes time to reformat documents, create new files, and remove old files. I assume that most of the editorial material would be written as part of another project.

Maintenance time for a World Wide Web server can range from 4 hours per week to 40, again depending on how active you make your site. Note that most of this time is *editorial* time. Once your Web site is up and working, technical maintenance can be as little as an hour or two per week. Your Web site will also generate additional email, to your webmaster and to anyone else whose Internet address is listed on your Web pages. Allow another 4 to 30 hours per week to process these.

This does not include any overall management time. If your company is big enough and your Internet activities are important enough, you may want a part time or full time manager of online communications—usually a non-technical person with excellent communications skills. Look for someone who can quench flames and not start them, and who is sensitive to the needs of your customers.

## 10. The "Hey, I know what I'm doing" fallacy

One of the great things about the Internet is that you get instant, unvarnished feedback directly from your customers and prospects.

One of the stupid things about some companies is that they ignore it.

 *Your network is only as good as your users say it is.* If they say it stinks, it stinks. If they like most of it but harshly criticize some, don't take it as a personal attack. Stash your fight-or-flight response in your bottom desk drawer, and change what has been criticized. Then give them more of what they like.

Companies that ignore their customers' wants soon get into trouble. The Internet gives you insights for free that you'd have to pay a market research company a lot of money to uncover. It delivers them faster, and without three pages of prefatory psychobabble that researchers use to justify their fees.

Expect criticism, and *welcome* it. You won't get criticism from someone who is apathetic about your offerings. You'll get criticism from people who want you to *improve*—even when their language would incite a saint to attack.

Treat responses from your customers as valuable research, and put it to work. As the founder of the great advertising agency Ogilvy & Mather said in his book *The Unpublished David Ogilvy* "...There is no great trick to *doing* research. The problem is to get people to *use* it—particularly when the research reveals that you have been making mistakes. We all have a tendency to use research as a drunkard uses a lamppost—for support, not for illumination."

## 11. Security breaches

In 1988, the infamous Internet Worm caused hundreds of thousands of dollars of damage to Internet-linked computers. It scared a couple of dozen companies off the Net. Most came back. A few stayed away.

Internet security and break-ins are important enough to warrant two entire chapters, 6 and 7. Actually, it's even more important than that.

## 12. The "Badges! We don't need no stinkin' badges" fallacy

Some companies think the laws don't apply when they're on the Internet. So far, they have been found guilty of fraud, libel, false advertising, obscenity, and other offenses.

A little background may keep you and your directors from landing in jail, paying huge fines, and being sued and paying your lawyers tens of thousands of dollars. If the fines don't get you, the legal costs will.

Brock Meeks found that out the hard way when he became the first person sued for Internet-based defamation. His newsletter *Cyberwire Dispatch* accused Suarez Corporation Industries of running a "scam" by offering free Internet access through a dummy company called Electronic Postal Service. Respondents wouldn't get free access, but instead a solicitation to pay $159 for a book and some software—a bait-and-switch operation. Suarez had been accused before of perpetrating misleading marketing ploys. Suarez sued Meeks for defamation. In August 1994, Meeks settled out of court by reimbursing Suarez $64 for its court filing fee and agreeing to fax questions to the company if he planned to write more articles about it. That sounds good for Meeks, but he had to pay $25,000 to attorneys, effectively wiping him out financially.

The least settled issue is jurisdiction. Whose laws apply in cyberspace? This is not a trivial issue. As I write this, one man is in federal prison as a result. Robert Thomas of Milpitas, California was sentenced to 37 months in prison for obscenity, convicted by a jury in Memphis, Tennessee. His wife was sentenced to 30 months. Thomas had never been in Memphis, but the "local community standards" of Memphis were applied because a federal investigator retrieved files from Thomas' computer in California to the investigator's computer in Memphis. (Thomas used an electronic bulletin board system and was not on the Internet, but there are legal and technical parallels between bulletin board systems and the Net.) Thomas broke a law in Memphis without actually going there.

It is easy for your business to break a law someplace. Encrypted files are illegal in Spain. If a citizen of Madrid retrieves an encrypted file from your FTP server in Florida, is your company liable for breaking Spanish law? What if your employee sends an encrypted email message to someone in Spain? In some countries, insulting religious leaders is punishable by death and insulting politicians by a prison sentence. If a policeman in such a country retrieves an insulting file from your Web site in New York, should your company suffer the consequences? Copyright laws differ from country to country. What country's copyright laws apply on the global Internet? Civil codes that regulate business transactions are another source of concern. This is an especially important issue for multinational corporations, which could find a branch in one country liable for an Internet message posted by an office in another country far away.

A December, 1994 seminar at the Practicing Law Institute in New York concluded that publishing electronically may lead to libel actions far from the publisher's physical location, simply because the Net makes stories available at remote distances.

Governments and law enforcement agencies have not yet realized that the Internet is a borderless worldwide phenomenon. Like falling rain, the Net affects a place without originating in it. Carey Heckman, codirector of the Stanford Law and Technology Policy Center, believes that the current controversy is a temporary barrier on the path to what Carey calls "the death of geography." We are years away from any kind of definitive legal conclusion on this issue.

## What the heck is this "Acceptable Use Policy" stuff?

When investigating the legal issues that govern the Internet, one of the first things you will hear about is "Acceptable Use Policy." This term is batted around enough to be called AUP for short. There are actually two kinds of AUPs.

The first was an Internet-wide policy, a vestige of the pre-commercial era of the Net when the National Science Foundation's NSFNet was the main Internet backbone. It said that NSF's part of the Net—which carried almost everybody's traffic—could not be used for profit. Fortunately, as of May 1995, NSFNet went away. For-profit providers now carry most traffic, and the old NSFNet Acceptable Use Policy only applies to companies whose access provider is an educational institution, nonprofit agency, or government entity which still applies that old AUP.

The second kind of AUP is very different and is more important to your business today. This is the Acceptable Use Policy—even if it is called by another name—that your Internet access provider expects you to follow. This AUP is not a law, but as a guideline for your activities, it forms the first level of regulation for the Internet. It is a contractual way to manage your relationship as a user or provider. If you violate it, you can be kicked off the system. By using the access provider's services, you agree to follow the rules set by your provider. Your provider can terminate your relationship if you don't. Read the agreement with your access provider to make sure you know what rules apply.

Your provider's policies may or may not specify that you practice *netiquette*, the Internet's code of conduct, but in either case you should keep in mind the practical consequences of not following these established rules.

The most obvious example of misconduct is conducting a mass email advertising campaign to people who haven't asked to receive your message (known as *spamming*). This violates netiquette. The consequence is that you will receive hate email in such vast quantities that it could crash your system and your provider's system. Your provider could then sue you for negligence toward its system, because you knew that your actions would hurt its business.

## Tort law on the Internet

*Tort law* is a broad area remedying wrongs between parties. Tort law also includes breaches-of-contract between you and your provider.

What other laws apply to your access provider? Surprisingly, access providers are *not* regulated by any commisssion.

"Access is not regulated by anybody," points out corporate attorney Thomas Cervantez. He represents startups, espcially online businesses, and is with the California firm of Pillsbury, Madison and Sutro (415-983-1505, **tomc@global.net**). "That's why you can go to a thousand different providers and for the same thing get a thousand different prices." He believes U.S. government regulation of providers is only a matter of time. He says some bureaucrat will do it, "Because we're the government—we *like* to regulate things"—even though the current unregulated system works.

Internet law is still an infant, but Net tort cases have already been prosecuted and won against businesses. What you can't do off the Net, you can't do on it. The same laws still apply. False advertising, fraud, negligence, misrepresentation, and trademark infringement are tort-based actions that some companies have committed on the Net. Of course, you'll want to plan your company's activities to avoid engaging in these actions.

False advertising is covered under a blend of federal and state regulations called unfair competition laws. Brian Corzine (also known as Brian Chase) won the dubious distinction of being the first person nailed by the Federal Trade Commission for false advertising on the Internet. A federal judge found him guilty and halted sales of his phony $99 credit repair program.

Your company can also be liable if it engages in product substitution (offering one product and palming off another as the offered product), trade name or trademark infringement, trade dress infringement (making your product or Net site copy the *look* of another company), and character rights infringement. You violate character rights if you use a photo of a famous person to sell your product on your Web page without permission. Even dead people have rights. Companies that used Elvis Presley's picture found this out the hard way when Elvis' estate won huge damages from them. Thank you, thank you very much.

Fraud is another tort liability that can apply to your business on the Internet, and also to your customers. From a legal standpoint, fraud is deception involving "knowing misrepresentation" of a material fact. In other words, there was an *intent* to deceive.

If your customer gives you a bogus credit card number over the Internet, your customer is liable for fraud. If your Gopher server claims that your product does something when you know it doesn't, your customer can nail you for fraud. Fraudulent offers on the Net have generated complaints from consumers and businesses around the world. In several countries, national and local consumer watchdog organizations are waking up and poking at Internet businesses, actively searching for fraud.

Misrepresentation is a tort area related to fraud. Your company can be liable for misrepresentation if you fail to truthfully represent facts about a product, service, or situation, and if your lack of truthful representation is detrimental to the person or organization that receives your representation. (Whew!)

Misrepresentation covers those hazy areas where a business slathers exaggerations on its product description, and when companies fail to disclose the negative aspects of their offerings. I have seen a lot of this on the Net, often from companies big enough to know better. I'm surprised that more lawsuits haven't been brought for Internet misrepresentation. When people find out how profitable such lawsuits can be, there will probably be a rash of them.

Negligence happens in the real world when a person or a company is negatively affected because another person or company failed to take care in an action. The careless company is liable for negligence when its judgment failed to meet a legally recognized norm for such actions. On the Internet, negligence will be new legal ground.

 If you do something (such as spamming and receiving 100,000 pieces of hate mail) that crashes the system of your access provider, you are damaging your provider's business and you can be sued for negligence. The consequences may be grave: Your provider's system also supports companies other than your own, so if your actions crash your provider's system, other companies can sue *your provider* for negligence that hurts their businesses.

Here's another hypothetical example of Internet negligence. "What about an Internet product catalog company, which sells the products of other companies?" asks attorney Cervantez. "Say that product catalog company fails to make sure it has a backup system and its system crashes right before a key trade show for its customers. If the industry standard was to have a backup system and the Internet product catalog company didn't, it could be sued for negligence."

Product liability laws vary from country to country. In the United States and other countries, you can be liable for *selling* a defective product that harms someone even when your company did not *manufacture* that product. Culpability lies in making the defective product available.

There are gradations in liability, from total (You sold this. It caused harm. This is all your fault.) to partial. (How much was the user's fault? How much was the manufacturer's?) For a business on the Internet, product liability issues are the same as they are in the real world.

## Intellectual property on the Internet

Probably the richest area of the Internet, from a lawyer's point of view, is intellectual property law. Software, patents, books, videos, music, photographs, trademarks, fictional characters, copyrights, Web pages—all are intellectual property.

Copyright law gives the creator of a *tangible* work the right to exclude others from using the work. Note the word "tangible." Copyrights don't apply to ideas or to ways of doing things. They apply only to the finished, executed product.

Whether someone puts a copyright notice on a finished work or not, copyright protection applies immediately upon creation of the work. Obviously, you should attach a copyright notice to anything you don't want copied. And you can choose from a variety of notices if you want to make something freely available but still retain rights to it. Some notices may be more practical than others.

If your company is on the Internet and displays or offers copyrighted property belonging to someone else, and if you haven't obtained permission to display or distribute that work, you are liable for damages. In a well-publicized case, Playboy Enterprises was awarded $500,000 from a company offering *Playboy* magazine photos online.

This can happen even if someone outside your company placed the copyrighted material on your Net site. There have been several cases in which users placed copyrighted software (OS/2 Warp, Microsoft Windows) in software archives, making the archive site liable for copyright damages. If you plan a similar service, give yourself some protection by posting a prominent disclaimer that users cannot post copyrighted material without your permission. And always get written permission before including any copyrighted material with your Net offerings.

Under copyright law, a catalog, database, or directory (such as a list of vendors from a newsgroup) is considered a *compilation*. This is defined as a selection of facts grouped in an organized order. If a sentence is copyrighted, a new copyright can be available for it when it is included in a new compilation. It's important to note that a compilation's copyright protects *all its components*, including pictures.

The way a compilation's components are arranged is also protected. If your competitor features a product in its catalog or Web page and your business sells the same product, you can advertise it as long as you do not copy the illustration, text, or arrangement that your competitor used. You and your competitor can both use the same pictures or descriptions from your vendor, as these are normally copyrighted by the vendor and made available for reuse.

# Internet copyright notices

For full protection of anything your business puts on the Internet—whether it's a file in an FTP server, a product FAQ, or a page on your Web site—you should put a copyright notice on it. To be valid, all copyright notices must have three things: 1) Either the word "Copyright" or the symbol ©. 2) The name of the copyright holder. 3) The year this work was first disseminated. In addition, it doesn't hurt to add the phrase "All rights reserved." This protects your rights under the copyright laws of some South American countries.

You may have seen some publications on the Internet with more lengthy copyright notices, including distinctions of who can and who cannot copy the material and under what circumstances. Here is a sampling of special-purpose copyright notices:

- Copyright 1996 by Your Corp. All rights reserved. Federal copyright law prohibits unauthorized reproduction by any means and imposes fines up to $25,000 for violations.

- Copyright 1996, Your Corp. All rights reserved. This material may be copied online but may not be reproduced in print or on a CD-ROM without written permission from Your Corp.

- Copyright 1996 by Your Corp. All rights reserved. This material may not be duplicated for any profit-driven enterprise.

- Copyright 1996 by Your Corp. Unlimited permission to copy or use is hereby granted subject to inclusion of this copyright notice.

- Copyright 1996 by Your Corp. This material may be freely copied and distributed subject to inclusion of this copyright notice and our World Wide Web URL **http://www.yourcorp.com**

For maximum protection, you should register your material with the Copyright Office. If you sue someone for infringing on your copyright, you can collect statuatory damages only if you have registered your material before the infringement took place.

An original compilation of names and addresses is copyrightable, even when the names and addresses are in the public domain. For this type of compilation, only the arrangement is protected, not the names and addresses themselves. In the same way, your home page arrangement of links is protected, even though the links themselves are in the public domain.

The same holds true for trademarks and logos. If you want to use another company's trademark in your Web page, get written permission first. Trademark law is messy in the United States. There are federal laws that offer nationwide coverage, but there are also individual state laws covering trademarks. Some trademarks are registered only in one state or group of states.

International laws add another layer of trademark confusion. This situation is bad enough for companies not online. Companies on the Internet are in a swamp. If a trademark is infringed on the Net, nobody knows *where,* physically, the infringement took place, and therefore nobody knows which courts and which laws have jurisdiction! Expect court battles and state and federal laws over this issue.

Trade secrets are another area of intellectual property law. Your company might protect strategies, future product plans, manufacturing methods, or other processes by keeping knowledge about them within your company. This gives them legal protection as trade secrets. But keep in mind that if someone in your company discusses your trade secrets on the Internet or posts documents about them, they are no longer confidential—and you are no longer protected. Trade secrets are major targets for industrial espionage on the Net.

To protect yourself from legal imbroglios over intellectual property issues, you need to remain alert regarding two quite different issues. First, remember that the Net is a *public* communications network, so you need to keep a tight

# Clearing copyrights: Who gives permission?

Even when you want to use photos or text on your Web page only for display and not for resale, you still need to obtain permission first. If you want to use a professionally-recorded song or a clip from a video or TV show, there can be hidden rights that you need to include. For instance, when you include a music recording, do you need to license rights only for your country or for the world? This is a gray area in Internet law.

Another gray area is how much someone can charge for use of material. So far, there are no standard rates for Internet reuse, so you may be able to get things cheaply, or be quoted a sky-high fee.

**When clearing text:** You need to obtain clearance from the copyright holder (usually the publisher or the author), possibly from the holder of foreign language or foreign territory rights, and possibly from the author—even if the copyright is in a publisher's name.

**When clearing still pictures:** You need to obtain clearance from the copyright holder, possibly from any people seen in the picture, and from the owners of any logos or trademarks included in the picture.

**When clearing recorded music:** You need to obtain clearance from the music publishers, the musician's union, possibly the record company, and possibly the performers. Fees can be higher if you accompany the music with visuals.

**When clearing a video or movie clip:** You need to obtain clearance not only from the copyright holder or holders, but also the actors' union, and people heard or seen (including stunt performers and doubles), the writers, and the directors. If music is heard, you also need the musician's union and the music publishers.

With any tricky clearance situation (especially a music recording or video clip), you can save money in the long run by hiring a clearance professional. Fees will depend on how many clearances need to be obtained and how tight your deadline is, and range from $200 to thousands. This is in addition to the actual fee you will pay the rights holder for a license to reuse the material itself. For a smaller fee, some clearance professionals will advise you on which material in your planned Internet project might run into rights difficulties, and which alternatives might cost less.

One of the few firms with experience obtaining Internet rights and clearances is Total Clearance, a company headquartered in Mill Valley, California (415-389-1531, **totalclear@aol.com**). The company's founder, Jill Alofs, started out handling clearances for Lucasfilm Ltd. and LucasArts Entertainment Company. Now her company obtains clearances for the reuse of all types of materials in all media for more than 1,500 clients. Total Clearance recently cleared more than 3,000 clips for the Parker Brothers CD-ROM version of Trivial Pursuit.

rein on your own intellectual property so you don't lose your rights by improperly making works public. Second, someone in your company needs to accept formal responsibility for making sure your company and its employees don't infringe on someone else's rights.

## *Contracts on the Internet*

Historically, business contracts were either written or oral, and implied or explicit. Now contracts are electronic.

In an online contract, it's important to specify which laws govern the contract. Besides defining the physical locality of the laws that govern your contract, in the United States you should add whether the Uniform Commercial Code or any other statute or law applies to the contract. UCC regulations cover all contracts relating to goods, but not for services. Services are usually covered by state laws. The UCC defines responsibilities for rejecting or accepting goods and most other areas of commercial transactions, and plays an important role in settling commercial disputes in the United States.

In his book *The Law of Electronic Commerce*, attorney Benjamin Wright points out that the Uniform Commercial Code says that an agreement for the sale of goods priced at $500 or more is not binding unless the contract is in writing, and that an email contract should qualify as a written contract. There are two problems. Email contracts have no equivalent of an authorizing signature, and without effective security, email can be altered—making contract enforcibility questionable. Wright recommends putting a clause in any electronic contract saying "a properly transmitted message is deemed 'written,' and a designated symbol(s) or code(s) within the message is deemed a 'signature.'"

This could apply to digital signatures. Digital signatures are encrypted by the signer, and include a checksum that shows if the electronic contract was altered, even by as little as a comma.

When you form a contract or process a payment transaction online, you are legally conducting electronic data interchange, called EDI for short. The U.S. law that covers EDI is called the Electronic Funds Transfer Act. It applies to most business transactions conducted over the Net, and it is long and complicated. If you really want to be diligent (after all, this law may apply to your company), go over a copy of this Act with your lawyer. Additional state laws cover forged electronic funds transfers.

Many agreements made online are "shrink-wrap" contracts, also called "unconscionable contracts or contracts of adhesion, where you don't have any negotiating going on," explains attorney Cervantez. "Courts don't like this."

There are two potential problems with a shrink-wrap contract. With most other contracts, negotiations happen before an agreement is signed. A shrink-wrap contract is a take-it-or-leave-it deal. No negotiation is involved. A court may view this as unfair. The second issue is one of timing. Does the buyer learn the full terms of the deal only *after* the contract was entered? This is

# Digital signatures for electronic contracts

Digital signatures are now available. They can be included with digital contracts as proof of the sender's identity and that the contracts are unaltered. They can also be used with other electronic documents, such as purchase orders, or even on regular email messages.

The encrypted signatures look different on every message you send, so they can't be duplicated. And checksums within the signatures show that your electronic document hasn't been altered.

The digital signature for each document is generated from a private key code you alone possess, and from the text in your signed document. That way, you are guaranteed that your document has not been changed and exactly matches the document you agreed to. Even the tiniest change—capitalizing one lowercase letter, or taking away a single space—will invalidate your digital signature. Other parties to your contract can never claim that it was revised after signing, because the signature would reveal any modification. Since the content must not be changed, cutting your digital signature off one message and pasting it to another wouldn't work, because the digital summary would change.

Since your digital signature itself can't be cracked, your communication is secure from tampering, so you have less need of a secure network.

often the case when software is purchased. Courts may view this as not disclosing information to the buyer before the purchase, which may make the transaction unfair.

One way to avoid this is with the two-step approach that America Online and Prodigy use to cover themselves. They accept signups online, and then confirm the commitment offline.

## *Federal laws*

Internet business brings many U.S. companies into the export field for the first time. If this is true of your company, be aware of the Export Administration Act of 1979. It includes lists of products that cannot be exported unless your business has an export license, including some computer products, electronics, and software. Besides telling you *what* you can't export, it also tells you *where*. You can send almost anything to France, England, and Germany. You can't send much to Libya.

Two federal laws cover computer crime that may affect your business. The Computer Fraud and Abuse Act prohibits unauthorized use of computers owned by the federal government, computer acts that are detrimental to commerce, and computer acts that reveal information that infringes upon a person's privacy. This law was amended in 1994 to cover access without authorization to any computer used in interstate commerce, which includes all Internet computers. Information theft is a felony.

The penalties for violating this act are serious. You can go to prison if you use a federal computer. Recently, a technician with the Lawrence Livermore Laboratories was arrested under this act for using a government computer to download erotic pictures. The technician was fired, which was just a wrist-slapping—he could have been jailed.

The Electronic Communications Privacy Act prohibits electronic eavesdropping. It forbids unauthorized access of electronic communications facilities, and prohibits someone with limited access to electronic communications from intentionally exceeding those limits.

In addition, many states have laws addressing computer crime. If someone uses your computer system to commit a crime, or if you become suspicious that this may happen, contact your local law enforcement agency. Being aware of a crime and taking no action makes your company liable for criminal charges as an accomplice. In a sole proprietorship or a partnership, this exposes management to personal criminal liability.

Even in a corporation, in rare instances directors or officers of the corporation many be personally charged with criminal liability if corporate systems are used to commit a crime, even if that use is unauthorized.

# Ten Steps to Internet success

We've covered the awful things that can go wrong and how to avoid them, but you can't write an Internet success story by avoidance alone. You need to know what steps your business should take to implement a triumphant Internet project—"steps" rather than leaps. For something as potentially complex as a Net project, a step-by-step approach is the best plan.

1. *Evaluate your existing needs and resources, including hardware and software, and the availability and skills of your people.*

Start out by finding what you need and what you have. Talk with your staff; you may find an employee or co-worker who surfs the Net at home and can give advice. Involve people across departmental boundaries; the more departments with even a little involvement in your ideas, the more will support your finished result. As every successful politician since Julius Caesar has known, broad-based support is essential to final success. Make an effort to involve nontechnical people from the very start.

Do a data survey of your business. Find out what data your customers, suppliers and staff will want to access on the Net and then find out where in your company that data lives.

2. *Select a simple, visible pilot project. Define its scope. Set a target timeline, with deliverable steps and required compatibilities.*

Budgeting is tough, especially when you budget for something you've never done before. Don't think you can budget to the exact dollar or even the exact hundred dollars. The unexpected will crop up. The most important part of your timeline will be the definitions of your deliverables and the milestones you set for them, not any projected dates. Be flexible with delivery dates. Expect your project to be late and over budget, and allow for it with ten percent or more of your budget reserved for unforeseen contingencies.

Remember to start small, as small as you possibly can. A small project is much easier to control. You're steaming into uncharted waters, and you'll get stuck in tight bends if your ship is the Queen Mary.

### 3. *Get support from your management—both financial support in the form of budgeted funds, and endorsement of deliverables.*

Ask for support based on business reasons, not technical reasons. Tie your project into the big picture. How will it support your company's long-term goals? Conservatively, what quantifiable benefits can managers expect after using the Internet for one year? Evaluate your company's culture. If it's a rigid hierarchy (a 'command and control' model), expect resistance.

### 4. *Gather a small project team willing to work hard and produce quickly.*

Committees take time. Unless you have a very small company, your first Internet project is no time to build a company-wide consensus. Hand-pick a tight crew who can get along together and who will thrive on pressure.

When appropriate, recruit your elite commandos from different departments. Your Net project may have work that requires different kinds of expertise: technical, marketing, operations, accounting, or sales. A diversity of skills—if they are the particular skills you need—will make it easier to assign specific tasks.

### 5. *Pick a project manager to assign tasks, meet the schedule, maintain a budget, and oversee testing.*

Choose wisely. As in most business situations, a great manager will increase your chances of success more than any other factor. It won't hurt if your team leader has actually been on the Internet for a few months and has read this book.

### 6. *Create detailed specifications.*

Working from your list of deliverables, your manager and team should create detailed specifications. Depending on your project, these may require research by the team. One of the decisions to make at this point in time is how much, if any, of this project should run on your own computer and how much should run on a computer managed by your Internet access provider. Other important issues at this stage are security measures and the types of reporting you will implement.

### 7. *Evaluate and select consultants, an Internet access provider, software, and hardware.*

Your detailed specifications give you the criteria you need to select the pieces to assemble. Since you have a clear idea of what you want, it will be easier (and less costly) to hire consultants at this stage to do tasks that your team lacks expertise or time to handle. At this stage you should still be flexible. A consultant or your access provider may suggest alternate ways to meet your objectives that streamline your workload or save money.

### 8. *Develop your prototype and put it online.*

After all those steps, finally you get to do something! By this point, you've done your homework and you have advisors when you need help. If you use your own technical staffers, prototype development will be their busiest stage. Development is where things get exciting and intense. To keep your Internet project team energetic and to build momentum, celebrate each milestone as you reach it. And watch out for *feature creep,* the innate urge to add just one more thing. It seems harmless but is deadlier than any ghoul dreamed up by Stephen King. You should have reached the stage of *feature lock* before you come to step 8. Be iron-willed about refusing to add features after feature lock, no matter how appealing they seem or how easy your staff says the features will be to add. Save them for your next project.

Then comes the magic moment when your experimental version first goes online. Let pioneers within your company try to break it first, before you expose it to the outside world. It will help if you can roll it out gradually. When your project goes live on the Net, let a few people know. Quiz them closely about their experiences on your site. Incorporate improvements based on their reactions before announcing your site to the world. Expect problems—there always are some at first.

And expect to conduct training for whomever your Internet project will touch, within your company or customers outside. When training, give people information they can use *immediately*. Let them understand that the Internet is not something to fear. The Net is useful and it's fun. Make sure your own

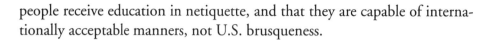

people receive education in netiquette, and that they are capable of internationally acceptable manners, not U.S. brusqueness.

## 9. *Promote your site.*

It is often a mistake to promote your Internet site before you have it up and running. Too many problems can happen. Too much can change. But as soon as your site goes live, pull out the bells and whistles, and honk all the horns! Make as big a noise as you possibly can.

Promote your site both outside your company and inside it. Make sure your employees know about it. Make sure that any staff members who deal with your customers can answer questions about it. Set up "guided tours" for staffers who lack Internet access on their own, and for senior managers. Start an employee suggestion contest with prizes for those who come up with ways to improve your site.

Outside your company, promote your Net site in as many ways as possible. You'll find lots of ideas on ways to do that in the marketing chapters of this book.

## 10. *Listen to the feedback and grow your site.*

The Internet is interactive. You will get feedback. Some will be direct, such as email messages from people who have used your site. Some will be indirect, such as statistics on file download rates or number of visitors to your site. Some may be sales figures, or cost savings as your Federal Express bill goes down.

Plan from the beginning to collect that feedback, to analyze it, and to apply it. From your seed project, you can grow your Internet business to serve your company and your customers in many ways. The feedback you receive will be your surest guide.

# How to Avoid Break-Ins and Fraud: The Basics

*"Where large sums of money are concerned, it is advisable to trust nobody."*
Agatha Christie

In talking to businesspeople about Internet security, I've found that most have one of two points of view. They either assume that nothing will ever hurt their company, or they worry endlessly that their Internet business(es) will be attacked simultaneously by Saddam Hussein, Charles Manson, and the Bermuda Triangle.

Those are two extremes, and reality lies in between. Any computer linked to the Internet is exposed to nearly four million other computers, maybe more. Most of those computers are used by everyday people just getting their work done. But *thousands* of Internet computers are used by Bad Guys. Evildoers. Spies. They are not all-powerful and all-seeing, but they can wreak some havoc. Most of them will never visit your site. But, as William Cheswick and Steven Bellovin point out in their book *Firewalls and Internet Security*, "It is this way with computer security: the attacker only has to win once."

So the bad news is that your business can be vulnerable on the Internet. The good news is that with common sense and a little work you can block all but the most able and determined attackers.

 "Who cares if my computer gets invaded?" one manager asked me. "It only cost a coupla thousand dollars. I can get a new one." He misses the point. Internet security is not about protecting your computer. It's about protecting your *information*.

If you have any information you don't want a competitor to see, you'd better worry about security. Contrary to what TV shows tell you, most successful computer attacks don't come from bored and brainy kids. They come from industrial spies out to make money.

Maybe they'll copy your information and sell it. Maybe they'll just *change* it. Some hackers simply want to annoy you. For example, in one Fortune 500 corporation, hackers changed the computer startup files to display X-rated photos during startup. They also altered the corporation's email system so managers couldn't use it.

Other hackers are out to do serious damage. Not too long ago, hackers broke into a steel plant's network and lowered the quality of the steel it produced by sabotaging its quality-control software. Incidents like these are making businesses painfully aware of something called *data integrity*. That's the assurance that your data has not been changed.

Of course, you also want to protect the *confidentiality* of your information. And you need to be sure of the *authenticity* of traffic you receive from the Net, making sure that messages are from the people they claim to be.

The shocking thing about Internet security is that most businesses who are broken into *never find out about it*. One government study estimated that 97 percent of computer penetrations remain undetected. Some data is missing, or a program won't work, but the victim never realizes that the problems were caused by an Internet break-in. Most companies don't have the proper monitoring software in place, and those that do don't review the security reports and never know what hit them.

## Preventing outsiders from ripping you off

1991: The United States Government Accounting Office reveals that during the Gulf War, military computers linked to the Internet were broken into by hackers from the Netherlands. They copied U.S. military data about Gulf War soldiers, military equipment, and new weapons under development.

1993: A hacker hides programs in the computer of Internet access provider Panix. For weeks—or perhaps months—the hacker's programs collect the passwords and account names of Panix customers. When the break-in is discovered, Panix has to shut down its computer for three days, closing Internet connections for its customers, who in turn have to change all their passwords and check to see if they, in turn, had been broken into.

1994: Hackers install a sniffer program to watch the Internet links of the University of California at Berkeley. The sniffer collects more than 3,000 passwords and account names in 14 hours.

1995: Hacker Kevin Mitnick steals 20,000 credit card numbers from Internet access provider Netcom, who made the mistake of storing credit card numbers on the same computers it allowed the public to enter.

The most visible computer crime-fighting organization is the Computer Emergency Response Team (CERT). On an average day, CERT handles three reported Internet security breaches. Those three are just the tip of a much bigger iceberg. Most businesses are afraid to announce a break-in, and it is estimated that only 15 percent of breaches are actually reported.

Ernst & Young took a survey in 1994. It found seventeen companies with computer security losses totaling more than $1 million in the past year due to stolen business information and destroyed data. Several additional companies reported serious losses to Ernst & Young but would not disclose the amount.

In case you hadn't tumbled on to it yet, I'm wising you up to the fact that serious damage happens all the time, and it can hit your business as sure as the bloke down the block. Don't get all knock-kneed, but don't be a cakebrain either. There are dangerous criminals out there who feel less regret selling your customer files than you would re-using a postage stamp.

At this point, you may be saying, "Hey, wait a minute! I use America Online (or CompuServe, Prodigy, Niftyserve, or the Microsoft Network), and I haven't heard of those kinds of problem there."

You're right. These kinds of problems happen more rarely on those commercial services. Security breaches are less frequent, smaller-scale, and less-publicized. There are two reasons for this.

The first reason is that the commercial services are *centralized* networks, while the Internet is a *distributed* network. That may sound like a meaningless technical distinction, but it's actually a simple, clear-cut difference and easy to understand. (See Figure 6.1.)

When you send a message or a credit card number on a commercial service like CompuServe, your message goes directly from your sending computer to CompuServe's central computer. It can't go anyplace else, and there are no other computers between yours and CompuServe's. Then CompuServe's computer reads the address on your message and sends it out. If the address is another CompuServe subscriber, your message goes directly from CompuServe's central computer to your addressee's computer. Again, your

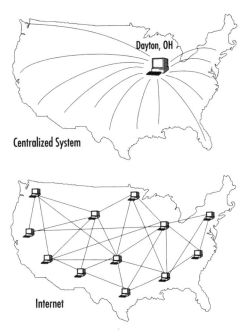

**Figure 6.1** *In a centralized network like CompuServe, traffic travels to and from a central site only. The Internet is a distributed network. Its traffic travels through other sites to reach its destination.*

message cannot go anyplace else, and there are no additional computers between CompuServe Central and your addressee's computer.

In short, your message goes right from you to CompuServe and straight from CompuServe to its destination. It's tough for anyone else to get ahold of your message, so it's relatively safe.

On the Internet, your message takes a much different route. In fact, several routes. As *San Francisco Chronicle* columnist Robert Rossney described it, "The information sent from one computer to another gets broken up into a zillion pieces, scattered across the network, and then reassembled at the other end, just like the transporter on *Star Trek.*"

When you send an Internet message, your computer breaks it into smaller pieces for efficiency. It sends the pieces to your Internet access provider. Your provider's computer looks at the address on each piece and sends it to whatever available computer is nearest your message's final destination. Depending on which computers and network links are open, that can be a different computer for each piece. Those computers forward your pieces to closer computers. Soon all your pieces reach your destination's computer, which glues them back together.

In short, one Internet message goes through several computers and several routes to reach its destination. You can't predict how many computers, which computers or which routes message pieces will take. *Any of those computers can read your message and change it.*

The second reason that America Online and its counterparts have fewer security problems is that the commercial services are much smaller than the Internet. All of the commercial services *put together* are less than half the size of the Internet. There are simply fewer people on them and fewer computers to break into. America Online customers are mostly people in their homes. There are fewer businesses, so break-ins cause less damage.

Call 'em what you want—hackers, crackers, spies, or scum—they are outside your company and looking for trouble. If you manage an Internet project, part of your job is to keep them out. Lucky for you there are only so many ways scum can break in through the Net. Let's take a peek at the doors you need to watch—without going into technobabble overkill.

## *Password attacks*

Your first line of defense is your software's password protection. Sloppy management of passwords opens doors to far more digital crooks than any other means. Most of the so-called brilliant hackers are actually good at guessing or getting passwords. It doesn't take a giant brain to stop these yeggs. With a couple of hours' planning and never ending vigilance you can plug password security holes. Keeping vigilant is the hard part. I'll provide details on password security later in this chapter.

## *Software attacks*

The second most popular port of entry is your software. You can have more holes than Swiss cheese in your operating system software, communications software, and applications programs—and those holes attract rats. You can plug holes by installing a protective "firewall" between your computers and the Internet, and by deploying your software carefully. There are some programs you should avoid if possible (Telnet, Sendmail), and others (like Finger) that your technical gurus can strip down for safety. Your technical staff will need to invest more time securing your software than in any other defense.

## Eavesdropping attacks

Passive attacks based on eavesdropping are on the rise. This popularity is fueled by the increase in Internet credit-card traffic—eavesdropping is the easiest way to steal card numbers. Eavesdroppers don't even need to break into your system to access such important information. They sit outside and use software called *packet sniffers* to scan your incoming and outgoing traffic. Packet sniffers recognize patterns like credit card numbers, your product names, and specific people's names. When the sniffer spots a familiar pattern, it copies your message and sends it to the eavesdropper. The reliable way to beat these spies is to encrypt your Internet traffic. Encryption makes your messages look like gibberish. Packet sniffers can't spot patterns because scrambled gibberish has none. Encryption is built into some operating systems such as Macintosh. In others it's easy to add.

## Forgery attacks

Forged messages are also on the rise. It is trivial to fake or change an Internet message. Forged Internet messages are called *spoofs*, a deceptively cheerful name. It makes them sound harmless, when some cause serious pain:

- The premier of Ontario, Canada, Bob Rae, was startled to find an explicitly sexual message from his return address posted on a widely read newsgroup. Political opponents used the forged message to embarrass him in the Ontario legislature.

- An evildoer sabotaged more than 30 customers of Internet access provider Net Access in Philadelphia. Apparently an unhappy Net Access customer, the culprit spewed racist forgeries across several Usenet newsgroups, as though the innocent customers had made racist insults. Each victim was bombarded with hate email from all over the world. Some lost business as a result.

- The most financially damaging spoof to date accused the Stratton Oakmont firm of investment bankers and its president of fraud and criminal activity in an October 1994 stock offering. The offering's share price dropped 40 percent in less than a month. Stratton Oakmont sued Prodigy for $200 million in damages, since the spoof was mailed from an expired Prodigy address. The forgery may have been posted by a short-seller to profit from the stock plunge.

Encryption helps defeat spoofing, as do *digital signatures*, which are like high-tech notary public seals, proving that a message came from only one person and that it has not been altered in any way. A digital signature is easy to include with most email. Don't leave home without it.

## Denial-of-service attacks

The least common type of Internet attack is called a *denial-of-service attack*. This means you get bombarded with hundreds or thousands of messages—sometimes huge ones—that clog your Internet site so nothing can get in or out. Large-scale attacks of this type can even shut down your Internet access provider's entire connection. There is no high-tech defense against a denial-of-service attack, but if you read this book carefully you won't need one. These attacks come in response to obnoxious behavior by a person or company. If your people are good neighbors on the Net, you should never need to deal with a denial-of-service attack.

## Virus attacks

Computer viruses have been around long enough so they are no longer big news. You probably already have at least one virus protection software program. If not, get one. Your virus protection vendor will send you updates to catch and kill new viruses as they emerge. Make sure all upgrades are added quickly, and make sure all software from the Net passes your virus checker before you allow it to touch other programs.

## Credit card scams

When your company takes credit cards over the Internet, you are vulnerable to all the usual credit card scams plus creative twists unique to the Net. We cover cardsharps in detail later in this chapter.

In many ways, the most serious and hardest-to-defend attacks are those based on security holes in your software. Sometimes the most innocent-seeming software is the most dangerous. Who'd ever suspect software as simple-looking as Finger? Yet Finger was the point of entry for the infamous Internet Worm virus that crippled thousands of computers and cost hundreds of thousands of dollars to clean up. Finger remains a favorite target for hackers today.

How about MIME, which lets you send email with pictures? Automatic execution of MIME email can be very dangerous. MIME messages can hide commands to take over your computer. Your World Wide Web server software is also vulnerable. Bugs in certain Web servers let outsiders retrieve any file on the Web server's computer. Those files could include your password file or other confidential data.

You will need to provide your technical staff with books that go into program-by-program detail on software security. We only scratch the surface here. However, keep three rules in mind to minimize software security risks.

1. **Keep Internet software away from your other software as much as possible.**

When you start out on the Internet, it may make sense for you to run as many services as you can on your Internet access provider's computer. Almost all access providers perform this service for a fee. Keep your FTP, Gopher, and World Wide Web servers on your provider's computer.

Instead of using SMTP for email—which requires that your computer is always connected to the Net—use UUCP if your company size justifies doing so. You can set UUCP to connect to your access provider's system every 15 or 30 minutes to send and receive email. This is more secure, and you don't have to run Sendmail, which is famous for security holes.

If you are going to run your Web server on your own computer, run it on a standalone computer if possible. This sacrifical computer should not be connected to the rest of your company computers, or if it is connected, it should be separated from your other computers by a firewall. *Whatever you do, make sure not to store any customer information on the same computer as your Web server, especially credit card numbers.* This is very, very, very important and is one of the most basic protection steps you can take. Never store credit card numbers on *any* computer connected to the Internet.

If you offer a Web, FTP, or Gopher site reachable by people outside your company, and you want to connect that site to computers within your company, *separate your open site from the rest of your network with a firewall.* If you can't afford a firewall, you also can't afford to clean up after the damage an invader could cause. Keep Internet servers away from your own network unless you have a barrier between them.

Think twice before connecting computers that hold your sensitive information, like accounting programs and R&D data. Consider an alternative in departments with secret data. Perhaps you can have your employees walk to an "Internet desk" to use vulnerable connected computers. This may be a little more inconvenient for your employees, but it's a lot less work than cleaning up after a nasty break-in.

### 2.   Keep it simple.

Complex software is more likely to have security bugs. Use simple programs when you can. Use as few programs as you can. As William Cheswick and Steven Bellovin say in *Firewalls and Internet Security,* "Programs that you do not run cannot hurt you."

When analyzing your system, don't trust complicated things. Trust only simple things like files and short programs. When your technical people program security rules into router filters, they should use short rules.

### 3.   Take advantage of security software tools.

There are terrific software tools available to increase your security. Many of them are available for free on the Internet. Check out the Unix software program COPS, which searches your system and finds security flaws. A program called ASET for Sun computers forces users to use hard-to-crack passwords.

One of the most valuable security tools can come to you via email. Your security administrator will want to subscribe to the mailing list from the Computer Emergency Response Team that emails CERT advisories. These advisories warn of all newly discovered software security holes and tell where to get patches to fix them.

If you follow the guidelines I've listed here, you should reduce your risks due to outside invaders from the Internet. The unfortunate part is that those Internet hackers are not your greatest danger. More computer security breaches come from another source, far more hazardous and harder to manage. Your toughest security challenge will come from these other culprits.

They are waiting to break into *your* system. They have passwords and can log on. They know the names of your files and where they are located. According to all studies, they cause thousands of computer security violations each year. Some are minimal. Hundreds do serious damage. Who are they?

They are your own employees.

## Preventing inside theft and breaches

You've read about hacker Kevin Mitnick stealing the numbers of twenty thousand credit cards from Netcom. Fortunately Mitnick was arrested before he did anything with them. But another case makes Mitnick look like small change.

In September, 1994, the U.S. Secret Service busted Ivy James Lay for stealing the numbers of *fifty thousand* credit cards from MCI Communications Corp., and selling the numbers to dealers, generating $50 million dollars in bogus charges. How did he do it? Lay was an MCI employee, and he programmed one of MCI's PCs to capture credit card numbers from MCI customers.

 By far the greatest number of computer security incidents are caused by employees. This holds true for Internet security violations as well as for non-Internet situations. Many incidents causing data loss are accidental. They can be prevented with more thorough training and better procedures. Deliberately caused computer security violations are harder to prevent, because they can happen for many reasons. And the perpetrators can be managers as well as staff.

Some employees violate computer security because they are angry. These violations can be unusual and are often difficult to catch. In Chicago, an unhappy Encyclopedia Britannica editor took revenge on the book's computer files. He put Mohammed's biography in place of Jesus.' Then he wrote unflattering biographies of Britannica managers and placed them in the book as regular entries.

Some employees are just sloppy. When I was with Computer Literacy Bookshops, we received a demonstration disk from a small software distribution company. When a manager popped the disk into a computer to try out the software, she got a big surprise. The disk had an elaborately printed label with instructions, but the software inside was no demo. Instead she found a support technician's resume and files of bestiality and homosexual sex material downloaded from the Internet. It looked like the support technician who made the disk had copied his personal directory instead of the demo directory—a careless mistake that reflected poorly on the software distribution company.

There is obviously a lesson to learn from these examples. Your business is much more vulnerable to computer abuse from employees than from outside invaders. Employees have more opportunities. They know the juiciest targets. They can damage your company in creative ways not possible by outsiders. And just as the Internet empowers employees to be more productive, it helps errant employees do worse damage in more ways.

So how do you prevent computer security abuses—especially Internet abuses— by employees? You extend the same guidelines you use for non-computer security. First of all, limit the information employees can reach to what they need to do their jobs. A manufacturing draftsman doesn't need access to your accounting files. An accounts payable clerk doesn't need your customer list. You would naturally restrict these employees from having complete access to all information from all departments.

When putting limits on the kinds of information employees can reach on the Internet, you have two ways to restrict access. You can limit the types of Internet services a person can reach, and you can limit the sources of data that flow into your company. Internet services are the easier to restrict of these two categories. Perhaps everyone in your company doesn't need Internet access. Those who do may mostly need email access. You don't have to give FTP, newsgroup, Gopher, Telnet, and World Wide Web tools to all your people. Limiting data sources will require assistance from your technical staff. Many companies, for instance, bar access to all newsgroups whose names start with **alt.**. This may be overkill. The **alt.** newsgroups include many valuable business resources, especially for software and hardware technical support. But prohibiting all newsgroups whose names start with **alt.sex.** would probably not harm your business. Blocking **alt.sex.** groups might have prevented that support technician from filling the software demo disk with his private files.

Besides newsgroups, you may want to filter out sites for games, gambling, and other recreational activities. These may be Web pages, Gopher servers, or FTP sites that have addresses you can input so your router or firewall blocks incoming and outgoing traffic with those Internet addresses. (On the other hand, if your company hasn't deleted *Solitaire* and *Minesweeper* from Microsoft Windows, why bother?)

One of the best motivations to keep employees from timewasters like these is embarrassment. Chances are people won't grab photos from **alt.feelthy.peectures** while other employees look over their shoulders. But at an isolated computer in a private office, there is less fear of being caught with your pants down, so to speak. This is another argument in favor of making the Internet available to employees only on computers at a few strategically located communal desks. The higher visibility of a communal computer discourages non-business Internet projects. Use of the Internet for some personal use is to be expected. It's nothing to make a fuss over. But the possibility of discovery certainly can eliminate the temptation for extreme abuse of Internet privileges.

Another watchful eye on employees should be maintained by your security administrator. Your company may not have someone with that exact job title, but someone should audit the log reports of Internet activity. If that person notices a sudden burst of email and file transfers to one of your competitors, take action. But if no one reviews your reports, you'll miss the most important indicator you have of sudden unexplained activities on the part of one of your employees.

# Password protection

The main reason any computer system is broken into—whether on the Internet or off—is because somebody guessed its password. And I hate to upset the delicate sensibilities of supermarket tabloid writers, but guessing passwords doesn't mean you're a mastermind. An eight-year-old child can do it.

 The number-one reason hackers break into computers via the Net is that the computer's owners never bothered to change the standard, vendor-supplied passwords that come with software. Software vendors provide a temporary password or two to use during setup, like TEMP, ADMIN, or SETUP. The idea is that you install the software and then replace their passwords with your own. That's the idea, anyhow. Believe it or not, *thousands* of sites never remove the vendor's passwords! Hackers have lists of them. If your system administrators haven't removed them, you might as well give your Internet site a drive-through window.

The number-two way for hackers to penetrate a site is by trying obvious, easily guessed passwords. The first thing a hacker will try is GUEST. Other popular guesses are ROOT, GUARD, ADMIN, ADM, SYSADM, SYSOP, VISITOR, and the ever-popular PASSWORD. Attackers try these guesses because they often work. Next they'll try site-specific guesses: company name, manager names, email addresses, and birthdates.

You want to prevent your people from using such easily guessed passwords. Make sure your Internet users know how to pick safe passwords. Any computer security book can give you guidelines.

To enforce selection of safe passwords, your security administrator can get free software that checks proposed passwords and won't let your people use any that are easy to guess. More important is education for all your Internet-using employees on choosing hard-to-guess passwords and keeping them secure.

Part of security is disabling passwords when an employee leaves. At many companies, an employee's password is disabled the instant he or she gives notice, or, when an employee is fired, while the manager gives them the news.

Check that the employee has only one password. This caused a problem for the Wollongong Group, whose former employee Ming Jyh Hsieh was arrested three months after being fired. She shared a password with five other employees. It wasn't changed when she left, so she dialed in and used it. She was caught in the act of stealing software from the company.

This brings up another important issue about passwords. You should change them often. This is called *password aging*. It prevents incidents like the one the Wollongong Group experienced, and limits damage when an attacker or an unauthorized employee captures your passwords. You can have employees choose a new password every 60 days, or even better, every 30 days. This can be done on a volunteer basis, but is more effective if you use software that forces workers to change their passwords when the time limit expires.

The safest passwords are those that change every time you log on. These are called *one-time passwords*, and there are a couple of different ways to implement them. S-Key, public-domain software that generates one-time passwords, is rated highly by experts in Net security and encryption. S-Key is free, and it's easy to install and use (**ftp://thumper.bellcore.com/pub/key**).

Security Dynamics (617-547-7820) sells inexpensive SecurID cards ($50 and up) that time-synchronize with its ACE/Server security software ($2,000). The SecurID cards have 6-digit numbers that light up and change every 60 seconds. To log on, you whip out your card and type in the number plus your password. The server software matches your incoming number with its own number, which also changes every sixty seconds. These cards are easy to use.

To keep your passwords from being stolen, don't store your main password file on a vulnerable Internet-accessible computer. Bad Guys have used several different Internet tools to steal passwords. FTP, Telnet, and Finger are the worst offenders, but UUCP and other software has also been used. The book *Firewalls and Internet Security* goes into these problems in detail.

Be careful about logging attempted logins. When people accidentally type their passwords on the wrong line—which happens often—it will show passwords. If a hacker grabs your log report file, you are wide open.

Watch out for bogus messages from a system administrator or supposed Internet authority (even your access provider) asking you to set up a guest account or change anything about your password file. If you get a message that sounds even remotely suspicious, get a phone number and call the person back. Make sure that the phone number is the normal number for your access provider or whomever.

And remember that people don't need to access your computer or your network to steal your passwords. Passwords have also been stolen from backup tapes and disks.

## Audit trails

Even when you protect your computers with firewalls, encryption, and a bullet-proof password system, someone somehow may still break into them. Angry employees with passwords may try sabotage, or intruders may fast talk their way in. That's why you need *audit trails*.

Every accountant is familiar with audit reports—or should be. In accounting systems, audit trails let auditors trace the flow of cash through your company and reconstruct the who, what, where, when, and how much of financial transactions. It was a computerized accounting system audit report that launched Cliff Stoll on his Internet hunt for a German spy ring, as he recounted in his book *The Cuckoo's Egg*.

You might not be attacked by international spies, but a competitor or hacker can do just as much damage. That's why any computer you link to the Internet needs to generate its own audit logs. Even the most secure system should record what traffic passes through it and the sources of that traffic. Your audit reports may also be your basis for defense in a lawsuit, or be helpful if your company undergoes an EDI audit or a data processing audit.

Some Internet server software automatically creates activity logs. With most computers, you will need to add software to capture and record Internet transaction information. In an ideal world, your computer's operating system would handle this for you. That is the most reliable way, and the least work to set up. In current computers, this is rare but worth looking for. For instance, Tandem NonStop Computers have a built-in audit function. For any file that you choose, the Tandem system can post every completed transaction to an audit file. I wish every system made it that easy.

What will your system need to record? Enough information to let your system administrator reconstruct the who, what, where, and when of Internet transactions. Your system needs to record not just unauthorized access attempts, but every login and logout. (It was a forged but seemingly authorized transaction that sent Cliff Stoll on his chase.) You'll want the "from" address for each incoming transaction, even though "from" addresses can be forged. And, you'll want to know which files or databases were accessed and especially if any were altered.

Get the date *and* time of each transaction. Timestamps are crucial in reconstructing crimes and catching culprits. Get timestamps for both incoming and outgoing Net traffic. I know of two cases in which businesses used timestamps to nab errant employees. In both cases, data processing managers were able to compare timestamps with payroll timecards to pinpoint the delinquent staffers.

You'll need more detailed audit records if you do sales on the Net or if you make electronic payments. These kinds of transactions affect your cash flow, so you'll need to record transaction amounts, and if you make international sales, currency types. Your accounting department will want specific information to meet your financial software's audit needs. Sales transactions may also need to generate information needed for inventory audit reports.

Whatever type of audit logs your system creates, look for the ability to pull reports *on demand*. Some systems generate logs only once a month, or only weekly, or only at night after your system has been shut down. Emergencies are not this polite, and audit reports are like hospital emergency rooms. You don't know *when* you'll need them, but when you do, you need them *now*. You can't tell when a hacker will hit, or when a virus will take over your disk drive, or when a screaming customer will call you. Chances are bad things will happen when your system is at peak load and the Net is at its busiest.

Just as you can't predict when you'll need audit logs, you can't predict for what time period you will need them. Perhaps you'll discover a Trojan horse software program in your computer, quietly collecting all your passwords. Its creation date may say it sat there undiscovered for two months. Who put it there? If you save log records for only two weeks, you can't find out. Keep your audit logs for at least three months. Six is better. Besides, your system administrator can analyze historical records to spot patterns and trends.

Beware of systems that won't give you audit reports that are *up to the minute*. Some systems will only give you reports showing yesterday's activity, or worse, last week's. When a problem hits, you'll want to kill it while it's fresh. Yesterday's audit logs won't help you clear out a disaster that erupted in the last fifteen minutes. Make sure you can run up-to-the-minute audit reports at any time you want, and without shutting your system down.

Audit logs will help you catch attackers, but even the best logs won't keep Bad Guys out. For that, you need to build a wall. I'll explain how to do this in the next chapter.

# Firewalls, Encryption, Credit Cards, and Digital Cash

*"Even if you're on the right track, you'll get run over if you just sit there."*
Will Rogers

If your business was small and had just one computer, it would be relatively easy for you to protect your information from the Internet. You would carefully set security. You would use that one computer every day and be familiar enough with it to notice any dramatic changes. And you would never be careless with your password.

## Filters and firewalls

With two computers, security is more difficult to maintain, but still manageable. With four or five, it would be time-consuming to configure and maintain security, one computer at a time. With twenty, it's impossible. You not only have to patrol twenty connections to the Internet, but you must secure communications *between* your computers so an attacker can't find a hole in one computer and do a runaround. That is where filters and firewalls come in.

### *What is a firewall?*

Simply put, a firewall gives you a single chokepoint through which all incoming and outgoing Internet traffic must pass, allowing you to control it. A firewall prevents break-ins from the Net, and a good firewall helps keep confidential data from being sent out.

You can configure your firewall to allow only email to pass in and out, protecting your internal network against any non-email attacks. Or you can allow other kinds of Internet services under approved conditions. You can also use a firewall's audit tools as a wiretap to trace hacker attacks. You can even set a firewall to bar traffic from the Internet, while still allowing your employees to access the Net without restraint.

In the ideal situation, the Internet and the Bad Guys live outside the firewall. Also outside, on a dedicated sacrificial computer, are the "dirty" network services (hackable and publicly reachable services such as Web and FTP servers) offered by your company. Only authorized users and approved Internet services pass through the firewall, and they are closely and automatically monitored. Your company's computers are inside the barricade, protected.

Although firewalls defend your business, you pay the price of limiting access to some Internet services, or making the Internet less convenient to use for your workers. Other firewall costs include its purchase price (though you can get some software-only firewalls for free) and its maintenance costs. In addition, setting up and then maintaining a firewall takes time and technical expertise.

If your company uses a router, you can program it to use *filter* software. Filters can spot and discard some types of incoming traffic that you regard as a potential security threat. A really good router will let you filter *outgoing* traffic as well as incoming. You can also use router filters to divide your network into subnets and restrict what type of traffic flows between subnets, thus maintaining internal security between company divisions.

A router with filters costs less than a more elaborate firewall and takes less work to maintain, but it is much easier for Evildoers to penetrate and control.

## Who needs a firewall and who doesn't?

Not every Internet site needs a firewall. If your business has only dial-up Internet access via modem, a firewall may be overkill. You also can get by without a firewall if your Internet activities meet all of these guidelines:

- If you run any servers (such as WWW, Gopher, FTP, Telnet, Finger, or mailing list) that outsiders can access only on your Internet access provider's computers, or a on separate standalone computer that is not connected to any of your other systems.

- People inside your company can reach the Internet only on standalone computers used for no other purpose. A possible exception may be to let Internet email reach your computers, while other Internet services are blocked.

- No customer information (especially credit card numbers) or any other confidential data is stored on any of the computers you connect to the Internet.

- For email, you use a UUCP mail server that dials up your access provider, exchanges messages, and then hangs up. Some Net security experts might disallow this last guideline, because hackers have broken into sites with UUCP. But in general, I find dial-up UUCP safer than the alternative, SMTP email.

Note that you can ask your Internet access provider to install and run a firewall for you, especially if you run your servers on your access provider's computer. There is a charge for this, but it saves you the hassle of firewall maintenance.

If you do business on the Internet without a firewall, be extra security-conscious. Watch your passwords. If you can, use a software program like S/Key to create one-time passwords. Always use the latest release of your networking software, because it will have bug fixes of known security holes. Turn off and restrict as many Net services as you can. Get the list of dangerous computer ports from the Computer Emergency Response Team (**ftp: cert.org/pub**) and block all the "sneak attack" ports that it recommends.

## *Pieces of the security puzzle*

There are several different types of solutions to the "which firewall approach is best?" dilemma. I have detailed the pieces of this puzzle for you:

**Filters and routers.** Filters look at each piece of Internet traffic and check its port number, the service (Telnet, Web, FTP, etc.) it requests, the protocol (TCP, etc.) it wants to use, the sending source, and the destination. After checking this data against rules you have programmed into it, the filter either stops the piece of traffic or lets it pass. You can set a filter to block all traffic coming *from* a particular destination, or all traffic headed *for* a particular destination, among other parameters. Filters by themselves are not a firewall. A router is a piece of hardware that takes incoming data traffic from several places and sends it to other places. For example, a router can take messages coming from all the computers on your LAN and send them out to your Internet access provider, and vice versa. You can also run filtering software on a computer instead of a router. This is the easiest and lowest-cost solution to implement. Figure 7.1 illustrates how routers work.

**A gateway.** (These are also called application gateways, application-level gateways, proxy servers, and proxies.) Gateways are more secure than routers.

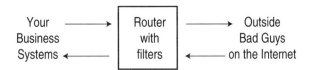

**Figure 7.1**   *Depending on which router you have, you can set a router to filter and block traffic going in, traffic going out, or traffic in both directions. The simplest level of protection, this is also the least secure.*

You can log and control all incoming and outgoing traffic down to, for instance, restricting outbound World Wide Web access to authorized individuals. With routers, traffic still passes directly between your network and the netherworld. A gateway actually stops the traffic and examines it before forwarding. An advantage of gateways is that they can forward SMTP email, eliminating the need for a separate computer to run email.

**A sacrificial computer.** This lamb sits exposed outside your firewall and runs all services accessible by outside people.

**A combination of routers, gateways, and computers.** As a step up from single-router protection, companies use every imaginable combination of routers, gateways, and computers. The book *Firewalls and Internet Security* is your best guide to many of the alternatives.

Filters are comparatively inexpensive and can be a usable solution, depending on what they are designed to protect. Filter software comes with your router hardware for no extra charge.

A twist on the router approach is a strict but secure two-router approach. This technique sets up *both* routers to allow outbound traffic only and block all inbound traffic. Your internal network talks only to the inside router, which talks only to the outside router, which talks only to one exposed sacrificial computer outside your network. Even if a trespasser were to take over your exposed computer and use it to breach your outside router, the interloper couldn't break through to your inside router. Your network would be safe.

Another two-router approach puts a gateway computer between two routers, as illustrated in Figure 7.2. Your exposed outside router talks only to the com-

**Figure 7.2**   *This more secure firewall employs two routers with a gateway machine in the middle. The inner router on the left protects your business in case a trespasser breaks into your gateway. The outer router on the right protects the gateway from outside attack.*

puter in the middle, which talks to both routers. This double defense is more costly to set up than a single router, but gives you much greater control and more thorough security.

Something similar to this approach is used by Motorola, which has about 90,000 employees with access to the Net. For security, it uses a double firewall to put two blocks between the Internet and Motorola's internal network. In addition, Motorola employees must use a special, restricted software application to connect, and they must be listed on an access control list.

One of the best protection tactics is to use an external sacrificial computer to handle mail, newsgroups, Web, Finger, and Gopher services. *Use the address of your sacrificial computer as the one you advertise for outside access.* Any address you advertise will be the one most often probed by attackers, so it makes sense to send them where they can do the least harm.

Configuration errors are the most common problems with routers and firewalls. When you purchase a product, it usually comes with all options open, allowing all traffic in both directions. You must disable unwanted options one step at a time. This requires in-depth knowledge of network protocols and application software. You can also disable your competitors' domains, so they can't enter your site.

Studies have shown that most data loss is caused by employee errors. You can place limits on the damage potential of employee errors by using firewalls or filters to segment your network into separate sections. Users from one section should not be allowed to enter another unless they need specific data and unless they have authorization. Usually, an internal barrier is set up to keep people out of other department's files.

In spite of what firewall vendors tell you, firewalls *will* inconvenience your users to some extent. How much so depends somewhat on which firewall product you use and even more on how you implement it.

## *How to buy a firewall*

How do you buy a firewall? That reminds me of the old vaudeville joke, "How do porcupines make love?" The answer is the same: very carefully.

Advertisements for one product, Firewall-1, claim that it is completely effective and allows no leaks, breaches, or compromises. Maybe it's good, but it wouldn't be that secure if it were defended by Klingons. The technology isn't invented yet that can keep out all of the attackers all of the time. Watch out for marketing exaggerations like these. Never believe that a vendor's system is as good as it claims unless you see some *unbiased* proof.

To sort through the distortion, you need someone who knows this stuff. Purchasing a firewall is a technical job for a technical person. Don't send your purchasing manager out with a shopping cart to buy a firewall unless your purchasing manager has a degree in computer science.

Do some homework before you shop. First you need to answer the question "What information are we protecting?" Figure out how bad it would be if that information were lost, copied, or changed. That'll give you a basis for calculating how much money and time you want to spend on Internet protection. Remember that your upfront costs for firewall hardware and software will be followed by setup costs, training fees, and ongoing expenses for hardware maintenance, software updates, and staff time for somebody to keep the dingus up and running. Different firewall products will require different amounts of staff time for upkeep—a potentially decisive cost factor.

With that background in hand, take a look at some of the security sites mentioned in this book, especially the firewalls mailing list archive.
Address: **ftp://ftp.greatcircle.com/pub.firewalls/archive**

A FAQ on firewalls is also available on the Web.
Address: **http://www.tis.com/Home/Network Security/Firewalls**

The avalanche of products coming out is tremendous, so you'll have a lot to choose from. With so many new products coming out all the time, there is no way to give you a complete rundown on every specific product. I will highlight a few recommended by technical people I know.

- Gauntlet is a complete applications gateway product by Trusted Information Systems, one of the most reputable firms in the Internet security field. This company's Web site has solid, useful informations about firewalls and is a good first stop in your shopping trip. For more information, go to **http://www.tis.com**.

- The same company also makes a good Unix software package, the TIS Firewall Toolkit—and it's free. The Toolkit is modular, so you use what you need and delete the rest. It lets you control the direction of allowable FTP transfers and provides other protection against FTP and Telnet assaults. It also provides front-end software to block direct access to Sendmail and keep out mail bombs. For more information, go to **http://www.tis.com**.

- The main advantage of Firewall-1 from Qualix Group (**http://www.qualix.com**) is its easy-to-use interface for configuring traffic flow. Firewall-1 looks at which applications are being accessed and filters packet headers. That's no great shakes, because expert intruders can defeat packet filters. Firewall-1 also provides an application gateway, which is the strongest part of its defense.

To give you an idea of cost, a basic router can cost $1,300 to $9,000 or more, filters included. Gauntlet costs $15,000 and Firewall-1 costs $20,000.

For any Internet security product on your consideration list, ask your potential supplier to describe, with technical detail, how it handles each of the 42 show-stopper bombs listed in *Firewalls and Internet Security*. Brochures for Sidewinder, a type enforcement product, specifically discuss these points. Other vendors will provide the information if asked.

Here are some important questions to ask for all firewall products:

- Will it connect to the hardware and software you have, and the access provider you use?
- Does it have enough throughput so it won't slow down your Internet activities?
- Will it meet your needs for security?

When considering a router to use on a firewall to run filter software (or, for that matter, when considering running filter software on a computer), there is a subtle-sounding, but important distinction for your technical people to check. A router can apply filters to *incoming* data and/or *outgoing* data:

- when it comes *into* the router
- as it *exits* the router

Notice that there are actually *four* alternatives here. Not all routers can handle all four. Check yours.

Here are some questions to ask when looking at filters:

- Will it filter input, output, or both?
- Can it inspect packets for source port, destination port, and protocol?
- Does it let you control the order in which it applies filtering rules?
- How easy is it to set up and change rules?
- Does it log rejected packets? (Few do.) What kind of information does it give in log reports?
- Will it filter established connections?
- Can it reject source-routed packets?

If you decide to set up a gateway, be aware that your gateway machine will need lots of memory—at least 16 megabytes. More is better. For high-volume situations, plan on 64 megabytes of memory. A gateway will also require lots of fast disk space, and "fast" is the key word here. Get the fastest you can find, because when you have a fast Net connection and plenty of memory, disk access will be the bottleneck that slows down your whole site.

Here are some questions to ask potential gateway vendors:

- Do you need special versions of your applications to work with the gateway, or will it work with the vanilla versions? If you need special versions, how much work will it take to modify your applications to work with this gateway? (Don't take the vendor's word for this. Get on the firewalls mailing list and get real-life answers from its customers.)

- Can you set it to allow only outbound FTP?

- Ask to see documentation for access control, filtering, and logs. Is it complete and understandable?

- How understandable is the operator interface? (It's generally quite cryptic.)

- What kinds of information do the logging reports provide?

- Does it authenticate both outgoing and incoming traffic?

- What kinds of traffic will it authenticate? Can you add your own custom authentications?

### A word of warning

Once you install a firewall, don't assume your site is hackerproof. Firewalls don't block viruses. They won't stop attacks in which a program is emailed or copied to a computer inside your firewall and then executed.

A trespasser may still sneak in, so don't rely only on your firewall. You still need to back it up with access log reports and alarms, and you still need to control which people and which programs have access to which files and which other programs.

## What to keep outside your firewall

You can dramatically decrease your chances of being eaten alive by attacking alligators if you keep certain Internet software programs on a dedicated, sacrificial machine outside your Internet gateway. If your company has no firewall, these processes are prime candidates to run on your Internet access provider's computer instead of your own.

Show this list to your network administrator. Potential offenders include:

- The *sending* portion of your SMTP email software
- Any World Wide Web server accessible by non-employees
- Any FTP server accessible by non-employees
- Any Gopher server accessible by non-employees
- Any mailing list server accessible by non-employees
- All Finger servers
- Especially all Telnet servers

## Type enforcement

Routers and gateways filter data based on information in the header of the message. This is a major weakness. Even newbie hackers learn to alter a message's header information to give whatever source address the hacker chooses. This is called *identity spoofing*. A hacker can create a fake source, fictional routing information, and a phony ID. The other strengths of firewalls offset this vulnerability to some extent, but firewalls still have no idea what an Internet message actually contains.

A newer approach to Internet security is based on technology called *type enforcement*, which is used to inspect the *content* of messages in addition to headers. It looks at what is actually inside a message, whether the message is text, like email, or binary files, like a software program. This lets a security administrator configure a type enforcement device so Internet traffic of any type with certain contents—say, a probe for your password file—is routed to a destination you choose—such as a security trap. These configurable routes are called *assured pipelines*.

This approach to content inspection means that customer files and product development files can be restricted from going out on the Net. Viruses are also easier to block with type enforcement. You can use type enforcement to forbid selected activities, no matter what destination was originally on a piece of Net traffic, thus disarming attacks by identity spoofing.

Secure Computing Corp. (**http://www.sctc.com**), a pioneer in type enforcement, was first (I believe) to the market with its product: Sidewinder. Priced at $30,000 and up, Sidewinder is really an application gateway with type enforcement and extra features to automate intruder detection. It inspects both inbound and outbound traffic, and scans the contents of messages. Note that Sidewinder cannot scan encrypted traffic. Sidewinder monitors real-time for signs of a break-in. When it spots a possible trespasser, Sidewinder sends a "silent alarm" to your system administrator to warn that a possible attack is taking place. I think Sidewinder is a valuable, but slightly overpriced product, and I hope that a high demand will help Secure Computing to lower their prices.

As I write, there are few type enforcement products available. There will probably be more by the time you read this. You should find up-to-date information on vendors from the firewall mailing list.

# Encryption

Encryption transforms your data, whether in transit on the Net or stored on your computer, into an unreadable mass of letters and numbers. This seeming gibberish is easily translated back into readable form, but only by the person (or software program) that has the specific software *key* to decrypt that particular chunk of information.

## *Why encryption?*

Since the Internet is a distributed network—that is, open to the public—your messages are exposed while in transit. You can use encryption so that no one except the intended recipient can open your message. Another threat comes from trespassers into your system. With encryption, you can scramble sensitive files like your password file to make them harder for invaders to use.

Encryption is the most practical and safest way to protect your secret information. Of course, you should not relax your vigilance totally just because you have a good encryption program in place. Your encrypted program is only as safe as its keys. And even when an attacker doesn't have your encryption keys, there are sometimes ways to bust down your encrypted walls.

Companies use encryption to secure everything from credit card numbers to legal documents. Encryption lets companies use the Internet as an alternative to a private leased-line network. The Internet alternative, Virtual Private Data Networks (VPDNs), offers security across the shared public networks of the Internet.

Encryption also can be used to create *digital signatures*. You can use your digital signature to authenticate messages when you post them to newsgroups. Digital signatures support *nonrepudiation*, a legal term meaning that the sender of a message with a digital signature cannot later deny having created the message and repudiate any terms or agreements contained in the message. The Macintosh operating system has built-in digital signature capabilities. Called DigiSign, this little gem lets a user sign an electronic document or message that proves that it could come only from that person.

Note that encryption is not legal in all countries. Encryption is illegal in France unless you give the government a copy of your key and get a written government permit. Spain forbids encryption, period. Spanish businesses are pressuring their government to change this soon.

## *A field guide to encryption species and their habitats*

Changes in the field of encryption can be tough to keep up with. I've provided you with an explanation of the different types of encrytion systems to help you understand the technology.

**Secret Key**. In a secret-key system, the same key that encrypts a message is also used to decrypt it. The keys must be exchanged in secrecy, because anyone with the key can read the messages. Some companies use public-key software like PGP to encrypt a secret key before sending it, and then use the secret key for subsequent messages, since secret-key encryption is faster than public-key encryption.

**Public key**. Several different kinds of encryption are called "public-key systems." This type of system solves the problem of securely distributing decryption keys. A good example is the PGP (Pretty Good Privacy) encryption system. With PGP, it takes about 5 minutes to first create your two keys (one public key and one secret, private key). Each of your two keys can read a message encrypted by the other key. You will have one public "key ring" to store all your correspondents' public keys, and you will store your own secret

# Break into your own network

For a quick test of your system's security, see if a tiger team of your own technical staffers can break into your site.

You must have your system up and running and plugged into the Net. Ask your technical staffers to enter your system from off-site, perhaps from their homes.

On the day of your test, disable your testers' passwords and accounts so it won't be too easy. Otherwise, keep your network security exactly as it is in real life. Leave other passwords the same. Don't increase defenses just to stump invader wannabes. The whole point is to probe your normal protection.

You want to duplicate the network setting that any stranger would confront. This means that it's okay for your simulators to get help from other people and to use any software tools they can find—just as real hackers do. A program called Internet Security Scanner (ISS for short) is available for free on the Net and can scan your entire domain or part of it and look for holes. Another free program, Crack, can analyze your encrypted password file to find passwords.

The one restriction to place on your staff before the test is that they refrain from doing anything illegal or anything that's hard to put back in order.

Your technical staffers may find this a rewarding task of their creative powers, and afterwards should better understand how to protect your company's systems.

key. Next you send your public key to everyone you correspond with. They add your public key to their key rings. When someone wants to send a message to you, he or she encrypts it with your public key. Only your secret key can unlock it. When you send a message, you use your addressee's public key to encrypt your entire message, or your own secret key to sign it with a digital signature. Then your addressee can use your public key to make sure that the message is really from you. To spread your public key around, you can post it in your .plan or Finger file or on a Web page. There are also PGP public-key repositories, which hold thousands of of public keys so other people can reach them. Once you add a person's public key to your key ring, you can send that person encrypted messages as well as decrypt messages from that person and verify that his or her digital signature really did come from that person. Lotus, Apple, Microsoft, and other companies have settled on public key encryption as a standard solution.

**Key escrow.** This is not an encryption species, but a habitat where encryption keys live. Trusted Information Systems (TIS) in Maryland (**http://www.tis.com**), a highly rated provider of firewall and security software, has a key-escrow system that lets businesses store keys in escrow. In this way law enforcement can access keys with a search warrant. The government doesn't escrow keys (preventing governmental abuses) and there are no databases of escrowed keys. The TIS key-escrow system provides a kind of insurance, so if you lose the key to an encrypted file, you can get it back. This way if an employee forgets a key, or has an accident, your company can still go to a bonded data recovery center and recover its encrypted data.

**DES (Data Encryption Standard).** DES was invented by IBM in the 1970s and adopted as a U.S. government standard. Any change to a message encrypted with DES turns the message into a mess of random characters that have nothing to do with the original message. DES is a secret-key system. Although generally secure, DES messages can be decrypted by a huge computer system or thousands of small ones working together. This makes some businesses nervous. Only a large corporation or a national government would have the resources to decrypt a DES encrypted message, but still, if you are competing with a large American, Japanese, or French corporation, you might want to take another approach.

**Triple DES.** This is a heavier-duty, tougher-to-crack version of DES that uses a key three times as long as DES. This secret-key technology can secure your most valuable data.

**IDEA (International Data Encryption Algorithm).** Invented in Switzerland in the 1980s, IDEA uses a longer key, making it resistant to brute force attacks, and a unique algorithm patented in many countries. For business uses, you must license IDEA from ASCOM Tech AG in Switzerland. PGP uses IDEA.

**RSA (Rivest, Shamir, Adleman).** RSA Data Security, Inc. lets you choose the size of your public key. With a 512-bit key, your messages are secure from all but large corporations or national governments. 768-bit keys are probably secure from everything but the NSA, and maybe even them. With a 1,023-bit key, your data is safe from pretty much everyone. Microsoft, Apple, and other companies are including it in their products.

**PEM (Privacy-Enhanced Mail).** Not really an encryption type, this is an Internet standard for sending encrypted email and email with digital signatures. It lets you plug in whatever encryption method you wish to use.

**RIPEM (Riordan's Internet Privacy-Enhanced Mail).** This is a version of PEM that uses RSA to encrypt secret keys, and DES or Triple DES to encrypt email. Get RIPEM software free by emailing to **rsares@rsa.com**.

**Kerberos.** Available for free from MIT, the Kerberos authentication system helps secure a company-wide network by providing a way to avoid sending readable passwords across the Net. The problem with Kerberos is that it is annoying to use. Every time you do anything, you need a different key and have to give your computer a password. To avoid logging in again and again, some Kerberos users never log out, leaving their computer open and their password accessible to anyone who walks up to it.

**PGP (Pretty Good Privacy).** PGP is very secure public-key software that is becoming widely used in the United States and Canada, and even though it is theoretically illegal to export, in other countries as well. Governments do not like PGP. It is too hard to crack, which is precisely why businesses like it. It is also easy to use. The U.S. government classified PGP as a weapon and forbids its export. The free version of PGP can be downloaded at sites outside the

United States, making export controls irrelevant, but the U.S. government refuses to recognize reality and change its policy. PGP is available for DOS, Mac, Unix, VAX, Amiga, and other operating systems. For commercial use in the U.S. and Canada, you must buy PGP from ViaCrypt Products, 602-944-0773, **viacrypt@acm.org**. For non-commercial use, you can download it for free from hidden Net sites. To get PGP you must first read a file called **README.Dist** at **gopher.eff.org/11/Net_info/Tools/Crypto**. On the World Wide Web, use **http://www.eff.org/pub/Net_Info/Tools/Crypto**. For more information about PGP, try **http://draco.centerline.com:8080/~franl/pgp/pgp.html** or **http://www.quadralay.com/www/Crypt/PGP/pgp00.html** or try the Usenet newsgroup **alt.security.pgp** to answer questions.

**RC2 and RC4.** These are two new and and as yet unproven private-key encryption schemes from RSA Data Security, Inc. Expect to hear more about these systems in the future.

**Secure Sockets Layer (SSL).** Netscape Communications designed this protocol, which uses the RSA algorithm to encrypt data. SSL also authenticates servers and clients for Web, email, newsgroup, and FTP transactions. It is approved for export by the U.S. government. There is a U.S.-only version and an exportable version. A demo of the security features is at **http://home1.netscape.com**. The first SSL version did not support nonrepudiation; the current version may.

**Proprietary encryption schemes.** Some software applications like Lotus 1-2-3, Microsoft Excel, Microsoft Word, and PKZip come with built-in encryption. These offer only a low level of protection. Hackers consider them encryption for babies. You can even buy (or download from the Net) software tools that decrypt them. They are better than nothing at all, but should not be used for sending truly valuable data across the Internet.

**Clipper.** The real name of this well-publicized encryption scheme is Skipjack, but sticking Skipjack on a computer chip called Clipper got all the publicity, so most laypeople use the name Clipper for the whole darn shooting match. The U.S. government—to be specific, the National Security Agency—wants all good Americans to use Clipper and no other method of encryption. Well, for now DES is acceptable, but the NSA expects DES to wither and die. The NSA claims that the Clipper encryption algorithm is pretty much unbreakable, but we don't know for sure since they won't let anyone see it. It's secret. To use Clipper, you have to buy a special computer chip that does the encrypting and decrypting. You can pick your own keys (only 80 bits long) for encrypting, but when you use Clipper to send an encrypted message, the chip will send your key plus a unique key burned into your individual chip to two U.S. government escrow agents. The government is supposed to get a warrant if it wants to read your encrypted messages and retrieve them from the escrow agents. One disadvantage with Clipper is the possibility that the NSA may have its own secret way to read your message without obtaining a search warrant. If you need high-level security and are not worried about the U.S. government reading your email, Clipper should work for you. You can legally export Clipper so you will find this especially useful if your business has branches overseas.

**DSS (Digital Signature Standard).** DSS is an NSA encryption scheme for creating digital signatures to prove that an Internet message was not altered and was sent by the person who claims to have sent it. As I mentioned earlier, there may be some reasons for your company not to use NSA's Clipper; there are *definitely* some reasons why your company should not use DSS. See the sidebar panel *DSS—the Digital Signature Standard* for details.

## Credit cards and digital money

Why is there so much talk about the problems with credit cards on the Internet? Why can't you just have customers send your their credit card numbers by email? Or type them in a form on your Web page?

After reading the previous chapter, you should have a good idea that you are more at risk taking a naked credit card number over the Net than when you take a credit card number over the phone, via fax, or through postal mail. With ordinary Internet email and Web transactions, you can't prove that a customer is who he or she claims to be. You can't prove that the order you received carries the same information your customer originally sent. Someone could have altered it. Your customer's order and credit card number could

# DSS—the Digital Signature Standard

The United States government's National Security Agency (NSA) and its National Institute of Standards and Technology (NIST) want you to use DSS, the Digital Signature Standard. Here's why you should avoid DSS.

NIST conducted an investigation to determine the most effective digital signature, with the intent of recommending the best technique as a national standard. After first favoring a technique from RSA that covers both digital signatures and message encryption, the NIST abruptly changed course when the Security Agency butted in.

The NSA is the super snooper agency that, among other things, monitors phone calls, radio, and email between the United States and other countries. We're talking major eavesdropping here. The NSA invented DSS, its own way to create digital signatures.

DSS won't protect your privacy by encrypting your messages. You can only use DSS to verify your message by including your DSS signature with a message. The government's own General Accounting Office said "for a broad range of digital signature applications, (DSS is) less efficient than RSA." Also, DSS technology possibly violates RSA's patents, and RSA warns that it will sue any company that uses DSS.

In spite of the shortcomings, the NSA bullied NIST into recommending its weaker DSS technique instead of RSA's offering. From the Security Agency's point of view, DSS has one strength that overwhelms its weaknesses. You cannot use DSS to make a message secret. Any business will see that as a disadvantage, but remember that NSA's job is to monitor thousands of messages daily, looking for threats to U.S. security. If messages are encrypted with RSA's system, *NSA can't read them*.

If your message contains a credit card number and you are sending these numbers in the open, NSA doesn't care. Anything that interferes with NSA's ability to read messages is a threat to its purpose. It wants you to use DSS precisely because it gives less protection than RSA.

have been copied on its way to you. In a fraud situation, your customer can deny that he or she sent the order to you and you haven't a leg to stand on.

And that's not to mention card number theft. The Hi-Tech Crime Network, a group of police officers dealing with technological crimes, reports that the number of arrests of hackers dealing in stolen credit card numbers is rising steadily. Since your customer is liable for only $50 per card in fraudulent billings, you, the merchant, are stuck holding the bag for the rest. The one good thing about MCI's fifty-million-dollar card theft incident is that it hit a company large enough to stand the pain. A loss that big would close the doors of most businesses.

## *Billed accounts*

If your customers are businesses instead of individual consumers, you have a different Internet payment alternative, and probably have most of the mechanisms already in place. That solution is to bill your accounts. Perhaps you bill accounts monthly, perhaps weekly, perhaps every time your customer makes a purchase. In any case, your billing procedures can be adapted for Internet purchases with a minimum of fuss and little risk.

That's *little* risk, *not* zero risk. I've seen a case where a business received a large merchandise order to ship to a long-standing institutional client. There was just one tiny difference with this order. It came from an authorized Internet address and carried the name of an authorized buyer, but the ship-to street address was a slightly different from normal. The order was taken by a new order entry employee who forgot to check the ship-to address and sent the merchandise. It was a forged order and the business was never paid. The slightly different address was a house down the street from the institutional client. It was rented by a thief for a short time. He received merchandise from several vendors at that address for two or three weeks and then moved. He was caught by the police, but the businesses still lost their merchandise.

To prevent this from happening to you, require that all new billed Internet accounts are opened by a signed document sent to you either by fax or by postal mail. That document should list the names of any authorized buyers, the email addresses of those buyers, all authorized ship-to addresses, and purchase amount limits if any. Any changes to those initial items should be made by sending you a signed change request via fax or postal mail. *Your order staff should verify with your customer by telephone before making shipments to the changed address.* Send an email confirmation of each order when you receive it and an email shipping notice when you make a shipment to your Internet customer.

To increase security, your customers can use Privacy-Enhanced Mail, digital signatures, or encryption to make their orders. The most efficient alternative may be for you and your customer to use a secure method of Electronic Data Interchange (EDI) across the Internet.

## *Credit cards: problem areas*

Credit cards are a different story. If someone steals your customer account information, the thief can steal from your business only. Credit card numbers, however, are like money. Not only are there lots of places to use them for purchases, they can be sold on the black market.

As in other businesses, Internet businesses report that credit card numbers are most often stolen by order desk employees. In most cases, it is easy for your merchant bank to pinpoint which business is responsible for a bad charge. If your business is the likely source of a card theft, the first place any outside detective will look is on your staff logs. What employee was on duty when this credit card came in? Who has access to your credit card information? Ask the classic questions any police detective uses to find suspects: Who had an opportunity, and who had a motive? As a preventive measure, it is in your own interest to limit employee access your customers' credit card information.

 In any case, don't store card numbers and account information on an computer exposed to the Net. Credit card files are becoming favorite hacker targets. Move your customers' card numbers off your Internet computer as quickly as possible. If you store card numbers even temporarily, it is a good idea to split the numbers and expiration dates into separate files, and to encrypt them.

Software vendor The Corner Store stores credit card and customer information on a separate computer, completely unconnected to any network. Its orders come in via the Net to one computer and are moved frequently to a floppy disk. An employee transfers the disk with the sensitive data from the Internet-linked computer to the isolated computer.

Daniel White, Ernst & Young's national director of information security effectiveness reported in the November 14, 1994 *Wall Street Journal* that an identical procedure is followed by an Ernst & Young client. It receives orders over the Internet from large retail chains. Orders arrive on a standalone PC. An employee moves the orders to a disk, scans them for viruses, and takes the disk to another computer not connected to the Internet, protecting the company from hackers and viruses.

When making credit card sales over the Internet, besides safely receiving card information via email or the World Wide Web, and besides designing Web forms to collect information from purchasers, you need to worry about the rest of the transaction. What do you do with that credit card information once you receive it? The best scenario is to validate the cardholder information and pass the transaction data and validated information to your payment-processing company for payment authorization—ideally doing both while your customer is still online, so you can send your customer an order confirmation and not keep him or her waiting.

You need to do this whether you run the software to do so on your own computer, or on a computer managed by your Internet access provider. In the second case, things are a little different, and you must plan procedures for your access provider to collect the data and then pass the data to you. In either case, you will also need to integrate your software with credit card-processing and approval systems and with software to calculate sales or VAT tax. You will then need to plan a way—manually or electronically—to pass transaction information to your order processing system, inventory system, and accounting system.

If you accept Visa cards (most merchants do), the VisaNet authorization system must approve each transaction. Your software will need the ability to provide required information for Visa's PCS:2000 program. The company that clears your Visa transactions will require a transaction number (called the "unique transaction identifier") generated with the VisaNet authorization, the authorized amount, the VisaNet authorization response, and the VisaNet validation code for each transaction it clears. For Internet merchants, each authorization must include a customer address verification request. You must provide at least the ZIP or postal code for each Visa customer.

Many companies accepting credit card orders by mail or over the telephone verify cardholder addresses. For Internet merchants, too, this procedure reduces risks—and on the Internet, you need all the protection you can get. Card fraud rates have always been higher for mail-order and telephone sales than for in-store sales. I know of no formal research on Internet card fraud rates. I asked merchants who sell both over the Net and by mail order about the problem, and many reported worse fraud on the Internet.

Craig Adams of Noteworthy Music ought to know. His company was named by the *New York Times* as the first merchant to make a secure Internet credit card transaction, using PGP software to sell a copy of the Sting CD *Ten Summoners' Tales* on August 11, 1994. Noteworthy Music sells music CDs from its World Wide Web page **http://www.netmarket.com/noteworthy/bin/main**.

"People are more willing to steal and cheat when there's no personal contact," explains Adams. "On the Internet there's no benefit of having an operator using intuition, which comes from talking to a person. On the phone the operator can get a sense of when someone's trying to pull a fast one, and the customer is more inhibited talking to a warm human being. The machine takes out the human element that guilt or conscience plays a part in."

Still, says Adams, cardsharps are "a very small percentage of Internet buyers. We have guys who try ten, twenty, or thirty times with different names and different credit card numbers but using the same address or two addresses. We've had a guy from New Zealand who tries every week."

Noteworthy Music verifies addresses for all Internet credit card orders. This is easy for U.S. credit cards, but the Internet brought many international customers to Noteworthy, and verifying cardholder addresses is more work in other countries. "In the U.S., banks have people who deal with addresses," Adams explains. "It's not as easy overseas. You call the issuing bank, get somebody in bookkeeping—who might not speak English—you read them the information and wait on hold for an answer. If one piece of an address—even one number—is wrong, it's all wrong. The bank won't correct you because people give banks wrong addresses to try to get people's real addresses." In some countries, banks don't track cardholder addresses the way U.S. banks do. As an example, Adams says that "In Germany, banks don't change credit cardholder addresses when they move unless they issue you a new card." This means that a merchant will often need to decline a perfectly legitimate German customer because the customer's old and new addresses don't match.

Address verification is important for the first Internet order you receive from a customer, but your risk goes down with a repeat customer who establishes trustworthiness over time. This is one of the ways in which you can benefit from tracking customer history. It saves you from making verification calls, which are especially time-consuming and expensive for international customers. "We track history," says Adams. "We only verify cardholder addresses for new customers. For established customers, we will ship to different addresses, especially when people order Christmas gifts."

Banks in all countries will hopefully improve verification procedures over the next year, now that Visa's PCS2000 Customer Payment Service requires you to request customer address verification as part of each sales authorization. Other card companies will probably follow Visa's lead. Address verification takes extra work, but the decrease in chargebacks makes it worthwhile.

An Internet merchant, like any other direct marketer, can verify addresses and still get ripped off. One scam hit the Leslie Shoe Company twice in one day. Two new customers ordered on two credit cards. One card's order went to an Illinois address, the other to an address in Virginia. Both asked for overnight delivery, providing their own Federal Express account numbers for delivery billing. Both orders were shipped to the correct name and address for their respective credit cards. That night, two phone calls to Federal Express asked to reroute the packages to a third address in Baltimore, Maryland. The orders were fraudulent. Not only was Leslie Shoe liable for the purchase price, but also for the Federal Express charges! Fed Ex and United Parcel Service both offer this rerouting service. You can guard against such delivery devilry by using *your own* Fed Ex account number for shipment to first-time customers in addition to verifying and shipping to their cardholder addresses.

## Unencrypted cardnumbers via email and the Web

Most of the companies taking naked credit card data over the Net are small companies. Big companies know better. They don't want to expose themselves to the risk. You may think, "Hey, wait a minute—that doesn't make sense. A big corporation could more easily afford to pay for a bad card's fraud." That would be true, if only one card number were stolen at a time. That isn't how it works.

You've already read how packet sniffing software "sniffs" Internet traffic, searching for card numbers. A hacker doesn't just toss a packet sniffer out in the Net at random. Usually, a packet sniffer is stationed outside a site that traffics in unencrypted card numbers. Logical, right? So the sniffer collects lots of card numbers from just a few merchants. A large company with a higher volume of credit card transactions would be a much more juicy target, and if hit, would suffer a larger loss than a small company selling, say, only $20,000 over the Net each week. That doesn't mean that if your business is small you won't get hit. That doesn't mean it won't hurt. You're still at risk taking naked numbers, and you still can be wounded.

What is your risk from taking unencrypted card numbers? Here's how to calculate your exposure to loss:

       Average Net cards per month
   × Average unused card balance
   + Staff time
   + <u>Lost future sales</u>
       Card loss exposure

Let's explain this formula. Suppose a packet sniffer sits outside your Internet site undetected, collecting credit card numbers for a month. Figure out on the average how many credit cards you expect to enter your site over the Net in one month.

The credit cards stolen from MCI were charged an average of $1,000 apiece. Often stolen cards are used until their credit limit maxes out, and most cards have more credit available than $1,000. A card can often have an unused balance of more than $5,000 available, especially a card owned by an Internet user, who is likely to be more affluent. Let's say an average unused balance of $5,000 per card. Multiply your credit-cards-per-month figure by $5,000. If you want, you can subtract the $50 per customer the law allows you to charge them for a fraudulent transaction—although your customers will not be happy with you if you do. You may lose more than $50 per customer in profits from future sales, depending on the nature of your business.

Then add your cost for staff time to straighten out a card theft problem. Then add an estimate for how much you will lose in sales from customers whose cards have been stolen. Base this not just on a single month's sales, but on the average total lifetime value per customer. (If you don't know the lifetime value of your customers, set one of your marketing staff to figuring it out. Without this key measurement, you'll never know if a new customer acquisition project is profitable or costs more than a new customer is worth.)

So what if, for some reason, you can't accept encrypted credit card numbers? Maybe your business is in France or Spain or another country where encryption is illegal. What then?

Follow the example of software retailer The Corner Store, which sells OS/2 and Windows NT software over the Net. Some Internet customers encrypt credit card information before sending it to The Corner Store. Other Internet customers send their orders via the Net, but give their credit card numbers over the phone or by fax. The Corner Store has a third group of customers— the ones who interest us here—from whom the merchant accepts naked credit card numbers sent over the Net, *but in pieces*. To reduce the risk of sending naked numbers over the Net, The Corner Store asks its customers to send the credit card number in one email message, and to send the card's expiration date in a separate message. The Corner Store's order desk personnel quickly remove incoming orders—especially the card numbers and dates—from the merchant's Internet-linked computer to an isolated computer. There they re-unite the card number, expiration date, and customer order by matching the "sent from" email addresses.

Note that this procedure does not eliminate the risk of theft, but merely re-duces it. Still, the broken pieces do not match the patterns that packet sniffers normally search for, making ordering more safe. For you, the merchant, having your customers split the card number from the date before sending them gives you the advantage of a very easy-to-implement solution for email customers, and World Wide Web customers as well. Your Web order form can be set to similarly scramble the order of card numbers and expiration dates, providing the same minimal level of protection. Keep in mind that this is not your only option. There are other, safer Internet order procedures that do not use encryption but avoid sending naked card numbers over the Net. I'll discuss those options next.

## *Credit cards: avoiding loss without encryption*

The safest way to take credit cards without using encryption software, and the method that has been used the longest on the Internet, is a two-stage order operation.

There are many variations on this theme, but they all boil down to the same essentials: Your customer sends you the order over the Net, but sends the credit card information via fax, phone, or snail mail. Although some of the largest Internet merchants use a two-stage order operation, it is so simple it can still be used by the smallest merchants, as well.

For a classic, fine-tuned example of a two-stage operation, take a peek at Computer Literacy Bookshops' Web page, **http://www.clbooks.com**. Look for the instructions on how to order. You'll see carefully worded instructions, letting customers know that the order procedures are in place to protect them. You'll also see a "Preregistration Form" that customers can print and use to send account information by fax or postal mail. Note that the form is designed to be used both by new customers and by existing customers who want to change account information, and that the instructions further down the form state (in a more friendly tone of voice) that account changes will not be accepted over the phone or via the Internet. Computer Literacy Bookshops uses an email version of this form to send to email buyers, and a printed version is included in Computer Literacy's catalogs. An advantage of the Computer Literacy system is that it does *not* require the customer to memorize yet another bloody password, as many two-stage order operations do. (Maybe that should be an Internet acronym—YABP.) We'll see how this works next.

Home Shopping Network's subsidiary the Internet Shopping Network (ISN) uses a YABP two-stage order system. Prospective customers can:

1.  Print a membership form and fax credit card data.

2.  Telephone a human during business hours and give card information over the phone.

3.  Use a Web browser.

For all three of these sign-up variations, the prospect's credit card information is retained on file for all future sales, so the customer sends it only once. We're covering non-encryption alternatives here, so ignore the Web browser option for the moment and concentrate on the first two. ISN sends each new customer an email welcome letter with the customer's "membership code" password. The welcome letter states the street address to which all purchases ordered with that customer's code will be shipped, and thoughtfully closes with: "All of the information you have given us is considered confidential and will not be disclosed to anyone outside ISN. We will never send you unsolicited email and we will always respect your privacy."

From the standpoint of a customer who doesn't have a fax machine, the ISN's telephone method offers the possibility of immediate gratification, of being able to open an account instantly by calling an ISN person and then going right back to the computer and placing an order. (ISN does not take orders over the phone.) The drawback of ISN is that it requires its customers to keep yet another password and safeguard that password. The drawback from the merchant's point of view is that having a signed form puts the merchant in a better position in case of disputes, and telephone signups don't create a signed form.

A company called First Virtual Holdings offers a different twist. A prospective customer phones First Virtual with credit card information and sends a confirming email message. First Virtual emails the prospective customer a password. The customer uses that password to make purchases from any Internet merchant that accepts First Virtual for payment. When the customer makes a purchase, First Virtual sends him or her an email message listing what was purchased and the price, and asking the customer to confirm the authenticity of each purchase. The customer confirms with an email reply; First Virtual bills the credit card and pays the merchant.

For merchants to accept First Virtual purchases, you pay First Virtual $10 and go through a simple sign-up procedure. When a customer buys something from you, First Virtual deposits funds directly into your checking account. Sellers also pay .29 per charged transaction plus 2 percent of the charged amount, and $1 each time a deposit is made to your account. First Virtual is a technically sound concept, and is secure. It is extremely simple for a merchant to sell using the service, but First Virtual has not strongly marketed its service. It has not signed a critical mass of merchants. It is not well-known to consumers. It may prosper, but based on early results I will be surprised if First Virtual survives the coming consolidation of Internet payment methods. For information on First Virtual go to **http://www.fv.com** or call them at 619-234-1300.

Two-stage order operations like the ones I've discussed here are secure. Some, like Computer Literacy Bookshops' use no password and so provide nothing for crooks to steal. Those two-stage operations that require passwords do not use words that follow credit card format, and so the passwords are less likely to be sniffed by hackers. If a merchant-specific password is stolen, it can only be used at that merchant or group of merchants. It can't be used worldwide and can't be sold on the black market. Since a merchant-specific password has no resale value, it is a less inviting target for thieves.

## Credit cards: Encrypted transmission

Encrypted orders are becoming easy on the Internet, and for the foreseeable future should be the way most credit card purchases are handled. (Of course, on the Internet the foreseeable future lasts about two weeks.)

Using encryption for an Internet sale assures a merchant of three things. First, that the order has reached you without being altered in any way. Second, that any enclosed credit card numbers, customer information (would a competitor want your customer list?), and order data was not copied while the order was en route. Third, if the order includes a digital signature, that the order was sent to you by the person who claims to have sent it, and not some bozo who plucked a card number off carbon forms he found in a trash bin. Remember that an order with a valid digital signature supports *nonrepudiation*.

Three things are necessary for you to process encrypted sales orders from your customers. First, your customers must have software to encrypt their orders. There are several email and Web alternatives available. Second, you need a secure way to receive decryption keys from customers and a safe place to store them. Third, you need a way to receive customer orders and decrypt them.

There is software available to handle all of this. The problem is that there are too many variations for most merchants to support. Here's a rundown on the seven most popular methods (in no specific order) of handling sales orders and credit card numbers via encryption.

1. **Pretty Good Privacy (PGP) software**. The first secure credit card transactions on the Internet were made using PGP software. The customer has PGP and sends the merchant the encrypted PGP order and a copy of the customer's PGP public key. The merchant uses the key to read the order and processes it like a normal order. This requires both the customer and the merchant to have PGP software. A more sophisticated implementation of PGP is used by Noteworthy Music in its Web home page. Initially available only to customers using X Windows and Unix software, Noteworthy's Web site accepted card numbers typed into interactive forms. The typed information was encrypted before transmission to Noteworthy's server. For the process to work, customers still had to have PGP software on their computers. PGP implementations like this are workable, but easier-to-use software—some of which works with PGP—is more practical for most Internet businesses.

2. **Privacy-Enchanced Mail (PEM)**. Most major email software packages support or plan to support this industry-wide standard for sending secure email. Several Internet merchants now receive orders with PEM. The fast spread of free email software that uses PEM (especially the popular RIPEM) makes this a quick, easy way for your business to take email credit card orders over the Net. I have not yet heard of any merchant figuring out a way to combine PEM and Web ordering. Even a small company can take advantage of PEM.

3. **Netsite Commerce Server**. If your business uses Netscape Communications' $5,000 Netsite Commerce Server software, your customers using the Netscape Web browser can establish a secure link with your Commerce Server and send credit card info to you by simply filling in a Web form. Your Com-

merce Server sends the card data to First Data (or another payment processing service), which processes the transaction in real-time. The cardholder information is verified and the purchase authorized while the cardholder is still online. No human intervention is needed to receive the order or to verify card information. Public keys are passed as part of the transaction, but your staff doesn't need to deal with them. The Netsite Commerce Server automatically links with different payment processing companies to automate the entire payment transaction process. The Commerce Server can secure transactions only with Netscape Web browsers at present. This is a limitation, although since the majority of Web browsers in use are Netscape browsers (according to one estimate, 75 percent of them), not as detrimental as you might think. Other browsers may use SSL, the Netscape security architecture, in the future, and Netscape Communications has pledged that the Commerce Server will support Secure HTTP (discussed shortly) and any other industry security standard that evolves. The first version of SSL did not support nonrepudiation. If your company uses InternetMCI or MarketplaceMCI, your credit card encryption and processing runs through a Commerce Server. The software is available for Unix, Windows NT, and Novell IPX systems. Annual support costs $1,000 to $50,000. For information, send email to **info@netscape.com**. For more on payment processing with the Commerce Server, send email to **banking@netscape.com**.

4. **Secure Encrypted Transactions**. CompuServe subsidiary (and seller of Air Mosaic software) Spry, Inc.'s secure Web server software supports an architecture called Secure Encrypted Transactions, or SET for short. This credit card-handling architecture conforms with the Secure HTTP standard described next. For more information, call Spry at 800-777-9638 or check its home page at **http://www.spry.com**

5. **Secure HTTP (SHTTP)**. This is an industry-wide standard for secure Web transactions developed by CommerceNet and supported by Spry, Inc., Netscape Communications, and other companies. SHTTP servers operate similarly to the Commerce Server software described earlier, but versions from smaller companies and free versions lack the back-end support to verify cardholder information and authorize payments automatically. SHTTP lets you use a variety of encryption schemes. Server software supporting SHTTP

will be available for most operating systems. Good free versions will be out in late 1995. For maximum security, when you receive an encrypted SHTTP transaction, decrypt the information on another computer, separated from your Web server by a firewall. For an online interactive demo of an SHTTP credit card transaction, go to **http://www.commerce.net/information/ex-amples/examples.html**.

6. **Open Market**. This company uses a technology created at MIT. It also sells a Web server for processing credit cards transactions. It sells for $5,000. Open Market is used by the commercial online Lexis/Nexis databases with its customers. For more information, go to **http://www.openmarket.com**.

7. **Microsoft/Visa standard**. Microsoft and Visa are jointly developing software that authenticates the identity of both customer and merchant, and encrypts transmitted data using encryption schemes from RSA Data Security Inc. This software should be available for sale in 1995. There are two versions, a client version (which will be built into Windows 95) and a server version for merchants to use. Microsoft will release the technical specifications, hoping to create yet another industry standard for secure Internet transactions.

## Virtual money, emoney, digital cash, and friends

Call it what you will, there has been tons of media hype about ecash. Some of the things described as virtual cash are really variations of secure credit card schemes. The system used by First Virtual described earlier has received a fair amount of ink, but it is really just a secure and well-engineered way to buy on the Net and have it billed to your credit card.

A real virtual cash scheme is more than just billing to a credit card. The simplest explanation of virtual cash is that it's like using a bank ATM machine, without an ATM card. When you draw money from your bank account with an ATM debit card, you give a Personal Identification Number, called your PIN by those in the transaction processing biz. With digital money, you just use your PIN number. I'm oversimplifying, because there are several variations.

What it boils down to is a secure way to buy and sell over the Net that does not necessarily involve credit card billing. There are ways of crediting and debiting accounts that exist only on the Internet. The final product must be something that is accepted widely, easy to use, and impossible to counterfeit.

There are a host of ideas for virtual money on the Net, ranging from hare-brained to downright amazing. It is too early yet to predict success for any one plan.

- **CyberCash** is a front-runner. CyberCash was started by Internet pioneer Dan Lynch and Verifone founder William Melton, and is backed by several large financial institutions. A customer must have special software to use CyberCash, which could be invisibly built in as part of Internet email and Web applications. To sell something to a CyberCash-using customer, you send the customer an electronic invoice describing the purchase and the price. The customer takes your invoice and adds a credit card number or a debit account PIN. CyberCash encrypts your invoice and the account information and sends it back to you. You add a merchant identification number and send it to CyberCash. Funds are deposited in your account as though it were a traditional credit or debit card purchase. CyberCash transactions will provide a secure audit trail. For information, send email to **info@cybercash.com** or on the Web, go to **http://www.cybercash.com**.

- **NetBill** is a joint venture of Carnegie-Mellon University and Visa. NetBill is designed to address the need for companies buying and selling high-volume, low-cost products on the Net. Normal credit card transactions charge way too much for a company to charge amounts like .25 or .10 apiece for small amounts of information. NetBill transactions will cost much less to process than today's credit card transactions, as little as .01 for each .10 purchase. NetBill transactions are designed to be simple to process for merchants, who will never see a credit card number and won't necessarily know the customer's name. For more information, go to **http://www.ini.cmu.edu/netbill**.

- **NetCash** creates *electronic tokens*, which are designed to be as easy to use as money. NetCash can work entirely through email, but is also easy for you to accept from your Web page. Developed by a company called Software Agents, Inc., NetCash uses coupons that customers purchase from the company's NetBank. These coupons can be purchased electronically or by postal mail. NetCash coupons are a string of characters that look like this: `NetCash US$ 25.00 M898900Z89032F`. When a customer sends you a NetCash coupon via email or enters it into a form on your Web page, you can cash it by emailing it to the NetBank, which will deposit funds in your regular bank account. Each coupon is good only one time. The drawback is that even though the NetCash system has built-in safeguards, which I have not described here, coupons are susceptible to forgery. There is a need for electronic tokens like this, but this first version of NetCash may not be its ultimate implementation. For more information, send email to **netbank-info@agents.com**.

- **DigiCash** offers a more secure way to buy and sell electronic coupons. To use DigiCash, a customer must have software that is given away for free. Your customer buys electronic coupons from the DigiCash bank and gives them to your business to make a purchase. Your business redeems them at DigiCash's bank. The advantage of DigiCash is that its electronic coupons are all verified the instant you receive them, and are nearly impossible to counterfeit. Another advantage is that DigiCash transactions can be completely anonymous. A customer wishing to remain unknown can do so. Several Internet merchants use DigiCash on a trial basis. For more information, send email to **info@digicash.nl** or set your Web browser to **http://www.digicash.com**.

- **Mondex**, a product of the National Westminster Bank in the U.K., lets users carry a fixed amount of anonymous digital currency. Many versions of digital cash are only available in U.S. dollars, but Mondex automatically handles currency exchange. It is being tested in England with McDonalds, Mobil Oil, Laura Ashley, BP Oil, Sears, and other large companies. For more information, go to **http://www.mondex.com/mondex/home.htm**.

# What to do when trouble strikes

Most computer break-ins are spotted by network administrators and not by business users. Network administrators might see suspicious log reports showing attempts to grab your password files or to log on with top-level security. Or they may see repeated accesses of Finger or many failed attempts to run certain programs. When businesspeople find an intrusion, the symptoms are usually missing or unusable files, or odd error messages. It is rare for a nontechnical person to link these clues to their cause without technical help.

Your company should have a short prepared guide outlining how to respond to any suspected computer attack. All employees with Internet access should have a *printed* copy at their desks. (An online version does no good when a virus freezes your computer.) Your attack response guide should have 24-hour phone contact information for all people who need to be notified, and quick descriptions of what to do. In general, you should follow these steps:

1. Contact your in-house network administrator. The administrator on duty needs to decide if a break-in has happened, or if your symptom actually is caused by another sort of problem. If you are under attack, the administrator needs to move as fast as possible to prevent damage from spreading and to catch the culprit, in that order of priority. If your company's computers are on the Net 24 hours a day, someone needs to be available 24 hours a day to handle this. Have at least *two* backup people available in case the designated contact is unreachable. An hour's delay can be fatal.

2. If your network administrator thinks that there is even a small chance that an intruder has hit, call technical support at your Internet access provider. Your administrators (including your backup people) should have 24-hour phone numbers for access provider support. Your provider can help with damage control, and can also check to make sure that other sites from that same provider aren't under attack.

3. As a counterpoint to this, your Internet access provider also needs 24-hour phone numbers for your network administrators. If another business alerts your provider to an attacker in your site, wouldn't you like

to know about it? If your company's Net site only operates during office hours, you might think that your regular phone number will suffice, but that may not be enough. Perhaps your computer is only linked during the daytime, but do you have a home page on your provider's computer? It will run 24 hours and is vulnerable to attack 24 hours. Will you use mailing lists? Lists usually run at night for faster processing. (And, in my experience, only break down in the wee hours. Sigh.) Even when you have limited Internet access, play it safe by giving your provider 24-hour contact information.

4.  If your security has been breached, *immediately call the Computer Emergency Response Team (CERT) at its 24-hour hotline: 412-268-7090.* CERT staffers can tell you if other sites anywhere in the world have suffered the same problem and are a solid source of advice on how to proceed.

Your administrator should have this information ready before calling CERT:
-   Internet addresses of your computer or computers compromised
-   Brand name and model of the computer, its operating system, and communications software
-   What security hardware and software you use
-   Any log reports showing evidence of the attack, including timestamps
-   Other computers or sites that may be implicated in the break-in
-   Whether you contacted the other sites, and contact information if you did
-   Whether you have contacted law enforcement agencies
-   What specific help you would like from CERT

5.  If your system administrator decides that a break-in happened and serious damage has resulted, he or she should contact appropriate non-technical managers to let them know about the situation.

6.  If proprietary information has been stolen or damaged, a non-technical manager should contact your local law enforcement agencies. Don't exaggerate the damage. You will need to describe what has been sto-

len or damaged in detail. If at all possible, attach a monetary value to your loss, and realistically estimate how much it will cost your business to recover from the attack. Your network administrator should take part in this discussion to address technical issues.

7.  Managers need to decide what, if anything, to tell employees about the attack. If employees are suspected, you will want to withhold non-essential information until the situation is resolved. Finger-pointing will do no good after an attack, but instructions on how to prevent further break-ins may help you in the future.

8.  If you suffered a loss covered by insurance, someone will need to contact your insurance company. Paperwork from the law enforcement agency may be helpful or even required.

One final tip: Before trouble strikes, your security administrator should review the CERT security checklist and security FAQ. You can find the checklist at **ftp://ftp.cert.org/pub/tech_tips** and the security FAQ at **ftp:// ftp.santafe.edu/pub/SIG/Security/FAQ.Z** and at **ftp://rtfm.mit.edu/pub/ usenetbygroup/comp.answers/comp-security**.

---

## A hacker's plan of attack

So what do these hackers do when they break into your machine? Here are a typical intruder's goals:

*   Break in
*   Hide evidence of the break-in
*   Steal your passwords
*   Take control of your computer
*   Open new doors for re-entry
*   Steal your data
*   Leverage your computer to break into others

---

# Email: Quickest Bang for Your Buck

*"You could take out every one of the three hundred to four hundred computer applications that we run our company on and we could continue—but if you took out our email system, Sun would grind to an immediate halt."*

Scott McNealy, Chief Executive Officer, Sun Microsystems Inc.

W hen you bring the Internet into your company for the first time, you'll want to start with the service offering the lowest risk, the highest visibility, and the quickest return on your investment. That service is email.

- Email is the cheapest way to tighten relations between your company and your customers.
- Email is the fastest way to improve communication among employees within your company.
- Email can increase the level of technical support you receive from your computer and software vendors.
- Email makes it easier for your company to collaborate on projects with other companies.

Starting to get the picture?

If your company doesn't use email, you'll find that its money and time savings give you a strong starting point for cost-justifying Internet implementation. Color graphics on a World Wide Web page look prettier, but email is a workhorse that will deliver improvements across many areas of your company. Since its benefits are clear-cut and widespread, you should find support from a lot of people who want to get it up and running as soon as possible.

If your company already uses email but isn't linked to the Internet, you'll find your strongest support for linking from people who deal with persons outside your company. Talk with your technical staff, who often communicate with computer vendors, and—of course—your people in charge of sales and marketing. Nothing makes a sales rep happier than a fast way to boost sales!

## What email can do for you

Let's start with *saving money*.

Since you pay a more-or-less flat rate for your Internet account, with email you don't pay extra for each message you send—unlike phone calls or postal letters. (If you're even *thinking* of paying per-message charges, you didn't read Chapters 2 and 3 closely.)

That holds true not just for outgoing messages, but incoming ones as well. Your customers save what they would spend on long-distance phone calls or postage. And you don't pay what you would for 800 numbers.

With money saved from converting printed internal and outside newsletters to emailed versions, you can increase their frequency, which will make them more effective.

For some companies, savings from email alone have paid for their Internet connections. Lower costs have driven thousands of organizations away from paper mail. The trend is so widespread that the United States Postal Service estimates that about 30 percent of its business-to-business first-class mailstream has been diverted to fax and email since 1988. The amount diverted to email increases every month.

Can email reduce your staffing needs? Your honor, I display as evidence Rivkin Radler & Kremer, a $42 million law firm with 178 attorneys headquartered in Uniondale, New York, with offices in Illinois and California. From 1990 to 1994, the firm used email to cut its paralegal and secretarial staffs by more than 40 percent, while significantly increasing its billings.

The firm sees email as a money-saver. Its clients see email as a benefit, and as a reason to increase their business with Rivkin Radler & Kremer. The firm emails memoranda and legal documents to its clients. Documents go from its document management system (the DOS version of PC Docs) and cc:Mail out across the Net. Its customers receive the documents in their software (cc:Mail, Microsoft Mail, Lotus Notes, and other products). Delivery is faster, plus clients are freed from the useless grind of retyping data into their own computers. Clients no longer have to pay per-page fees for copies of documents, which can be a big expense in a complex case. Also, clients find email a more effective way to communicate with attorneys, who are often hard to reach by phone. (Ever played phone tag with a lawyer?)

Now Rivkin Radler & Kremer is working on providing clients with direct Internet access to billing information, which will help the firm get paid sooner.

If you want the least expensive way to connect electronically with your customers and your suppliers, email is the way to go. Internet tools like the

World Wide Web require more hardware horsepower and a larger network connection because they are interactive—users push a key, then sit and *wait* for your computer to respond. Delays are annoying. People expect your system to respond instantly. With email, on the other hand, no one fires off a message and expects an instant response. You have an hour or more to get back to them. You can use a small, cheap computer for email, as well as a slower and less expensive network connection.

Companies are moving to email for reasons that go beyond cutting costs. The best advantage of email isn't the savings; it's that email *works better* than phone calls or paper mail. Email increases productivity—dramatically, in some cases. Email is much faster than paper mail. You don't have the delay of printing a copy or copies. Instead of waiting days for delivery, it takes minutes or just seconds, even across long distances. In fact, Internet inhabitants have dubbed postal mail "snail mail," to point out its slowness.

People see email as more timely and more important than printed matter. They might stack and ignore printed documents, but people read your email message soon after it arrives. This makes email your best way to distribute urgent or time-sensitive information.

Another advantage of email over snail mail comes from the current transformation of the nature of documents themselves. You can pull an email message into your word processor, spreadsheet file, or database more quickly than you can retype it from paper. And with less errors. This makes a big difference any time you need to swap documents with another company or with a far-flung site of your own company.

For example, when venture capitalists Kleiner, Perkins, Caulfield & Byers raised $250 million for a limited partnership in 1994, they used the Net to send legal documents back and forth with its attorneys. In a Nov. 14, 1994 *Wall Street Journal* article, Michael Curry, the company's chief financial officer, said, with email, "I've traded spreadsheets with CFOs in our portfolio when I needed to confirm the ownership structure of their companies." Sharing legal and financial information can be a major benefit if your company is communications-intensive.

# A little email goes a long way

The shocking thing about Alain Pinel Realtors is not what the company *did* but what it did it *with*.

When the real estate sales company was founded, from the start it wanted to be technically advanced. This was natural—it's located in the heart of Silicon Valley, California. It equipped its sales agents with workstations and built custom software to improve sales effectiveness.

In 1991, Mark Richards, chief information officer, decided to connect the company to the Internet. At the time, it had two offices and about sixty agents. Now it has grown to five offices with 300 agents who use the Internet extensively, selling $750 million in real estate in 1994. You'd expect the company's Net connection to be expensive and high-powered. *But Alain Pinel Realtors did it all with a little 19.2 baud modem!*

What is the company's secret? Email.

In 1991, Alain Pinel Realtors already had a Wide Area Network in place to link both offices, so initial Internet costs were less than $200 per month for a dialup connection with service provider Netcom and a few hundred dollars for that 19,200 bits-per-second modem. Initially, the company used email only internally. The next step came when it exchanged email with outside companies, chiefly mortgage companies and title companies. Some companies were reluctant to link on the Net and took lengthy persuasion.

In 1992, the Internet floodgates opened when clients discovered that Alain Pinel Realtors had an email address. The company found a lot of its Silicon Valley customers on the Internet, and the Net was their *preferred* method of communication. Pinel put its Internet address on all business cards. Sales agents actually got clients simply because their cards listed that address.

"When Realtors got clients by having an email address on their card," recalls Richards, "email use by our staff spread quickly. The hard part was getting the agents to read their email on a regular basis. That took about a year."

What it took was a lot of training. No one in the company has a technical background, except Richards, who notes, "Most people come into our company as computer illiterate." He hired six nontechnical people as instructors/system administrators and trained them. They taught classes to the rest of the staff almost every day, on the Internet and on the company's custom software.

In the company's email software, agents can define a group of people and email to that list. The company discouraged agents from getting carried away and "emailing the world" because of the backlash that could cause.

Today, many of Pinel's Realtors use email as the primary means of interaction with half of their clients. "Few companies use email as pervasively as we do," says Richards. "It gives us the competitive advantage of having a better way to coordinate with people."

The company network has grown to 370 nodes sending thousands of email messages per day. It still uses the same 19.2 baud modem. "We can get away with that because 99.9 percent of our Internet use is text email," Richard explains. "Our current system automatically dials up our service provider every 15 minutes to download incoming and upload outgoing email." This is called a *UUCP connection*.

Alain Pinel Realtors' computers use the Next operating system, because of its NextStep tool for building custom software rapidly. "NextStep was the only way we could do two dozen custom applications in-house," explains Richard, especially since the company has no programmers. "Over time, we will migrate to Windows running NextStep on top of it for custom applications. More canned applications for real estate are coming out for Windows. Everything we buy now is Intel-based laptops. They will run Windows 95 with NextStep."

One last point of comparison: Email provides more accountability than snail mail. Yeah, sure, your postage meter can tell you more or less what your department spends on postage. But with email, you can run analysis reports that give you accountability per person down to the byte. (That's one single English character.) You can break usage down by the day and by the hour. This makes it easier for interdepartmental billing, for client billing (if you charge customers per message or per kilobyte), and for projections.

Email also has advantages over phone calls. I can answer five or six email messages in the same amount of time it takes me to return one phone call. No busy signals, no receptionists to get through, no waiting on hold. When I want to respond to an email message, I just press the "Reply" key, type my response, and press the "Send" key. My message is addressed automatically, is delivered automatically, and is in the addressee's mailbox in seconds. And I pay no long-distance phone charges. It's hard to beat that.

On the phone, you have to think on your feet. Sometimes you say things you wish you hadn't. Sometimes you don't have an immediate or proper response. Contrary to a phone call, in an email message you can think about what you want to say, before you send it. It's easier to seem smart when you have time to work on it.

Now, all of the above reasons are well and good, but as a marketing man, I find that they aren't the best email benefits to me. There are two marketing reasons to use email that rise above all else.

1. **When companies use email, they multiply the number of customer contact points without additional incremental cost.**

Think about this for a moment. Email spreads direct contact with your customers across your company. The implications are vast. Your customers and prospects gain a depth of service and a tighter interrelationship with your company than you can achieve by any other medium.

And your company gains a depth of insight into what your customers want—and what they don't want—that comes not from guesstimates, but from *firsthand interaction* with your clients.

2. **You can reach large groups as easily as one person.**

This is a slight exaggeration, but not much. To send your email message to 1,000 people instead of one person takes only a little more work. I've been doing publicity and direct mail advertising for enough years to appreciate how much easier, faster, and cheaper this is than any other alternative. There are caveats about Internet mailing lists, but if you mind the rules, the rewards will surprise you.

One other thing I like about Internet email is this: messages are easy to pass around. If you see something you want to share with others, the Net makes it easy for you to copy and forward that message. When somebody likes one of your messages, they can forward it.

This is the typed equivalent of good word-of-mouth on the Net—what some call good "word-of-fingers." It's a free bonus on the Net. When you send out something successful, it snowballs and generates a greater response than you could have created on your own.

In summary, get email if you want to speed up communication. It reduces decision-making time. You can reach a lot of people quickly—and it's cheap.

# Yeah, but why *Internet* email?

Would you use a telephone system that only connected you with the people in your own company? Then why use an email system that doesn't link you to the rest of the world?

Email on the Internet carries your words to more of the world than any other computer communication—even more than the other services of the Internet itself. As of early 1995, only 88 countries had access to all the services of the Internet, but 169 countries had access to Internet email.

It's truly *worldwide* communication—and then some: Astronauts on the space shuttle can receive and send Internet email.

Don't get the idea that the Internet limits you to reaching only other Internet users. From the Internet, you can email directly to people who use most other forms of email: CompuServe, America Online, Prodigy, MCI Mail, Microsoft Mail, Lotus cc:Mail, DEC All-in-One, and Minitel, to name a few.

From the Internet, you can even send email that reaches people's *fax* machines—and without paying long distance charges.

There's a less tangible reason to use the Internet, too. As every issue of *Wired* magazine reminds us, the Internet is *cooler* than any other network. Its denizens see the Internet as the only "real" network. Internet people look down at "lesser" networks' users as if they were mental croutons.

## Three problems with email

Like everything else in life, Internet email has its weak spots. You can follow Caesar's example with Gaul and divide them into three areas: security, reliability, and compatibility.

### 1. *Security: The Internet is a public network, not a private one.*

The Net is as private as a glass shower stall in the middle of Times Square.

 Email is not secure. Unlike postal mail, *other people can read your mail.* This can happen by accident or on purpose, and your readers may be people with access authority (like your company's system administrator), or people without authority: hackers, industrial spies, or just a wrong address to whom you accidentally sent secret data.

This is why you are told not to put confidential information in an Internet email message. And why it's not safe to send your credit card numbers in email.

Those are problems with *outgoing* mail. You also need to know a couple of things about *incoming* email. First, email return addresses can be faked. This is called "spoofing." It sometimes involves forged messages from celebrities, such as a purported message from author Stephen King to the **alt.horror** newsgroup. Spoofed messages have also been created to hurt the reputations of business people and everyday people. The same snooper who can eavesdrop and read your incoming email can also change email messages.

Fortunately, solutions to email's security loopholes have arrived. They are called Privacy Enhanced Mail and Pretty Good Privacy. There is also a variation of Privacy Enhanced Mail called RIPEM. I covered these secure email products in the previous chapter.

Obviously, you won't use these public-key encryption products for all your email, but they are good to secure your email with regular correspondents such as major customers, suppliers, consultants, and offices in remote cities.

## 2.  *Reliability: Internet email is not 100 percent reliable.*

Your Internet messages will usually reach addressees anywhere in the world within minutes, often within seconds. But not always. Since Internet email is passed along from computer to computer to its final destination, if a computer or a network link goes down holding your message, sometimes it can take days to reach its addressee.

You will notice this especially if you often do large (more than 1,000 names), time-sensitive mailings to an email list. Every few mailings, one or two people will complain that you should have sent your message earlier because they didn't receive it in time. Investigation will reveal that the message took a few days or a week to reach the complainers.

Rarely, an Internet message will simply disappear. When you have a complex document to email, make sure you keep a backup copy so your information can't be lost. Email software makes this simple to do. You don't need to copy everything, but ask yourself, "Would I feel pain if this document were lost?" If you would, make a copy. If not, don't.

## 3.  *Compatibility: Everything on the Net works together—except when it doesn't.*

The Internet was started back in the early 1970s, and has computers from every manufacturer running every operating system imaginable. Some computers on the Net are nearly 20 years old. Everything *almost* works alike. You need to keep this in mind when you send a message to someone. The limits of your recipient's computer and software determine what he or she can read.

If you keep two simple guidelines in mind, your messages should be readable by everyone:

***Keep the line length of your messages 80 characters per line or shorter.***
Some networks truncate lines longer than 80 characters. Many email packages automatically limit outgoing line length to fit this limit, or, like Lotus cc:Mail, let you choose your message width. If yours doesn't, and you don't want each line of your message chopped off, just hit the return key to end each line before it grows too long. 70 characters should work. The sample message in "Anatomy of an Email Message" in this chapter is 70 characters wide.

***Know how long a message your addressee's system can receive.***
America Online and the European network EUnet limit incoming message size to 102,400 characters. (That's a lot of characters. To give you a point of comparison, the original manuscript for this chapter was more than 100,000 characters long.) Several sites limit incoming messages to 65,536 characters (called 64 K, for 64,000). A few places set a size limit as low as 10,240 characters.

To compensate for these limits, keep messages emailed to AOL and Europe shorter than 100,000 characters unless you know that your recipient's system can handle a longer message. When you mass-mail a message to an email list, keep your message shorter than 65,536 characters—which shouldn't be too difficult.

A couple of other oddball compatibility problems may affect the integrity of a message from time to time. When your message passes through an older Internet computer, the system might drop attached files, or get confused by a perfectly valid node name longer than 6 characters, and bounce your message back to you. These problems are uncommon, and will grow less common over the next year as newer hardware and software replaces the present museum pieces.

# How to get top management involved

In the early days of the telephone, the chief engineer of the British Postal and Telegraph System (then the world's biggest telecommunications organization) dismissed phones as a needless luxury. He said, "I have one in my office, but mostly for show. If I want to send a message, I employ a boy to take it."

Modern versions of this attitude still exist. If you want to get senior managers to use email, you may have to go to extra lengths to accommodate them. Obviously, it's an advantage when you have managers who are savvy enough to jump right in and send their own email. It's a valuable customer relations tool. Rachel Unkefer, president of Computer Literacy Bookshops Inc., publicizes her email address of **pres@clbooks.com**, and asks customers to contact her directly if they have any problem. That kind of accessibility goes a long way toward making customers trust a company.

For senior execs who refuse to deal with their email first-hand, you can come up with workarounds. Former Apple Computer honcho John Sculley didn't read his own voluminous email. He had two assistants answer it. Hewlett-Packard CEO John Young used a different approach. His assistant printed his email and put the hard copies on Young's desk for Young to read and answer.

The trouble with approaches like these is that the executive who avoids direct involvement with email loses the advantages of immediate, person-to-person contact with employees and customers. A manager with a hands-on approach to email learns a lot more about what really goes on, especially what goes on in the minds of his or her customers.

Writer Sherman Stratfor pointed this out in an article called "The New Computer Revolution" in the June 14, 1993 issue of *Fortune:* "The common ailment of the corporations that got hit on the head by two-by-fours—particularly IBM, Digital, and Compaq—was distance from customers. They ended up making products customers didn't want. The lesson here, that applies to every industry, is that successful companies depend utterly on customer feedback. At winning outfits from GE to Wal-Mart, a primary goal is to create structures—from flattened management to email systems linking employees with customers and suppliers—that increase that closeness."

It might take private training to get your executives to use email. It might take a daily visit from an email "coach" for a few weeks to get a manager up to speed. But the benefits are worth it, for the manager, for your company, and for the visibility and success of your email project.

There is one type of manager who is better off *not* using email. If you have a top manager who enjoys confrontation and actually *likes* to be obnoxious, that person on email can give your company a bad reputation, generate flames, and get your entire company blacklisted and barred from whole sections of the Internet. You could spend a lot of time cleaning up the damage. Keep bullies away from email.

This is especially true if your company has international customers. Compared to the United States, other countries' manners are more formal and standards of politeness are more important. Someone who just seems rude or impolite in the United States can get you into real hot water internationally.

## Anatomy of an email message

To discuss how to apply email in your business, you need to know what the different parts of an email message are called.

All email messages have two parts, the *header* and the message itself, which is called the *body*. Most messages have an optional third part, called the *signature*, or *sig* for short. (See Figure 8.1)

## Fourteen company policy considerations

Email will touch more people in your company than any other Internet service. It is a good idea for you to create formal company policies for employees and email, because it will be widespread, because your employees' email will represent your company to the outside world, and because of the ethical and legal aspects of dealing with your employees and email.

You benefit from having policies worked out in advance. This makes it easier on your system administrator, who can apply policy guidelines to make the rush decisions that come with email administration. Formal guidelines avoid

**Header:** Tells who sent the message, when it was sent, who it's for, its subject, and how it traveled to its destination.

```
Return-Path: <perine@detect.com>
Received: from moon.earthlink.net by mwmlaw.geonet.com
        (8.6.9/SMI-4.1/Geonet) id VAA20224; Thu, 6 Dec 1928 10:07:51-0800
Received: by mwm.geonet.com (Smail3.1.28.1 #28.2)
        id <mOrUTAI-000LFfC@moon.earthlink.net>; Thu, 6 Dec 28 10:08 PST
Message-Id: <mOrUTAI-000LFfC@moon.earthlink.net>
Content-Type: text
Date: Thu, 6 Dec 28 10:07 PST
X-Sender: perine@detect.com
To: sidney.wise@mwmlaw.com
cc: samuel.spade@detect.com
From: effie.perine@detect.com
Subject: Meeting today with Sam Spade
X-Mailer: <Windows Eudora Version 2.02>
```

**Subject:** What this message is about. Your subject gets your message read, so it is important. Some email software truncates long subjects, so keep your subjects short.

**Body:** The message itself.

```
Sid, will you be in your office this afternoon?  Sam would like some
legal advice _before_ the coroner's inquest on Miles' death.
Please have your secretary call me to set up a time.
```

```
Effie Perine, Office Manager                    effie.perine@detect.com
-----------------------------------------------------------------------
Spade & Archer, Private Investigators                 Phone 415-555-2300
Hunter-Dulin Building, 111 Sutter St.                      "Our Specialty:
San Francisco, Calif. USA                        Confidential Investigations"
```

**Signature:** Automatically added to all Ms. Perine's outgoing messages by her email software. Stored in a file called *sig file*. This sig is five lines tall. Four or five lines tall is a good size for a sig.

**Figure 8.1** *A typical email message has three major sections—the header, the body, and the signature, along with the important subject line.*

lawsuits. Your policies will prevent errors by letting employees know what they are expected to do.

Your email policies should become part of your company documentation and your employee training for all who are allowed email access. Your company training needs to cover not just the technical part of how to use email, but also the ethical and liability aspects. Your company documentation should include a set of rules stating clearly what is allowed and what is not when sending email. From a legal standpoint, it may be beneficial to you to clearly state the consequences of failing to follow company email policy guidelines.

### *1. Make sure your staff understands email is not secure.*

First, let your people know that email is *not* private. Email is often copied and reposted, much to the sender's dismay. As Carol Welsh of the Computer Museum says, "Don't say anything in email that you wouldn't want to read on the front page of the *New York Times.*"

Ask Tonya Harding. She made front page news during the 1994 Winter Olympics when reporters snooped in her email. Your employees may not have reporters poking in their mailboxes, but email industrial espionage is on the rise. Maybe your competitors snoop.

Let your workers know that email may be used as legal evidence. The most famous example was during the Iran-Contra hearings, when Oliver North thought he had deleted his email. Actually, a backup system had saved his messages, which were used as evidence against him. Email was also used as evidence when Microsoft Corp. was investigated by the federal government. U.S. Justice Department investigators sifted through thousands of email messages from Microsoft employees, dating back years. And email has shown up in court as evidence in divorce cases.

### *2. Write guidelines on what to include in email and what to exclude.*

 You need to define what is and what is not permissible for your staff to discuss in email messages. A written policy can protect your company from legal liability due to actions of employees. Hallmark Cards, Inc. gives all email users a written policy that forbids harrassment, including any remarks that can be interpreted as sexual harrassment; offensive or insulting remarks; emotional responses to business correspondence; and personal information or gossip about the user or someone else.

The most common offense is sexual harrassment, which has resulted in many multi-million dollar lawsuits. With printouts of the offending email as evidence, most are settled out of court. Some companies' policies specifically prohibit "electronic valentines" of any sort, and ban any mention of sex or of a person's physique.

Depending on your company's network setup, you may need to differentiate between email sent *inside* your company or site, and email sent *outside*. Email is not as open to prying eyes when it stays on your company's internal computer network, and when it travels only to outside computers linked with your internal network on a leased line.

If your company is privately held, you may not want sales figures mentioned in email. Should people mention wage figures in email? How about customer names? Certainly you don't want to leak any of your customers' proprietary data entrusted to you. What about new products and services that your company has under development? Give employees a written guide to what is and what is not emailable, what stays within your company and what can go outside. The more explicit you make your guide, the less chance that someone will unintentionally give away corporate secrets.

### 3. If your company will monitor employees' email, tell them about it in writing.

Laws differ from country to country, but in the United States, employers do have the right to monitor email sent on company-owned computers. Email is governed by the Federal Electronic Communications Privacy Act of 1986, which recognizes that companies sometimes need to read messages to make sure that no industrial espionage is taking place. The company paid for the email, so it owns the email.

 Make employees aware that people *within* your company may have access to their email. A system administrator, for example, normally has access to messages. Other people in your company may have access as well. This needs to be made clear to your employees *in a written notice*. If you tell them about it ahead of time, they'll say, "Yeah, sure, no big deal." But you might encounter some anger if they find out by surprise, even if your monitoring is perfectly legal. A simple phrase will do, such as, "From time to time, your email messages may be read by company managers for various reasons."

As there is no U.S. law preventing an employer from reading an employee's email, there is no law that states an employeee must be told when his or her email is inspected. Even so, if there is even the slimmest chance that your company might monitor employee email, you avoid legal brawls and bitter staff confrontations by letting people know about this possibility in advance.

A woman named Alana Shoars who used to work for Epson America sued the company, saying that it violated her privacy by reading her email. She lost. The judge ruled that the company's property rights took precedence over Shoars' privacy rights. Even so, Epson America paid tens of thousands of dollars in legal fees, which it might have avoided just by giving Shoars a written notice that someone might read her email.

## 4. *The legal consequences of reading employees' email differ from those of doing anything with it.*

Reading an employee's mail is one thing. Taking action with an employee's mail is very different. When you find a message that you want to copy, forward, or make public, you should discuss it with the employee first, *before* you take any action. There can be severe legal consequences if any of the employee's rights are violated. This varies depending on your local labor laws and union regulations.

## 5. *Decide who in your company will have Internet access and what kind of access they will have.*

Who gets email? Who gets the World Wide Web? Some people will forcefully demand complete Internet access. Some will want email as a status symbol. Other will shun it as a source of more work. Someone in your company will need to create decision-making criteria for who gets what and why.

This doesn't need to be a formal, written document, but put some thought into it. The current trend seems to be that all employees—at least, those with computers—get email access, but only the ones who *need* other Internet tools can use all Net services. As the CFO of one large corporation told me, "Everyone should have email, but only a few get full access. I don't want the guys in the mailroom spending all day playing computer games."

You will find, with rare exceptions, it pays to give email to all your staff who have a computer. Email will be especially important to anyone who has contact with the outside world: sales representatives, purchasing agents, R&D, accounts payable, accounts receivable, customer service, and marketing people. Remember your telecommuters—for them, email is a life-or-death matter.

Then decide which people get access to all the other Internet services. Obviously, your technical staff will need full Internet access to support your own Net efforts. Your marketing people—or whomever will be in charge of maintaining the contents of your Internet presence—will need full Net access to test and monitor your offerings—and your competitors'. You might be surprised to see how much Net activity deals with accounting and finance (maybe that's predictable, given accountants' passion for precisely organized data), so that lets in your number crunchers. A good browse of this book will give you an idea of what the Internet has to offer the different departments in your business. If you're not sure, err on the side of restraint. It will be easier to add more services later than to take them away.

There is something to keep in mind when you give an employee email access to the Internet but not access to other Internet services. If your employee looks for them, alternative ways *using only email* can be found to use these services: Archie, Veronica, WAIS, mailing lists, Gopher, FTP, Usenet newsgroups, Finger, Whois, and even the World Wide Web. So keep your eyes open—your restrictions may not be as thorough as you think.

If you want to provide email access for your staff who don't work on computers, you can do this in a limited way. Whether they have a computer or not, all Sprint/United Telephone of Florida employees have an email address. Sprint/UTF sites make terminals available where the computerless can log in, retrieve their email, and log out.

## 6. *Decide who will deal with customer email, then define procedures for them to use.*

Who talks with customers in your company now? When your business uses email, the number of customer contact points will multiply quickly. Your clients will touch people in more departments across your company than before, including people who don't otherwise deal with cutomers. You need to plan for this.

Which email addresses will be publicized to your customers and which will be withheld? Will departments such as customer support and sales make the email addresses of all departmental personnel available to customers? Or will departments give customers a single address as a point of contact? This last approach has advantages, which you can see in Chapter 16, *Customers, Sales, and the World Wide Web.*

Define procedures and standards. When you receive an email message from a customer, how long will it be before someone returns a response? Some companies set maximum times, such as a response will go out within 60 minutes or 90 minutes—perhaps not an answer to the customer's question, but at least an acknowledgment that "We have received your question, and are working on it." Retailer Hammacher Schlemmer's standard is 5 minutes.

Let people know about the different tone of voice appropriate for people outside your company's home country. Customers from the United States and Canada usually prefer casual email and are offended by too-formal messages (because that shows you don't *like* them), but customers from most other countries prefer formal email and are offended by casual messages (because that shows you don't *respect* them).

When a customer emails a complaint, who receives it? Who gets copies of each complaint and its response? (These can be very useful for sales, marketing, and customer service planning.) Someone should prepare statistical reports on emailed complaints. Who will prepare reports? How often? What do you want to track? Who gets the finished reports on complaints? Who decides what actions to take based on your findings?

It is a good idea to store copies of all email from customers. Where do you want to store them? How long do you want to keep them? (Different lengths of time for different types of clients?) How do you want to arrange them—by date, by customer, or by type of message?

## 7. Pick a firefighting team and have them draft procedures for email flames.

 An irrationally intense, angry email message is called a flame. No matter how carefully your company treads, you may be flamed. You need a plan to handle flames.

Designate a firefighting team that will create procedures and respond to flames. It is important to prevent anyone from responding to a flame with another flame. That will just make things worse. Any employee who receives a flame should contact his or her supervisor or a designated firefighter immediately, and the supervisor should read the flame before a response is made. Keep copies of all flames and responses. After the incident is under control, your team should meet to discuss ways to prevent a recurrence of the situation that triggered the flame.

You might conduct a "flame drill" to test your procedures and find ways to improve them.

## 8. Let your employees know how their email addresses will be assigned.

People get emotional about their names, and with email, your address *is* your name. Employees will be concerned about their email addresses. You can prevent outbursts and wasted time answering the same questions over and over by letting everyone know ahead of time the formula by which their addresses were chosen.

## 9. Decide whether or not you want to standardize signature files.

Some companies let employees write and design their own sig files, so outgoing email messages all are different. Other companies define a style or a few rules that all email signatures must follow, but allow employees creativity within those limits. Other companies make all sig files follow an exact format, with no personalization allowed except the sender's name and phone number.

In most ways, sig file content decisions are marketing decisions. The marketing part of this book covers sig issues in more detail.

There is one legal aspect to consider when you set your policy for email signature files. Employers can be liable when an employee sends abusive or offensive email. As a way of limiting legal liability, some companies require their employees' signature files to say "These opinions are my own, not necessarily the opinion of my employer." Few businesses do this. Whether your business needs to depends on conditions specific to your company.

## 10. *Decide how to handle employees' personal email.*

It is silly to pretend that your employees will not send some personal email. That is human nature, and you need to allow for it. As long as it doesn't interfere with their work, be prepared for a reasonable amount to occur.

## 11. *Any person with email should log off a computer before leaving it.*

There is a risk in leaving your email program up and running when you're away from your computer. Someone can use your email account to send embarrassing or legally actionable messages. Admittedly, in many companies this is unlikely. But depending on how many people work at your site and what the physical layout is (bullpen vs. private office), you may want to require employees to log off their computers before leaving them unattended.

## 12. *Work with your network administrator to define procedures for shared computers.*

As telecommuting grows in popularity, it becomes less cost-effective to have a full-time computer for an employee who is rarely around to use it. There is a growing trend for employees to share computers. Each of these employees will still need a personal email account. Your service administrator can set up multiple mail accounts on a single computer. This is trivial with Unix, but takes more work with other operating systems. For instance, Microsoft Mail for Windows requires your system administrator to set up a Workgroup Post Office on a separate computer and then set up all shared accounts on the Post Office computer.

### 13. With your system administrator, set accumulation limits on the age and amount of saved email.

If you let them, some people will never delete any of the email they receive. Old email swallows acres of disk space if you let it accumulate. Your system administrator will want to archive messages to a backup disk and delete them from the computer periodically. If done without warning, you'll hear more wailing than two weeks of *All My Children*. Prevent it by telling people ahead of time that they have $x$ amount of disk space assigned to them, and that if they go over that limit, their older messages will be removed. People in some positions will need more disk space than others. Allow for that, and plan to give managers more space. But most employees' saved email messages should total 500 kilobytes of disk space or less.

You may think this is irrelevant if you just use a dialup account with a service provider and store email messages on your service provider's computer instead of your own. You will still need to set limits. If you leave your messages in your mailbox too long, some providers will delete them.

### 14. Set goals for training to accomplish, and remember training in your budget.

When planning Internet projects, people often forget about training. Training is important, time-consuming, and costs money. Without training, your email software will be useless. Plan hands-on training for all people who will use email. Train them either one-on-one or in small groups, with one computer per trainee. In my experience, hands-on training is the only kind that shows results for email software.

Make a list of what specific actions someone needs to know to use your email software. Break those down into a series of step-by-step lessons. Make "cheat sheets" for your employees to use after the classes. After people have used email for four months, give them a second class on more advanced topics.

If your company includes people with different amounts of experience with email and the Internet, you might have separate classes for those with little or no background and those with more experience. That way veterans won't make newbies feel slow, and the vets won't be held back by beginners.

## Personnel management uses

For all the talk about the Internet connecting your business with far-flung places, you will find that many of the most productive uses of email will be for communications *within* your company.

Employee newsletters are a good example. Instead of typesetting, printing, and distributing a newsletter on paper, you can send internal newsletters by email. It is so much easier to edit and distribute an emailed newsletter, that you can send them more frequently. In turn, increased frequency lets your newsletter cover more *immediate* news—which is the single most important key to effectiveness in employee newsletters. Employees must come to rely on your newsletter to break important news first. To do that, your internal newsletters must be fast enough to beat the grapevine to the punch. With email, you can.

Email also simplifies *customizing* your newsletter. For instance, you could include core articles that all employees receive, insert technical articles in the versions received by your technicians, add a story about changes in your sales compensation plan for the salespeople and a description of new payroll taxes received only by people in the locations where the tax applies. For employees without computers, supervisors can print the newsletter and distribute it to them. Read the story on the following page about Sprint/United Telephone of Florida for an example of how one company does this.

Employee phone and address directories can be sent by email, ensuring that your contact information is always up-to-date. Expense reports can be submitted to supervisors by email, who can correct them, approve them, and

# Employee news for less

The most thorough employee propaganda program I've come across has two remarkable aspects: First, the level to which it saturates managers and employees with needed information on core business issues, and second, the small effort and cost it requires in relation to the amount of news it delivers.

Not surprisingly, this program is run by a communications company. The startling thing is the major role plain old email plays in the Sprint News Network. Sprint/United Telephone of Florida built the Sprint News Network (SNN) to spread news to its own 5,800 people, who are scattered throughout the state of Florida. The Sprint News Network's foundation is email, which delivers five of seven internal SNN media.

The backbone of SNN is an emailed newsletter, *SNN Today*. It goes to all employees three times a week—more often when hot news breaks. Sprint/UTF employees without email receive *SNN Today* from their supervisors, who distribute paper copies of the newsletter to all email-less subordinates. Some supervisors print multiple copies and hand them out to each employee. Some print a single copy and route it through their department. Others print a single copy and post it on a corkboard that all subordinates check daily. This is a simple and effective distribution plan, and can easily be imitated by other companies.

*SNN Today* is not lengthy. Its goals are frequency and immediacy. Preparing and emailing the newsletter takes about 80 percent of one person's job, and others contribute some articles.

"Employees appreciate the immediacy of it," says Lloyd Karnes, Sprint/UTF's manager of strategic communications. "That's the key. It used to be that when we'd get an important announcement or a big event and we'd have to notify 5,800 people spread all over the state, it was a big project and took a lot of people a lot of work. With email, it's just a matter of pushing a button. What makes the difference is that we have built a structure to handle news of that kind. Because *SNN Today* comes out so often, people rely on it and expect it to have the important news."

During the first two hours of each business day, executives receive an additional email newsletter, *SNN Leadership Briefings*. It includes stock market information, industry news, and Sprint-related business news. Also emailed from time to time is *SNN Leadership Letter*, specifically for Sprint supervisors. It covers corporate policies, procedures and news, and contains general articles on management skills.

A fourth email newsletter, *SNN Today and Tomorrow* is delivered weekly to everyone in the company. While the regular *SNN Today* delivers the lowdown on current news, this sibling newletter deals with issues that will affect employees in the future, including reengineering, quality improvement, and process improvement. That's how management gets the word out to staff. But how can Sprint/UTF employees talk back to management?

That's where an email free-for-all called "Quanda" steps in. Quanda is the equivalent of 12 private, staff-only newsgroups for Sprint employees. Quanda works like any other Internet discussion group. Employees post questions to anyone in the company, all the way up to top executives, and see answers to their questions and those from other employees. "It's wide open," explains Karnes. "People can say whatever they want." His communications department monitors Quanda to make sure that vice presidents and department heads respond to questions asked of them. "We get good ideas from employees that I don't think the company would have come up with without Quanda. Several ideas have become policy."

Karnes reports much healthy debate of issues through Quanda, which helps the company reach a consensus on important matters. He says it took time for some people to grow comfortable with the give-and-take: "The idea that someone can pose a question to the president of the company, and someone else will jump in and make an answer for him."

To run Quanda and company email, Sprint/UTF uses Digital's All-in-1 software on a VAX computer. A feature called Group Conferencing comes as part of All-in-1. Sprint/UTF uses Group Conferencing to run its email discussion groups, and so it calls them "conferences."

Karnes' communications department also prepares slideshow-like presentations that it sends through standard phone lines to PCs and TV monitors for employees to view. They call this the *SNN Vision Channel,* which despite being flashy and high-tech, is still practical. Karnes' staff creates graphics and type on a central PC using TVI DeskTop graphics and scheduling software from Target Vision of Pittsford, New York. They send the finished images across phone lines to more than 140 TV monitors in 31 buildings across the state, and to 24 LAN servers that route the Vision Channel pictures to 500 PCs. On PCs, employees view the slideshow images by subject, or use the images as screen savers. Three days a week, *The 60-Second Sprint*, a one-minute presentation, covers company news. The other two days, *Sprint Financial News* shows how the company meets the financial goals of its business plan.

These Vision Channel presentations are custom-tailored for each site. Each location receives company-wide news, followed by specific news for its Sprint/UTF region, specific news for its local district, and even news specific to its *building*.

The seventh piece of the Sprint News Network is a monthly print publication, *SNN Intercom.*

"Our goal is not just to say who is Employee of the Month and do that kind of morale-boosting," Karnes explains. "We want everyone to know about the *strategic core issues* of our business." From the perspective of Karnes and his company's executives, their business is so competitive that the only way Sprint/UTF can reach its objectives is if the company presents a unified front of information to all employees. The Sprint News Network is a central piece of that strategy. It has earned high marks from management and staff alike.

email them to accounting for payment. Changes in an individual's insurance coverage can be emailed to that person. The steady stream of paperwork to and from managers can become email, making it easier to manage.

Recruiting is another important management use for email. You can email a job vacancy description to dozens of "Help Wanted" spots on the Net. I list several spots in Chapter 13, and new ones open up literally every month. Some are general, but the greatest growth is in specialized job banks. For example, mathematicians, teachers, and accountants all have specific sites where you can post relevant openings.

Some sites charge companies a fee for posting openings, including those that your recruitment advertising agency will try to sell to you. However, there are so many free sites that you may not need the fee-based services.

## What to look for in email software

Which kinds of software will you need? First of all, each person in your company who uses email will need *mail client* software—the program that a person uses to send and read mail. To make things more confusing, email clients are also called *mail user agents*, or MUAs. I'll just stick with mail client.

In addition to mail client programs, you may need: *Gateway* software or hardware called *switches;* mail server software; mail transport software (called MTA for Mail Transport Agent); list server software (If you want to mail to lists of 200 or more names).

Client software is what every emailer in your company will use every day. What should good email client software do?

First, the basics. It should:

- Ask you to fill in the address of your recipient, usually by asking "To:".

- Let you name each message, usually on a "Subject" line.

- Let you write the text that is the body of your message.

- Show you a list of incoming email messages.

You should be able to do at least five things to each message after you read it:

1. *Reply* to the sender of a message without retyping an address.
2. *Forward* the message to other people.
3. *Save* the message to disk.
4. *Print* it.
5. *Delete* it.

- The client program should give you an address book. This lets you save often-used addresses and pop them onto messages automatically. You don't need to retype or even remember them. It saves on Post-It notes.

- The client should automatically add one or more signature files to your outgoing messages.

- Does it have understandable documentation? Check the table of contents and the index.

Any email client software you consider should handle the basics above. If not, scratch it off your list.

Not all client software provides every feature below, but these features are worth searching for:

- Some people get 500 email messages on a busy day. Yikes! Check to see if your software has a *mail handler* or a *mail filter*, two names for the same thing. This option automatically sorts incoming mail according to criteria you define, and puts messages in mailbox folders for you to review. That way, you can read your high-priority folders when you don't have enough time to look at all of that day's email. Most mail filters check addresses and subject lines. Some inspect body copy as well.

- Does your client software have a *bozo filter*? This checks the sender's address on each incoming message you receive. If a message comes from an address you have specified (as a "bozo"), it deletes the message or puts it in a *bozo folder* for later review. This is also called a *kill file*.

- Part of sorting mail is *message threading*. If you send a message to three people, they reply back to you, you reply to them, and they return another reply, it is useful for you to be able to review the entire correspondence in sequential order, separated from your other email. Good message threading will let you do this.

- Does it spellcheck your outgoing email? Some client programs have a built-in spellchecker. Some let you attach any spellchecker you choose. Some Unix programs let you attach any *word processor* you choose.

- While you use another program, will your client display an onscreen message telling you that incoming mail has arrived? This is extremely useful, especially for customer service people and people who deal with urgent situations.

- Your client should let you create an alias or nickname and have mail to it go into a designated file, or go to a group list. For instance, could you set up the alias **finance** so any mail sent to that address goes to everyone in your finance department? Could you direct all mail sent to **info@yourcorp.com** to your service manager? Could you create an alias so **miles.a@detect.com** and **m.archer@detect.com** both go to the same person?

- Are aliases the only way your client software gives you to build a mailing list? Can you build more than one list? What's the maximum number of names you can add to one list?

- Can your client software create and receive messages using international character sets? This allows messages in languages like Japanese, Arabic, and Russian, which do not use the Roman characters that English uses.

- Automatic forwarding sends email for a vacationing employee to someone else. When an employee leaves your company, have his or her email forwarded to someone until it drops off. Some email software has a vacation mail feature to accept any incoming messages for a person and send a "Hi, I'm on vacation and won't be back until June 17" message.

- Some Internet email software lets you request return receipts for important messages you send. When your recipient receives and opens your message, you receive an email message telling what day and time your message was opened. Some software can give you a reminder if the message you sent remained unread for a number of days you define. Some vendors call this *certification*.

- You want your mail client to let you attach a file to a message you send. This is an important feature. Some programs do it easily. Some can't do it at all. The problem is that Internet email can handle only text, not graphics files or software programs. To send a nontext file (called a *binary file*), you have to first translate the binary information into text. This is done one of two ways: Uuencode or MIME. The recipient then translates the file back into binary files and uses them. Check to make sure your client handles Uuencode, MIME, or both. Then check to make sure it recognizes and translates them automatically. It's a pain in the anatomy to translate files by hand. Note that some companies don't allow MIME email for security reasons.

- Does the software include encryption with PGP (Pretty Good Privacy), PEM (Privacy-Enhanced Mail), or the Kerberos authentication system? Will it also encrypt attached files?

- Support:
  - Toll-free number for support.
  - Support by email.
  - 24-hour support. (Yes, please!)

Your choices for email client software depend on three things. First, are you are going to use Internet email all the way to the desktop clients, or make your existing email client software (whether it runs on your mainframe, mini or LAN) work with Internet email? If the latter, you may need costly gateways and switches, discussed in Chapter 2 and in the next section.

Second, what operating system are you going to use? And last, what kind of Internet connection do you have? If you use Unix, you have more than a dozen email clients to choose from: Mail (also called Berkeley Mail), SunSelect Mail, Elm, Pine, Mush, Zmail, XMH, Mail Tool, and others. Many of them are free.

If your Net connection is an IP account, you can use a highly rated product called Eudora. Mac and Microsoft Windows versions are available now, and OS/2 and Unix versions are under development. Eudora includes mail sorting and management tools, is easy to use, and has links with Microsoft Mail, cc:Mail, and other products. Shareware versions of Eudora are available from several Internet and Web sites, but are not supposed to be used by businesses. The commercial version is available from Qualcomm: 619-587-1121 or email **eudora-sales@qualcomm.com**.

If you have a dial-up shell account, your service provider probably provides a Unix mail client program such as Mail, Pine, or Elm. If you'd like to use Microsoft Windows software instead, check out Delrina Corporation's Internet Mail Manager client software. It is very easy to set up, requiring almost no configuration. It doesn't do newsgroups, but it is an impressive, easy-to-use mail client. You can get Internet Mail Manager only as part of a suite of communications packages from Delrina. You can contact them at: 895 Don Mills Road, 500-2 Park Centre, Toronto, Ontario; Canada M3C 1W3. Phone: 416-441-3676, Fax: 416-441-0774.

OS/2 comes with IBM's UltiMail Lite Internet email client, which is functional. If you like the Lite version, take a look at the full-fledged UltiMail product, which has many more features. You can also pick up special-purpose Internet email clients. For instance, SNPP, the Simple Network Paging Protocol, lets you send email to pagers. There are a handful of clients that use SNPP to send email to your beeper. In addition to the client software, this requires a separate gateway program.

## Working with the software you have

If you already have mainframe or LAN email client software, the good news is that there are software and hardware solutions to make your existing email talk with Internet email.

The bad news is that in most cases it is more difficult—and more expensive—than an all-Internet approach. You will need to buy either software called *gateways,* or hardware called *switches.* A gateway will usually support only one client software package, for example, linking Lotus cc:Mail to the Internet. If your company uses several email clients, it may be cheaper for you to get a switch, which can link several email clients with the Net.

 Most gateways and switches are expensive. Many are also time-consuming to install and operate, and do not work well.

For example, the Microsoft Mail gateway from Microsoft and the cc:Mail gateway from Lotus both cost more than $3,000, are only available as DOS programs—not Windows—and are buggy. The Microsoft Mail gateway has problems with long messages, and both gateways often lose attachments.

On the other hand, easy-to-use gateway packages for the Macintosh versions of Microsoft Mail and QuickMail are available, inexpensive, and reliable. It boils down this: To link your non-Internet email client to the rest of the world, you'd better look carefully at as many options as you can. Your choices depend on your operating system.

With support for Internet networking built in, Windows 95 handles email more easily than the previous release of Windows. Windows 95 features a "Universal In-box" for email, voicemail, and faxes.

Some companies, mostly larger ones, use email systems that conform to a communications standard called X.400. Using X.400 for email has some advantages over the Internet, and some disadvantages. The Internet can exchange email with all other computer networks. This is not true with X.400. It uses a different addressing scheme than the Internet, which makes it hard to link the two. There are software products to handle this for Windows, Unix, Novell,

---

## How to receive email without a computer

If you are dealing with a customer or a supplier who has no email, you may want to tell it about Email by Fax. This service lets people without computers receive email on their fax machines. When you subscribe to Email by Fax, you receive your own email address. Instead of going to a computer, all your messages print on your fax machine. The service charges only $5.00 per month, no matter how many messages you receive.

To find out more, call IDT at 201-928-1000, or fax 201-928-1057 to the attention of Howard Jonas, or send email to **howard.jonas@icm.com**.

---

OS/2, and several large computer systems. None of them is simple to install and maintain.

There is a soaring demand from businesses to link Internet and non-Internet email systems. Software and hardware vendors aren't blind to the need, so hundreds of programmers are feverishly writing code. New products are released every week, and existing LAN client programs are getting upgrades and add-ons to more easily join the world of Internet email.

## Flames and mail bombing

One of the more "entertaining" aspects of email is that people using email tend to lose their self-control surprisingly easily. Somehow, email lends a feeling of anonymity and safety. Often email users become more emotional than they would in a face-to-face talk. People will write things to you that they would never dream of saying to your face.

A good result of this is that people can form close relationships by email without ever meeting each other in person. That's great for customer relations.

The downside is that people become angry easily while reading email, and may send you abusive responses. Writing inappropriately angry email is called *flaming*. You can be flamed for something you regard as completely trivial.

Here's an example. After writing an article for *The New Yorker* about Microsoft chairman Bill Gates, writer John Seabrook received this email message:

```
"Crave THIS, asshole:

Listen, you toadying dipshit scumbag . . . remove your head from your rectum
long enough to look around and notice that real reporters don't fawn over
their subjects, pretend that their subjects are making some sort of special
contact with them, or worse, curry favor by TELLING their subjects how great
the ass-licking profile is going to turn out and then brag in print about
doing it. Forward this to Mom. Copy Tina and tell her the mag is fast turning
to compost. One good worm deserves another."
```

Even more surprising, Seabrook said he received this venom from a "technology writer who does a column about personal computers for a major newspaper," according to a followup *New Yorker* story Seabrook wrote, called "My First Flame."

If you or your company are flamed, *don't flame back!* Fighting fire with fire only makes things worse. It generates more flames and can lead to mail bombing or other destructive Net tactics. When you are flamed, the first thing to do is to *cool the situation down* immediately.

The same holds true if someone thinks that you have flamed him or her: Chill out!

Flaming is in the eye of the beholder. If someone feels that a message from you was a flame, it was. Don't try to say, "But I didn't mean it!" That didn't work when you told it to your mom in the second grade, and it won't work in business. If someone accuses you of flaming them, your best response is to apologize, find out *exactly* what trigger made the recipient feel flamed, promise to never do it again, and mean it.

If you get in a flame war or are accused of *spamming* (sending advertisements to inappropriate Internet places), you may be mail bombed. Don't confuse mail bombing with letter bombing. Letter bombs are physical explosives delivered by snail mail. Mail bombs are delivered by email. Sent as revenge, they are designed to overload your system.

Mail bombing is normally done in one of two ways. One tactic is sending the target huge files. For an example, read the sidebar on the facing page.

# Mail bombing and its effects

From: TerryH@ix.netcom.com (Terry Haggin)
Newsgroups: alt.stop.spamming
Subject: Re: sick of all the long-distance phone price spamming
Date: 18 Jan 1995 19:12:57 GMT

Great group,

What I like to do with the spammers is to put 100 megs in a file then
paste it onto my active system. When I come across a fresh spam, I open
it, then mail them the 100 megs of gobbledegook. I have OS/2 so I can just
go on with what I am doing while the 100 megs of junk is being mailed to
them. That should slow them down.

Terry
>
>


Newsgroups: alt.stop.spamming
From: ddern@world.std.com (Daniel P Dern)
Subject: Mail-bombing hurts innocent bystanders (Was: Re: sick of all
the...)
Summary: Crashing systems that other people rely isn't appropriate
Date: Thu, 19 Jan 1995 15:22:00 GMT

In article <3fjp7p$6bd@ixnews2.ix.netcom.com>,
Terry Haggin <TerryH@ix.netcom.com> wrote:
>What I like to do with the spammers is ...
>... mail them the 100 mgs of gobbledegook,

While this may be gratifying, unless you're certain that the spammers
are the only ones on the target system, what you're doing may well
result impairing the service of other, innocent users on that system.
Coping with mailbombing to preserve service to non-spamming users can
easily require time and effort by sysadmins there. I don't think
this is solving the problem properly, therefore. The first act
should always be complaining to the postmaster and cc'ing the user
(or vice versa).

And then we go sneak up on their homes late at night and blast 'em
out of bed with 10,000 watts of Barry Manilow, or maybe William
Shatner intoning McArther Park. Assuming we're not concerned about
bothering the neighbors (there goes that pesky problem again...).

DPD
—
Daniel Dern (ddern@world.std.com) Internet analyst, writer, pundit & gadfly
(617) 969-7947 FAX: (617) 969-7949  Snail: PO Box 309 Newton Centre MA 02159
Author, The Internet Guide For New Users (McGraw-Hill, 1993) - info & stuff
at URL=gopher://gopher.dern.com:2200 (a.k.a. "Dern" area on
gopher.internet.com)

The second method is sending thousands of smaller messages. Automated mailing software makes this easy to do, and it is effective. Companies have been mail bombed with more than a hundred thousand messages in a short time. This overloaded the victim's access provider, forcing it to shut down service to *all* companies handled by the provider. Since email can be sent to fax machines, mail bombing has also been done to victim's fax lines, rendering them useless.

Your only defense against mail bombing is to avoid the behavior that triggers it. If you don't send flames and you don't spam, you should be safe.

# The 10 commandments of email

The Internet has been around for 25 years, and like any large group, has evolved its own rules of the road. The rules for email are straightforward and after you've been on the Net for a while, make perfect sense.

The rules of behavior on the Internet are called *netiquette*. Make sure that the emailers in your company know these rules and how to apply them. The Net has its own sense of frontier justice. Flames and mail bombs punish businesses that blatantly violate netiquette, and there are other penalties for those that break more subtle rules. These include loss of customers, prospect alienation, removal from mailing lists, active uncooperation in resolving technical problems, and a bad rap on newsgroups.

It makes good business sense to follow the rules of the Internet. Here's a summary of ten email rules you should know:

## I. Thou shalt not spam.

The term "spamming"—sending unwanted advertisements—comes from a Monty Python comedy routine in which every dish on a restaurant's menu includes Spam, no matter how inappropriate. It is similarly inappropriate to email your advertising to people who don't ask for it. Remember, on the Internet, people *pay* to receive your messages. The recipient of an Internet spam feels as though you interrupted his or her dinner with a *collect* phone call sales pitch.

If you spam, you will receive flames, be mail bombed, have your fax machine jammed with hate faxes, have your phone lines tied up (modems can be programmed to autodial your voice line and jam it), alienate prospects, lose repeat customers, get your entire company permanently cancelled from newsgroups, and possibly get kicked out by your access provider.

If you want to email anything that even *remotely* resembles an advertisement, send it only to people who have *asked* to receive it.

## II. Thou shalt not flame.

When you write from a business, don't flame. If you are flamed, don't flame back. There are no valid excuses. Period.

## III. Thou shalt not waste bandwidth.

An Internet saying is, "Talk is cheap. Bandwidth is expensive." Bandwidth—the Internet's carrying capacity—is limited. Sending useless or excessive messages fills the pipeline and slows the Net down for everybody. Useless messages also waste another limited resource—the time required to deal with them. Efficient use of Internet resources is viewed with approval.

This is part of the reason that spamming draws hate mail. Email is being sent to people who won't use it—a waste of resources. Concern with waste carries down to the signature file at the end of your messages. Your sig should ideally be four or five lines long, six or seven at the maximum. Since it will be repeated on hundreds of messages, a long signature wastes bandwidth and is therefore rude. Large sig files are an especially hot topic for the thousands of people who pay for each incoming email message they receive based on its *length*.

If your signature is ten or more lines long, you can expect to be flamed for it. (There are actually *two* Usenet newsgroups devoted to the discussion of the long sig file problem.)

## IV. Be brief.

Write short messages. Use short sentences. "The most beautiful sentence? The shortest." —Anatole France, as quoted by Dashiell Hammett.

## *V. Thou shalt not SHOUT.*

Typing your message IN ALL CAPITAL LETTERS READS LIKE YOU ARE SHOUTING AT SOMEONE. People hate that. Besides, as any student of advertising research knows, readability drops horribly when you use all caps for body copy. If you want someone to read your message, avoid all caps.

## *VI. Make thy "Subject:" clear.*

In many ways, the Subject of your message is its most important part. A recipient will choose whether to read your message or not based on what the Subject line says.

You should write a Subject line that tells why your addressee should read your message. Make it clear and specific. "Hello" is a bad subject line. "Meeting on Dec. 8 about falcon" is a good one.

Keep in mind that many people use software that sorts incoming email automatically based on what's in the Subject line. When you include a project name or other specific name in your subject line, it increases your chances that your message will be sorted into the proper file and will actually be read.

## *VII. Thou shalt not wash thy linen in public.*

Remember that what you write in an email message may be copied and posted to newsgroups, printed in the media, and sent to your worst competitor. Keep your secrets out of your email.

## *VIII. Thou shalt use the right voice for thy addressee.*

On the phone, no one can see your face, but your feelings are still clear. Why? Because the person you talk to can hear your tone of voice. Email is the written word, and no one can hear your voice. Misunderstandings from email are common, and often occur when the writer wasn't careful with his or her *written* tone of voice.

For example, a knowledgeable computer programmer at Computer Literacy Bookshops often emailed store managers with instructions for software. He thought he was being short and direct. Readers found his instructions brusque and almost rude. One spoke with the programmer about it, and the next emailed instructions were prefaced with the phrase, "Gentle suggestion:"

Isn't that a beautiful phrase? It turns a barked command into helpful words from a friend. My gentle suggestion for managers is that they take care with their email, making sure they adopt a supportive tone. Orders seem harsh when emailed, and your employees may resent them. Try phrasing a command as a question and see what results you generate. Or make a "gentle suggestion" of your own.

All emailers need to watch their words—not just managers. Sarcasm doesn't work in email, so avoid it. Avoid vulgarity—it can come back to haunt you. Humor is risky. Match your message's formality to your addressee. You wouldn't speak the same, for instance, with the chairman of the board as you would with your best pal. Don't use the same email voice either.

You especially need to tailor your email voice when you correspond with someone from another culture. Sarcasm and humor don't travel well across cultures. Use the other culture's manners. For instance, don't display anger or say "no" directly to a Japanese person—you will seem very rude.

One final gentle suggestion: Reread your message before you send it to catch things that may be misinterpreted. You can ask yourself, "Would I say this to this person's face?" I have saved myself a lot of grief by making this a habit. Amazing gaffes jump out at me when I read my mail a second time.

## IX. *Look twice before thou leapest.*

If reading an incoming message makes you see red, reread it carefully *before* you respond. Its sender may not have said what you think. *Don't* assume every message that catches you off-guard is a flame. It might be failed humor or unclear phrasing.

In his book *Navigating the Internet*, Mark Gibbs tells how he became angry when a woman emailed "I resent your message" to him: "Like a gold-plated, five-star idiot, I phoned and asked her, 'What the hell do you resent?' I then spent the next ten minutes jabbering my apologies. I had mistaken 're-sent' for 'resent'."

## X. *Honor confidentiality.*

Ask for permission before you forward someone else's message to another user, if you think there may be the *slightest* chance they'd be embarrassed or would feel you've violated their confidence.

# Mailing list servers

You already know you need a UUCP or SMTP server to handle your regular email. Your email software should also let you build mailing lists for email.

But with a mailing list server you can put email to work in other ways. You can set one up like a fax-back service: Your customers can send email to automatically receive your brochures, catalogs, and price lists. Because no human intervention is needed, you can offer this as a 24-hour service. Your customers specify what they want in their email, and your server sends it to them.

Here's how it works. You build informational files. Make one a company FAQ list, answering frequently-asked questions—your hours, your location, contact information, information about your products and services—whatever your prospects and customers ask the most often. Make a file for each of your press releases. Make one for what PR types call a "company backgrounder." You might want another that's a directory of who to contact in your company for what reasons and how to reach them. You can add files listing dealers who carry your products, product reviews, support notes, and information about add-on products.

Your mailing list server will read incoming messages. An incoming email containing one standard command returns a list of all commands someone can email to your server. Another standard command returns a list of all files that your server can send them. A prospect may ask for, say, your death-ray installation instructions, and your list server will send them back. The message that the server returns does not necessarily have to be a pre-existing file. Your server can generate and assemble information on demand.

In other words, a customer could send you an email request for your product catalog, and your list server could pull together your most up-to-date product descriptions and prices, build the catalog file on the fly, and email it to your customer. It could even send back different prices (and sales contact information) based on your customer's location. This use of a list server is sometimes called an email archive or a list archive.

This principle of "send one message in, get a bunch of messages out" has other applications as well. For instance, on a collaborative project, a mailing list server can coordinate communications. You can program your server to take messages from anyone working on a project, and distribute them to everyone on the project list. Thus, everyone on the project sees the same information, and no one gets left "out of the loop."

Or you can create a public discussion group, if you set up your list server so it can receive any sent messages. Your discussion-type lists can be *moderated*— which means that someone inspects and approves every message before it goes out—or unmoderated.

A list server will also automate signups to your lists. People who want to get your information, or a specific subset of your information, can send email to your list server software and your server will automatically add them to the right list or lists.

For example, Computer Literacy Bookshops run a list server that will automatically add your name to different lists. To receive advance notices of free lectures in northern California stores, send an email message to **events_carequest@clbooks.com**. To receive notices of free lectures on the East Coast, email to **events_va-request@clbooks.com**.

Mailing lists are extremely popular. There are more than 10,000 mailing lists on the Internet—no one is sure exactly how many. More than 2,000 of them are open to the public. You can set up small lists—using Internet addresses— with cc:Mail, Microsoft Mail, or Sendmail, but these require you to do a lot of the work by hand.

For a single short list of 200 to 300 names, you can use the above software, and update or edit your list by hand. People who want to subscribe to your list, have questions, or want their name removed from your list can send email to the person who manages your list. This doesn't require technical expertise, and can be done by a clerical employee with good writing and customer relations skills. However, it's good to have a knowledgable technical staffer available to answer questions, especially when responding to error messages, or when problems crop up. (Murphy's law says most list problems happen when you need to send an urgent mailing. I have scars to verify that.)

It's nice to offer the extra personal touch of processing by hand, but for each address added, deleted, or changed, someone must open a message from that addressee, read it, write down the requested action, type an email reply to the addressee, send it, and type that day's changes to your list. This takes at least a minute per name, often longer. For a thousand-name list with typical churn, you're looking at from two to three hours of tedious work per day.

Automated list management isn't as friendly, but it saves staff time and it is more accurate—no typos when adding an address to your list.

For lists longer than 200 or 300 addresses, you'll want more capable mailing list software. The most popular on the Internet are three products: Listserv, Majordomo, and ListProcessor. Without human assistance, they respond to subscription and cancellation requests, send and retrieve archived messages, and help take care of undeliverable messages that the network bounces back to your list. A human can act as list moderator and choose what messages will be sent to the list.

Sending to email lists is efficient, but contrary to some hucksters' claims, it is *not* instant. It takes time for your computer to combine your message with your list of addresses and send the finished products. If you have a list of significant length, it can take hours or even days to process your names. The amount of time depends on the message length, your connection speed, and the number of names on your list.

For whatever mailing list server software you are considering, for whatever operating system, ask these questions before you decide:

- Can this server software handle both moderated and unmoderated lists?
- Can this software check the addresses of incoming software so I can generate private lists?

- Can I split one long list into several shorter ones?
- What kind of error recovery does this software provide? What happens when the power fails or the Net connection goes down in the middle of my mailing?
- How many days or weeks will it take my system administrator to learn how to manage this software?

Less crucial, but still something to look for, is the ability to send messages in digest form. An email digest is one long message that contains several complete messages. They are not shortened versions, but often include a summary of what is in the long message file. Digest format offers your recipients a choice between receiving several smaller messages and a few long ones—an important consideration for the millions of people whose bill is based on how many messages they receive.

When planning mailing list activities, remember that you will need to reserve ongoing staff time to update your list, clean up mistakes, deal with your Internet access provider.

Depending on how large your lists grow, whether they are moderated or unmoderated, and how often you mail to them, someone will need to spend from 2 to 15 hours per list each week, updating and editing. If you mail to a list less often than once every two weeks, someone will need to spend 2 to 4 hours per mailing to prepare for the mailing, clean up bounced mail, and deal with other situations that pile up after a mailing.

To keep your list alive and healthy, you will always need to budget time and resources for it.

# Watch out! Internet Marketing is a Different Animal!

*"The Internet is a freeway into millions of homes. Direct marketers must literally ask themselves if they know what to do with this new technology. The Internet is a fascinating animal if you understand it, but I really don't think many people do, not just yet."*

Robert DeLay, president of the Direct Marketing Association

A "fascinating animal," indeed. The Net is a new and different species that marketers aren't sure how to handle.

Byron Abels-Smit of Aspen Media observes, "The Internet is not just a new medium, but a new *kind* of medium. It's like when television was new, at first advertisers treated it like print. Early TV commercials were just type and a voiceover. That only changed as people learned how to effectively use television for marketing. Newspaper rules didn't apply for TV. In the same way, print media and TV rules don't apply to the Internet."

We learn about something new by comparing it with something we already know. So, let's compare the Internet with traditional marketing channels, using such criteria as customization capabilities, cost, and prospect coverage:

- **Print media.** After something is printed, it becomes outdated eventually. But since it is easy to change Internet information, it is more often up to date. Print offers a low level of customization to match prospects' individual needs—you can do split-run advertising, but you can only fine-tune a split run into broad general categories. The Internet, on the other hand, lets you tailor exactly which information an individual receives, building custom information on the fly based on that prospect's behavior. Print media cost more per impression than the Net. Print can only send information, it cannot receive—an Internet server can do both. Print media requires a delay of hours to deliver information. The Internet delivers information almost instantly. What the Internet and print have in common is that both are *high-density* media (offering a large amount of information), both use the written word, and both require layout and visual design.

- **Broadcast media.** By its nature, broadcast is not customizable; radio and television can't communicate different information to different prospects. The Internet can. Broadcast media cannot *receive* information. The Internet can. Broadcast alone cannot complete a sale. An Internet site can handle the entire sales transaction process. Radio and television are *low-density* media; they cannot communicate a large amount of information, as Internet sites can. What the Internet and broadcast media have in common is that they both can deliver information instantly over a wide geographic area to many prospects.

- **Direct mail.** Direct mail is somewhat customizable—you can send different letters to different prospects, but the Internet is more so. There are long delays between preparation of a mail campaign, delivery of information, and subsequent response. There is almost no delay between the creation of an Internet marketing campaign, its delivery, and its response. The cost-per-impression of direct mail is enormous. The Internet's cost per impression is far less. What direct mail and the Internet have in common is that both are high-density media, both use the written word, both can be made to deliver only to targeted prospects, both can complete a sales transaction, and both are highly measurable. Also, inappropriately targeted direct mail can be seen as somewhat of an intrusion, and inappropriately targeted Internet marketing even more so.
- **Telemarketing.** A telephone salesperson can sell to only one prospect at a time. An Internet site can sell to hundreds of prospects at once. The cost-per-impression of telephone sales is higher than Internet marketing. Telemarketing is only a medium-density form of media. Both telemarketing and the Internet can customize and communicate different information to different prospects, and both can receive information, as well as send. Both can complete a transaction, and both are highly measurable. Telemarketing and the Internet share another characteristic: When inappropriately done, both are perceived as an exasperating intrusion.

When comparing similarities and differences between the Internet and other marketing channels in this way, it becomes apparent that the Internet actually has more in common with telemarketing than with any other channel. The second-closest match is direct mail. The Internet is a form of direct marketing.

What is direct marketing? The Direct Marketing Association defines it as "an interactive system of marketing which uses one or more advertising media to effect a measurable response and/or transaction at any location." The Internet is definitely "interactive," and the transaction tracking possible on the Internet fills the bill for "measurable response." In the definition, the phrase "at any location" means that your customer does not have to travel to a physical store to make a purchase. That is certainly the case on the Internet.

This doesn't mean that the only type of marketing your business can do on the Internet is direct marketing. You can use the Internet for image advertising alone, or just to provide background information. But to make full use of the marketing potential of the Net, you will need to measure response and track sales sources for Net-generated sales. Direct marketing is different from mass media marketing. If your business has no in-house direct marketing expertise, you may want to hire a consultant or an advertising agency with that background. If you plan on hiring a marketing staff to work on Internet marketing, look for candidates with direct marketing experience.

When a business uses traditional advertisements together with salespeople, the two complement each other: The mass media advertisements reach a large audience, while the salespeople provide custom information service and process the sales transactions. Most businesses need a blend of mass media advertising and salespeople to have a complete marketing capability. This is not true of Internet-based marketing. The Internet can reach a large audience, provide custom information, and process the sales transaction by itself. For these reasons, some say that the Internet is more a market than a communications medium. I believe the Net is both. It is a market and a medium, and your business will thrive if you view it the same way.

Let's take a deeper look at how the Internet is different from traditional marketing approaches.

## The Internet is misunderstood because it seems technical

In her newsletter *Marketing Technology*, editor Kristin Zhivago pointed out a key Internet difference in marketing: "The Internet is not your normal marketing vehicle. It is more technically demanding than any marketing vehicle you have ever used."

She's right. You don't have to learn how to program computers. But to market on the Net, you need to know how to reach and respond to people, and that requires learning some technical terms and being comfortable using email, the World Wide Web, FTP, newsgroups, and Gopher.

To understand the Net there is no substitute for actually spending hours on it. For example, you need to read enough newsgroups to understand not just how they work, but more importantly for marketers, *how people using them feel*. If you don't have enough hands-on experience actually surfing the Net, finding information, and communicating with Internet people, you will never understand the intense emotional bond that has pushed the Internet to grow so fast so quickly. Remember, email has become the *preferred* method of business communication of Net users. This is not just a rational, logical decision. It is also an emotional decision. What makes people enjoy email so much? If you don't use email yourself, you will never be able to apply email effectively as a marketing tool. The same holds true for newsgroups, mailing lists, and the World Wide Web.

This lack of understanding in marketers leads to interesting blunders and mistakes on the Net, and to a lot of dumb-sounding statements from marketing people.

One came recently from Woolward & Partners, a San Francisco agency that handles mostly high-tech clients. In a story about client Logitech, Inc., a company sponsoring an Internet-based magazine for teenagers, Francesca Castagnoli was quoted as saying: "Being on the Net first gives you the status of respected elder statesmen. The people who come on later look like tourists." Wrong! Anyone on the Net for three months knows that people care about your content, not how gray your beard is. Especially screenagers.

Here's another case of missing the boat: Camille Johnson, senior vice president and media director at ad agency Goldberg Moser O'Neill, in defending traditional ad media, was quoted as saying, "You can put together a sophisticated interactive program full of all sorts of detailed product information, but there's only so much hard data consumers want to know about Dreyer's Ice Cream." She would never have said that if she had spent two weeks on the Web.

This misses the point that Internet marketing is about *communication* and *interaction*, the foundations of emotional intimacy. If you understand the Net, you can use it to build a stronger emotional tie between you and your customer. And people can get pretty emotional about ice cream, which is a non-rational comfort food. For an example of involving food marketing, take a look at **http://www.hot.presence.com/hot**. You'll find a fun site called Hot Hot Hot selling bottled hot sauce—and doing it so entertainingly that it generated international media coverage!

## The Internet gives you *two-way* marketing

We mentioned this earlier, and will elaborate on it here. For marketers, the Internet's interactivity is both its greatest strength and its biggest source of puzzlement. If you've been designing print advertisements all your life, it'll take you a while to figure out what to make out of this interactivity.

Try thinking of the Net as a conversation between you and your prospects and customers. Phineas Gay, of Internet marketing agency Direct Results Group puts it succinctly: "Internet marketing is *dialogue*—exchanging information—as opposed to *monologue*—which regular advertising is."

In other words, don't talk *at* your Internet customers. Talk *with* them. When you make information available, always provide a way for your readers to respond. Ask how they feel. Solicit responses. Every FTP file, your Gopher readme file, and others should tell how to get more information, and provide your traditional contact information (address, phone, fax, email, Web address). Different prospects want different information, so give them choices. The Net's ability to provide customized information will help you do this. Providing choices will *give your prospects the feeling of control.*

This feeling of control helps your prospect understand your marketing messages. In a recent study by P.L. Wright, subjects who could control the pace of reading and pause to evaluate the information could better explain what they read and could also more clearly define their own points of agreement and disagreement than people who read the same material in a timed video presentation. The more strongly the readers cared about the topic, the more the feeling of control increased comprehension. Wright's findings echo Jean Piaget's and Seymour Papert's theory that the more someone can manipulate and control a presentation, the more that person can internalize it.

The interactivity of information presented on the Internet increases readers' perception of being in control. Anything you do to add to this perception increases a prospect's emotional involvement with your site. Look for opportunities wherever you can to provide your customers with opportunities for control and feedback. Ask for customer comments about your site. Ask them about your service. There are an infinite number of ways to use the Internet to increase your customers' involvement. Publisher Catbird Press went so far as to put drafts of a novel online so the public could comment and suggest revisions.

In traditional marketing media, prospects don't take your communications as personally as they do on the Net. This intense involvement can lead to intense responses. This can be good, but the emotionality is also what leads to flames and anger as well. Internet customers can be more volatile than your other clients. That's why it's especially important for all your marketing people on the Net to learn about *netiquette.*

"Netiquette is not just about the niceties of behavior or avoiding embarassment. Netiquette is like the double yellow line in the middle of a highway," said Internet pioneer Howard Rheingold. He's right. Your prospects on the Internet will not tolerate the kind of obtrusive advertising found in other media. Make sure your marketing communications will be welcomed before you post or email them someplace. Always ask permission before emailing advertising or literature to someone. Millions of people pay for each message *received.* They won't be happy to pay for a surprise mailing from your business, and since the Internet makes it easy to respond, you will hear about it. So might thousands of your sales prospects.

You can get short-term sales and tons of hate mail or you can build a loyal, long-lasting base of repeat Internet customers. Which would you rather do? Fortunately, two pathetic lawyers from Arizona served as global guinea pigs, sparing the rest of us tons of pain. Posting messages to inappropriate places is called a *spam attack,* and the lawyers spammed thousands of Usenet newsgroups with an ad that offered help in getting a U.S. immigration Green Card. The lawyers made some quick sales, but did nothing to build their prospects' goodwill. They received tens of thousands of hate messages, and upset Internet people used modems to jam the lawyers' phones and fax machine—an example of the backlash made possible by the Net's interactivity.

This sort of newsgroup spamming is harder to do now. Newsgroups are protected by software programs called *cancelbots,* which patrol the groups and remove messages posted on large numbers of newsgroups. Besides cancelbots, the Net offers other punishments for those who abuse its interactivity. Keep in mind the importance of stuff like flames and mail bombs that I covered in earlier chapters. Wise companies follow the rules of netiquette because it is in their own self-interest to do so. They don't need the pain. ("Gee, I'd wondered why big companies haven't slathered ads all over the newsgroups. I thought it was just because they were polite." Yeah, right. I'm sure Microsoft folds its napkin after every meal.)

Here is an example of an actual spammed advertisement and its aftermath. I This message appeared on a newsgroup that exists solely to discusss the PageMaker desktop publishing software package.

```
Newsgroups: alt.aldus.pagemaker
Subject: FREE PAGER!
From: (name deleted)@aol.com
Save 10-45% on your long distance service every month.
Attention
Now you can receive big discounts on your long distance calls that other
companies only promise. NTC Dial-1 ressisential and business long distance
services and travel cards offer 6-second billing, prompt payment and volume
discounts combined with great domestic and international rates.
FREE PAGE OFFER LIMITED BY TIME
For more information:
e-Mail
(name deleted)@aol.com
```

"But what's so bad about one little message?" You mean, besides the spelling? This group is about PageMaker. The spammed message is not. It's like a stranger interrupting a Baptist revival meeting with a sermon praising Druids. People read this newsgroup to find out about PageMaker. Some of them pay for each message. They paid to read this commercial. And this spammer is not the only person who does this. Other businesses try, and newsgroup readers feel that to prevent their groups from becoming a sea of advertisements with only occasional islands of news, they must respond forcefully to each and every inappropriate message posted.

Heated responses to an inappropriate newsgroup posting like this are normally emailed directly to the sender of the message, but one person slipped up. He accidentally posted his flame to the entire PageMaker group instead of sending it directly to the person who wrote the above spam.

```
Newsgroups: alt.aldus.pagemaker
Subject: Re: FREE PAGER!
From: (Reply name deleted)
Here's a helpful piece of advice: Get the hell out of our newsgroup with
shit like that before one of us finds out your phone number, ok?
(Reply name deleted)
```

This is a very mild flame. It was one of dozens of messages sent to the spammer. My guess is that a reader of the **alt.aldus.pagemaker** group noticed that the spam came from an America Online subscriber. (The spammer's Internet address ends with **@aol.com**.) That person forwarded the spam to the postmaster of America Online, who must have told the spammer to send an apology to the spammed newsgroups or America Online would terminate his account. America Online puts up with no nonsense. If an AOL subscriber blatantly violates netiquette, AOL kicks the subscriber off its system. The spammer subsequently posted an apology and promised never to spam again.

As a marketer, the thing to remember about this exchange is the message from the offended newsgroup reader. It is a reminder of the interactive, two-way nature of Internet marketing. In the same way, your prospects will get angry if you misuse the interactivity and praise you if you apply it properly.

## The Internet markets to different demographics

And who are these people to whom you market interactively? Net folks are upscale, well-educated, more highly paid than average, and early technology adapters.

Around 1976, researchers with The Yankee Group discovered a demographic cluster they called "Technically Advanced Families," or Taffies for short. "They represent about 10 million families who are already putting pieces together," explained Yankee Group managing director Howard Anderson in a December, 1994 *Upside* interview. "Any new service or product that succeeds, succeeds with this group first. For example, only 14 percent of the American homes now have a modem, but 54 percent of Taffie families not only have a modem, they are bitching and screaming that it's not fast enough. When some families are glued to the radio on snow days to see if school has been cancelled, the Taffie families have already queried the school computer on the Internet and rolled back to sleep."

A large proportion of Internet users are based in government, non-profit groups, and higher education—organizations whose culture downgrades commercialism. They distrust businesses to begin with. To win new customers, you have to overcome that attitude first.

It will be worth your while. Don't make the mistake that a *San Francisco Chronicle* reporter did and assume that academia, for instance, is not a lucrative market. Solange Van de Moer of Infinity Marketing (and one of the most experienced Internet marketers anyplace) corrected the *Chronicle's* assumptions. "There are 46 million people in the United States between the ages of 18 and 29, including graduates and undergraduates. That is a very important market. It spends $125 billion yearly in *discretionary* spending. To come to the conclusion that because they're mostly in academia they don't spend any money is *ludicrous*."

Van de Moer says the *Chronicle* ignored "Marketing Rule Number One: Know your customer. Most customer service problems and strategic marketing errors happen because companies don't know their customers." She relates that Infinity Marketing's experience is that Net users are predominently young and male, "Probably not great for Avon cosmetics, but it *is* good for sellers of information, or for products which require information to purchase."

However, Judith Resnick, who studies Net demographics, says that women are growing faster than any other demographic group. This is backed up by the experience of the *Electric Examiner*, the online version of San Francisco's other daily paper, the *San Francisco Examiner* (**http://www.sfgate.com**). One of the most popular spots in the *Electric Examiner* is Women's Web, which directs readers to resources on the Net for women. Another demographically revealing piece of data from the *Electric Examiner* is that its main Web page use time is 6 a.m. to 3 p.m. PST, with an 11 a.m. peak. This means that most readers reach this Web site during business hours, while they are at home or at school. The *Electric Examiner*'s Web server saves domain names of readers, so its marketers can see what kind of people visit. How many are from the business domain **.com**? How many from the academic domain **.edu**? They found the highest percentage of *Electric Examiner* readers are at high-tech companies—two-thirds of its readers are **.com**.

Business-hour use of the Internet is confirmed by Barry Parr of *Mercury Center*, the online version of Knight-Ridder's *San Jose Mercury News*. Parr sees the Internet as a completely distinct market from the commercial services such as America Online, based on *Mercury Center* use, which has sites both on America Online and on the Internet. *Mercury Center* on America Online is busiest in the evenings, when people use it at home. *Mercury Center* on the Internet is busiest in the middle of the day Monday through Friday, when people use it at work. "A year from now," said Parr, "that's not going to be true. Folks from America Online and CompuServe will spend as much time on the Web as people from the Internet. It will be a 24-hour operation."

Companies of all sizes are on the Net, good news for businesses whose customers are other businesses. In the U.S., there is a trend of more home-based businesses opening every year. This group of companies is a fast-growing market, with 3 to 3.5 million positively identified in the U.S., and the real number closer to 10 to 12 million. Canadian research is not as clear. A survey by Syntony Marketing identified 242,000 people who stated that they operate a home business in Canada, but the total is probably closer to one million when you consider the rapid rate of new home-business startups. Many new business trends begin in the U.S. and migrate to other countries. Home-based businesses may be one. And many home businesses use the Net to communicate.

Unlike print ads or TV, Internet people are information junkies. They want as much information and as great a level of detail as you can present. Long copy sells on the Internet.

There is a clear demographic skew in Internet users toward younger people. This was backed up by a 1994 survey sponsored by the Institute of Electrical and Electronics Engineers (IEEE). It found that 44 percent of Americans were interested in receiving mail by computer, among them 21 percent who were "very interested." The interesting thing about the survey was that the strongest demographic differential was neither sex—about the same percentage of males and females are "very interested" in receiving email—nor income levels, but *age*. Almost 40 percent of 18-to-24-year-olds were "very interested" in email, but the percentage dropped to 32.8 percent in the 25-to-34 group, 18 percent in the 35-to-49 age group, a mere 9.1 percent in the 50-to-64 age group, and only 8.8 percent in the 65-and-over age group.

When you market on the Internet, many people you reach are members of Generation X. They have a distaste for blatant advertising and see through overly commercial messages.

For demographics on Internet size and World Wide Web use, FTP to **ftp:// nic.merit.edu/nsfnet/statistics**. You'll find text and graphics showing monthly gross before April 1995. World Wide Web use nearly tripled from July to November of 1994, and doubled in one month, from September to November of 1994. Readership of Usenet newsgroups is also growing. Network Wizards, a company in Menlo Park, California, counts the number of hosts on the Net and estimates how many people have accessed these host systems. Take a peek at **http://www.nw.com** to see their numbers.

The Internet has a population larger than any city in the world, and bigger than many countries and states. Its population is so diverse that mass mailings just don't work. Thousands of different networks make up the Internet, and the people who use them have hardly anything in common except literacy and the use of a keyboard. You've got right wingers, left wingers, and middle-of-the-roaders. You've got Jews, Christians, Moslems, Buddhists, Hindus, and nonbelievers. You've got people who hate animals, professional livestock handlers, and people with 14 cats. Companies often spend a fortune to pinpoint the kind of target markets you can pick up for free on the Internet.

The most realistic view is to remember that the Internet is really not one big market, but a bunch of markets from large to tiny. The great strength for marketing is that you can narrowcast and pick exactly the kind of prospects you want for your message. If you offer a World Wide Web site, your prospects will be *self-selecting*; if you promote your site, and they are interested in what you offer, they will come to you.

## The Internet markets to the world

The concept of boundaryless marketing is one of the most difficult to convey to non-Internet users. On the Net, it is not just easier or less expensive to reach prospects in other countries. When you use the Internet for marketing, you quickly discover that borders simply don't matter!

Convincing politicians of this fact is extremely difficult, with the result being that many countries have silly laws restricting cross-border marketing. More uselessly, some are thinking of regulating Internet marketing, forgetting that the Net is beyond the control of any one country.

The Federation of European Direct Marketing (FEDIM) is working with European governments to guarantee marketers equal access to the Net. Some European countries tried to regulate the Internet under television rules, claiming that any moving image on a screen is television, including online computer services. As television, the Net would come under restrictive rules about content, with a guaranteed percentage of local content! This is nuts. What are they going to do, tie up Frenchmen and force them to post more newsgroup messages? Fortunately, saner minds prevailed.

France is the country with the largest percentage of online sales, but few of those go through the Internet. France's Minitel network is a $2 billion business for France Telecom. Some 15 percent of all French direct purchases are made through Minitel, another 25 percent by phone and the remaining 60 percent by mail. Compare this to the U.S., where sales via the Internet, CompuServe, America Online, and all other services together add up to less than one percent of total direct sales. French people are used to buying online.

Most messages on the Internet are in English, but not all. Estimates of English use among Internet users range from 75 percent to 85 percent. People from many countries speak their mother language plus English. Many Japanese—especially Japanese Internet users—are comfortable with English. The Japanese education includes six years of written English, and Japanese are interested in and apt to buy from other countries.

## The Internet markets faster

On the Internet, the timespan between concept, execution, and customer response is sometimes so short that it's startling. No other media can match this two-way speed of delivery.

Internet advertising agency Poppe Tyson's Web page (**http://www.poppe.com**) puts it this way: "On-line information is all about instant gratification—all the information you what, whenever you want it, in any sequence you like. On-line selling, if properly designed, can be the ultimate in thoroughness and responsiveness. And it can get customers to their decision faster."

Speed matters on the Internet. People get used to fresh information, delivered quickly, and near-instant responses. Word-of-mouth travels with shocking speed. When something hot (or truly awful) is discovered on the Net, an email blizzard alerts people all over the planet. In a matter of days, it's old hat.

This creates an Internet phenomena known as *flash crowds*. The term comes from a story by author Larry Niven. Flash crowds happen when an Internet site receives a sudden, huge surge in visits, followed by an equally sudden dropoff a week or two later. A site's listing on the *NCSA What's New Page*, for instance, has sent an extra 10,000 to 20,000 visitors in one week to some Web sites. When new listings bump the Web sites off the page, the visitation rate immediately drops, almost to previous levels.

Novelty and newness have strong drawing power on the Net. The search for freshness gets more extreme with people who spend more time on the Net. For such people, it is literally true that something added to a Web site two weeks ago is old, and information a month old is positively ancient. This is why you need to constantly update your Internet site. If you want to generate repeat business, you want repeat visitors. To get repeat visitors, you need to feed them a steady stream of new information. Your Web site should be updated at least once a week. More often is better.

Internet customers will also judge you by the speed of your response. Do you ask for customer feedback? Then you need to respond to it, and quickly. Assign responsibility to someone for maintaining Internet customer dialogue. This person or people should read and respond to customer email every day, or even better, several times every day. The standard for the customer service department of retailer Hammacher Schlemmer is to answer all customer email within five minutes.

Like so much else on the Internet, responsiveness is a two-way street. If you respond more quickly to your Internet customers, they will be more responsive to you.

## The Internet markets inexpensively

Although we've covered this before, let's review one more time how the Internet stacks up against other marketing media:

- Relatively low setup cost
- Low cost of updating information
- Low cost of providing customized information
- Low cost of transaction processing
- Extremely low cost of delivering information
- Negligible cost of providing information to an additional prospect
- Low cost of increasing the quantity of information
- Little additional cost to deliver a high density of information

## Internet marketing options

To old-school marketers, one of the confusing aspects of the Internet is that, unlike any traditional media, you have many different things to do and many different ways to do them. If you create a print advertisement, you know it will run in a printed publication. On the Internet, you might use Gopher, newsgroups, or an email list to spread your words, or MIME or the World

Wide Web to deliver graphics. It might help to think of the Internet as a collection of somewhat different media rather than a single medium.

As far as what you can actually do on the Internet from a marketing point of view, all activities can be roughly grouped into the following five levels in order of cost, complexity, and amount of time to implement:

## 1. Netlurking and publicity

This is the easiest method of Internet marketing and it costs the least to do. All you need is email and access to Usenet newsgroups. Monitor the newsgroups where your customers hang out. When someone asks a question that you can answer, be helpful and do so. (Provide real, usable information, not just instructions to buy your product.) Your answers should have your sig file, which will carry your business and name before your prospects. This sounds so simple as to be useless, but I have talked to several businesses selling more than a million dollars a year that use netlurking as their primary—and in some cases, only—method of marketing.

T.R. Sills, operator of The Entrepreneur Connection (**mailto: trsills@ccgate.hac.com**) says that hundreds of dollars in print advertising generated half the response that one posting on the Net brought in. Sills checks business newsgroups daily, looking for posted business questions to which he can provide an answer, such as telling someone how to perform his own patent search. Sills' answers trade knowledge for publicity.

If your posted answers provide genuine, useful information, you will not be flamed, you will be welcomed. You can also use the Internet to email electronic press releases to appropriate (that's the key word, *appropriate*) sites, especially to print magazines and electronic publications that cover your industry.

I'd add the need to provide email lists to your customers in this beginning category as well. It costs a little, but if you can regularly deliver useful information to a list of prospects and customers, the sales generated will usually be much higher than your effort and expense.

# UnCover: An Internet marketing success story

CARL Systems, Inc. of Denver, Colorado, markets software that automates library catalogs. In 1988, it launched a product called UnCover, a database of the tables of contents from thousands of scholarly journals. The database was available only through the Internet. People in the industry thought CARL Systems was crazy to offer no print equivalent, saying that the Internet wasn't big enough to be a "real" market. Naysayers predicted that UnCover would never break even, let alone generate a profit. Fortunately for CARL Systems, the pessimists were wrong. By early 1993, UnCover had grown so profitable that CARL Systems spun it off as a separate company.

The UnCover database was originally on the CARL computer in Denver, Colorado. Customers paid an annual fee based on the number of people within the client company who had access to UnCover. Access has soared from 500 hits per day in 1990 to thousands now.

In early 1990, UnCover added a new service: delivery of articles. Customers could find an article in the UnCover table of contents database, order it online and pay for it online via credit card, all in one transaction. The company set up internal systems to process the anticipated order volume, and linked with a bank so it could verify credit cards while its customers were still connected online. This added substantial overhead to each UnCover transaction, but let CARL Systems expand its prospect base from educational institutions and corporate libraries (which paid a monthly bill for UnCover use) to millions of small companies and individual researchers. Articles are delivered via fax for about $8.50 each. Since beginning its new service, UnCover has sold and delivered tens of thousands of documents. Document delivery is so profitable that UnCover has made its original product free. Company management reasons correctly that its free table of contents database is now a promotional come-on for buying articles. This clicks with the experiences of other companies, which again and again show that giving information away for free is one of the most effective lures for Internet customers.

How else does the UnCover Company (**http://www.carl.org/uncover/ unchome.html**) use the Net as a marketing tool? It provides updates over the Net to customers on new services. It trains new customers how to use its system. It lets customers check order status, review their account history, and check their current account balance. It maintains a mailing list to answer customer questions and to elicit customer suggestions for improvement. And the company teamed with Journal Graphics to offer an online index of transcripts of television news programs over the Internet, selling the transcripts for payment. The new service is available only over the Internet, and it is a success.

## 2. *Showing your products and services*

You may be familiar with "fax on demand" services. This is the Internet equivalent, and in the case of a Web site, with the added impact that color graphics deliver. It's a low-cost alternative to literature fulfillment, and you can update it instantly and always add more information to it.

There are three things you'll need to do. First, you have to translate your exisiting literature into HTML (for a Web page) or ASCII format (for a mailing list server, or an FTP or Gopher server) and arrange your literature for maximum Net usability. Second, you need to allow time to monitor customer responses to your site, review what worked and what didn't. Then apply that information to fine-tune your content and format to keep your site useful, interesting, and easy to use. Third, you need to educate prospects and customers about where they should look and what they should expect. If you don't tell them what you want them to do, they won't do it.

Note that most Internet sites of this type, especially World Wide Web home pages, fail to generate a desirable level of response. If you use the Internet to showcase your products and services, you must be prepared to promote your site on a continuing basis.

## 3. *Processing orders and inquiries*

When used for lead fulfillment and human-assisted order processing, the Internet lets you rapidly gather customer feedback about your products, marketing, and customer service. What answers are missing from your literature? You'll quickly find out, because your Internet customers will tell you. Handling orders and inquiries on the Net can be a useful customer service. If done properly, it fosters interest and generates goodwill among your prospects.

You'll need to allow for staffing needs so customer service reps can devote time every day to answering questions on the Net. You'll quickly see the need to develop a library of stock answers and form letters for questions you hear repeatedly. You'll need to set up a mechanism to track sales leads and pass them to your sales or marketing people. When using the Internet for this level of marketing, allowing time to support your customers and your Internet site will be the crucial ingredient for success.

## 4. *Processing payment transactions*

At this level of marketing, the Net lets you create electronic "mail order." Your customers can place an order without direct human intervention. This is a significant increase in time and money invested compared to the previous level. And security becomes a much more serious issue.

To succeed at transaction processing, your back-office order fullfillment is extremely important. Besides credit card processing or billing, you also need to plan for sales tax management and the physical shipment of products—probably internationally. At this stage, the reliability of your Internet access provider becomes mission-critical, because when your provider is down, your cash flow drops dead. Depending on your sales volume, you might look for two or more phone lines to link to your provider, or, use two providers so if one provider goes down, your orders still come in.

## 5. *Actually delivering products and services over the Net*

This is only suitable for certain kinds of businesses. Software, information reports, consulting, and research of all kinds can actually be delivered over the

Net. Several companies deliver online versions of books over the Net, and QuoteCom (**http://www.quote.com**) sells stock information, delivered by email.

The challenges of online product delivery are internal and external security, the need for a secure delivery method, and export control. (Export regulations depend on your product or service, the laws of your country, and the laws of your customer's country.) For some products, *copy protection* is also an issue. This prevents your customer from turning around and reselling your product to others without your permission.

## Ten steps to marketing on the Net

The wrong approach to Internet marketing is to take your existing marketing materials, scan them, dump them on a Web page, and walk away. You won't reach many prospects, and those who you do encounter won't be too impressed. Here is a ten-step process to help implement Internet marketing that generates more positive results.

**1. Investigate and analyze the Net as a marketing medium.**

We're talking hands-on experience here. Reading this book by itself (or any other book, for that matter) will not give you a clear understanding of how the Internet works and how to use it effectively as a marketing tool. Grab a keyboard and jump in.

**2. Define your Internet objectives to fit with your other marketing efforts.**

Treat Internet marketing as a *supplement* to your existing, traditional marketing methods, not as a *substitute*. There are few markets in either the consumer or the business-to-business arenas that offer enough Internet penetration for you to go all-Internet and drop other methods of marketing communications.

So don't expect the Internet to do everything. It won't. You will still need salespeople. You will still need customer service. You will still need other forms of marketing communications. And, more than ever, you will need to coordinate all parts of your marketing effort so they all reinforce your movement towards your overall goals. Don't let the pretty little Web pictures make you lose sight of the more important big picture of your business objectives.

# Internet marketing guidelines

These guidelines are suggested by the New York office of Ogilvy & Mather Direct, whose Interactive Marketing Group is the largest, most experienced, and best-regarded (the only one to receive a four-star rating from *Advertising Age*) agency for creating interactive advertisements.

"Unbridled commercialization will likely crush what is most precious about the Internet," the group stated. "These guidelines are offered as a starting point towards the responsible participation of marketers on the Internet."

**1. Intrusive email is not welcome.**

No one should receive a message they haven't either asked to receive, or more generally, want to receive. If a user requests information from companies that sell ski equipment, the companies within this category should be able to send this user relevant information. They may offer to add the user's address to their list server, but under no circumstances should an inquiry result in an automatic subscription.

**2. Internet consumer data is not for resale without the express permission of the user.**

Unlike commercial services, where it is clearly understood that data generated through consumer interaction is being sold to marketers, Internet data should remain the private property of the user.

Using the ski example, the fact that I have requested information via the Internet should not de facto allow the ski company to resell my behavioral data to, say, SAAB—which may be interested in reaching ski enthusiasts.

**3. Advertising is allowed only in designated newsgroups and list servers.**

The most objectionable form of advertising on the Internet comes in the form of off-topic commercial postings to newsgroups and list server conferences, usually cross-posted to dozens or hundreds of groups.

These postings generally draw harsh flames from readers, but such feedback may not be sufficient to stop this type of abuse.

Those who post off-topic commercial solicitations should be warned once, then filtered at the source from any commercial postings.

4. **Promotions and direct selling are allowed, but only under full disclosure.**

Marketers should be free to offer promotions from their own domains, but users should be given an opportunity to clearly review the rules, guidelines, and parameters of the event before they commit. Promotions should be subjected to the same guidelines as above—all promotions should be self-selected.

We suggest the recommendations be consistent with those developed for analog merchants by the Direct Marketing Association, and modified or enhanced to reflect the unique attributes of electronic delivery.

5. **Consumer research is allowed only with the consumer's full consent.**

Marketers should be able to conduct consumer research as long as respondents have ready and easy access to information outlining the uses and implications of participating in the market research survey.

6. **Internet communications software must never hide concealed functions.**

Several years ago, a commercial online service was accused of using its terminal software to scan users' hard disks for text that appeared to be an address. The program would then allegedly collect this data, and, unknown to the user, send it to the service for use in compiling mailing lists.

As client/server applications become more prevalent on the Internet, the opportunity for this type of abuse increases.

**3. Determine how you want your prospect to respond.**

We are not talking some generality like "have warm, fuzzy feelings about our company." That is vague and useless. Instead, be specific. Where do you want your prospect to go? What do you want that prospect to do? What steps, in what specific order? How will you measure if your prospect has done this? If your prospect's response isn't measurable in some way, you will never know if your Internet marketing works or not.

**4. What is your competitive advantage?**

You should already know this. It should be one, short, memorable sentence. Short, because Internet people move quickly. A typical Generation X male Internet user paying $3.00 an hour to use the Internet (some pay more), will not sit still long enough to wade through two screens of boilerplate to find out just what (if anything) makes your company different from its competitors. And, please, don't say something vague like "People helping people help people." Yuck! Be specific. Computer Literacy Bookshops offers "the world's largest selection of computer books." That's short and tells you how that company differs from the rest. Don't worry about being cute. Just be clear.

You need to know your competitive advantage before you plan your Internet marketing so your Internet projects can all reinforce that advantage.

**5. What are the key benefits of your product or service that most sharply convey that advantage?**

Again, you should already know this. For Internet marketing, you may want to look at your key benefits from a different angle. Which benefits would be most important to a prospect who uses the Internet? This may cause you to reorder some priorities in a way that will make more impact on the Net.

**6. Outline how you will communicate those benefits and your competitive advantage.**

Will you use a World Wide Web server? Will you build a customer mailing list? What Internet tools will you use?

**7. Figure out what information you need to present.**

You can Internetize listings of dealers, contact information for sales reps, data sheets, support information. If you keep up-to-date product information on your Net site, your distributors and resellers have uninterrupted access to the facts they need to promote and sell your products.

Look at the information you already have, and look at what new information you could create. When starting out, don't go overboard. Select only the most important information that would be easiest to deliver on the Net. Look for the information that will generate the biggest results, and for what is most "doable."

### 8. Turn it into digital versions.

The cost of presenting information on the Internet is influenced by how much information your company already has on disk. If you have the information you need already in electronic format from your catalogs, press releases, product specifications, or newsletters, it's easy to copy the information to your Internet server. Don't get too elaborate. Start simple.

Note that if you have a lot of information, an FTP server or Gopher server can be easier to set up than a World Wide Web server. To create a file for FTP or Gopher, your information just needs to be in the common ASCII format. For the Web, someone needs to translate all documents into HTML.

### 9. Put your information on the Internet.

Put your files in one directory on your server (give them helpful filenames; Z9893422.txt doesn't give your customers a clue) and you're set. Name your directory something easy to remember. As your content grows, open up subdirectories under your main directory. Add some free stuff. Giveaways are a cheap way of generating goodwill among the Internet community, and also good "word-of-net" publicity.

### 10. Promote, promote, promote.

Remember, most Internet sites—especially Web pages—are undervisited. If you want yours to be a winner, you need to put your email address and home page address on your business cards, letterhead, advertisements, and brochures. Make your Internet addresses as prominent as your 800 number. Publicize your site to print media and to electronic publications on the Internet.

# How to Generate Internet Publicity that Works

*"When I turn my computer on, money comes out of it. And I never spent a penny for advertising."*
Paolo Pignatelli, owner of Internet merchant The Corner Store

This might seem like an odd statement, but on the Internet it's hard to tell publicity from advertising. There is often a considerable debate over whether a certain thing is or is not an Internet advertisement, so classification becomes a matter of opinion.

In printed magazines, the line of demarcation is simple. If you pay for an insertion, it's an advertisement. If you don't pay, it's publicity. But on the Internet, some types of communication are considered advertising even though they are free. In fact, Internet people will complain loudly if you violate a non-advertising space with a free advertisement. The very term "free advertisement" suggests that there must be another differentiator besides the paid/free distinction.

The somewhat arbitrary classification I will use for this chapter and for the next chapter is simple. I will cover the types of communication that Internet people usually refer to as advertisements in the advertising chapter. And I will cover other marketing communications that are not considered advertising in this chapter.

It's like a famous quote from Montaigne: "A word is half his who speaks it, half his who hears it." In other words, if your reader thinks it's an ad, it is.

## Traditional publicity, Internet style

The job title may be publicist, public relations manager, or media relations specialist, but the core job duties are the same in businesses all over the world.

One of the most frustrating parts of the job is when you spend a lot of time creating a stupendous story idea just to pitch it to one of the media gatekeepers and get turned down. That's when angry PR people say, "Oh! If only I were a publisher!" Well, guess what? You can be. As Tim O'Reilly, president of book publisher O'Reilly & Associates said, "On the Internet, *everyone* is a publisher."

There are so many ways to publicize your business on the Internet, it is truly amazing. On the Net, your problem is not "How can I find one way to get the word out?" but "There are so many ways! Which do I choose first?"

And you have one other problem. It is life or death for you to understand Net culture. Every good marcom person knows that to win a customer, you can't expect the customer to learn your language. You must speak the customer's language. In the same way, you must learn the language and customs of the Internet. Since the Internet is interactive, if you punch people's buttons on the Net, they punch back, only harder. You won't make too many sales that way. Go out on the Net and study it for a couple of weeks (especially the newsgroup **alt.current-events.net-abuse**) before you send out any electronic publicity.

"So I can use email to send press releases to everybody on the planet and post them to all of the newsgroups, right?" Not exactly. In fact, not at all. Most places on the Net consider press releases to be advertisements, and many newsgroups forbid any type of advertising or anything even close to it. Don't think you can send press releases to the general public on the Internet. With a few exceptions (explained in this book's advertising chapter), you can use the Internet to send press releases only to media contacts.

## *Distributing your press releases on the Net*

The easiest way to send press releases electronically is to build a list of email addresses. You probably already have a contact database, whether it's on Rolodex cards or stored in a dBase program. If your contact list already has email addresses, that gives you a start. Your network administrator will need two files, one with your email address list and one with an ASCII text version of your press release (not a file in your word processor's format). Your email software will combine the two files and send them out.

That's a brief description of how to do it. Here is a cautionary note. Many reporters and writers have email addresses, but do not like to receive emailed press releases. Others prefer email versions. (Columnist John Dvorak said that he won't even look at a hard-copy release.) You will need to talk to each person on your list and ask how he or she would prefer to receive releases.

I know of no specific study that says whether emailed releases or printed releases generate more coverage, but some publicists swear that using postal mail produces a far greater response than sending email releases. This may differ depending on the types of media with which your business deals.

You might like to build different kinds of lists for different purposes. Perhaps one for media contacts and one for dealers—if those are people who receive your printed releases now. You will also want to send your electronic releases to sales representatives and other appropriate people within your company. You can ask customers and prospects if they would like to receive your news via email, and you may be surprised at how many will sign up. Don't put customers' names on your emailing list unless they *ask* to be on, though. Along the same lines, it is a good idea not to offer your list to other businesses to send out their releases. Some people get upset when they receive email from an unfamiliar source, much more upset than they would get over receiving postal mail from a company they didn't know.

When you send out email press releases, you will generate responses by email. People who respond by email usually want a quicker response time than someone who responds by mail. For a point of comparison, think of an emailed publicity response as being slightly less urgent than a telephone call. Emailers will expect your response within 24 hours, the faster the better. Since most businesses hear variations of the same questions again and again, canned responses can save you time and keep your prospects and customers happy with your promptness. These canned responses are just standard text files that you can pull into your email software, customize with a person's name and other specifics, and send out.

Besides canned responses to questions, make emailable versions of the other components of your press kit. A backgrounder about your company, lists of dealers, product information, price lists, executive bios, and other handouts will all be useful in electronic form. Your electronic press kit will need one other document that Internet users will expect. It is called a FAQ.

## Creating a FAQ

FAQ stands for "Frequently Asked Questions," and your FAQ document will be a list of them in question-and-answer format. Take a look at some of the FAQs out there to get a better understanding of how to format your own.

Your FAQ will be read online. People mostly read the first part of online documents and often don't make it all the way to the end. Put your journalism school classes to use by putting your most important information and most often-asked questions right up front. I recommend starting your FAQ with a brief (ten to twelve lines) summary of what's to come.

Update your FAQ information often—at least once a month. Twice a month is better. Highlight new material by putting *NEW* in front of it. A FAQ should not be a sales sheet, but a background piece about your company and your products. It should not be longer than the equivalent of five to seven pages of typewritten press release copy.

Once your FAQ is complete, you want to make sure it is seen. You should include your FAQ as a file in your FTP and Gopher servers (if you have them) and as a page on your World Wide Web server. You can also set up a mail server to automatically hand out your FAQ to anyone who sends email to **faq@yourco.com**. You can contact organizations that offer archive sites of information on your industry and ask if they'd like to provide your FAQ.

## *Formatting emailed announcements*

When creating Internet press releases and any other electronic publicity materials, there are a few things to keep in mind. First, there is an important distinction between the headline of your story and the Subject line of your story. The headline is the traditional journalistic head you put above the first page of the body of your release. The Subject line is what your addressee sees when he or she receives an incoming email message. Your addressee will make the decision to open or not to open your emailed release based almost entirely on what you type as your message's Subject. Most email software gives only a fixed amount of space to display a message's Subject, and cuts off what doesn't fit. Some software has room for forty characters, and some only twenty. So make your Subject short, catchy, and put the most important words first. You can put more information in your message's headline.

At the top of an emailed press release, you don't need to put the same contact information that you would include in a hard-copy press release. By default, an email message starts with email header information. Screen real estate is limited, and many of the people who open your message (one publicist I know says way more than half) will never look beyond your first screenful of copy. Start immediately with your headline, and follow with the most urgent, high-impact information your story contains. Since you want to have as much of your message as possible on the first screen—the only part of your message that most of your readers will see—don't format your headline so it takes up several precious lines of first screen real estate. Make it fit on as few lines as possible.

Another point of loud debate is how long your announcement body should be. Some people say your message should all fit on one or two screens of type. Some say it doesn't matter. Book publisher O'Reilly & Associates has had experience longer than almost any other company sending Internet press releases, and uses three to four screens. My experience is that announcement length should depend on the type of announcements you send, to whom you send them, and how often you send. This may sound obvious, but include only *useful* information. Cut out the company boilerpate. People view emailed messages as a more personal communication, and resent fluff. If you send only to reporters who expect press releases, they expect longer material. For the general public, I'd keep announcements two screens long, or three at the most. If you send two or more announcements a month, shorter, two-screen messages will be better received.

At the bottom of each emailed press release or announcement, place your contact information. This is usually just the signature file of the marcom person who wrote the message. The one thing important is to have a *person* to reply to, not a *department*. For example, saying that your announcement is from "Marketing Department, Yourco., email marketing@yourco.com" will not work. You need a person to whom recipients can respond, and that person's own email address and direct dial phone number.

## Electronic newsletters

I mentioned before that you might generate coverage for your company in one of thousands of electronic publications produced on the Net. These range from simple three-screen quickies to elaborate electronic publications.

In addition to getting ink in other peoples' electronic newsletters, you can start your own. A good newsletter attracts prospects, helps convert prospects to customers, and helps to keep customers buying. A newsletter is good for cross-selling, promoting a family of products to a customer who normally buys just one. As people subscribe to your electronic newsletter, you also add names to build your email list.

Jaclyn Easton emails a weekly newsletter, *Log On USA's Electronic Program Guide*, to publicize her radio show *Log On USA*. Her newsletter is short—four screens long—and contains tips about new sites on the Internet, CompuServe, Prodigy, America Online, and Microsoft Network. It mentions the upcoming *Log On USA* radio program, and contains a small, clearly labeled section of one-paragraph advertisements. Advertisers on the radio receive "air time plus a bonus mention in the *Program Guide*," explained Easton. "It's a great tool when I sell advertising."

Easton receives requests from Internet sites and bulletin board systems to copy her newsletter for their readers. Most publicists would jump at the chance, but Easton has a reason to keep tighter control. "I don't allow people to repost the newsletter, so I can track circulation more closely and tell advertisers," she explained, "Although someone did ask permission to translate it into Braille, which I allowed." The free newsletter has a circulation "in the thousands and growing every day," including people in remote locations who never hear the radio show.

Even though Easton's newsletter is short, it takes time every week for her to write and to check every tip. "It takes so much longer to prepare than you realize," Easton warned. Most electronic newsletters require you to sign up by email, but *Log On USA's Electronic Program Guide* does not. Easton offers email sign up (**logonusa@logonusa.com**) and also allows people to subscribe using her toll-free 800 number. "People might not have a computer handy to subscribe," Easton explained, "but everyone is near a phone." Only 10 percent of her readers subscribe using email, while 90 percent subscribe using the phone number. One-third of the phone subscribers call from cellular phones while listening to the radio show.

To succeed, each issue of your electronic publication must deliver news, not fluff and promotions. Don't view it primarily as a selling tool. View it as an opportunity to demonstrate that your business delivers value. Don't run self-congratulatory articles, or articles based on press releases. They turn off readers.

Tell people about your company's future plans—not promises, but concrete information with figures and facts. You will get good reactions from stories about specific customers and what they have accomplished with your products. Suggestions on how to avoid and handle problems also draw a good response. Include a "Letters to the Editor" section, and encourage your readers to email their ideas to you. Genuinely interesting letters—not empty praise—can interest your readers and reduce the amount of writing for you to do.

Frequency is better than length. A newsletter with a little good information that comes out often—once every week or two—will generate more response than a bigger newsletter that appears less frequently. Besides, a newsletter longer than about ten pages will have problems going to some readers whose systems can't handle long email messages. If you publish your own electronic newsletter, make it as easy to do as possible. Don't get ambitious. Keep it simple and frequent.

As a finishing touch, you can get an International Standard Serials Number for your newsletter. An ISSN number costs nothing, makes you seem more established, and helps librarians catalog your newsletter. (Yes, libraries do store electronic publications.) National libraries provide ISSN numbers. For more information about ISSN numbers and instructions (in English and French) on how to get one for your publication, go to **http://www.well.com/www/issnic**.

## Sig files

The standard chunk of information at the end of an email message or a newsgroup posting is called a *signature file* or *sig* for short. Your email software or newsreader software should let you create a standard signature file once that will be electronically rubber-stamped at the bottom of every message you send. Sig files will be part of every email message your business sends out and every newsgroup posting made. Any customer or prospect who corresponds electronically with your company will see your people's sig files again and again. They are small but potent punches of publicity.

You need to decide if you want to create a standardized sig file format for everyone in your business to follow, or if you will allow employees to be creative and come up with their own. There are a few simple guidelines. Long sigs irk many people, so keep it short. Four to five lines is best. You can get away with six, but will hear complaints if your sig is ten or more lines long. Some email systems truncate any line longer than 80 characters, and a few less than that. Your sig will be safe from the scissors if you keep each line 70 characters wide or shorter.

What information should you include in your sig? Well, the first thing is your name, and the second thing—surprisingly—is your email address. Several email systems strip the header information off the top of every incoming message, so your recipient may have no way to reply to you if you do not repeat your email address in the body of your message or in your sig. You will also want to include your business name, other contact information, a brief description of what your business does, or a company slogan.

Here is a sample sig file from attorney Lewis Rose of the firm of Arent Fox. In only six lines, Rose squeezes in a considerable amount of information. All methods of contact are covered except ESP.

```
Lewis Rose                                  202-857-6012 (voice)
Arent Fox                                   202-857-6395 (fax)
1050 Connecticut Avenue, NW          lewrose@netcom.com (email)
Washington, DC 20036                  Advertising and Marketing Law
Advertising Law Internet Site URL: http://www.webcom.com/~lewrose/home.html
Moderator of Net-Lawyers Mailing List: net-lawyers-request@webcom.com
```

A less informational but more creative sig was created by movie director (*The Wizard of Speed and Time*), animator, and special effects genius Mike Jittlov, who includes his email address and the name of a newsgroup for his fans, along with a picture—created entirely with normal keyboard punctuation—of a wizard sprinkling pixie dust. Note that Jittlov's sig is only 64 characters wide, so it will fit on the smallest computer screens without getting chopped off. This sig is also six lines tall.

```
                                      ___.-'.*.'-._ _____
Mike Jittlov - Wizard, etc        .    . + * .o   o.* '.'. +.
Hollywood, California, USA        '   *   . ' ' |\^/|  `. * . *
jittlov@erehwon.caltech.edu      (: May All Your \V/  Good Dreams
   <& alt.fan.mike-jittlov>      and Fine Wishes /_\  Come True:)
                                                _/ \_ ==========
```

Jittlov's sig is entirely appropriate for his business, dealing in motion pictures and fantasy. For some professions, you may need a less entertaining sig. Attorneys and bankers, for instance, should avoid art, quotations, and anything that would cause their sig to be labeled "too cute" or "too cartoony".

Of course, your sig is not chiseled in stone and you can change it whenever you please. Before creating your sig files, you may want to review the information on sigs in Chapter 8. The results your publicity will generate in mailing lists and newsgroups will depend greatly on using sig files that clearly communicate exactly what your firm has to offer prospective customers.

## Internet marketing's greatest secret: newsgroups without flames

Newsgroups are like discussion lists except that instead of coming to you via email, you go to them to read them. This is great. You can pick and choose the messages you want to read. A newsgroup gives you an electronic equivalent of a cork bulletin board, where messages are *posted* instead of sent. You don't have to deal with every message, as you do when a discussion mailing list dumps dozens of messages in your emailbox.

But the best thing about newsgroups is that they are *targeted*. There are about 13,000 Usenet newsgroups, each with its own specific topic. This automatically classifies newsgroup readers into market segments according to newsgroup topics. If you can't find a newsgroup that speaks to your prospects, you can create one of your own that does. Publicity in newsgroups may generate more sales than any other weapon in your Internet marketing arsenal.

Newsgroup publicity generates significant sales for The Corner Store, a retailer of OS/2 and Windows NT software "When I turn my computer on, money comes out of it," says Corner Store owner Paolo Pignatelli (**paolop@pipeline.com**). "And I never spent a penny for advertising." Publicity on Internet newsgroups and CompuServe forums are the main thrust of marketing for his company. Pignatelli and his wife look on the newsgroups for questions. When Pignatelli cannot answer a question, he delegates the answer to someone else. He finds information-seeking messages from hundreds of people, "talking out loud and hoping somebody will listen to their thoughts." If his company can answer a question or direct someone to useful information, even when the answer or the directions have nothing to do with

The Corner Store, the answers—which are read by thousands of people in addition to the specific person addressed—create good will toward Pignatelli's business. Through this approach he has built a reputation for The Corner Store as a knowledgeable and helpful business.

In spite of all the messages The Corner Store has posted to newsgroups over the years, the company has never been flamed with hate email. Not once.

This idea of reading newsgroups where your prospects hang out, searching for questions, and posting answers for the world to see is the most successful method of marketing on the Internet. I have talked with many businesses whose Web pages were unvisited, whose mailing lists had few subscribers, and whose Gopher servers were shut down due to lack of interest. But every single company that I spoke with that invested time to answer questions on newsgroups *and that played by the rules of the newsgroups* reported that sales from grateful customers more than paid for the staff time spent in newsgroup publicity. There may be no newsgroups where your customers can be found, so this is not a strategy for every business. But if your customers read Usenet newsgroups, this is a valuable publicity technique.

Do not mistake this discussion as a "thumbs up" for posting press releases on newsgroups. *Press releases are not considered publicity by people who read newsgroups.* They are considered advertisements, and can cause anger and hostility instead of gratitude. I'll talk about posting press releases on newsgroups in Chapter 11.

It is estimated that 10 million people read newsgroups, but of course, not all of them read every group. Most just read a couple of groups on topics they care about the most. Newsgroups are read by many more people than those who actually post messages. The most-read group is **news.announce.newusers** with more than 1,200,000 readers. (For current statistics on newsgroup readership, generated by a program called Arbitron, go to **http://www.tlsoft.com/arbitron**.) Don't judge just by numbers. The important thing is to look for a tight fit between a newsgroup's readers and your prospects. A group with 500 readers intensely concerned with the product you make will generate more paying customers than 100,000 readers interested in how to kill Barney the dinosaur (**alt.barney.die.die.die**).

Which newsgroups should your business use for publicity? To find out, read the instructions on the Web page that tells you how to find the right place to post: **http://www.cis.ohio-state.edu/hypertext/faq/usenet/finding-groups/faq.html**. If you are looking for customers, find out what they read. Learn what your customers' top ten newsgroups are. Assign staff to read them regularly and contribute to them.

If your business sells to customers in your local area, there are some newsgroups that provide information for specific geographic areas. These local newsgroups provide a more focused market for some businesses. They start with a prefix to indicate the area they serve. For instance, **aus.theatre** covers live theater in Australia, while **ba.motorcycles** covers an obvious subject for people in the San Francisco Bay Area.

When you find newsgroups that seem like places you'll want to contact, first do some *netlurking*. This refers to the practice of reading messages without posting anything yourself. Always read enough messages so you get a feeling for the topics discussed and the people discussing them. Are they your customers? If not, try another group. Do your competitors post to this group? How do subscribers of this group treat other companies that post? What kinds of messages generate flames and arguments? If the group fits, you have one more thing to do: Look for the group's FAQ list or lists, and read them. There is no faster way for you to make your company look foolish than to ask or answer a question that is already on the FAQ list. Some groups post their FAQ monthly. Chapter 4 of this book tells you where to find archives containing FAQs of many groups.

Some people say that you should subscribe to a newsgroup and read all its messages for two weeks before you post anything. There are faster ways to learn about most groups. If a group generates 100 messages in one day and you read all 100, you will have a good idea of the character of that group. Instead of reading messages one day at a time, some software will also let you read several days of messages. This is handy because you can get a feel for a newsgroup in an hour or less, instead of subscribing for two weeks.

Internet people hate blatant, intrusive advertising, but actively seek information and electronic contact with experts. Your goals should be to establish the people in your company as trusted, helpful experts and to develop name recognition in your target markets.

To build trust, you must follow the newsgroups' rules. Otherwise, with one posted message you can outrage all your prospective buyers and lose your whole target market at once. With newsgroups, you might not get a second chance. Cancelbot software deletes offending messages and can block offending parties *and their companies* from ever posting on that newsgroup again. Individual readers who don't like your messages can list your name or your company name in their kill file. A *kill file* prevents any future messages from a particular person or Internet domain from ever being seen by a user. This is not to mention the fact that posting offending messages on newsgroups can get you flamed and mail bombed with hate mail. The same wonderful communication speed that spreads good news about your company can also be used to smear your reputation worldwide in a matter of hours.

When you post a business message to a Usenet newsgroup, *stay on topic*. Start your message with a short, to-the-point description of how your message fits the group's main topic. Don't try to cover everything about your product, service, or event. Just give the briefest possible response to the issue that you are posting. Don't post off-topic messages that do not address the specific needs of the group.

Many newsgroups allow no commercial announcements. Don't try to disguise a press release-type of announcement as something else; readers will get angry and may kick you off the group. In some groups, you shouldn't post messages or announcements at all. For instance, **alt.binaries.pictures** is reserved just for graphics files, and **comp.binaries.ms-windows** is strictly for Windows software programs. Posting your message to a newsgroup not related to your message's topic is spamming.

## *14 rules for publicity on Internet newsgroups*

1. Don't post advertisements or anything that someone might *think* is an advertisement. Ask the test question: "Will a reader feel grateful to receive this information?"

2. Before you first post to a newsgroup, read the group's FAQ and review 100 to 150 messages or so to get a feel for what passionately interests the group. The practice of reading messages without posting your own is called *netlurking*, and is the best way to find out what is really going on. Be sure to read a group's FAQ before you post a question or an answer to one.

3. Keep your newsgroup message short—two screens or less (48 lines) and to the point. Shorter messages download more quickly and so get chosen and read more often. Keep it 70 characters wide or less—some software truncates longer lines.

4. Stick to the actual subject of that group—based not on the group's name (newsgroup names are often misleading), but on what you found by netlurking.

5. Remember that thousands of people will read what you post to a newsgroup.

6. When you respond to a message, don't repeat the whole thing. Just quote relevant passages, or summarize it.

7. If someone flames you, don't flame back.

8. Posting articles in more than one newsgroup at the same time is called *cross-posting*. Only cross-post to newsgroups that have something to do with the subject of your message. Keep cross-posting to a minimum. Excessive cross-posting will automatically trigger cancelbot software to remove your message.

9. Don't post the same message twice in the same newsgroup. Post your message once only. Don't email a followup note to make sure that readers saw your first one.

10. Don't reprint copyrighted material.

11. Don't copy and reuse posted messages without permission. Remember, under current copyright law, even uncopyrighted text is still owned by its original creator.

12. Don't post messages that say only "I agree, " or "Me, too."

13. ALL CAPS IS SHOUTING AND PEOPLE HATE IT.

14. Always end each message with your signature file.

## Creating your own Usenet newsgroup

The procedures to create your own newsgroup are complex. They differ depending on what newsgroup *hierarchy* prefixes the beginning of your group name, such as **comp.** for computer topics or **rec.** for recreation. If your business deals mostly with local customers, you might want to create a group under your local hierarchy, such as **austin.** for Austin, Texas, **melb.** for Melbourne, Australia, or **pdx.** for Portland, Oregon. Most local areas have no local newsgroups. *Starting and sponsoring a set of groups for your area can be a valuable promotional activity.* It takes less work to run an unmoderated newsgroup than it does to run a discussion mailing list.

Anyone can create a newsgroup under the **biz.** or **alt.** hierarchies. For example, SBT Accounting Systems (**http://www.sbtcorp.com**) sponsored the formation of the newsgroup **biz.comp.accounting** for "discussions between users, developers and recommenders of accounting software," said Diane Causey of SBT. "Our goal is to provide a resource for people who need information about computerized accounting: available software, development trends, technical and implementation issues, and industry news." This lively group offers candid discussions of the strengths and weaknesses of all manufacturers' accounting systems—not just SBT's products. It has become one of the best places to go for research before you buy an accounting software program. Because SBT sponsors the group, its prospective customers are more aware of the company and its offerings. SBT also makes an archive of past postings from the group available through its home page, which increases visits by SBT's target market to the SBT Web site.

The **alt.** groups are widely distributed, but many business sites don't allow **alt.** groups, making them less valuable for business-to-business communication. If you start your own newsgroup, extra readership may make it worth your while to start it under one of the core hierarchies—the most-established newsgroups—even though this takes longer and requires more work. Creating a core group requires that your group not duplicate the subject of any existing group, that a vote be taken, and other procedures that can take three months.

For instructions on creating a newsgroup for worldwide Internet distribution, the best step-by-step information I've found is in *The Usenet Book* by Bryan Pfaffenberger (described in Chapter 4). Pfaffenberger doesn't specifically give instructions for creating a **biz.** group. You can find those along with more information on the **biz.** hierarchy in the Usenet FAQ archive at **http://www.cis.ohio-state.edu/Services.html.**

If you start your own newsgroup, you may be tempted to have someone from your firm act as moderator. It is better to avoid this and either run an unmoderated group (as SBT does) or use a moderator from outside your company. A moderator tends to inhibit constructive criticism, especially when the moderator is an employee of your company. This defeats one of the main benefits of running your own newsgroup, getting honest criticism quickly.

# Mailing lists and list servers

Internet mailing lists offer four types of publicity opportunities:

1. You can participate in other organizations' *discussion* mailing lists and publicize your company.

2. Your business can run an *announcement* mailing list.

3. Your business can run your own *discussion* mailing list as a publicity vehicle.

4. Your business can run a mail *archive server.*

All four accomplish different goals, making it important to understand the differences among them.

## *Participating in others' discussion mailing lists*

Some people confuse discussion mailing lists with a newsgroup. A newsgroup can be seen as a *place* you visit to read posted messages. A discussion mailing list *delivers* posted messages to you as email. Messages posted to a newsgroup are seen by the world. Messages posted to a discussion mailing list are seen only by subscribers to that list.

A discussion mailing list is operated by an organization using a list server software program. Everyone who participates emails messages to a central email address. The software takes that message and sends a copy to every person who subscribes to that list. Many lists are *moderated*, meaning someone reviews each incoming message before sending it to subscribers.

You can generate publicity on discussion mailing lists the same way that you generate familiarity with your business by posting on newsgroups. First, find a mailing list that is read by your prospects. In most cases, you will need to subscribe to a mailing list and read its messages for a while to find out if it has what you are looking for. Some mailing lists have archives where you can review past messages to evaluate a group, but relatively few archives exist, and some are open only to list subscribers. Third, after you are familiar with the list, post helpful information when appropriate.

Each discussion list has its own style and rules, depending on whether the list is moderated or unmoderated, how often readers post messages, whether they write formally or informally, and whether advertising-type messages are permitted. As with newsgroups, it pays to tailor your communication style to match your readers. Few lists allow advertising.

Most mailing list subscribers read only a few of the messages they receive from a list. They decide whether or not to look at your message based on three factors:

- The title of your message as shown in the Subject line
- The name of the person who sent the message
- The length of the message; shorter messages get more readers

To get your message read, your Subject is most important. A Subject like "Message for You" or "Hello" will get you a readership of zero.

It is easier to get kicked off a discussion mailing list than a newsgroup. When you subscribe to some mailing lists, you receive a notice about what kinds of material should be posted and what kinds should not. If you don't know if your posting would be right for a list, you can ask. Just send email to the discussion host or list moderator and ask for an opinion. (Don't send your query to the list itself, though. Instead of just being a private message for the host, your question will be exposed to the entire readership.)

Because a list owner can easily throw you out, it is very important to watch your netiquette when posting to a discussion list. Follow that list's guidelines. Don't make pointless comments about other people's messages like "I agree." (I confess that as a newbie, a list kicked me off for that very sin.) And don't insult your competitors. This behavior is viewed as rude and can get you kicked off a list.

## Running your own announcement mailing list

If your business sends announcements by postal mail, you may be able to use the Internet as a replacement. Even better, if a high percentage of your customers use Internet email, you can send them regular announcements to remind them about you. Computer Literacy Bookshops holds free lecture events in its stores with top speakers on technical topics. Two weeks before each event, Computer Literacy emails a brief, two-screen announcement of the upcoming free event to its list of subscribers.

The key is to get people to *ask* to subscribe to your list. If you add email addresses of your customers who have not requested your mailings, you will get a lot of angry customers. People don't like unsolicited email. If you decide to build an announcement list, it will require constant promotion to add new subscribers.

Your list can be open to the public or private and by invitation only. You can send brief announcements or entire newsletters—anything that is not perceived by your readers as an advertisement. Any message you send should provide a benefit to your subscribers and have real value. If the information you provide has enough value, you can even charge people for subscribing to your list.

Unless you use your list to send a newsletter, keep your announcements short and frequent. If you don't stay in touch at least every 2 to 3 months, recipients will forget they gave you their address and you may get a flame asking, "How did you get my name?"

An announcement list does require work to write and enter the announcements and to maintain the list of subscribers, and some work by your technical staff to send each mailing. Since only your views are propagated, mailings can occur at predictable times and the workload can be predicted and balanced. This is not as true of the other types of Internet mailing lists.

## *Running your own discussion mailing list*

A discussion mailing list is an inexpensive way for your business to provide an electronic channel for discussions of interest to your business. You can open your discussion lists (with one software program, you can run many lists) to the public or keep them private and by invitation only. You can have discussion lists for your customers and support staff, or simply for internal use by your employees. They are a useful way for people on a project team to communicate, especially on collaborative projects between your business and other companies.

Running a discussion list requires a list server software program, as discussed in Chapter 8. You can run the software either on your own computer, on a computer run by your Internet access provider, or on a computer provided by a completely separate service bureau company. Unless you have technical staff to monitor your list server software, I recommend farming out mailing list management to another company. Like most other Internet services, prices and quality vary, so shop around. Distance is no factor. You may find a better provider in another country.

Before you start your discussion list, plan the type of list you will want to offer. Whom will you target as subscribers? What topics will your list address? How will you promote your list to generate signups? Will it be open to the public, private and open only by invitation, or open only to members of certain companies or organizations? Do you want to offer subscribers the option of receiving the messages in digest format? Digest lists gather and post messages in bunches, sometimes in condensed form.

Do you want your list to be moderated (someone screens all messages before mailing them to subscribers) or unmoderated (senders' messages are emailed directly to everyone on the list without human intervention)? If your list generates a high message volume, moderating creates a lot of extra work for someone.

When you have made your choices, write a policy and instructions for subscribing. These will be useful tools when you publicize your list. Write a FAQ list. You will also need to make a subscriber welcome message, with instructions on how to unsubscribe, a description of your list, and who to contact for problems. Here is a good example that I received:

```
Welcome to the adlaw mailing list!

If you ever want to remove youself from this mailing list, send the following
command in email to "adlaw-request@webcom.com":
     unsubscribe

Or you can send mail to "majordomo@webcom.com" with the following command in
the body of your email message:
     unsubscribe adlaw vince@emery.com

Here's the general information for the list you've subscribed to, in case you
don't already have it:
[Last updated on: Tue Nov  1 13:30-46 PST 1994]

Thank you for joining the Advertising Law Internet Site Mailing List. This
mailing list will be used by the Site's maintainers to send announcements of
new articles, speeches, testimony, regulations, court cases, and related
materials to subscribers. The list may also be used by members of the list to
post questions about advertising and marketing law issues or related matters.
The list is moderated and the moderator retains the sole discretion to deter-
mine whether any particular post should be passed on to the list.

The list is not intended to create an attorney-client relationship between the
maintainer of the list and subscribers. Information at the Advertising Law
Internet Site and on this list is not intended to be used as legal advice and
is not the substitute for consulting an experienced lawyer with expertise in
the relevant subject matter.

With that out of the way, you can post to the Advertising Law Internet Site by
sending email to the following address: adlaw@webcom.com

Thanks for joining us. If you have any questions, please send me an email at
lewrose@netcom.com
```

Notice that this message is customized for the subscriber. The unsubscribe instructions include my own email address, and the message tells when it was last updated. It tells where to send a message so everyone on the list can read it, and tells where to send a private "off-list" message to the moderator. This welcome message makes a good reference for you when you write your own.

Some discussion lists send a FAQ to all new subscribers and provide an archive of previous postings. To create an archive of your discussion list messages, you can use a Unix program called Hypermail, which can sort and index past messages so server visitors can search them by date, thread, subject, and author. For a copy of the program and more information, **ftp://ftp.eit.com/ pub/web.software/hypermail**.

## *Running your own mail archive server*

The same software that you use to run a discussion mailing list can also be used to email documents to anyone who requests them. When people say *list server* and *mail archive server*, they are talking about the same software, just configured to handle different duties. When used as an email archive server, the software is sometimes called *mailbot* software.

This automates document distribution, and makes your press kit and other information available 24 hours to anyone around the world. We discussed this type of mailing list server in Chapter 8, and they are especially valuable as publicity servers. Once again, you don't have to put an email archive server on your own computer. Service bureaus rent space for between $1 and $10 per document per month, usually with a ten to twenty document minimum. This makes it affordable for small companies to make information available by email. Look for a service that does not charge per-request fees for this service.

As with other types of Internet services, if you want your mail archive server to be successful, you must work to promote it.

The question is, do you really need this service if you also have a World Wide Web site? In most cases, probably not. A Web page presents information more understandably for consumers and business people than the commands and different email addresses needed to retrieve documents from a list server. However, an email archive does offer advantages in some situations: It can present a large quantity of documents inexpensively, deliver them to people who don't have World Wide Web access, and it doesn't require you to reformat documents into HTML or PostScript.

## *Maintaining email lists*

This is a true horror story. Names have been changed to protect the guilty. Joleen Davis, manager of the announcement mailing list for Flavored Colas Inc., opened her email one morning and gasped in shock. The night before, Flavored Colas had emailed notices to its customers. Joleen had expected the usual bounced messages that follow a mass emailing. Instead, she received a flame denouncing the company in the vilest terms for sending unsolicited email, and a request to remove the recipient from Flavored's mailing list.

Joleen searched through her mailing list, but the address of the flaming writer did not appear on it. She wrote a sympathetic reply, telling the flamer that Flavored Colas never put anyone on its list unless that person specifically asked to be added, and that she had searched the email list and not found Mr. Flamer's address. Then she emailed the reply to him.

(Do you see the start of a problem? Flavored Colas had no formal procedure for Joleen to follow when flamed. A preplanned technical and management firefighting team should have been called immediately.)

Within an hour, Joleen received a second email from Mr. Flamer, more vile than the first. Mr. Flamer accused Flavored Colas of stealing people's email addresses from the Internet and bombarding everyone at Mr. Flamer's company with unsolicited email advertising. Joleen called her supervisor, Sam Bell.

With Sam, Joleen searched Flavored's entire email list for Mr. Flamer's address. They couldn't find it. They found three other list subscribers whose email addresses came from Flamer's company, but nothing for Flamer himself.

Joleen wrote a polite email explanation of what she had done. Sam reviewed it carefully and Joleen sent it to Mr. Flamer, hoping that it would satisfy him.

That afternoon, Joan Topnotch, a senior executive at Flavored Colas, opened an email message to read a horrifying attack on Flavored Colas. It was unsigned. Joan looked at the sender's address at the top of the diatribe and was startled to find it had been sent from an address *within Flavored Colas itself*. Joan asked someone walking by, who happened to be Sam Bell, to take a look.

Sam noticed that the sender's address was Flavored Colas' announcement mailing list address. Could it be the list? He ran to the technical supervisor and asked to check the outgoing email. To his horror, he found hate mail going out to all the people on Flavored Colas' customer announcement list! The technical supervisor stopped the mailing, but the message had already gone out to 600 customers. Mr. Flamer had taken over Flavored Colas' mailing list.

 Here's what happened: To send a message to an email list, you send the text of your message to a program that combines your text with the addresses on your list. The address of that program appears on all outgoing messages. If you don't secure that program so only trusted users can access it, anyone with that address can take over your software and send email to your entire list.

A more technically knowledgeable manager reviewed the addresses in Flavored Colas' list and found what had caused Mr. Flamer to get upset. One of the three addresses from Mr. Flamer's company was **all@flameco.com**. Someone at Flameco, probably thinking that everyone in the company would be interested in Flavored Colas' announcements, had subscribed to Flavored Colas' list using a group name that delivered every message it received to *everyone* in Flameco.

 Have your software or an employee inspect new addresses before putting them on your mailing list. Don't accept group names such as all, everyone, group, co, dept, everybody, company, or corp.

List server software can be tricky to set up and run. There are a lot of log files and configuration files to watch, puzzling error messages to solve, and unhappy subscribers to handle. Set it up wrong, and instead of sending out 500 messages one at a time, your system will try to send out all 500 at once. That'll put a serious drag on the rest of your system. If you set up a list server in-house, be sure you have an experienced person with the time to maintain your software.

## *Tasks for a list owner*

For each of your mailing lists, you must pick one person to be the list owner. The owner doesn't have to be a technical person, but you'll find it a time-saver to have a technical staffer as the list owner for large lists. The list owner will manage the way your list is organized, control adding and deleting subscribers to your list, and can act as moderator to review and approve each message before it goes out to your list. You may want to have a separate person act as list moderator. Your list owner doesn't need to work on the same computer where your list resides, but can be located anyplace where he or she can make email contact with the list server. The list owner's duties can be handled by remote control via email if your list software is located on your service provider's computer instead of your own.

Your list will have several addresses: one for the list owner, one for broadcasting messages to your list (only if your list is a discussion list), one to receive error messages, one to receive messages about the list. This last may be the same address as the list owner, or it could be a separate address for a list moderator.

People who don't send an exactly correct command to your server will get an automated rejection, and the list owner will get a *bounced message*. Unless your list is only for computer geniuses, invest the time to make your error messages understandable by the uninformed. The most crucial part is to make the *response* you want absolutely clear. If you don't tell somebody what you want them to do, chances are they will do something else. Test your error messages on your non-technical staffers. Ask them, "What would you do if you saw this message on your computer?"

Check your server's log files often, especially for bounced email from people who tried to subscribe or unsubscribe once, made a mistake, and didn't try again. You can turn angry, silent subscribers into contented ones by processing those bounced messages by hand, and sending them a friendly personal email note to tell them what you've done.

Make sure bounced messages won't be sent to your list *subscribers* by mistake. Run a test to make sure. Bounced email is most often caused by a simple (and sometimes hard to spot) typo in the address. The second most common cause is that computer systems or the links between systems are temporarily down, blocking the route to your addressee. If your message bounced back to you and you have double checked the address and swear that it's letter-perfect, try resending it in a couple of hours.

There is another cause of bounced messages. When you send a mailing, you may get error messages back that say "Unknown host". This could be a typographical error in which the name on the right of the "@" sign in someone's email address is misspelled. But what if you send email to a name ending with an obviously correct address, such as **@ibm.com** and it comes back with the message "Unknown host"? When you get that error message but you know the host name is accurate—especially if you get a whole stack of error messages for several people at different companies—it may be a problem with your Internet access provider. If your access provider has configured its software incorrectly or held on to your message for too long, the message will bounce back to you. To prove that it was your access provider's fault, you will have to document when you sent the messages that gave you the "Unknown host" error, to which addresses, and when they returned to you. Be skeptical if your provider says this problem was your fault if it happens frequently.

It pays to invest time in maintaining your list. People move, people lose interest, and addresses change. Always update your list after every mailing. If your list deals with customers, archive all your changes and change request messages. The archive gives you something to fall back on if you have a problem like Mr. Flamer.

## Miscellaneous mailing tips

When you send any mailing, you should send any local addresees first. That means that people in your company on that list should receive their copies of your mailing before outsiders do. This gives you extra eyes to spot if there is a problem, so you can stop processing before it covers the rest of the world.

Store your mailing list file on-site, but for many companies it will be faster to send a mailing if you upload your list to your access provider's system and run it remotely. Check with your provider to see if this would work for you. For security, maintain your list on a computer separated from your Internet connection. Move a copy of your list to your Internet account, then upload it to your service provider. Rather then leaving your list for anyone to read or copy on your provider's computer, delete it after your mailing.

Depending on your hardware and software setup, list processing may slow down your computer system during business hours. Sending to a long list, or sending long messages, can take hours. Send 'em at night.

## Giving away free stuff with FTP

FTP stands for File Transfer Protocol. It's a way for you to provide files for people to copy to their own computers. Giving away free stuff via FTP is a very popular way for companies to publicize themselves to Internet users, especially since an FTP site can cost very little. An FTP site open to the public is called an *anonymous FTP* site, because members of the public can enter it anonymously, without giving a name or a secret password. FTP moves data more quickly than attaching a file to an email message. There are more email *transactions* on the Internet, but each message is small. In terms of sheer *volume* of information transported over the Net, FTP is the unchallenged champion.

There are thousands of anonymous FTP sites. Among the most publicized are the giant archives sponsored by Sun Microsystems. Called SunSITEs, there are three of them—in Tokyo, London, and the University of North Carolina—that distribute everything from software to White House papers, sports archives, and of course, Sun's publicity. To take a look, use FTP or Gopher to: **sunsite.unc.edu**.

You can put any kind of file on an FTP server: graphics, video, sound, software programs, documents. Most companies that have only small (under 50K) text files make them available via Gopher or a Web server rather than FTP, but FTP is the method of choice on the Internet for moving larger files and software programs.

In spite of the wide use of FTP, the World Wide Web has become the Internet access method of choice for most consumer and business users of the Internet. How can you decide whether to provide an FTP site, a World Wide Web site, or do both? Here are the differences: An FTP site presents to a visitor a list of files and directories. To find out what the files are and which directories contain them, the visitor must retrieve a README.TXT file, open it and read it. A Web site visitor can read descriptions of all material and distinguish files through longer and more clear descriptions than mere file names. FTP visitors see file names and directory names, but no descriptive information. The Web's built-in navigation abilities make it easier and faster to search through material. It is easier and less expensive for you to produce an FTP site than a Web site. An FTP site requires only that you have computer files and make them available. All World Wide Web text must be converted to HTML or Adobe Acrobat format for your Web site visitors to read.

My opinion is this: Start an FTP site only if you have lots and lots of material available, especially lots of software, or if you market to technical people, especially to computer programmers. On the other hand, businesspeople and consumers find FTP a chore, so build a Web site for them unless you have too much material to convert. An FTP site is reachable by most Web browsers, so you can combine both, and put explanatory information on Web pages with clickable links that take your visitors directly to your FTP archives to retrieve files.

In addition to providing an FTP site offering free files to the public, you can set up a private password-protected FTP site for company use. This site can be useful for non-publicity purposes, such as moving files back and forth between different sites or making software patches available for customers.

One disadvantage: FTP software is a major security concern. You can restrict access to files, but the security holes in FTP make it a good candidate to either be on your Internet access provider's computer or on a sacrificial computer of your own placed outside your company's Internet firewall.

Most Internet access providers will set up an anonymous FTP site for your business for just the cost of renting disk space. This can be less than $10.00 a month. If your access provider wants you to pay disk space plus a fee for the amount of data downloaded from your FTP site, or wants you to pay a "per-access" charge, find another provider. Usually access providers charge a small setup fee and a per-megabyte monthly storage fee. One potential problem to check with your provider's anonymous FTP space is to see how many users can access it at one time. You might have a problem if several companies share a provider's FTP server but simultaneous FTP use is permitted for only 20 or so people. Additional fees may be also charged, based on how much disk space you use, how many people will have access and how often, and how often you change or add to your FTP files. Prices vary wildly, so get at least three quotes.

Besides access providers and service bureaus for FTP sites, you also have the alternative of running FTP server software on your own computer. FTP server software is available for almost all operating systems. FTP software is easy to set up. Like any other kind of Internet server, running an FTP server requires a commitment to ongoing maintenance. Someone will need to add new files, delete old files, remove empty directories, and the like.

You'll need to plan a logical and easy-to-understand structure of files and directories, so your visitors can tell what you are providing and can find what they need. Start your site and each major directory with a README.TXT file providing indexes and describing the contents of your site.

When naming your FTP directories, take Archie into account. Archie is a search program that allows users to search across the Net for files with a name that the user has specified. Often, users can't remember the company that has the information they want, but they know the subject. Name your files with subject names instead of people's names, company names, or gibberish like WEAP3796. In other words, use "search sense."

When choosing files to include in your FTP site, don't think you can just copy a bunch of shareware and freeware from other FTP sites and people will beat a path to your door. Most of that stuff is already available in many well-publicized locations. To get any attention, your site will need to have unique material that people want but cannot get elsewhere, or information that may be available elsewhere but is not organized so as to be most useful for your prospects. Think in terms of the needs of your market. What can you provide for them that they will be most grateful for?

## Providing Finger files

Finger is an Internet software program originally developed so people outside a company could find out information such as: who was logged onto the computer, what their Internet address was, and other information. Unfortunately, Finger became a major security risk. It became a favorite target of hackers and computer viruses.

Today, some businesses provide no Finger information at all. Others, however, use Finger to deliver marketing information. If the technical data so beloved by hackers is stripped from Finger, you can provide contact information, your order desk phone number, hours of business, and other information. For a simple example, Finger **info@clbooks.com**.

Your Finger file information can be amplified by attaching a **.plan** file, which can provide more data and can update information continuously. Some Finger servers give weather information, sports scores, or stock market quotations.

In most cases, the extra effort is probably not worth it. Finger is a rarely used Internet tool, and provides little interactivity compared with other Internet services your business can provide. It is not essential for your company to provide a Finger server at all. If you do provide Finger information, make sure your technical people block all security holes. And don't spend a lot of money and time providing complicated Finger data. Most people won't ever see it.

## How to publicize your Internet offerings

Your Internet activities will not succeed unless you publicize them. Remember, when your site gets publicity, your business gets publicity. When your business gets publicity, you make money. You have to promote your Internet site as much as your 800 number or more.

First, cross-promote. It costs nothing extra to list your Web home page on your email signature files, and to list your mailing list and customer service email address on your Web site. Follow through with everything printed. All offerings should list your home page address at a minimum.

Check out the list of print magazines in Chapter 4. Get samples and contact the most likely candidates to see if they will cover your company's Internet offerings. (Print editors these days are most easily swayed by Web sites.) Don't think because your site is only in English that editors in Japan or Germany will not care. Most Japanese can read English, and magazine editors in both countries are interested in anything genuinely new.

One of the best-promoted Web sites I've seen is the Advertising Law Internet Site operated by the law firm of Arent Fox. First, take a look at the site's name. Arent Fox specializes in a particular area of law and wants to make sure prospects know it. The firm listed its site in all the directories and search engines on the Net. It got publicity in printed magazines that cover the Internet, publications that cover marketing and advertising, and legal journals. One of the Arent Fox Web pages offers browsers the opportunity to sign up for its Adlaw mailing list, which is a mailing list that publicizes its Web page! The mailing list tells prospects about new information and encourages them to visit the Web site again. The resulting business has more than paid for Arent Fox's Internet presence.

The easiest, fastest, and cheapest way to spread the word about your company's Internet offerings is on the Internet itself. Here is a directory of places for you to publicize your company's Internet presence. This is just a starter list; as always, addresses may change. If you find any errors or changes, or if you discover something new you'd like to share, email me (**vince@emery.com**).

**To publicize any kind of Internet site:**

- The InterNIC *Directory of Directories* tries to list everything and includes Internet-wide Whois. For instructions on listing your business, email to: **admin@ds.internic.net.**

- The *Net-Happenings* newsletter. To subscribe, email to **majordomo@is.internic.net**, leaving the body of your message blank except for **subscribe net-happenings**. To read articles, go to **http://www.mid.net/NET**. To submit listings, go to **http://www.mid.net/NET/input.html.**

- Open Market's Commercial Sites Index will list your Internet site in a searchable database and on its own "What's New" page, subject to its editor's approval. It will also list pages you create for new products: **http://www.directory.net.**

- The Internet Mall will list a five-line description of any Internet site that *sells* something over the Net. For more information, go to **http://www.mecklerweb.com/mall.**

- For Japanese sites, the Japan Network Information Center includes Japanese Whois and other resources to list your company. For more information, go to **http://www.nic.ad.jp/index.html.**

- In Spain, go to **http://www.uji.es.spain-www.html.**

**To publicize your Gopher server:**

- Make sure your Gopher filenames contain keywords that will make it easy for Veronica searches to find you.

- Get listed in the Gopher Jewels located at **gopher://cwis.usc.edu**; look in **other Gophers and Information Resources.**

**To publicize your FTP site:**

- Your Web server should point to your FTP server.

- Publicize your site in the FTP sites directory. To get a copy of the directory with instructions on how to list your site: **ftp://ftp.ucsc.edu/public/ftpsites.**

- To publicize your FTP site's offerings on Archie, send email to **info-archie@bunyip.com.**

**To publicize your newsletter:**

- Never post your full newsletter to a Usenet newsgroup. You can put out a notice that a free new issue is available and briefly summarize its contents.

- Find Internet archives of information for your industry and ask if they'd like to store your newsletter. Most will if your newsletter has worthwhile information.

- Gleason Sackman's NEWSLTR will distribute your complete newsletter to hundreds of sites worldwide. For information, email to **newsltr@vm1.nodak.edu**.

- The Association of Research Libraries will distribute your newsletter through its NEWJOUR-L service. Email to **newjour-l@ e-math.ams.com** for information.

- The CICnet Archive of Electronic Journals and Newsletters will archive your newsletter and make it available. For information, Gopher to **gopher.cic.net**. Here are three more archive sites:

- Library of Congress **gopher://marvel.loc.gov** Go to: **Research and Reference (Public Services)**

- University of Waterloo **gopher://uwinfo.uwaterloo.ca** Go to: **Electronic Resources Around the World**

- University of Bath **gopher://ukoln.bath.ac.uk** Go to: **BUBL Information Service**

- You can publicize Asian newsletters in *Asia Online*. Go to: **http://www.ncb.gov.sg:1080**

**To publicize your discussion mailing lists:**

- Get on the directory Publicly Accessible Mailing Lists: **http://www.neosoft.com/internet/paml**

- Email a short description of your list to **interest-groups-request@sri.com** and to **newlist@vmi.nodak.edu**.

- Get on Diane Kovacs' List of Lists: **ftp://ksuva.kent.edu/library** Go to the file **acadlist index**.

**To publicize your World Wide Web site:**

- NCSA What's New Page: **http://www.ncsa.uiuc.edu/SDG/Software/Mosaic/Docs/whats-new.html**. A listing here can generate a flash crowd at your site of 5,000 or more visitors, lasting only for one week. After you submit your information, it can take up to three weeks to appear.

- In Japan: **http://www.ntt.jp/SQUARE/www-in-JP.html**. You can also get on "What's New in Japan," at **http://www.ntt.jp/WHATSNEW/index.html**.

- In France: **http://web.urec.fr.france/france.html**

- In Belgium: **http://www.ufsia.ac.be/wgis/index.html**

- In Italy: **http://www.mi.cnr.it/NIR-IT/Reg-WWW.html**

- In the U.K: **http://scitsc.wlv.ac.uk/ukinfo/uk.map.html**

- JumpStation: **http://www.stir.ac.uk/jsbin/jsii**

- WWW Virtual Library: **http://info.cern.ch/hypertext/DataSources/bySubject/Overview.html**

- Lycos: **http://www.lycos.com**

- Yahoo: **http://www.yahoo.com**

- W3 Catalog: **http://cuiwww.unige.ch/w3catalog**

- Apollo Directory: **http://apollo.co.uk**

- Global Online Directory: **http://www.cityscape.co.uk/gold/indexdir.html**

- EINet Galaxy: **http://galaxy.einet.net.galaxy.html**

# How to Advertise on the Internet

*"On the Internet, if you only have a space ad from a magazine, (customers) will not come back."*
Steve Isaac, CEO of Martin Direct

Marketing, publicity, and advertising are all swirled together on the Internet in a mixture that many advertisers find hard to sort. The boundaries between angrily rejected advertisements and welcomed PR seem so *arbitrary* to advertisers experienced in traditional media.

In traditional media—print, television, and radio—the advertiser decides when something is an advertisement. On the Internet, your reader decides when your offering is or isn't an advertisement—and grief comes to advertisers who put ads where they don't belong! You may understand this from reading the previous two chapters. This chapter builds on that information. You won't get the full impact of this chapter without reading those.

David Carlick, Senior Vice President and General Manager of agency Poppe Tyson Advertising (**http://www.poppe.com**) explained one difference in the technique of successful Internet advertisers. "The business of advertising on the Net is more *invitational*," Carlick explained. "It takes a whole different mindset on the part of the advertiser: Be attractive rather than intrusive. Instead of positioning your Internet advertising around intrusive methods, position it to say, 'If you're interested in this, come and take a look.' In a way, this is database marketing turned inside-out. If I make my advertisement attractive by providing strong content, I don't have to target my prospects."

On a good Internet site, prospects are *self-selecting*. A site offering terrific tips on machine tool maintenance will be read only by people who maintain machine tools.

The Internet is causing a turmoil in advertising agencies. Comedian Fred Allen pointed out that "advertising is 85 percent confusion and 15 percent commission," and hardly anything on the Internet pays media commissions. "This is the rebirth of the agency," observed Carlick. "Agencies will be selling hours to build content. All of the advertisers that we work for want a lower-cost channel. On the Internet, the media now cost less than the content." And he pointed out what the lower media cost means to advertisers: "Your competitors will have a cost advantage if they use electronic media and you're still using paper."

# The Internet as a medium

"Advertising is communications over a medium to reach a target audience," said Carlick. There has been a lot of noise about the Internet as a general-purpose medium, which it is not. "The Internet serves *special interest needs*, which publishers have understood for a long time. Over the years, the amount of money advertisers have spent on general media has declined, and special interest (direct mail, special interest magazines) has risen."

The ease and low cost of providing content on the Internet has led to a splintering of the Net to serve an inconceivable number of microinterests. Robert Rossney described it in the Feb. 9, 1995, *San Francisco Chronicle* : "A lot of Web sites are useless. The Web is a lot like that 500-channel television that we hear about from time to time, except that there are more than 25,000 channels, and a significant portion of them seems to be run by undergraduates in the nation's many computer science departments. So there are at least four different sites on the Web where you can get the first 50,000 digits of *pi*. There's a woman at the University of Michigan who has put up a page with a picture of her pet ferret, Potpie, and several examples of his typing. And what are we to make of the unlikely Erik Tjong Kim Sang, who collects and distributes photographs of palindromic Dutch license plates?"

This splinterization of the Internet puts the lie to a lot of claims about why your business should advertise on the Internet. An advertisement from one unscrupulous Internet advertising company promises you will "Reach 25,000,000 New Customers!" Not only is that argument dishonest, it misses the point. All the people on the Internet won't visit your online advertisement, *and you don't want them*. You want only those people *interested in what you have to sell*.

This fundamental difference about the Internet is one that a great many traditional advertising agencies have a difficult time comprehending. On the Internet, you don't need a massive saturation campaign to reach your customers. You need, instead, to understand who your customers are and how to satisfy their needs.

Another fundamental distinction of Internet advertising is that it is *measurable* ; but being *able* to measure advertising response and knowing what to *do* with it are two different things. Most consumer advertising agencies simply lack the knowledge of how to track responses to advertisements and how to apply the results. Direct marketing agencies are aware of these things, but many of them don't know how to make their techniques work in the new medium. Direct marketers are accustomed to punching as hard as they can and as obviously as possible. To the upscale Generation X inhabitants of the Internet, blatant commercialism and overmarketing are distasteful. At best, these prospects will turn up their noses and walk away from you if you oversell. At worst, they will attack your business with a flamethrower.

A successful Net advertiser must imagine the internal conversation in your prospect's head, and turn it into an external discussion between the prospect and your interactive Internet advertisements. To sell your products, this discussion must sell your features, dramatize your benefits, answer all questions, present enough information to make a decision, and motivate your prospect to follow through with the response you want. The person who designs and writes your Internet advertisements has a tricky job.

Your ideal Internet advertiser is someone with at least a year of Internet experience, the direct response background to understand that the Net is electronic direct marketing, and a belief in the Shansi kung fu proverb that "Correct hitting is invisible. Your enemy should fall without seeing your hands move."

For a quick education on too-blatant advertisers who became roadkill on the info superhighway, visit "The Internet Advertisers Blacklist" at **http://math-www.uni-paderborn.de/~axel/BL.** Advertisers are pilloried here for committing two of the wost offenses to their prospects on the Net: sending unsolicited commercial email or posting inappropriate commercial messages to Usenet newsgroups. As an advertiser, beware that these are the two Net crimes you can commit that will cause you to lose the greatest number of prospective customers. If you avoid those tactics, your chances of being punished by Internet inhabitants are minimal. Information on a French-language blacklist is available from **pb@fasterix.frmug.fr.net.**

# Advertising with newsgroups and mailing lists

Most of the brouhaha over advertising on the Internet has to do with the World Wide Web, but for many companies that is not the most cost-effective method of Internet advertising. Honors there go to two lesser-known and less-expensive tactics: posting on Usenet newsgroups and creating email mailing lists. These two approaches are often blended to reinforce each other. And both must be used with extreme caution by advertisers.

Almost everything you post on a newsgroup that directly promotes your product or service will be considered an advertisement—any press release, for example. There is no way for an advertiser to fight this perception. The logical thing to do is say, "Okay, people will think my information is an advertisement. So where can I post it?" Fortunately, there are several places.

## *Newsgroups for advertisements*

There are different kinds of newsgroups that are suitable for posting advertisements. But they reach different audiences and are structured for advertisements on different topics. Several advertisement newsgroups have names that start with **biz.marketplace**, such as **biz.marketplace.computers.mac** and **biz.marketplace.international**. Any kind of *on-topic* commercial advertisement can be posted to the "**biz.marketplace**" groups, and they are free. Two different and helpful "Usenet Marketplace FAQs" are posted to all of the **biz.marketplace** groups every five days. They are helpful to read beforehand if you want your advertisements to work.

In addition, there are more than 100 classified ad newsgroups, all free. All have either **forsale**, **marketplace**, **classified**, **auction**, or **swap** as part of their names. **misc.forsale** has more than a quarter of a million readers, the highest of any advertisement newsgroup. Some are worldwide but topic-specific. Some are specific to a geographic locale, such as **bln.forsale** for Berlin, Germany and **fj.forsale** for Japan. Some are for a specific topic *and* for a specific locale, such as **pdaxs.ads.tickets** for selling tickets in the Portland, Oregon area. Some groups have a policy that only private individuals, not businesses, can sell items. When you want to post ads from your business, check the group's FAQ first, or if you can't find a FAQ, post a message asking if a business ad is appropriate. (**misc.forsale** has a good FAQ that explains how to buy and sell on all newsgroups.)

Some of these newsgroups are very busy. Some have only one ad posted every couple of months. Your message stays on most service providers' computers for a few weeks, so you should not post more often than once every month. Don't cross-post to several groups at once. When you sell a product available only in your local area, target a local newsgroup. If a newsgroup doesn't start with a geographic prefix, it is worldwide. Use a Subject line that tells what you are selling. Provide enough description of your product so someone can tell if he or she wants it. Finally, and importantly, *post on-topic only*. If you have a lawnmower for sale, be smart enough not to post an ad for it to **rec.bicycles.marketplace**. Sending your ad to an unlikely buyer is a waste of your time.

In addition to newsgroup ads, you can run classified ads on the World Wide Web as well. Check out the classified advertising page at **http:// www.imall.com/ads/ads.shtml**. For more classified ads, go to **http:// www.yahoo.com/business** and look under **Classified Ads**. Some electronic publications like *HotWired* (**http://www.hotwired.com**) provide classified ads; most charge for this.

## *Advertising on other newsgroups*

New York microbrewery Spring Street Brewery Co. posted information about its $5,000,000 initial public offering of stock on newsgroups and received 20,000 inquiries. It then emailed inquirers an electronic version of its prospectus. Spring Street did not post its prospectus to advertisement newsgroups, but to a small number of carefully selected business and investment newsgroups. As with any announcement of a prospectus, its postings warned that "this is not an offer to sell nor a solicitation."

Posting advertising on other newsgroups is skating on thin ice. If you follow the FAQ rules of your target newsgroup, if you compose your message carefully, and if—and only if—your message ties in closely with that newsgroup's topic, you can post some advertisements to some newsgroups and not anger and drive away your prospects. You must pick and choose your newsgroups carefully. For instance, **alt.business.import-export** has many announcements from companies around the world selling wholesale quantities of every conceivable product. These are on-topic advertisements for that group. If a long distance telephone company posted to that group, it would be off-topic and a waste of readers' time.

 If you post off-topic, you spam. You will lose customers, get flamed, and possibly get your message canceled by cancelbot software. This last one requires some explanation. There is no equivalent to it in other media. When you place an ad in several inappropriate newsgroups, you trigger one of several different cancelbots. Cancelbots remove your offending message, warn appropriate system administrators, and post a message like this in the **alt.current-events.net-abuse** newsgroup:

```
From: Cancelmoose[tm]
Subject: Spam Cancelled (cme@io.org (Candian Music Exchange), **INTERACTIVE
MUSIC TALKER/MUCK**)

This 161 message spam has been cancelled from 161 newsgroups. It was not
crossposted. 1 copy and headers follow. Note that this user also has a differ-
ent 30 message spam that is not being cancelled at this time (hopefully they
will clean up some of their own mess, and learn how to crosspost). This is
*NOT* a statement that a 30 message spam is acceptable.

This is not being done because the message is an ad. This is not being done to
censor a critic. This is not being done because I am offended by the words in
his message. To stop a man from speaking his views in the public square is
censorship. To stop a man from speaking his views when he amplifies his voice
161 times the normal volume is not. Cancelling spam is not censorship:
spamming is disturbing the peace.

*Please* be sure to write to the postmaster at the offending site, and tell
them you do not approve of this behavior. If spam cancelling eliminates the
outrage people feel about spam, then it will cease to be a problem to the
uninformed sysadmin. This will cause bigger problems down the road when they
stop educating their users.

Even though this spam is cancelled, please complain *politely* to
postmaster@io.org.

The commercial or noncommercial nature of this spam did not influence its
cancellation. Spam is determined on number of newsgroups posted to, and not
the content of the message. I sincerely hope these people will learn to
crosspost and find a better way to get their message out to the net.
```

(This message has been slightly condensed.) I don't know what happened to the offending advertiser in this case, but many Internet access providers will close your account if you spam. America Online is quite efficient about this. AOL users who spam have their accounts terminated immediately. To avoid mishaps, before posting to any non-advertisement newsgroups read the rules for posting on Usenet newsgroups: **http://www.cis.ohio-state.edu/hypertext/ faq/usenet/posting-rules/part1/faq.html**

A handful of other tips on advertisements: Don't post to a general-purpose newsgroup. For maximum effectiveness, tailor the content of your message to the content of the newsgroup. Explain at the beginning of your message how your announcement directly relates to the topic of that group. If your announcement is an out-and-out advertisement, label it as "Ad:" in the Subject line of your message. There is no need to overstate or exaggerate the benefits of your offering. Understatement will pull better than overdramatization. Cool it with the exclamation points!!!! They make you look silly!!!! And ****too many asterisks**** are just as bad.

My personal experience is that you will get a bigger response from newsgroups by posting, instead of blatant ads or press releases, the type of messages described in the previous chapter. Other businesses report the same. Waterbug Records is a good example. Waterbug owner Andrew Calhoun spends time on folk music newsgroups and conducts personal email with folk music lovers—up to 400 messages per day. Folksinger Cosy Sheridan credits this Internet marketing with building her into a rising star. Her fans agree. A T-shirt entrepreneur cashed in by selling a shirt saying, "I heard about Cosy Sheridan on the Internet." Calhoun noted that the people who use a newsgroup are the most intense, dedicated fans of whatever that newsgroup's topic may be. They spread the word to others; kind of an electronic trickle-down effect. You may catch a newsgroup follower's attention with an advertising message, but you won't generate the same kind of devotion that comes with sustained contact.

It's what Jim Barrick of KeyNote Software called "The pass-around factor. Good word-of-mouth spreads quickly on the Net. So does bad."

## *Electronic mailing lists*

Apparel manufacturer Joe Boxer Corp. dropped its 800 number in favor of using its email address to communicate with customers. In 18 months, the corporation received 20,000 email responses. It then asked everyone who sent it email if they would like to subscribe to its emailing list. The company uses email to conduct focus group-type research, and to email product announcement advertising.

There are two ways your company can advertise using email lists: build your own list of customers and prospects, as Joe Boxer Corp. did, or send announcements to other organizations' discussion email lists. There are very few discussion email lists that accept advertisements. The best way to find a list that accepts advertisements is to subscribe to lists that address your company's industry, and carefully read the signup information the list sends you. Read messages from the list for two weeks to see if anyone else posts advertisements. If you have even the slightest doubt about whether you should advertise on a list, send an email note to the person who hosts the list and ask. You can get kicked off a mailing list far more quickly and completely than from a newsgroup, and once you are kicked off, it's permanent.

There are email lists of people who *want* to receive advertising. Inside Connections offers businesses access to an email list of consumers who want to receive emailed announcements for particular types of products. For information, email to **inside@tyrell.net**.

## Advertising with a Gopher server

Before the introduction of Mosaic, Gopher was the fastest-growing method of getting information on the Internet. Now its growth has slowed, but Gopher is still a popular way to reach information. A Gopher server is very efficient and can serve many users at the same time, even with a cheap computer on a slow connection. It is easier to set up a Gopher server than a World Wide Web server because you don't have to create HTML files; you can use any kind of files. You can even conduct sales transactions with Gopher. There are entire Gopher malls on the Internet.

If your company has limited resources and has to make a choice between putting up a Gopher server or a Web server, consider these points: A Gopher server is easier, faster, and cheaper to set up than a Web server, and also easier to update. Most Web browsers can also access your Gopher server. However, a Web server will attract far more visitors, and informal research has shown that visitors to Web sites spend more time at a site exploring its offerings than they will at a Gopher site.

From the point of view of a visitor using Gopher, your Gopher site would be a list of directories and files, with single-line descriptions of what is in each. The Gopher presentation of computer file menus is understandable, but not as visually exciting as a World Wide Web site.

A newer version of Gopher, called Gopher+, lets you add Microsoft Word, PostScript, Rich Text Format and ASCII text documents that can be viewed online if your visitor uses Gopher+ client software. Gopher+ can display graphics, play sound files, show videos, and let readers fill in interactive forms. Gopher+ also has built-in security and verification for people who use a Gopher+ client. Few people do. The stampede to the World Wide Web left Gopher+ in the dust. There are tens of thousands of World Wide Web servers, about 10,000 Gopher servers, and less than 1,000 Gopher+ servers.

To estimate costs for a Gopher server, you need to know how many files you will want on your server, about how much disk space the files will occupy, and the types of file formats you will use. Gopher Jewels, listed in Chapter 4, gives you a list of Gopher sites to explore and will give you some ideas on how to design your own. Several books listed in Chapter 4 have extensive information on how to set up a Gopher server.

## Advertising on the World Wide Web

The University of San Francisco requires that all business majors take a course on information technology, which includes the use of the Internet. What does it cover? "We just use the World Wide Web. We don't use any text-based tools at all," said Lev Efendioglu, Professor of Management. For most businesspeople, the World Wide Web *is* the Internet.

This is becoming true of consumers as well. My Aunt Rosemary doesn't like computers and doesn't own one. She visited me while I wrote this book and said she heard that transcripts of the O.J. Simpson trial were on the Internet. I opened my Web browser and went to the EINet Galaxy search engine. I found the address of the Simpson transcripts, clicked on it and we were there. She found the transcript of the police interrogation of Simpson and was hooked. The appeal of the Web is seductive, universal, and simple to convey. The Web does this by making a tremendous amount of information reachable with easy, instant navigation and an attractive visual display. Even people who don't like computers, like my Aunt Rosie, are attracted to the World Wide Web.

What can a World Wide Web site do for your business? It can do anything you do with printed matter, and then some. It can create awareness for your company and your products or services. It can deliver reference information about what you have to offer. It communicates your "image" more graphically than email. (Email looks like a classified ad.) It's like a 24-hour front desk for your business.

You can put your catalog online on the Web, and can constantly change it. You can add or remove individual items at any time without having to adjust the rest of your catalog. You can change prices and give different prices for different customers. The ability to update continuously eliminates much of the expense and workload of traditional catalog creation and distribution. Internet catalogers can respond immediately to changes in market demands.

If successful, your Web server will probably be seen by more people every month than any printed brochure or newsletter your company publishes. And you can find out which information readers access most often, an advantage you lack with a printed newsletter. In print, you can never tell what parts people read and what parts leave readers cold. Your Web site can deliver information that is completely up to date to your customers, and in turn can deliver instant feedback to you.

Your Web site can actually process a complete sales transaction automatically—without human intervention—and charge the sale to a customer's credit card or billing account. (Using the Web to make sales is much more complicated than advertising. Look for more about sales in Chapter 16.)

Although the World Wide Web is used mostly for external advertising, you can also use Web servers to spread information internally through your company. Levi Strauss uses LeviWeb, an internal server for all 10,000 Levi's office workers around the world. LeviWeb gives them instant access to the most up-to-date company policies, labor practices and human resources information. Hewlett-Packard uses more than 200 internal Web servers for similar information and to spread scientific and purchasing data worldwide.

Still, most businesses use the Web for advertising. Some have been very successful. Lew Rose of the law firm of Arent Fox said his firm's Web site attracted more than 19,000 visitors and that Arent Fox had produced "more than enough business from it to pay for itself for several years. In addition, the publicity from our site generated a tremendous number of very good speaking and writing opportunities." As a promotional item, Rose gives out his Web page on a disk.

Like many advertising people (I do this myself), Poppe Tyson Advertising's David Carlick is fond of numbered lists. When I asked him why a marketer would advertise on the Web, Carlick said, "1) You can define your own Web space and control it. 2) It's easy to update and keep current. 3) Web technology lets you establish a dialog with your customers. 4) Lowest-cost per visit by prospects—cheaper than flyers. 5) Lets prospects *self-select* the information they need. 6) Reaches influential people. 7) Can generate repeat traffic. 8) A surprisingly cheap way to learn about interactive marketing. If you're in marketing, you *must* learn about interactive technology. There is no way around it. 9) Help lower the cost of selling significantly. 10) You can count the exact number of lookers and the exact number of responses. When many companies compare print cost per inquiry or cost per sale with Net costs, their marketing budget will shift to the Net." He also gave three reasons for an advertiser to prefer the World Wide Web to traditional media: "Interactivity is more involving; deeper material; richer advertisement content."

This last point, richer advertisement content, is an important difference between the World Wide Web and traditional media. On the Web, *there is no limit* to the amount of information you provide. You aren't trapped within the confines of a fixed magazine page size or a 60-second spot. You can provide as many thousands of pages of information and illustrations as you need to explain the benefits of your product or service.

In fact, the best advertisers for the Internet are those who need to present lengthy information, whose customers make a "considered purchase." This is a sale in which information from competing suppliers is evaluated, such as with a high-cost item or one requiring a group-buying decision. For cases like these, as David Ogilvy likes to say, "Long copy sells." On the Web, you have the luxury of unlimited length without having to pay substantially more for it.

The Web attracts attention because prospects can view text *with pictures*. You don't need graphics to have a successful Web page, but illustrations don't cost much and don't hurt as long as they are used to reinforce your selling points and don't distract from them. For some Web advertisers, such as Hot Hot Hot (**http://www.hot.presence.com/hot**), the illustrations *establish* the selling point. This is true more often for consumer Web advertising than it is for business-to-business Web advertising. For many consumer Web sites, however, providing *information* that prospects want has proven more successful than illustration and design. Copy bears the brunt of the workload in Web advertising.

There are two levels of Web advertisements. The first presents simple information (a logo, contact information, overall information about the company, general information about products and services) and for most companies won't generate any business, in spite of hucksters' claims to the contrary. If your company presents only general information, regard it as a seed experiment, but don't expect to make money from it. The second level of Web advertisement adds value, which it can do by presenting information, entertainment, or both. A visitor to this type of site feels *satisfied* in some way for having visited. The visitor has been entertained or has received satisfactory information of some sort, perhaps having completed a sales transaction or copied a free software program. Viewer satisfaction with advertising is not an important consideration in traditional media, but it is crucial to Internet advertising, especially if you want repeat customers.

## Planning your Web site

First, a quick clarification of terms. What's the difference between a *home page* and a *Web site*? Your *Web site* will probably contain many individual pages. Although someone can enter your Web site from any page, the main portal of entry is your *home page*. It's like the main lobby of a building, the front page of a newspaper, and the table of contents of a book all rolled into one. Your home page sets the tone for your site, says who you are, excites visitors about your contents, and tells them where to find things.

As its production manager, Chris Gulker brought the *San Francisco Examiner's* Web site (**http://www.sfgate.com**) online. He said, "Your home page is like a newspaper front page, which is a highly refined technology. For best results, arrange your Web page and write your Web stories as journalists write newspaper stories, in descending levels of detail. Start with general information, then more specific information, and finally, yet more specific information. Readership of Web pages drops proportionately from the top to the bottom. When 25 percent of readers read any one story out of all the stories on a newspaper page, that story was a hit. The same holds true with Web pages." As an example, Gulker said that out of 1,000 visitors to the *Electric Examiner's* San Francisco 49ers Web page, the most popular story on the page would be selected by about 250 people.

Since Web advertisers can measure how many times a story is chosen, the *Electric Examiner* is able to tailor its content to increase visitor satisfaction. Gulker elaborates, "There was no response to stories about President Clinton, but any story with the word 'hacker' in its headline did great." A page with a big picture of Madonna on the cover of *Esquire* also had a tiny link to a virtual newsroom. Editors were surprised that the virtual newsroom far outdrew Madonna—an indication of readers' priorities.

In planning your Web content, take note of the *Electric Examiner's* most popular content, in order of popularity:

1.  Lists of links to other sites (about *ten times* as popular as number 4!).

2.  Photos and graphics.

3.  Stories with links to other sites (these outdraw unlinked stories by far).

4.  Stories about the Net, high tech, hackers, and so on.

5.  Any other content. "O.J. Simpson is the only ringer," said Gulker. "I'm sorry, but everything on O.J. sells."

Before you actually build your Web site, you need to plan it. Don't go running to a Web service bureau immediately. You could wind up with your Web presence shaped to conform to the service bureau's needs when it should be the other way around.

**Step One: Research and set goals.** First, study different Web sites. Visit your competitors. You might like to purchase an in-depth analysis of three of the most successful Web sites (DEC, Sun, and Silicon Graphics) done by Datapro. Decide what you want to accomplish. Define your site's purpose and the scope of its contents. Start small. A smaller project is much easier to keep under control, especially if it is your company's first Web site. You can start with just a single page of contact information and an "Under Construction" sign. Then add more pages as you need them. If your company is looking at electronic malls, there are many additional considerations, which you can find in Chapter 16. An important question to answer is, "How will I measure my site to determine whether it is a success?"

**Step Two: Storyboard your Web site.** Producers of television commercials know the value of storyboards. In the design of a Web site, storyboards can save your life. They don't have to be fancy. You can build them with a legal pad, using one sheet for each Web page. For each page in your site, a storyboard page should show what graphics are displayed on that page, what kinds of text are presented, any push-buttons and what the buttons do, what kind of links are on that page, and any checkboxes or interactive forms that your visitors can fill in. Then you can shuffle your paper pages around to determine how you want to sequence your Web pages. You may come up with ideas for new pages or ways to combine pages. Your Web pages can have multiple links with each other. You might spot places to add links between pages. When you have an idea of what you want, create a smaller-sized version that shows the pages with arrows showing the links between pages and direction of travel. A real-life example, one of several created by WAIS Inc. for the DowVision Web site, is shown in Figure 11.1.

Use storyboards to organize your presentation first, then match the contents of your Web site with your concept, not the other way around. The more you present, the more expensive your site will be. Pay special attention to your

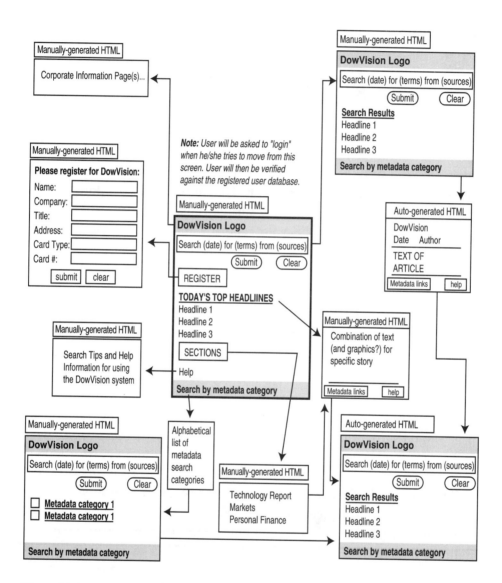

**Figure 11.1**   *This is one of several storyboards used by WAIS Inc. and Dow Jones to plan the DowVision Web site (**http://dowvision.wais.net**). The DowVision home page is the panel in the center. Arrows show all links that a visitor can use to go to another page. A header for each page tells if it is manually generated HTML (a standard page created in advance) or auto-generated HTML (a custom page created upon demand for a specific visitor).*

home page. It will be the first impression many Internet users have of your business. Remember that every link a visitor uses means a sometimes unendurable wait on hold for your visitor. The more waits, the sooner prospects leave. Plan your pages to cause as few waits as possible. Some Web designers suggest that a visitor should be able to reach any page from any other with *no more than four or five mouse clicks.*

If an advertising agency or marketing consultant is involved in planning your Web site, bring them in early in the storyboarding process. Early involvement (assuming they have Web experience) can cut your planning time by an order of magnitude or more, and can give you a better site. When you finish your storyboards, you will know how many graphics files you need, how many text files you need, and the other information necessary to move to the next step.

**Step Three: Estimate costs and locate your server.** At this point you can estimate costs and decide how much you want to do in-house and how much should be handled by outsiders. Farm out whenever possible, especially if this is your first Web project. The important decision here is whether your Web server should be on an in-house computer or on rented space on a computer managed by a service bureau or an Internet access provider.

Are you in a hurry? An outside service will be faster. Is this an experiment you might want to fold if it doesn't meet targeted results? If so, go outside and keep your investment costs low. Will you need to update your data more than once a week for a lot of data or twice a week for minimal changes? Stay in-house if you'll need frequent changes, especially if you will have live links to a database stored on an inside computer.

If you locate your Web server on an outside service bureau's computer, be aware that your service bureau can be *anywhere in the world.* You can send all of your files over the Internet to your Web server. Inexpensive service bureaus in California have led to a flood of immigrant Web sites. Web Communications Corp. in Santa Cruz, California (**http://www.webcom.com**) has attracted businesses from all over North America and Europe with low rates. Its fees start at $30 per month for a business server, and $100 per month for a larger corporate server.

As part of this step, hire any consultants you need. Be aware of the differences between technical expertise, design expertise, and marketing expertise. These are three different skill areas. You could add copywriting as a fourth.

Specialized Web service bureaus have sprung up to focus on serving businesses in specific industries. One is Aspen Media (**http://www.aspenmedia.com**), which concentrates on printers, graphic designers, advertising agencies, and other graphics resources. It provides businesses in its market with a free listing in Aspen's Web directory, and for a fee provides graphics-related businesses with Web sites on its computer. Aspen's site and connection are designed to quickly move huge graphics and video files, a necessity for online graphics portfolios. Aspen will even promote its clients' sites, listing them in online directories and on search engines. If your company looks for an outside service bureau to handle your Web site, check to see if there is a service like Aspen that focuses on serving your specific industry.

With a service bureau, consultant, or designer, you should negotiate. Published prices are usually not final. Service bureau charges may include setup costs, costs of creating Web files, monthly disk storage costs, credit card processing fees, per-download fees, and monthly maintenance fees. And ask related questions. What does its setup fee include? Is there an extra charge when you update your server? You will want to update your site as frequently as possible. Is there an extra charge for creating interactive forms on your Web page that visitors can fill out? Will your bureau do anything to market your site? It may be worth paying extra for this. The longer the lease, the lower the price. Many businesses start sites that flop and then, when they want to close them, realize they are trapped in a one-year lease. When you start your first Web site, consider it an experiment and don't sign up for longer than three months.

Every week or every month, your service bureau should give you daily traffic reports. These should measure hits for each file at a mimimum, and how many distinct *users* if possible. See what kind of reports your service generates. Get a sample. Are reports broken down to show activity by day? Are visiting domain names spelled out or in difficult-to-decipher abbreviations?

Potential show-stoppers: If you intend to integrate with a database, let a potential service bureau know. Database hookups are complicated and can have many ramifications. Check in advance to see if you can use your own domain name. Some services can accommodate your business only if you use the bureau's domain name, not your own. If you want your service bureau to accept credit card transactions, see if it has secure Web service software. If it does, will it process the credit card transaction for you, or only fax the credit card information to you? How much will it charge per transaction?

When you provide a change to your service bureau, there should be a minimum amount of time before your bureau puts your change in place on your Web site. This should be specified in writing. Other questions: How fast will your connection be? What security is used? How long has it been in business? Visit the bureau's own Web site. Is it slow? Who are its clients? Talk to at least three of them. Look at their Web sites. Are they slow?

Do a site visit (unannounced is best) if your candidate bureau is nearby. Standard payment terms are one-third up front, one-third upon delivery of the system, and one-third after it has been running for 30 days so you know everything works. You should get a price break if you provide finished HTML files.

If you shop, you can get a single page for under $500 or even under $100 (setup cost) if you keep it bare-bones simple. If you do your own pages, I've seen service bureau rents start at $25 a month, based on the amount of disk space used. If you hire someone to write your Web pages, the fee for HTML creators starts as low as $50 an hour, but CGI programmers and experienced Web designers usually charge $75 to $200 an hour.

Netscape, which has, according to some estimates, 75 percent of the Web browser market, has added the ability to do pages in Adobe Acrobat format (.PDF files, which stands for Portable Document Format), so you can use full-blown PostScript design on your Web pages. Expect to pay more for someone to design pages this way.

If you want to build your Web site in-house, you will need Web server software in addition to your own computer. There are good, free Web server software packages for almost every kind of computer operating system, but none of the free ones process credit card transactions securely. Netscape (**http://www.netscape.com**) sells its Netsite Communications Server for $1,500, which is not secure, and its Netsite Commerce Server—which can handle credit card payments—for $5,000. Netscape also sells more expensive higher-end servers, detailed in Chapter 16. Open Market Inc. (**http://www.openmarket.com**) sells insecure Web server software for $1,500 and secure software for $5,000. Open Market's software includes the ability to track transactions onscreen. Spry Inc. also sells a secure server.

**Step Four: Write, design, and build your components.** Once you have your costs figured out and have chosen a place to locate your server (either a service bureau or in-house), it is time to actually create the pieces. I cover this in detail in a following section.

**Step Five: Put the pieces together and go live.** As long as you let visitors know that your site is "under construction," they'll forgive you if the site has a few kinks in it. Think of your Web site as an ongoing work in progress. That's one of the great features of the Web. You can make changes more easily and more often than you can with a print or broadcast ad.

**Step Six: Promote your site, study your response, and enhance your site.** I'll say more about this later, so here I'll just stress that your Web site will require continual attention to ensure that your target audience is being served and that you are responding to its needs.

# Web design and construction

In the next few sections, I'll give some specific advice and techniques for designing and setting up a Web page. I'll include advice from real-world businesspeople who have already conquered the Web, and who use their own Web pages successfully to attract and retain customers.

## Web advertising design tips

Some people call Web sites "digital billboards." This is one of the most ridiculous things I've ever heard. If you treat your home page like a billboard, you won't get many people interested in it, your return visitor rate will be zilch, and you won't generate sales from it.

Your Web server can survey your customers, take orders, calculate sales tax and shipping charges, validate a credit card or account name, and even deliver products (consulting reports, software programs, pictures, and so on). Billboards can't do that. If you think of your Web site as a billboard, your whole *mindset* will be wrong when you plan your site. So don't.

The most important page for most sites is the home page. (If you take online orders, your order entry page is the most important.) Your home page is a limited but valuable piece of screen real estate, and it needs to convey a number of ideas at once. It should show a visitor at a glance what kind of business you are in, what your site has to offer, and why the visitor should explore further.

Most companies begin with a graphic banner showing their company name. This does not need to be gigantic. Many companies have a few lines of description of the company, but most visitors care more about what's available from your site. This is the place to put a table of contents for your Web site. Don't make visitors wade through a page of glib nothingness to reach another page that actually gives information or takes them somewhere. Put a menu right up front, on your home page. Also, Web visitors want to see things that are new. On your home page, list anything new or changed, and put a date by it. People who return to your Web site will usually scan your home page menu. If it shows nothing different from their previous visit, they will leave without looking further.

About 40 percent of your visitors might *not* look at your graphics files, so when you use a picture as a link, include an alternate route via a text link. If you are ambitious, you can provide text-only alternative pages for any graphics-heavy Web pages. But if you provide text-only access, here's what *not* to do: Many misdesigned sites have a "text only" link prominently displayed on their home pages. When you click on it, you download a text-only version *of the same page you have already downloaded*. When you go to another link, it takes you to another page full of graphics. What a waste. If your site is set up properly, clicking "text only" should take a visitor down a completely separate *set* of pages, none of which contain graphics files.

You will have visitors who speak different languages. If this is important to your business, make your Web site, or at least your home page, multilingual. Present your home page in English, with the option to click on a "Deutsche" link, for example, to see your home page in German. Many European and some Japanese links give good examples of this technique.

The biggest issue among Web page designers involves the amount and quality of graphics. Should you have beautiful jumbo graphics files that take several minutes or longer to download, or should you have as little graphics as possible so your pages download faster? As far as I know, no one has yet done a split-run test (which could be easily done on the Web) to answer this debate. In my experience, both camps are right. There are times when large graphics files are the better approach. The success of HOT HOT HOT proves that. There are other times when minimal graphics are preferable. A frequently used search engine like Yahoo would drive people nuts if they had to wait for a 40 K graphics file before they could use it. The same holds true for database searchers. Your choice depends on your target markets: Researchers and business users seem to be less patient with graphics lag than consumers.

Some simple math will give you a size budget for a Web page. You can set a goal of a number of seconds for total download time for a page, and size your text and graphic files to fit under that time limit. You need to take into account the kind of connection your customers have. If they use a modem, each download takes one second for the modem to *negotiate* the download with your Web server software. If your customers use ISDN or any faster digital connection, each download's negotiation will take less than one-tenth of a second on average. (How do you know what speeds your customers use to connect? Your Web site should generate activity reports to tell you. For your first Web page, you need to guess.)

Here are numbers for a sample page. For total time, we'll use the figure recommended by Webmaster Robert Mudry: a top limit of five seconds per page. Most customers for our imaginary site use a 14.4 Kbps modem, so five seconds gives us 72,000 bits of graphics and text to play with. But we need to subtract one second's bits for the modem to negotiate the text file download. 72,000 bits minus 14,400 bits leaves us with 57,600 bits. If we add a graphics file, that adds another download, so we subtract another one second's 14,400 bits, leaving 43,200 bits for two files, one text and one art. We could have a longish 20,000-bit text file and a good-sized 20,000-bit graphics file and still have 3,200 bits left over.

Great! Let's add a teeny green bullet as a highlight. It's only a 276-bit graphics file. 3,200 minus 276 bits should leave 2,924 bits left over, right? Wrong. We forgot that the bullet adds another modem negotiation, which takes one second and eats up another 14,400 bits all by itself. You now have a Web page that takes at least six seconds to view. This math may seem a bit much, but it shows how lots of tiny graphics files can take longer to download than a couple of medium or large ones. Web browsers have kill buttons, and it is estimated that between 40 and 45 percent of all Web users surf the Web with graphics turned off, or kill large graphics files and never see them.

If you want customers to look at your graphics files, keep in mind that people are most likely to wait for a small file of 5 K or less, and will usually wait for a 10 K file. You can employ some proven pricing psychology here with your file sizes. Web browsers show file sizes, and a 4,995 K file seems much smaller than a 5,000 K file. When you use Photoshop or other software to create your graphics files, you can adjust the size down a notch to keep below "price points."

Don't get carried away with fancy buttons! Paramount's *Star Trek: Voyager* home pages give you page after page of nothing but big 60 K files of pushbuttons before you see anything cool. No matter how slick you make pushbuttons, page after page of them will make your viewers angry. Each page should have some information, not just a handful of links to yet another page. One Web designer told me he tries to put at least three pieces of information on each page.

 If you want to make your visitors really mad, put up a dead-end link. A dead end takes you to another page, which turns out to be blank except for a sign that says "Under Construction" or something equally useless. A company that had information I really wanted on an overcrowded site (we are talking slower than a tax refund) forced me to go to a page three times that had nothing but a 45 K graphics file. When I finally got it, all it said was—you guessed it: "Under Construction." I was steamed. Apparently I'm not the only one, because a warning to avoid this deadly sin appears on nearly every list of Web design tips.

Now for some Web design miscellany: Part of going on the Web involves scanning your company logos and images into GIF files. This costs little, and you can reuse the same graphics for months or even years. Hot links, hypertext links, and anchors are essentially all the same thing. Links are usually in a different color and are underlined when they are text, but they can be pushbuttons, pictures, or even areas within a picture, such as countries on a map. Don't clutter your Web pages with too many pictures. Don't use a different icon for each bullet. Keep a good white space balance. Anything that looks like a button should work like one.

One final design tip from author Jaclyn Easton: "When you're done designing your Web page, go to Prodigy and look at it." You might design your Web page on a Power Mac, Sun workstation or SGI Indy, but most of your customers will view it under far worse conditions. Get a 9600 baud modem and review your work the way real people see it.

## Free art for Web pages

So you're not an artist and you don't have one in house? Try these sites for some art resources you can download for free:

- Sandra's Clip Art Server: **http://www.cs.yale.edu/HTML/YALE/ CS/HyPlans/loosemore-sandra/clipart.html**
- Department of Computer Science Icon Browser: **http://www.di.unipi.it/iconbrowser/icons.html**
- Anthony's Icons: **http://server.berkeley.edu:80/pub/AIcons/appl** (Some icons here are copyrighted and not usable. See the readme file.)
- Public domain Web art designed by Poppe-Tyson Advertising: **http://www.poppe.com/poppe/pt2-public_jpeg.html**
- Tony's Icons: **http://www.bsdi.com/icons/tonys.html**

## *Writing for the Web*

Web copywriting is 90 percent marketing and 10 percent technical tricks. Internet junkies are information junkies, and on most Web sites, the text presents the information. Web copywriting should be low-key, less pompous than a press release, and more soft-sell. One of the main jobs of writing for the Web is to use information and/or entertainment to *differentiate* your company from competitors. You will have competition on the Web because the barriers to entry are so low. How is your company different? What information (not hype) can you provide that shows that difference clearly?

Aim the copy on your home page directly at getting a visitor *into your site*, not at selling your company or its products. The place to sell products comes later. Your home page needs to tell what is inside, what is new, and how to get there. Your home page should also list contact information for your business: phone, fax, postal address, and an email address. It is amazing how many Web sites provide only part of this information. A few sites actually provide no contact information at all! In researching this book, I went over every page twice at the site of a company I wanted to contact. It listed absolutely no contact information, not even the Webmaster's email address. And I'll bet that company complains that it gets no business from its Web site.

For most writers, a Web site is their first experience with hypertext links. Writing with links in mind is fun, but don't get carried away and use linking every time a word—your company name, for example—appears. Follow the storyboards for your Web site. Link only the words needed to take people to and from the places listed on the boards.

Every link should have a description. If your link is in a paragraph of body copy, something in that paragraph should say what that link is. If you have a list of links to sites, add an explanation about each link. The ability to write copy to describe a file or a page is what distinguishes the World Wide Web from Gopher or FTP. It frustrates visitors looking for something on your site to click on one of your links and be detoured to an unwanted destination. Author Jaclyn Easton visited more than three thousand Web sites researching her book *Shopping on the Internet and Beyond*. She wasted hours of time chasing down vague links. The attitude of your customer, said Easton, is "Don't make me click at three bucks an hour and tap my toes for a full ninety seconds to find out that's not where I want to be."

When you provide a downloadable file and write a link for it, also write the size of the file next to your link. This holds true for all kinds of files, whether they contain software, graphics, or text. The price Web users pay for files lies in their download time. When you give someone a file without the size, it's like selling him or her something without giving a price. Without knowing a file's size, a customer will start to download it, get an idea of its size, and cancel the download. That wastes machine cycles for your Web server and wastes time for your customer. Just put the size in parentheses after your link: <u>Mona Lisa</u> (56 K).

Newspaper front pages are designed so the most important stories are on the top half of the page, above the fold. A story below the fold won't be seen in a newspaper vending machine. In the same way, on Web pages people look mostly at what is on the top of the page. People miss links, graphics, and copy at the bottoms of Web pages. Keep that in mind when writing for the Web, and make sure all your most important information is at the top of each page.

There are certain things that should be in the copy for each Web page. At the bottom, the email address and perhaps the name of your company's webmaster should be listed. The name *webmaster* is derived from "postmaster," and is the administrator in charge of your Web site. Your company name should be someplace on each page, perhaps with a way to contact your order desk. You may want to include copyright information on each page.

There are also two invisible pieces of copy to write on each page. All Web pages include HTML text at the top that does not display onscreen. In this copy, you need to include a title for each page. It should briefly describe the page ("Yourco 1995 Quarterly Financial Reports") and include your company name. Even though this title will not display on the Web page itself, it is the name that will appear in a bookmark if your customer wants to return to that page, and Web search engines will direct people to that page based on its title. The other thing to include in the nondisplayed text at the top of each page is the URL address of the page. When people save or print your page, this will give them the address so they can return.

## *Simple technical tricks*

You can create Web pages in a format readable by Adobe Acrobat, but most Web sites are created with a simple language called *Hypertext Markup Language*, or HTML, which uses *tags*. These tags are the commands embedded in your original text document that transform your text into a Web page. Your original document is called a *source document* by Web preparers. Any word processor can create a source document. Many word processing and desktop publishing programs can even produce Web-ready HTML documents. WordPerfect, Word, Lotus Notes, FrameMaker, and other programs have add-ons that let them do this.

HTML tags let you change type sizes, format paragraphs, add hot links, and tell where to place graphics, sound, and video files. HTML also lets you create tables of information and interactive forms that visitors to your site can fill in to provide you with information.

Cyberleaf, a product from Interleaf, Inc. (**http://www.ileaf.com**) automatically turns documents from Interleaf, FrameMaker, Microsoft Word, WordPerfect, and ASCII into HTML documents. It analyzes the styles of the original documents and matches them to equivalent HTML styles. Cyberleaf is available for Unix, Windows, and Windows NT.

You can generate HTML Web pages dynamically. This lets you provide user-specific pages—a custom page designed specifically for each reader. Dynamically generated pages require more expensive custom programming than your average HTML page.

Your Web software can also read a Web site visitor's domain name and display a different page based on what it finds. For example, your software could examine your reader's email address, and if that person's address is from Italy, display text in Italian. Or if the reader had looked at your page before and selected French text, your software could remember the reader's address and when the reader looked again, display French without asking. If you have a catalog page and your prices are different for different clients, your software can check your reader's email address, and based on that show the correct prices that apply to this specific client.

Most Web browsers can also use other Internet services, including Gopher, Veronica, Archie, FTP, Telnet, Finger, WAIS, email and even newsgroups. You can write links in your Web pages that, when clicked, take your visitor directly to your Gopher server, and even to a specific file on your server, or on your FTP, Telnet, or WAIS server.

If you have a graphic file that you want to use on more than one Web page, you can write your pages so that the file is downloaded onto a visitor's computer only once and reused by following pages. Doing this makes your pages display much faster than reloading graphics every time.

To incorporate an advanced feature into your site, you can use WebChat, which lets visitors have a real-time typed conversation with other visitors to your site. They can also send multimedia information back and forth, live. WebChat is free software. The site that offers it also has a live demo: **http://www.irsociety.com/webchat/webchat.html**

## After your Web site goes live

Once you have your World Wide Web site up and running, it's time to promote it, study the response you generate, and tweak your site to make it more productive. You will need to make the *editorial investment* needed to sustain interest, making frequent changes and additions to attract return visitors. Return visits don't just happen due to random molecular collisions. You need to *motivate* return visits, to provide customers with a reason to come back.

Companies have come up with ingenious methods to lure returnees. Contests have given away cars, software, and a bag of 10,000 pogs. Sun Microsystems tied its Web server into the 1994 World Cup Soccer playoffs, providing the latest scores and information on the teams and players.

Tom Mayer, marketing director of The Coriolis Group put an offer for a free issue of the magazine *PC TECHNIQUES* on the Coriolis Web site (**http://www.coriolis.com/coriolis**). The first two months, response was slow. Coriolis advertisements and catalogs listing its Web site address came out in the third month, and the site now racks up as many takers for its free issue offer every five days as it did in the previous two months.

John Russo of access provider GeoNet Communications said of the Web, "Unlike print media, you have to condition your customers to how often to expect new material. Then, to avoid disappointment you have to deliver to deadline, just like print media." Unless they provide extraordinarily rewarding information or entertainment, sites that change their Web pages only once a month will get customer visits only every couple of months. Sites changing every day receive return visits every few days.

One Web-only method of promotion that has grown popular is swapping links on pages with other companies. Some companies actually charge money to do this, but in most cases it is a straight link-for-link exchange. The problem that link swapping creates lies in measuring effectiveness. How can you tell if you have received any referrals from the other site? It is actually easy, if you have a technical person who knows how to program *redirects*. Here is how it works. When you swap links, you give the other company a special URL to link with. That URL points to a redirect file on your computer, which points to your home page. When a visitor to the other company's Web site clicks on your link, the customer goes to the redirect file, and without any knowledge or effort on the customer's part, ends up on your home page. Most customers will never notice that anything has happened. Your redirect file can count how many visits it receives and give you a tally. That tells you exactly how many referrals your swapped link generated. You can make as many redirect files as you need, so each redirect can keep track of a different swapped link.

Add this to the data you capture from *clickstreams*, the tracked paths of individual visitors through your Web site, and other data you collect from your Web site and customer email, and you will have a clear indication of areas to expand. Continually measure the impact your site has on your company, and keep telling management about that impact so managers will stay committed. Build on your first successes when you design your next project.

## Advertising and more with WAIS

WAIS (Wide Area Information System) is software that crosses boundaries. You can use it for publicity, advertising, sales, and customer support. It can present information as a Gopher server and as a World Wide Web server. It is free, and you can buy it.

WAIS sorts through databases, documents, audio files, and graphics files and builds indexes for them. Then WAIS links up with a Gopher or Web server and lets people look up information, and quickly delivers the requested information to them. You ask a *question* of a WAIS server, rather than click on a known address. When new additions or changes are made, WAIS indexes the changes and updates the information available for searchers. World Wide Web indexes must be built by hand, which is only feasible for smaller, manageable databases that don't change much. WAIS makes it possible to provide a large amount of information online, getting a system up and making it easy to keep up to date. It retrieves the material and generates Web pages on the fly to display it. It makes businesses online publishers.

There are two versions of WAIS: a free smaller model called freeWAIS, and a commercial version for large-scale online publishing projects. The commercial version runs on Unix, and a Windows NT version is due about the time this book comes out. The commercial version costs $15,000. Hardware for the Unix version runs $15,000 to $20,000. The NT version should run on less expensive hardware.

WAIS Inc. sells and supports the commercial version of WAIS. Its clients include:

- Encyclopedia Britannica (**http://www.eb.com**), which makes 44 million words of text available to subscribers. (After several experiments, Britannica found that the best place to put a search engine is right up front on its home page.)

- DowVision (**http://dowvision.wais.net**) by Dow Jones, which delivers the *New York Times, Wall Street Journal, Los Angeles Times,* wire services, and other services for $50 per month, letting subscribers design their own personal newspaper and receive it daily. The information on DowVision changes every few seconds.

- Sun Microsystems (**http://www.sun.com**), which uses a WAIS server to provide customer support, marketing, and sales documents. Sun distributes 40,000 documents a day over the Net.

- Novell (**http://www.novell.com**), which had 1,000 people on the phones for tech support, with an average call length of 30 minutes. Novell installed a WAIS server to cut calls. Its server now distributes 10,000 documents per day.

- CMP Publications (**http://techweb.cmp.com**), which put 17 of its publications online.

- Internet Shopping Network (**http://www.internet.net**), which uses WAIS to create its catalog electronically, avoiding printing and mailing, the major costs of catalog sales.

WAIS Inc. (**http://www.wais.com**) sells the commercial version of WAIS and lets you build your own system, or builds a server for you, for $50,000 to $250,000. This includes a billing module, so you can charge for your information, and software that captures statistics.

## Paying for Internet advertising

The tactics above all involve free access to communicate with prospects on the Internet. A growing number of sites offer you the opportunity to pay for the same access. Is it worthwhile to pay for ad space in cyberspace?

The pioneer in charging for Internet advertising is Tim O'Reilly, president of publisher O'Reilly & Associates. O'Reilly's 1992 release of the book *The Whole Internet User's Guide & Catalog* by Ed Krol was a catalyst in the subsequent explosion of Internet growth, and O'Reilly's *Global Network Navigator* was, I believe, the first World Wide Web electronic magazine. *GNN* charges for advertising. "We're making a substantial amount of money" on *GNN*, O'Reilly said. "It's a playground where we can learn what works and what doesn't work."

"The point of Web advertising," he continued, "is that people have got to *want* to retrieve it, which I think is great because it means that advertisements will have to have useful information." He was approached by Lonely Planet, which wanted to buy advertising in *GNN*. Lonely Planet wanted to put its advertisement in an ad for O'Reilly's Traveler's Tales books. O'Reilly believes that is the best kind of Internet advertisement—one so compelling that another business wanted to advertise in it.

But how can advertisers decide what Internet media to pay for and what to avoid? There is now no accepted method of measuring Internet "viewership."

Some people talk about hits, a very misleading figure. Others discuss the number of actual users visiting a site in a given time span.

Jack Edmonston, editor and publisher of *Computer Advertiser's Media Advisor* (fax 508-358-2798) wrote in *Business Marketing:* "High penetration would be useless to cable TV if no one ever turned it on. A survey of more than 5 million Americans with direct access to the Internet showed more than a third accessed it less than once a month. Only 12 percent of the survey respondents accessed it every day. And, using this picture, I believe that advertisers should evaluate—and pay for—interactive advertising based on the cost per thousand contacts generated, or 'CPMC.' This is like paying for direct mail based on the number of people who actually read it. Imagine how much cheaper your mailing program could be if you didn't have to pay for any mail that wasn't actually opened and read."

Gary Wolff is one of the producers of *HotWired* (**http://www.hotwired.com**) and is coauthor of the book *Aether Madness.* He believes that hits are an almost completely invalid way of measuring Internet viewership, pointing out that Adam Curry claimed 200,000 to 300,000 hits per day for Curry's Metaverse site, but most of the hits were generated by the multiple graphics files that any single Metaverse page contains. Wolff claims that *HotWired's* method of registration is more valid. "When *HotWired* launched," said Wolff, "in its first week readers *registered* at an average of one per minute." *HotWired* is free to readers and is supported by ads. It is divided into several sections. A banner advertisement runs at the top of each section, often linking to an advertiser's own Web site. One of the sections, "Coin," is nothing but advertisements. The electronic magazine opened with 14 advertisers, some of whom have since renewed their contracts, and several new ones have come aboard. *HotWired* grosses about $2 million per year.

The successes of *Global Network Navigator* and *HotWired* unleashed a stampede of advertiser-supported wannabes. Publisher Sendai Media has an online Web magazine called *Nuke* targeted towards males aged 15 to 30. Ziff-Davis asks $10,000 to $25,000 for a three-month advertisement in one of its electronic publications. Publisher CMP put 17 high-tech publications on the Web and sold advertising space starting at $5,000 per month. For that money, more than an entire Web server costs to run, most advertisers ran only small graphic files of company logos.

A more elaborate project is Knowledge Adventure World's *Interactive World's Fair*, a computer game that requires both a CD-ROM and an Internet hookup to play. Knowledge Adventure's (**http://www.kaworlds.com**) investors include Steven Spielberg. The company initially wanted to charge advertisers $100,000 to $500,000 for advertorial content in the game.

In the newspaper business, the bread-and-butter advertising—where most papers really make their money—is in the "Help Wanted" section of the classifieds. Bernard Hodes Advertising is one of the largest agencies in the recruitment advertising business. It came up with a new way to make money. Hodes charges its clients to run job openings on Hodes' own help wanted Web page instead of running many large print ads. Then Hodes runs small print ads in newspaper classified sections telling readers to look on its Web page instead of in the paper. The *San Jose Mercury News* was so upset by this tactic that it refused to run Hodes' ad. A number of newspapers now protect themselves by running all classified ads both in their print pages and on the Web.

There is no *Standard Rate and Data Service* book for the Internet to tell advertisers what they are getting into. There are no Neilsen or Arbitron ratings, no audited readership reports. There is no protection at all against getting charged unreasonable amounts for Internet advertising. The only company working on a standard third-party audit for Web ad media is I/Pro, which I discuss in the next chapter. Your company can run a big Web server on a fast line for $1,000 per month or less. Certainly if any Web site approaches you for advertising and its rates are higher than that, you should probe and find what the value added is—if any—that justifies the extra cost.

Cooperative advertising for Web space is another fast-growing area. Computer products retailer NECX Direct charges co-op to manufacturers to advertise in its online store, with fees ranging from $500 a month (to be one of three sponsors for a product category) to $2,000 a month (for a "customized showroom" with detailed product information, press releases, online technical support and name-capturing for the advertiser's mailing list). NECX Direct probably pays for its entire Web presence with this co-op and perhaps generates a profit.

There are many less costly alternatives available. Corporate sponsorship is effective on the Net, and surprisingly cheap. You can sponsor software with your company's name on it and give it away on the Net. There are no disk duplication fees and no printing costs, and if you set it up properly, your free giveaway can generate both email and postal mailing lists for future promotions.

The biggest advertising bonanza in the United States will be something that is already a cash cow in France. When French people visit the United States, they are astonished that we are so backward as to still have printed telephone directories. France hasn't had printed phone books for years. Instead, they look up numbers online using their Minitel network. Yellow Pages-type advertising in Minitel generates enormously profitable revenues for France Telecom. Here in the backward U.S., several large corporations are racing frantically to be the one company to put a national World Wide Web telephone directory in place, with annual advertising sales potentially in the billions of dollars.

## Selecting an agency

In August 1994, *Advertising Age* surveyed 280 corporate CEOs. Only 12 percent of them said that their ad ad agencies were ready to help their clients market via the "information highway" (a term that will disappear once the technology becomes commonplace, as "horseless carriage" bridged the technical comprehension gap early in this century). Nearly 50 percent of the CEOs thought *they wouldn't need an ad agency* when technology lets their companies talk directly with their customers.

Very little of the advertising done on the Internet is created or placed by advertising agencies. Most of it is created by Internet access providers and service bureaus, who understand the technology better than the marketing.

David Carlick of Poppe Tyson said that the difference between ad agencies and service providers doing your Web site is that "an agency figures out who to reach and how to sell to them. A service bureau says, 'What do you want on your home page?'" According to Carlick, the Internet was 10 percent of business at his agency at the start of 1995, but is projected to be 50 percent by year-end, helped by Poppe Tyson's track record of high-visibility Net projects, and because, he said, Poppe Tyson charges "very, very competitive rates."

I asked Carlick what a company should look for in an Internet advertising agency. He cited five important questions:

- "Do they have expertise and a commitment to the medium so you won't be their guinea pig?
- Do we have chemistry?
- Do they have the ability to understand my business?
- Do I like their work?
- Does my budget match their client requirements?

Avoid people who seem intimidating and who act like they know more than you do."

I would add to his suggestions one of my own: Look for background in direct marketing. It is hard to find an agency or a service bureau that fits those criteria. Besides Poppe Tyson Advertising and Ogilvy & Mather Direct's Interactive Marketing Group (**http://www.img.om.com/img/default.html**), few fit the bill. There are more designers and agencies jumping into the pool every day. Most are generalists, but more specialists like Aspen Media have been announced. Magazine designer Roger Black announced a company called Interactive Bureau in New York to design online magazines.

In the meantime, the best way to preview an agency is to check its Web site. You have quite a range to choose from. There is everything from Tenagra, with almost no detectable design but a rich level of information (**http://arganet.tenagra.com**) to fresh Clement Mok designs Inc. (**http://www.cmdesigns.com**) showing a Web page with 3-D QuickTime videos. New Internet agencies come online every week.

# How to Generate Vital Strategic Information With Internet Marketing Research

*"As a copywriter, what I want from the researchers is to be told what kind of advertising will make the cash register ring. A creative person who knows nothing about plus and minus factors, and refuses to learn, may sometimes luck into a successful campaign. A blind pig may sometimes find truffles, but it helps to know that they grow under oak trees."*

David Ogilvy, *The Unpublished David Ogilvy*

Every successful company does market research—whether it is formal or casual, logical or intuitive. Once on the Internet, your company still needs to answer the same questions as in your pre-wired days:

- Who are your prospects? How can you tell a likely prospect from a hopeless one? What information does a prospect need to decide to buy? What is the most profitable way to reach your most likely prospects with that information? Would it be more profitable to change your pricing strategy? How can you speed up your sales cycle?

- Who are your customers? Out of all your customers, how can you spot your *most profitable* customers? How can you make your less profitable customers more profitable? How can you convert one-time buyers into repeat customers? What do your customers *really* think about your company and its offerings? What are the main reasons you lose customers? What are the main reasons you lose sales? What new products and services do your customers want?

- How can you advertise and publicize more effectively? What characteristics do your most loyal clients share? Can you use this to pinpoint a common appeal to increase sales to your less-loyal customers?

- How big are your markets? Are they growing or shrinking? What is your market share? Is it growing or shrinking? What other markets would work for you?

- Who are your competitors? How well are they doing? How do your best customers feel about them?

To research these questions in the old days, you'd have to go to a library. On the Net, you rarely need to leave your desk. You get the same information—or better—in a fraction of the time and for pennies on the dollar.

You can use tools like FTP, Gopher, and the World Wide Web to locate information from governments, universities, corporations, industry associations, and data providers all over the planet. Topics range from census information and import-export statistics to advertising lineage and purchasing surveys. You can monitor Usenet discussion groups on topics that affect your company. There are about 10,000 of these newsgroups. A good one is like watching a focus group on steroids. You don't have to guess how participants feel—you *know.*

You can conduct marketing surveys on the Net. You can search through thousands of online newspapers, magazines, and journals. You can capture demographic, statistical, and behavioral data from your company's own Internet traffic. You can do split-run tests of advertising concepts, package designs, and pricing ideas.

The most direct form of Internet marketing research is also the most simple: tally your email. Count incoming email messages from your customers. This is what happens when you send email to the President of the United States at **president@whitehouse.gov**. All incoming messages are logged and read. The subject or subjects of each message are noted, as well as any pro and con points of view. Every day the White House staff reviews reports of messages, serving as an instant opinion survey.

If your company already conducts email correspondence with customers or prospects, it costs little for you to put a similar message tally operation into place. The most basic statistic—number of incoming customer messages per day—can be recorded to reveal patterns and trends. Recording message subjects and preparing a simple daily report can reveal much more. Since email is such a quick response medium, this can be a surprisingly fast way to identify potential problems as well as indications of new opportunities.

In an interview in the February 1995 issue of *Micro Times*, CompuServe vice president Tim Oren told how quick customer reactions by email keep him informed. He said one advantage he has, "...being an old research guy now moved into the online business, is that if I want to try something out, I've got two million people out there, some portion of which will try it out and tell me real quickly if I have a winner on my hands or if I've got a problem. Instant test-tube. No need to guess. No need to run the focus groups. If you can turn it on, just turn it on and go. Just post the disclaimers." *(He laughed.)*

That kind of instant interactive response is one factor that makes the Internet such a valuable tool for marketing research. You get insight—sometimes hard-hitting—into customer and prospect needs, and you get it quickly. When you have more specific needs than your email tallies can satisfy, you can conduct marketing surveys over the Net by using email, newsgroups, and the World Wide Web.

# How to conduct surveys

Using email is the easiest way to conduct a survey on the Internet. It's also cheap and fast. The caveat here is to be careful (see the tips below), so you don't anger perfectly good customers and prospects. Strive for surveys without flames.

First, don't be intrusive with your email survey. Remember that millions of people on the Internet pay for each message they receive or pay by incoming message length. Such folks will not be happy to find an unexpected 10-page questionnaire from you.

Keep your survey short. You'll get the highest response rate with a one-screen (24 lines long) survey. A two-screen (48 lines) will do almost as well. Beyond that, response drops off sharply unless you offer incentives. You don't need to leave lots of blank space for replies. Your respondents can insert that themselves. Here's a simple example of formatting:

## *The Wrong Way*

```
1. Was your Spade and Archer customer service representative:
   (chose one)
   A. Concerned and responsive

   B. Unconcerned and boring

   C. Hard-boiled

2. Please give any comments about the investigator(s) who handled your case.


3. What was(were) the name of your investigator(s).
```

That took 14 lines. Here's how to do the same thing in four:

## The Right Way

```
1. Your Spade and Archer customer service representative was: (delete all but one)
   A. Concerned and responsive  B. Unconcerned and boring  C. Hard-boiled
2. Please give any comments about the investigator(s) who handled your case.
3. What was(were) the name of your investigator(s)?
```

## What You Will Get Back

```
>>
>> 1. Your Spade and Archer customer service representative was: (delete all
      but one)
>> C. Hard-boiled
>> 2. Please give any comments about the investigator(s) who handled your
      case?
   He wouldn't play the sap for me.
>> 3. What was(were) the name of your investigator(s)?
   Originally Mr. Archer. After Mr. Archer was shot, Mr. Spade handled my
   case.
>>
```

How do you get names and Internet addresses to use for an email survey? If your company has its own mailing list, you can use it, but only if your survey covers the same topic that the mailing list addresses. Off-topic surveys make people mad, and generate flames or responses with bogus answers instead of usable ones. If your company saves prospect and customer email addresses, you may be able to use those. Don't use names from another company. People with no relationship to your firm will be hostile to unsolicited surveys from you. If another company offers its own list for your use, have the other company send your survey out from its Internet address under its own name, and structure the survey as one from the other company. Don't rent email lists. They are useless for surveys.

Don't send your surveys out "cold calling." If people don't expect your survey, they won't answer it. This especially holds true for prospects, who may not even remember ever contacting your business.

Instead, send a short prefatory message to your intended respondents. Personalize this message—don't make it seem to come from an impersonal bureaucracy. Make it informal. When getting permission to survey someone, you want to be casual even when asking someone in a country with an otherwise formal email style. Just keep it respectful. Say something like, "You contacted our company for information some time ago. I'd like to make sure that we sent you the right information and see what more we can do for you. May

I ask you a few questions by email?" If you want to send a lengthy survey (a dozen or more questions), say "a survey" instead of "a few questions." No use calling a pickle a pig.

Sign your message with a *person's* name. Don't say this message comes from some cold-sounding and anonymous department. And if you market to programmers or technical people (and there are a lot of them on the Net), don't say that your survey comes from a marketing department or sales department, or even use the words "marketing" or "sales." Those are dirty words to technical people. In many companies, technical and marketing people are bitter enemies. Use "customer support" or "customer service" instead of the m-word.

Email surveys go to people who have had some kind of relationship with your company. There are times when you will want information from people with a strong interest in a specific topic, people who may have no interest in your company at all. You can do this by surveying the discussion groups known as Usenet newsgroups.

 Of all the ways to conduct surveys on the Internet, newsgroups are by far the most potentially explosive. Mistakes here can generate hate mail, lose prospect goodwill, and get your *entire company* banned from newsgroups—not to mention ruining your survey. Do not attempt a newsgroup survey without reading this entire section carefully.

The first rule of newsgroup surveys is to pick your targets cautiously. Pretend you are walking in a minefield. Set your foot down in as few places as possible. Each newsgroup is completely different and runs by different rules. Don't judge a newsgroup by its name. Names will often mislead you.

For each newsgroup you select as a survey candidate, read about 150 messages or two weeks' worth, whichever is a smaller number. You may not have to actually subscribe to a newsgroup to evaluate it. Depending upon your Internet access provider and upon which newsreader software you use, you may be able to review newsgroup messages without subscribing. Some providers store a week or two of newsgroup messages online. If your access provider does this, you can read two weeks' worth of messages in 45 to 90 minutes or so.

This will give you a feel for the style and content of each potentially surveyable newsgroup.

Before you post a survey to a newsgroup, always look for its FAQ list—Frequently Asked Questions. A group's FAQ (pronounced "fak") will cover rules for posting—who can post (subscribers only?) and what can be posted. Most groups post their FAQs once or twice a month. There is an archive of FAQs for many groups at **http://www.cis.ohio-state.edu/hypertext/faq/usenet.**

The more closely your survey fits your audience, the less likely you are to receive bogus answers and angry replies. Restrict your survey to the appropriate interest groups for your survey's subject. Also note what geographical areas you want to cover. Most newsgroups are worldwide, but some are local to one area or country. For instance, newsgroups prefixed with "**au.**" are for Austin, Texas, and "**ba.**" stands for the San Francisco Bay Area. All groups beginning with "**fj.**" are discussions in Japanese about Japan, and "**de.**" stands for Deutschland—Germany—meaning discussions are in German.

If you want to post to a worldwide group but want answers from only one geographic area, say so in your Subject line. Put "Only for AZ please" if you want responses only from Arizona.

When you have selected your final list of potential newsgroups to survey, cut it down to only the best groups. When you send the same message to many groups at once, it is called *cross-posting* and is considered bad netiquette. You might say, "So what? I pick my nose at the dinner table, so I certainly don't give a hoot about Internet manners." Yeah, but the Internet has an enforcer. A type of software program called a *cancelbot* patrols newsgroups and keeps them safe from scum like you. Present company excepted.

Cancelbots check how many newsgroups received a message. If a message is splattered across the newsgroup landscape like so many bugs across a windshield, cancelbots remove the bad messages and warn the offender. Really bad offenders find their entire company-wide *domain* (yourco.com) blocked from newsgroups! Companies have been kicked off not only for spamming identical messages, but also for misposting many slightly "customized" versions of the same message.

Next you need to consider how to *present* your newsgroup survey. You have alternatives based on whether you are looking for information, reactions, or quantifiable statistics.

If you just want a simple answer to a question or three, present your survey as a posted question from an individual person. End the Subject line of your message with a question mark: **Price of jeweled falcon?** All newsgroup messages asking questions should do so. Posting a question from an individual in your company is also a good way to get a reaction to marketing ideas. "I want to know if anybody's had any experience with...", "Does anybody have any strong feelings about...", and "What would you think of..." are all good lead-ins for a short, informal question.

Within a couple of days of posting your question, you will have a few answers and possibly some reactions to your answers and to the topic of your question itself. Just sit back and watch the fur fly.

Your task is more complex when you want quantifiable statistical information. The problem with isolated questions—even if you ask a lot of them—is that you can't link the answers with other answers.

There is a problem with posting lengthy multiple-question surveys on a newsgroup. If you are successful in generating a response, no matter how carefully you instruct respondees to forward completed surveys to you instead of reposting to the group, many will miss your instructions and repost to the group. The group will become clogged with copies of your survey. People will be unhappy. Unpleasantness will ensue.

For complex surveys, you may find it more rewarding to post an invitation to participate. Respondees email to you if they wish to participate. To increase the response rate, your newsgroup posting can offer an incentive for participation.

Whether you conduct surveys using email, newsgroups, or the World Wide Web, the following rules hold true for all Internet marketing surveys:

- Only do consumer research with the agreement of the consumer. Many Internet users have strong concerns about the use of their names and addresses, and about how their information will be used. Tell your potential respondents about the uses and implications of participating in your survey. Be explicit. Let them know that their names and addresses will not be used for solicitation or sold to another vendor.

- Conduct them anonymously; Internet surveys can be biased by a respondent's feelings about your company. For instance, a survey on 486 microprocessors by someone whose Internet address ends with **intel.com** will pull different responses than the same survey by someone from **research.org**. This bias especially affects surveys done in your company's own World Wide Web site. Internet people respond more honestly than most, but it's harder to say negative things directly to someone. Being in someone's Web site is like visiting an aunt's parlor. When she asks, "How do you like my cat?" most people will answer "It's very nice," even if it slobbers, drools, and has ringworm.

- You can reduce the effects of that bias by conducting surveys in conjunction with a research company or an educational institute. Some of the most valuable Internet surveys are conducted by universities. Many are glad to work with private companies. For an example, visit the University of Michigan's survey of World Wide Web buyers: **http://umich.edu/~sgupta/survey3**. This was the first ever conducted survey of Internet buying habits. It is part of the University's Hermes project. On its Web page, Hermes openly invites businesses to participate and to suggest questions for future surveys.

To look at several surveys conducted on the Internet—mostly on the World Wide Web—visit **http://www.yahoo.com/Business/Products_and_services/ Contests/Giveaways.**

If newsgroups are the trickiest way to conduct surveys on the Internet, the World Wide Web is the safest. On the Web, visitors come to you, so you don't have to worry about seeming intrusive.

The drawback to the Web is that you have to find a way to convince people to visit your site to take your survey. If your site is busy, handling thousands of visitors each week, no problem. Just pepper your Web site with invitations to visit your survey page. If your Web site traffic is low, be prepared. You will need to work to actively promote your survey location to generate enough traffic to make it worthwhile.

The World Wide Web's capability for creating fill-in-the-blank forms makes it easy to write and design Web surveys. Plus, you can blend your survey results with the statistical data your Web site captures for rich and detailed results.

There are services and software products you can use to make Internet surveys more rewarding. One company, SmartChoice (**aurken@smartchoice.com**), makes a product called SmartPoll. Sun Microsystems and other companies use it for marketing surveys on product performance, service quality, feature preferences, corporate quality, and employee feedback. SmartPoll not only takes a survey, it provides analyses using different scoring systems to reveal hidden patterns in responses.

SmartPoll is available three different ways: as a Unix software program, for non-Unix companies as a standalone hardware/software product, or as a service bureau offering. Prices start at $425 for one-time polling of 100 participants. As alternatives to single-survey pricing, unlimited annual licenses and facility licenses are available. To take a look at a SmartPoll survey form, visit **http://copeland.smartchoice.com/scdemo/scdemo.html**.

Survey Said for the Web is a product from the company Marketing Masters. It's based on the popular software program Survey Said, which has thousands of users, including Digital Equipment Corp., Arthur Anderson & Co., BMW, Amoco, Dupont, and Ralston-Purina. It is the Windows version of Survey Said with added extensions and scripts that let you conduct surveys on the Web.

You can quickly create a survey in Windows. Survey Said takes your instructions and generates Web-ready HTML files. The program lets you store results either on the same server you use to conduct surveys or on another computer. (For security's sake, I recommend the latter.) You can download an almost-complete version of the software from **http://SurveySaid.ostech.com:8080**. This tryout version seems to have everything but the scripts that generate the HTML files. The product costs $1,000. For more information, call 414-788-1675, or email **jsmits@masters.atw.fullfeed.com**.

Something to remember in Web surveys is that your survey can be generated on the fly according to your respondent's previous answers. If your respondent says "Yes" to the question "Do you invest in bonds?" the next page can be questions about bond investments. If your respondent says "No," the next page can be something completely different. You can custom-tailor Web surveys for each respondent.

## Custom info delivered to you

You already know the Net is rich in information resources. There are so many that you can never find all of them. It makes sense to have someone else cull as many as possible. Any article that meets your criteria should be delivered to you—like an electronic clipping service, only faster, cheaper, and smarter. Customized news has been delivered over the Internet to peoples' desktops for more than three years. The generic name for one of these selection-and-delivery engines is a *newsfeed*. Newsfeeds are immensely valuable for any kind of researcher.

A free version monitors Usenet newsgroups for you. Called the Stanford Netnews Filtering Server, it saves you from monitoring newsgroups if you're looking for information on a specific topic. You tell the server what to look for (such as the name of your company), how often you want results delivered, and the volume of results you want. The Stanford server will search through thousands of newsgroups for you, emailing any messages that contain your search criteria. To use this free newsfeed, go to **http://sift.stanford.edu**.

If you want to monitor more than Usenet newsgroups, and you want more selection choices or delivery methods, take a look at the commercial newsfeed services. One of the top-ranked, Individual, Inc. (in the U.K., 44 1491 638 123, **sarah@individual.com**; in the U.S., 617-354-2230, **info@individual.com**), offers three newsfeed services: First!, Heads Up, and I-News.

Individual's newsfeeders comb stories each night from more than 400 English-language wire services, newspapers, and magazines, and deliver your choices to you. Contents ranges from generalized sources such as Associated Press, Reuters, Canada Newswire, Kyodo, the *Financial Times* of London, *Boston Globe, Los Angeles Times,* and *Miami Herald* to focused publications such as *Oil Daily, Defense Daily, Cancer Researcher Weekly,* and *Electronic Imaging Report.* Individual's subscribers can also search an archive of all articles published in the last six months.

More than 27,000 readers use Individual's top of the line offering, called First!. It delivers your information to Lotus Notes, as Internet email, or as a World Wide Web page. First! offers more custom service options than will fit in this space. The cost of First! depends on volume; for company-wide service, it runs $5,000 to $8,000 per year.

Individual's middle-tier service, named Heads Up, is designed for single subscribers. Heads Up combs through the same thousands of stories as First!, but instead of sending you complete stories, it gives you each article's headline and a summary. When you want a story's full text, you email, fax or call Individual. The service will send you the full text for $4.00 per article. Priced for single users, the base rate for Heads Up is $30 per month. It has 6,000 subscribers.

Individual's newest offering, a slimmer, personal service called I-News, already has thousands of subscribers. It costs only $15 per month.

The strengths of Individual's offerings are the large number of sources it searches and the variety of delivery choices it offers. Individual's Achilles heel is that you receive stories based only on *its* list of topics, not on your own. Individual lets you choose which topics to deliver from a predefined list of hundreds. If your topic is not on that list, forget it. You cannot search only for articles mentioning your company's name, or your company president's name, or your competitor's name. When this book comes out, I will want its reviews delivered to me via newsfeed, but I can't do that with Individual's services. However, another service called NewsHound will do that.

NewsHound is a newsfeed offered by the Knight-Ridder Corporation's online *Mercury Center* (408-297-8495, **http://www.sjmercury.com/hound.htm**). NewsHound does not monitor Usenet newsgroups, and it does not search as many publications as Individual, Inc.'s newsfeeds. But NewsHound will search for *any* topics, names, or words that you wish. And it not only searches articles, it also searches classified *advertisements.*

NewsHound searches often—once an hour—and emails directly to you the articles and advertisements that match your criteria. It monitors stories and most classified advertisements in the *San Jose Mercury News*, plus Knight-Ridder News Service articles from *Chicago Tribune, Detroit Free Press, Miami Herald, Philadelphia Inquirer,* and others. It throws in the *New York Times* News Service, Associated Press, Kyodo News, Scripps-Howard News Service, Business Wire, and PR Newswire. NewsHound charges $10 per month for up to five "profiles"— as it calls your search criteria—and bills fees to your credit card. You can adjust your profiles based on how well what you receive meets your needs. NewsHound also conducts article searches by date.

Barry Parr, publisher of the *Mercury Center* and NewsHound, is adding more sources, especially trade publications. "NewsHound is good for people following an industry or watching a company," he said. "It's not designed as an executive briefing service, since most sources are daily papers. It's valuable if you're in an industry and want to see how it's covered in different parts of the country. Since NewsHound sources come from different regions, it gives you a different perspective on a lot of topics. Not just the point of view you hear on the coasts. And NewsHound lets you track how press releases propagate."

Parr uses NewsHound himself. He monitors the online services industry—searching for stories mentioning "Internet," "online," "America Online," "CompuServe," or "Prodigy." Parr also tracks the personal computer industry, using NewsHound to find stories mentioning "Macintosh," "PC," "Intel," or "Motorola." This gives him news about price cuts and new products.

Another custom newsfeed comes from a company called Internet Profiles Corporation, or I/Pro for short (415-322-9600, **http://www.ipro.com**). I/Pro's service is called I/Want, and it's free. Fill out an I/Want survey on—of course—what you want, and receive a custom Web page every day. Like NewsHound, I/Want lets you give it any selection topics you can think up, rather than forcing you to pick from a list.

I/Want monitors Usenet newsgroups (but not ClariNet newsgroups), wire services, and—uniquely—World Wide Web pages. Key Web sites are inspected every day for changes by searching software created by the same developers who built the famous Yahoo searcher. I/Want grabs the Web, wire service, and Usenet information that matches your survey, cross-indexes everything, and builds you a custom daily home page with live hyperlinks. You want fries with that?

You may ask, "If it's so cool, why is I/Want free?" Well, I/Want ties in with other I/Pro products and services. Remember that; we'll return to I/Pro later. For now, note that each of these newsfeeds has its own strong points. Each searches different *sources*; each is based on different ways for you to provide *search criteria*; and each has different *pricing* and *delivery* structures.

These points are the ones you need to review when selecting a newsfeed—or newsfeeds. The almighty yardstick is the range of *sources* that your potential information supplier uses. Do the raw sources have the information you need? If the sources are weak, it doesn't matter how wonderful the indexes are or how low the price is. A bargain you don't need is a waste. Next, check selection criteria. The Library of Congress on a newsfeed does you no good if you can't pull what you want off its virtual shelves. Pricing and delivery are the least important points. Save 'em for last.

## Information from the Net

For an example, look at InfoSeek (408-982-4450, **http://www.infoseek.com**). InfoSeek offers a database of more than 2 million articles on Internet- and computer-related topics. To apply our criteria to InfoSeek:

- What are its sources? Usenet newsgroups, plus Business Wire, CW Publishing, Newsbytes, PR Newswire, *ComputerWorld, InfoWorld, Advanced Systems, Interactive Publishing Alert,* and more than 80 other computer publications plus databases and other resources. InfoSeek includes sources in several languages.

- How can you search it? By any criteria you specify.

- How does it deliver? You must go to InfoSeek's Web server to make searches.

- What does it cost? $10 per month to subscribe. Base rate includes 100 queries and retrievals per month. Additional public documents cost 10 cents each, and copyright documents cost between 5 cents and $5.00 each.

There are thousands of information resources available on the Net. Hundreds are commercial information providers like InfoSeek, Dow Jones, Lexis/Nexis, and Dun & Bradstreet. Thousands more are free: government resources, universities, industry organizations, or goodwill offerings from corporations. A surprising number are offered for free by private individuals.

The easiest way to find things is by using the World Wide Web. You can start from any five-star resource in Chapter 14 and point-and-click yourself to death.

The World Wide Web is the most seductive part of the Internet, but some of the most valuable marketing research information is accessible through less visual means, like FTP, Gopher, and Telnet. Plan to spend a lot of time getting to know the Usenet newsgroups, which have a seductive appeal all their own. They are rich in unexpected information. The *Wall Street Journal* quoted *Playboy*'s director of new media, Eileen Kent, on newsgroups' appeal: "It's like having your own private focus groups. Hef (*Playboy* founder Hugh Hefner) is nuts about newsgroups."

For a market researcher, one of the most rewarding aspects of newsgroups is the pool of knowledge from newsgroup subscribers. When you have a problem finding something, post it to the right newsgroup. You'll probably find what you need to know, plus seven related items you've never heard of.

Note that there are several newsgroups to which you cannot post, beginning with the prefix **clari**. These are produced as read-only groups by the ClariNet Electronic Publishing Network. ClariNet receives wire service and syndication feeds. It organizes the stories like Usenet newsgroups and sends them out, where newsgroup subscribers can read the stories just like regular newsgroup postings. International news coverage is ClariNet's most popular area, probably because it provides depth that local news media lack. If your company has its own Usenet feed, your firm will need to pay extra to receive ClariNet stories. Most companies receive ClariNet free from their Internet access providers, who pay ClariNet and make its stories available to their users.

It is important to realize that you will find *hundreds* of great research spots on the Internet. Plan from the beginning to catalog them intelligently for easy retrieval later. And plan your research site catalog method so it accommodates changes. Even if you solve the *New York Times* crossword puzzle in ink, use pencil here. Everything changes on the Net; names change, addresses change, and sites are combined, split apart, or sprout subsites. Entire businesses disappear with no word or warning.

## Statistics from your own Net sites

Your own mailing lists, your own FTP server, your own gopher, your company's home page, your own WAIS database: All these can generate usage statistics to provide revealing marketing information.

How many names are in which of your mailing lists? What is the growth rate per week? How many names cancel mailing list subscriptions each week? These are all simple to track. Your technical people can write software to automate mailing list tracking and reporting. Another mailing list question shouldn't be tracked weekly, but every time you do a mailing: What percentage of names bounced back to us from this mailing as undeliverable? A spike in this figure reveals a technical problem.

Out of all your company's Internet offerings, the most exciting marketing information can come from your World Wide Web server. When the World Wide Web was new, everybody talked about how many *hits* or *accesses* busy Web sites received. Companies bragged about receiving 10,000 hits per week, or 50,000 accesses per month, or even 200,000 hits per month. People batted these numbers around as equivalents of newspaper circulation or television viewership.

Reality slowly settled in. We sobered up. Hits are misleading.

Let's say you have a home page and one person, Jean Valjean, accesses it once. The way the Web works is that a file with text and instructions is sent first. *That's one hit.* Your home page has a banner on the top, a picture of a loaf of bread and two buttons. Jean's computer reads the instructions, which tell his software to ask your Web server for the graphics files of your banner, bread picture and buttons. Your Web server sends them. *That's four more hits.* Jean reads your copy and sees a link to a map of the Paris sewers. He points to the link and clicks his mouse, at which point his software sends a request to your Web server for the map page text. *One more hit.* Then it asks for the picture of the map and two more buttons. *Three hits.* Jean looks at the map, then clicks on a button to go back to your home page. Some Web software remembers previous pages, but Jean's doesn't. *Five more hits.* Then Jean leaves your home page to visit an FTP server for jewelry manufacturers.

Your Web site has had one visit from one person, but it totaled 14 hypothetical hits. Even if you count only home page accesses, that's two hits. And this was an oversimplified scenario. You can't rely on "number of hits" for statistical analysis of a Web site's traffic.

Fortunately, the cavalry is coming to the rescue.

First, for an example of the type of statistics your Web page can generate, go to **http://www.netusa.com**. It shows:

- Daily statistics for the last two weeks or so.

- Hourly transmission statistics (the day I looked, busiest was from 8 a.m. to 5 p.m., slowest was from midnight to 7 a.m.).

- Activity by domain (from a high of 26.32 percent for **.com** to lows of 0.01 apiece for South Korea and Slovenia).

- Activity by subdomain. (103 requests from Hewlett-Packard received a large 1.57 percent of all data sent, the most for any one company. 782 requests from access provider Netcom received 7.08 percent of all data sent, of which 643 requests [5.42 percent] were from Netcom's NetCruiser users. 107 requests from the University of Stuttgart in Germany outpaced all other schools.)

- The most and least requested Netusa files and error messages, from 5,713 requests for "All Icons" to one request each for several obscure files.

This looks impressive, but these kinds of statistics are based only on hits, and as we've explained, are of only limited use and reliability. Hit counts cannot answer key questions, such as: How many separate *people* visited this site? How much time did an average visitor spend? In what file or page did visitors spend the most time? Web browsers can enter and exit your Web site from any point, but which entry and exit points were most often used?

To capture and generate that information, your Web server needs to use CGI software (Common Gateway Interface).

Most Web servers are written in HTML. Remember Jean Valjean's different accesses? A server written only in HTML can't tell that those files were sent to the same person. It won't keep track of who asks for what. But if your Web server uses CGI, it can track your customer's path as your customer moves through your site. CGI knows where Jean went, how long he spent there, what buttons he pushed, and at what exit Jean left. *This is crucial information if you sell on the Net. Without it, you cannot build a running total of sales as a customer purchases your products. And you cannot link a customer's purchases with that customer's payment.*

That company I/Pro that we mentioned above (**info@ipro.com**) sells software and services that measure your Internet traffic and yield data comparable to that used by traditional advertising media. This information can be used to improve the response to your Web site and to cost-justify Internet marketing projects.

I/Pro offerings are split into several optional parts. For marketing researchers, one of the most rewarding is I/Count, optional software that works with your Web server to enhance its tracking abilities. I/Count does not require your staff to write CGI programs. It lets you separately track each visitor to your Web site. It tells you how many different people visited your site, entry points and exit points, time spent per screen, and profiles visitors by SIC code, ZIP code, and other information.

Even more detailed information is available with the company's I/Know system. This ties in with I/Pro's newsfeed service (I/Want, described a few pages back), which records registrants' demographic data. The I/Know system taps into that database to give you aggregate demographics about your Web visitors: age, occupation, job title. Another service called I/Audit conducts a detailed audit of the "readership" of your site. The resulting audit statement can be used to justify prices if you charge other companies for advertising on your Web pages.

# Market Testing

Without testing, your marketing efforts can be just as out of touch as if somebody had covered you with a rug. Market surveys and focus groups let your customers tell you how they *think* they will respond. Market testing tells you how they *do* respond. The Internet is an ideal medium for testing your marketing prowess. It costs little to run a test, you can test under controlled conditions, and you can see results in a few hours.

This astonishing speed lets you quickly adjust a test and run it again. Series of tests and refinements that take months in traditional media can be done on the Net in a couple of days.

When your company builds its own Internet mailing list of customers, you can replace much of your direct mail tests with email tests. You can email two messages with different appeals for a free white paper to equal numbers of names and judge the relative power of each appeal by how many requests each produces for the paper. You can use short filenames to each carry a product benefit, list them in a Gopher server, and see which benefits generate the most activity.

The most fruitful part of the Net for tests is the World Wide Web. If you have a CGI programmer available, your Web site can actually generate completely different pages for each visitor, and it can base those pages on the visitor's previous actions. Many businesses make sales on the Web, so those businesses can test the copy and layout that leads to a sale and find ways to improve both.

Keep in mind these foundational truths of market testing:

- Test just one thing at a time. More than one muddies the water.
- The marketing for every product or service is built around a core offer. The most important thing to test is your offer.
- Make sure your test quantities are big enough to give you valid numbers.
- Test to avoid gray "maybe" answers and to provide "yes or no" answers on major issues. For example, when testing prices, don't test amounts that are too close.
- Don't test trivia.

# 140 Cheap or Free Business Resources on the Internet

*"We are drowning in information and starved for knowledge."*
John Naisbitt, *Megatrends*

A**s more and more businesses establish a presence on the Internet, more
sites pop up to provide information, services, and products for those businesses. The collection of Web and Gopher sites, newsgroups, electronic books
and magazines, and programs in this chapter gives you a taste of what your
business can put to use from the Net.

The Internet changes constantly, so don't be surprised if you go to one of
these sites and find something radically different from what I describe. Or
you might find nothing at all. Addresses change; it's almost certain that some
of these sites will have moved by the time you read this—some might even
have dropped off the Net altogether.

If I've left out your favorite Net source for business information, or if you find
a mistake, let me know about it. You can reach me by email at
**vince@emery.com**. I will post all corrections, changes, and any amazing new
discoveries on my home page, **http://www.emery.com**, for you to read. Think
of it as your free update to this book.

Each item in this chapter was selected for its relevance for *businesses*. To clarify
which items I found the most helpful, I've used a five-star rating system. Stars
indicate *usefulness* and no other factor—not good design, not ease of use, not
pretty pictures. I looked strictly for what would most benefit a business. (Note
that this rating system is slightly different from the one used in chapter 4.)

You'll find that I give many of the items listed in this chapter relatively high
ratings (three stars or more). It's not that I am feeling particularly generous,
it's just that I don't feel the need to devote a lot of paper to lists of useless
online sites—nor do I think it would be fair to you to include garbage just so
the title of this chapter could read "200 Free or Cheap Business Resources"
instead of "140." When I do list what I consider to be a bomb, it's because it
looks or sounds deceptively useful, and I want to save you from wasting time,
as I did, trying to figure out why you can't seem to get much out of it.

Sources of general management information are listed first. Next come sources
of financial, accounting, and investing help, followed by sites about economics, and then ones devoted to international trade. Resources for marketing
and demographic research follow.

## *Your guide to the stars*

☆☆☆☆☆      Highest rating: extremely valuable for its topic.

☆☆☆☆      Lots of information useful to many businesses.

☆☆☆      Useful for specific purposes or to certain fields of business.

☆☆      Of some use.

☆      Of little value.

[NOT RATED] A source wasn't rated if it was under heavy construction when I visited it, or if I didn't visit it before press time. You might think these sites are great or you might think they're useless, but they're worth a mention.

Sources relating to logistics, R&D, and purchasing come next, then those on career development and human resources. Finally, a section called "Special Interests" provides information on resources that don't quite fit in any of the other categories.

Note that resources are listed alphabetically within a section. Also note that in places where an email message or subject requires your name or address, the information to be provided appears in brackets. If, for example, Jane Smith wanted to subscribe to a list that required the email message *subscribe [your full name]*, she would type *subscribe Jane Smith*.

Some sites provided in this chapter could have been listed in several different categories. I avoid such redundancy by listing each site in the category under which I think you would most likely look for it. Keep in mind, then, that if you're looking for, say, help on marketing to Western Europe, you should check out the resources in both the "Marketing and Demographics" and "International Trade" sections—and a quick look through the "Economics" section wouldn't hurt.

## Management resources

This section contains items of particular interest to company managers. If you're planning a startup, need help with a particular point of business law, or are interested in the broad issues of business on the Net, check out the resources listed here.

A-ha! Monthly ☆☆☆
http://sashimi.wwa.com/~notime/eotw/bus_info_sources/idea_assoc.html

This newsletter for startups, from IDEABase, gives answers to basic business questions and reprints quotes from articles about business. Includes business-to-business classified ads.

alt.business.misc☆

A newsgroup discussing starting and managing a business. 95% irrelevant ads.

Business law mailing list☆☆
Email to: bizlaw-l@umab.edu

This discussion mailing list deals with the law regarding business associations and securities.

BusinessNet at UMD☆☆☆
http://ub.d.umn.edu/~rvaidyan/resource.html

Directory of business resources on the Net, compiled by the Department of Management Studies at the University of Minnesota at Duluth. Includes marketing sites, Net publications, finance, economics, business law, etc. Updated often.

The Company Corporation☆☆☆
http://incorporate.com/tcc/home.html
Email to: corp@incorporate.com

This site full of useful information on incorporating in Delaware or other states is provided by a company that specializes in helping firms incorporate.

com-priv mailing list ☆☆☆☆
Email to: com-priv-request@uu.psi.com with the message *subscribe com-priv [your full name]*

This well-known mailing list covers the commercialization and privatization of the Net. It's sponsored by access provider Performance Systems International.

Cornell Legal Information Institute Archives ☆☆☆
http://www.law.cornell.edu

At this site, you can search and retrieve information from the Uniform Commercial Codes, the U.S. Copyright Act, and other legal texts.

econ-dev mailing list ☆☆☆
Email to: majordomo@csn.org with the message *subscribe econ-dev*

The Economics Development project is sponsored by the town of Littleton, Colorado. Its goal is to give small companies the tools and information they need to compete globally.

Electronic Commerce on the World Wide Web ☆☆☆☆
http://www.cox.smu.edu/mis/cases/webcase/home.html

This case study from the Edwin L. Cox School of Business, although originally intended for use by college students, provides detailed, practical information on how business is currently conducted on the Internet. You'll also find food for thought about how it might be done better.

Home Business Review☆☆☆
http://www.tab.com/Home.Business

The articles in this monthly electronic magazine are relevant to many small business, not just home-based ones. Because it accepts submissions from businesses that have a story they want to tell, the writing is uneven, but worth sorting through. The home page makes it clear that the magazine is funded by commercial sponsors—in other words, you could probably advertise here.

Interesting Business Sites☆☆☆☆☆
http://www.rpi.edu/~okeefe/business.html

Don't miss this well-maintained and well-organized home page of Bob O'Keefe, a professor at Rensselaer Polytechnic Institute's School of Management. One of O'Keefe's stated goals is to keep the list of links on this page down to just 50 particularly useful, relevant, and interesting sites. There's a lot to explore here—especially the sections on Net business success stories.

The Japan That Can Say No☆☆☆
Gopher to: quartz.rutgers.edu
*or*　　　　　ftp://ftp.wimsey.com/pub/japan_no
Choose: Economics, Business, Finance

A very influential book among Japanese executives, coauthored by Sony founder Akio Morita and politician Shintaro Ishihara.

Innovation's Guide to Management and Technology☆☆☆
http://www.euro.net/innovation/Management_Base/Man_Guide_Rel_1.0B1/Introduction.html

This nontechnical guide to management techniques and technology is really more of a reference than a guide. Still, it has some worthwhile information.

Mantec Dictionary☆☆☆
http://www.euro.net/innovation/Management_Base/Mantec.Dictionary.html

The largest Internet dictionary of management and technology, this reference has too many little icons, but it's still quite useful.

Organization and Management Theory☆☆
http://cwaves.stfx.ca/Subjects/Business/omt.html

Home page of the Organization and Management Theory division of the Academy of management of St. Francis Xavier University, Nova Scotia, Canada. Provides an archive of management-related software, newsletters, papers and conference information. Most information here is for academics, not businesspeople.

Print Publications on Business Use of the Internet ☆☆☆
http://arganet.tenagra.com/Tenagra/books.html

Internet consulting company Tenagra Corporation presents reviews of every book written in English about business and the Internet. (Hope I make it through with only minor scars!) Lots of other goodies at this site.

Psychological Operations in Guerrilla Warfare ☆☆
Gopher to: wiretap.Spies.COM:70/00/Library/Classic/guerilla.txt

What is this book by Tayacan doing among all the reports, case studies, and databases in this chapter? Just as the military tomes *The Art of War* and *The Book of Five Rings* have become management classics, this book has acquired a growing reputation among managers for its relevance to running a business.

U.S. Government Publications Index ☆☆☆☆
telnet to: database.carl.org
Choose: CARL Systems Library Catalogs, then CARL Systems Libraries - Western U.S., then CARL, then Library Catalogs, then Government Publications

Go here to search by keywords through citations for U.S. government publications produced since 1976 by the Government Printing Office. Maintained by CARL, the Colorado Alliance of Research Libraries.

U.S. Small Business Adminstration ☆☆☆☆
http://www.sbaonline.sba.gov

The home page of the SBA, this site has information on finding local Small Business Development Centers and SCORE volunteers, overviews of various government loan programs for small businesses, and links to many other sources of business information.

Washington & Lee Law Library ☆☆☆☆
telnet to: liberty.uc.wlu.edu and log in as *lawlib;* also give *lawlib* as password

A huge menu of more than 3,000 Internet resources, mostly law-related. Slow.

Yahoo Business Directory ☆☆☆☆
http://www.yahoo.com/Business

Despite the silly name, this is a valuable source of serious business information. You'll find a list of business consortia, 202 job banks and employment resources, electronic commerce resources, sources of information about intellectual property rights, an extremely useful directory of business directories, a section about taxes, and more.

## Financial, accounting, and investment resources

The resources listed here can help you plan investment strategy, manage finances, keep up with the latest in tax regulations, and more.

CTI Department of Accounting, Finance, and Management ☆☆
http://www.sys.uea.ac.uk/cti/cti-afm.html

Gives a catalog of software, instructions on how to subscribe to three email discussion lists (on business, auditing and marketing) for U.K. academics, and sells the journal *Account* and other publications.

Daily Market Report ☆☆☆
telnet to: a2i.rahul.net and log in as *guest*
Go to: Current System Information, then Market Report

This periodical presents an overview of financial markets, interest rates, foreign exchange rates, and more.


Department of Accountancy, Aberdeen University ☆☆
http://www.abdn.ac.uk:80/~acc025

This is mainly a link to many other sites, most regarding (surprise!) accounting and finance. The list is not particularly well-organized, but it is helpfully annotated.


Dun & Bradstreet ☆☆☆
http://www.dbisna.com

Good articles on the basics of business fraud, finding a job, marketing, vendor management, import-export and how to do business research.


EDGAR ☆☆☆☆
Address: http://edgar.stern.nyu.edu/edgar.html
Or try: http://town.hall.org:80/edgar/edgar.html

EDGAR stands for *Electronic Data Gathering, Analysis, and Retrieval system*, a huge database of all SEC-required corporate filings. You'll find more than 35,000 documents from thousands of companies that filed electronically.


Electronic stock quotes, graphs of Dow, and S&P 500 ☆☆☆
http://www.secapl.com/cgi-bin/qs

Almost live stock quotes (five-minute delay) are available here, plus historical data from the past 25 years. Also check out "The Podium," "Market Watch."

Ernst & Young Canada☆☆☆
http://tax.ey.ca/ey

Provides books *Doing Business in Canada* and *Managing Your Personal Taxes* (Canadian), plus Canadian tax and business information.

Ernst & Young U.K☆
http://www.ernsty.co.uk/ernsty

Not much here.

Federal Electronic Commerce for Acquisition Team (ECAT) Library☆☆☆
Gopher to: ds.internic.net/1/pub/ecat.library

If you want a hint of what the government thinks about online commerce, and especially if your business involves financial transactions over the Net, turn here for an explanation of ECAT, a draft of its Implementation Conventions, and periodic progress reports.

FEN mailing list☆☆☆
Email to: marr@clemson.clemson.edu or trimble@vancouver.wsu.edu

Get the free daily *Holt's Stock Market Reports* published by Financial Economics Network, summarizing 29 market indexes and averages, including Dow Jones, S&P 500, currency prices, and the most actively traded stocks. Subscribers discuss new markets, corporate finance, accounting, banking, small business issues, stocks, bonds, and options.

FINWeb☆☆☆☆
http://riskweb.bus.utexas.edu/finweb.html

A financial economics WWW server, with journals, papers and databases of finance-related information. Excellently annotated and organized.

*HedgeHog Online* Financial Market Advisory ☆☆☆☆
http://risc.cpbx.net/hedgehog/weltohh.html

*HedgeHog Online* is an investment magazine with financial market advice. This site lets you look at back issues for free, although there is a charge for new issues. You'll also find free samples of *HedgeHog*'s refreshingly opinionated tutorials on the technical analysis of market prices.

Internal Revenue Service home page ☆☆☆
http://www.ustreas.gov/treasury/bureaus/irs/irs.html

This site has tax forms, tax FAQ files, and provides information on where to get help. Many of the tax forms are acceptable for filing with the IRS.

International Accounting Network (Anet) ☆☆☆☆☆
http://www.scu.edu.au:80/ANetHomePage.html

This one-stop site for all accounting and auditing resources on the Net was created by Southern Cross University in Australia.

Investment FAQ ☆☆☆
Gopher to: quartz.rutgers.edu
Choose: Economics, Business, Finance

A collection of frequently asked questions on investing.

Infotech Information Technologies [NOT RATED]
Email to: infotech@fx.net

This company provides individual and business credit reports, Dun & Bradstreet profiles, arrest and conviction records, and other related information. You might also use it for its locator service by Social Security number.

Intelligent Market Analytics, Inc.☆☆☆
http://www.marketmind.com

This site supports an expert-systems software package for investors. You can download demos, manuals, and the software itself from here.

MIT Stock Market Database☆☆☆
http://www.ai.mit.edu

This Web site updates stock prices daily, giving you charts showing price/volume performance on 315 stocks and several mutual funds.

Network Payment Mechanisms and Digital Cash☆☆☆
http://ganges.cd.tcd.ie:80/mepierce/project.html

Look to this site sponsored by Trinity College Dublin's Department of Economics for information on the current status of encrypting credit-card transactions and using digital cash. There's a lot of good information to be found here, although I could do without all the little .gif buttons.

Nikko Securities Co., Ltd.☆☆
http://www.nikko.co.jp

You'll find Nikko Performance Indices, information on stocks, bonds, convertible bonds, J-MIX monthly Nikko Index reports, and data to download here. There are both English and Japanese versions. A slow site, and not all links worked when I visited.

Small business finance mailing list [NOT RATED]
Email to: afa-pub@wsuvm1.csc.wsu.edu. In the body of your message, type *SUBSCRIBE AFA-SBUS [Yourname]*

A discussion list about small business finance.

SUMMA Project☆☆☆☆
http://www.ex.ac.uk/~BJSpaul/ICAEW/ICAEW.html

Part of the International Accounting Network and sponsored by the Institute of Chartered Accountants of England and Wales (ICAEW), this site has lots of accounting stuff from all over the world.

Tax minimization tips [NOT RATED]
Gopher to: quartz.rutgers.edu

Choose: Economics, Business, Finance, then Lawnmower-Strategy

## Economics resources

The resources listed here help you sift through the mountains of economic data on the Net to find the stuff you're really likely to use.

Center for Economic Studies☆☆☆☆
Gopher to: gopher.census.gov
Choose: News and Analysis from the Center for Economic Studies

A source of news and analysis from the U.S. Census Bureau.

Econ Data☆☆
Gopher to: info.umd.edu
Choose: Educational Resources, then Economic Data

This is an archive of economic statistics from federal government agencies. You will need to copy the data and reformat it on your own computer. Before you look for data, check out the downloading instructions and tools provided.

Economic Indicators☆☆☆
Gopher to: gopher.gsfc.nasa.gov

Go to: Virtual Reference Shelf, then Economic Bulletin Board and Exchange Rates, then Economic Indicators

Check here for the latest on the U.S. economy.

Gross State Product Tables☆☆☆
Gopher to: gopher.lib.umich.edu
Choose: Social Sciences Resources, then Economics (*most recent date*)

U.S. Bureau of Economic Analysis tables that present the estimated value of goods and services for 61 industries in all states.

*An Inquiry into the Nature and Causes of the Wealth of Nations*☆☆☆☆
Gopher to: gopher.vt.edu:10010/02/141/1

One of the most influential economics books ever written, this classic 1776 work by Adam Smith (1723-1790) is still in the news—mentioned as one of the top 10 books all managers should read, according to Speaker of the House Newt Gingrich.

List of economics servers☆☆☆☆
http://sol.uvic.ca/econ

This is a gold mine of links to other sites. It's produced by the Department of Economics, University of Victoria, British Columbia.

NetEC☆☆☆
http://netec.mcc.ac.uk/NetEc.html

This site unites many networked projects in economics, with links to the full text of papers, FAQs, and a searchable CodEc with software programs for economics and econometrics. Many links to related Web sites.

Resources for Economists on the Internet☆☆☆☆
http://netec.mcc.ac.uk/~adnetec/EconFAQ/EconFAQ.html

This mammoth reference site also has dozens of links to other sites.

sci.econ.research archives☆☆
http://www.sun.com

Archives of the newsgroup **sci.econ.research** provide data and resources for mathematically-inclined economists.

University of Michigan Economics Gopher☆☆☆
http://gopher.econ.lsa.umich.edu
*Or* Gopher to: gopher.econ.lsa.umich.edu

This gopher provides a big source of economics data.

U.S. Commerce Department's Economic Bulletin Board☆☆☆☆
Gopher to: gopher.lib.umich.edu
Choose: Social Sciences Resources, then Economics

This site is always fresh, since some 700 files are updated each day. You'll find thousands of files about current economic conditions, economic indicators, employment, international trade, and money. Search for and download promotion files and resources, presidential announcements, news about the U.S. budget, and related news items.

U.S. Government Sources of Business and Economic Information on the Internet [NOT RATED]
Gopher to: niord.shsu.edu

World Wide Web Aerospace Business Development Center☆☆☆☆
http://arganet.tenagra.com/aero_bd.html

Check this site for everything on the Net relating to the aerospace industry, especially procurement Web sites. A great spot for NASA and DoD contractors.

*A Vision of Change for America* [NOT RATED]
Gopher to: wiretap.spies.com
Choose: Government Docs and search for Clinton's Economic Plan

This is a condensed version of President Clinton's economic plan.

# International/import-export resources

When you cut through all the hype about the Internet's ability to globalize markets and facilitate international business, what's really out there for you? The online books, periodicals, articles, and sites here will get you on your way toward answering this question for your business.

Association of Japanese Business Studies (AJBS)☆☆
Email to: listserve@pucc.princeton.edu with the message **subscribe japan@pucc.princeton.edu yourfirstname yourlastname**

The AJBS is an international association of people interested in the Japanese economy and Japanese businesses.

Basic Guide to Exporting☆☆☆☆
Gopher to: umslvma.umsl.edu
Choose: The Library, then Government Information

This free book is an introduction to exporting from the U.S. International Trade Administration.

British business research mailing list☆☆☆
telnet to: niss.ac.uk
Email to: business-research

A Mailbase discussion list for U.K. business and management researchers and academics.

Currency conversion program☆☆☆☆
http://gnn.com/cgi-bin/gnn/currency

The program at this site gives instant currency conversions from any one major country to any other, updated weekly.

DEVLINE☆☆
telnet to: LIB.IDS.SUSX.AC.UK and log in as HELLO GUEST.MARC

A service of the British Library for Development Studies, an international center for information on economic and social aspects of developing regions. Not as much information as I'd expect, but perhaps they'll have added by the time you visit here.

European business history mailing list☆☆
telnet to: niss.ac.uk
Email to: euro-business-history

A scholarly discussion of business history in the U.K. and Europe.

Foreign Trade Monthly☆☆☆☆
Gopher to: gopher.census.gov
Choose: News Releases on Trade, then Imports/Exports

One of many useful publications at the U.S. Census Bureau's Gopher site.

Gateway Japan On-Line☆☆☆☆
Email to: gwjapan@hamlet.umd.edu for access instructions

Extremely important site for anyone doing business with Japan, and provided by Gateway Japan, a nonprofit organization funded by the Center for Global Partnership. This is the only English-language source for some material, including Japanese government procurement announcements. Also provided is

Focus Japan II: A Resource Guide to Japan-Related Organizations. Although some of the material is in Japanese, this site's unique search engine lets you search in *both languages*. You can enter a word in English, and find all mentions of it in English and in Japanese. You can enter a word in Japanese and do the same. Much information here is free, but there is a fee-based section. This site is available by Gopher, telnet, ftp, and the World Wide Web.

General Agreement on Tariffs and Trade (GATT) [NOT RATED]
Gopher to: ace.esusda.gov
Choose: Americans Communicating Electronically, then National Policy Issues

You'll find the latest version of GATT here, including all the Uruguay changes. This site presents an executive summary as well as the complete version.

Hong Kong Business Directory☆☆☆☆
http://FarEast.Com/HongKong/directory.html

You can search this listing of 123,400 businesses via keywords to locate importers, exporters, companies, and individuals.

InterFinance Ltd.☆☆
http://intergroup.com/interfiinance/index.html

Financial intermediaries in Europe.

International Business Practices☆☆☆☆
Gopher to: umslva.ymsl.edu
Choose: The Libraryt, then Government Information

This free Department of Commerce reference book provides information on doing business with 117 countries. For each nation, you'll find out about import regulations, free trade zones, foreign investment policy, intellectual property rights, and tax regulations. You'll also find "International Background Notes" from the State Department at this same site, with information on the economy, government, people, foreign relations, and history of more than 100 countries.

International Trade Network mailing list☆☆☆
Email to: majordomo@world.std.com with info intltrade in the Subject line

Daily email on trade opportunities and import-export trends.

NAFTA [NOT RATED]
Gopher to: ace.esusda.gov
Choose: Americans Communicating Electronically, then National Policy Issues
Or Gopher to: umslvma.umsl.edu
Choose: The Libraryt, then Government Information

For a little light reading, turn here for the complete text of the North American Free Trade Agreement and all related documents.

NAFTA Implementation Resource Guide [NOT RATED]
Gopher to: gopher.gsfc.nasa.gov

Choose: Virtual Reference Shelf, then Economic Bulletin Board and Exchange Rates, then General Information Files, then NAFTA Implementation Resource Guide

Still sorting out the effects of NAFTA on your business? Get a copy of this, by the U.S. Department of Commerce's Office of Mexico.

National Export Strategy [NOT RATED]
ftp to: sunny.stat-usa.gov, log in as anonymous and give your email address as the password
Choose: Pub/Export

This report from the government's Trade Promotion Coordinating Committee outlines sixty actions to increase U.S. exports.

Offshore☆☆☆
http://www.euro.net/innovation/Offshore.html

This newsletter on offshore assets-protection by offshore specialists Cornez & Associates covers topics for business users with investments and operations outside the U.S.

Sumitomo Corporation☆☆☆
http://www.sumitomocorp.co.jp

This is a good source of statistics and research in English and Japanese, and even cultural information on subjects like kites—although you do have to slog more pages of indexes than I like to reach a final destination. An online copy of *Keizai Doukou*, a monthly economic newsletter (complete in Japanese, partial in English), reports on company activities. Not all links worked when I visited.

U.K. Treasury Internet service☆☆☆
http://www.hm-treasury.gov.uk
ftp to: Send email to FTPMAIL@HM-TREASURY.GOV.UK containing the single word HELP in the body.

For an insight into the British economy, download ministers' speeches, minutes of the Chancellor's monthly monetary meetings with the Governor of the Bank of England, reports of the Panel of Independent Forecasters, the Fundamental Expenditure Review, and press releases from here.

U.K. Treasury press releases mailing list☆☆
Email to: MAJORDOMO@HM-TREASURY.GOV.UK. Leave the Subject line of your message blank. The body of your message should be Subscribe PRESS [your email address]

You can also subscribe to the "What's New" mailing list at the same address for updates of new additions to the United Kingdom Treasury Internet Service. Leave the Subject line of your message blank, and type the message Subscribe WHATSNEW [your email address].

The World Bank☆☆☆
http://www.worldbank.org
Gopher to: gopher.worldbank.org

The World Bank's Public Information Service provides economic reports on many countries, policy papers, project information, a publications catalog, and more.

Worldwide commercial credit reports☆☆
http://www.dbinfo.co.uk/dbinfo

This is Dun & Bradstreet's site for international credit reporting.

## *Marketing and demographics resources*

As you cruise through the resources listed in this section, remember to keep in mind not just *what* information is presented, but *how* it is presented. After all, several of these sites are run by professional marketers, who presumably know a thing or two about creating interesting and eye-catching material. You might be able to pick up some ideas about what to do—and what not to do—at your own Net site.

Advertising Law Site☆☆☆☆
http://www.webcom.com

Check here for the actual text of laws relating to advertising, FTC rules, legal considerations affecting marketing, legal implications regarding your choice of a business name, and regulations covering 900 numbers and mail-order. This site also provides related legislative testimony and speeches. It's sponsored by Arent Fox, a law firm specializing in advertising law and intellectual property.

**American Marketing Association**☆☆
http://www.nsns.com/Mix

This is the home page of the AMA, with links to AMA-related sites. You'll also find a considerable amount of membership information at this page.

**Business to Business Information Exchange**☆☆☆
http://www.btob.wfu.edu

This site, sponsored by the Business-to-Business Special Interest Group of the American Marketing Association, provides information on marketing courses, books, articles, and associations, as well as links to other marketing-related sites.

**Dataquest**☆
http://www.dataquest.com
http://www.dataquest.com/weekly/main.html

How can a company that deals in information present so little of it? The main Dataquest home page has little information and just ads. Buried at /weekly/main.html you will find three-month-old issues of Dataquest's newsletter *Online, Multimedia, and Software Quick Takes*, but this newsletter indicates no particular understanding of the online world and has relatively negligible online coverage.

**Economics and statistics spreadsheets from the U.S. Department of Agriculture**☆☆☆
Gopher to: usda.mannlib.cornell.edu

You'll find statistics on such things as consumer food spending, product sales, meat consumption, and many more trends at this Gopher sit. You can download most files in Lotus 1-2-3 format or as text.

Internet Marketing Archives☆☆☆☆
http://galaxy.einet.net/hypermail/inet-marketing

This searchable index to a moderated list of marketing-related topics provides a relatively easy way to find out what other users think about marketing on the Internet. For example, a quick search for material related to the use of credit cards online quickly netted a list of 80 highly relevant discussions, sorted by size and correlation to the search topic.

MKTSEG marketing email discussion list☆☆☆
Email to: listserv@mail.telmar.com
with the message: subscribe mktseg (your email address)

Discussion of marketing and advertising to targeted segments. Topics include creative, media, research, database marketing, and direct marketing.

Mlink☆☆☆
http://mlink.hh.lib.umich.edu

On this server from the library of the University of Michigan at Ann Arbor, you'll find economics and census data.

MouseTracks☆☆☆☆☆
http://nsns.com:80/MouseTracks

Not only does it have great resources for marketing people, this is a business site with a sense of humor: "It is universally agreed that the Internet is the hottest new medium since the invention of stone tablets, or at least since *Melrose Place*." Highlights include the Hall of Malls (a directory of Internet malls), Nuts & Bolts on the technical aspects of Web marketing, List of Marketing Lists (a directory of Net marketers), and MetaMarket, a directory of firms selling services to other companies' marketers. Look under the education section for a complete sample issue of Kluwer's *Marketing Letter*. MouseTracks is brought to you by New South Network Services, which should get some kind of medal.

*The Possible Futures of Multimedia*☆☆☆
http://www.ac.com

This thought-provoking report, an online publication of Anderson Consulting's Technology Assessment Group, shows four alternative scenarios for multimedia and makes a strong case that one will probably come to pass. Other articles are available from the same site, including several case studies—intended primarily to showcase Anderson Consulting's services—that provide good examples of how to use reports as promotional tools.

Small Business Industry Profiles and State Profiles of Small Businesses☆☆☆☆
Gopher to: umslvma.umsl.edu
Choose: The Library, then Government Information, then Small Business Administration Industry Profiles (or Small Business Administration State Profiles)

Check here for Small Business Administration reports on trends and opportunities for U.S. small businesses, categorized by industry or by state.

softpub mailing list☆☆☆☆
Email to: softpub-request@toolz.atl.ga.us

Managed by the Software Entrepreneurs Forum, this list discusses marketing, packaging, and R&D for the software industry.

Up Close Publishing☆☆☆
http://www.upclose.com

This site provides U.S. demographics by state, metro area, county, city, town, and ZIP code. The company sells reports, but informative summaries are free.

U.S. Census Department☆☆☆☆
Gopher to: gopher.census.gov

You'll find tons of economic and demographic data and reports at this site. If your business involves selling to consumers, this is a good place to gather information for a marketing plan.

U.S. Census spreadsheets☆☆☆
Gopher to: bigcat.missouri.edu
Choose: Reference and Information Center

Download 1990 Census of Population and Housing data in both Lotus 1-2-3 and text format for cities, counties, metro areas, states, and the nation, with comparisons to the 1980 census.

U.S. Industrial Outlook☆☆☆☆
Gopher to: **gopher.lib.umich.edu**
Choose: **Social Sciences Resources**, then **Economics**, then **Industrial Outlook**
*Or* telnet to: **una.hh.lib.umich.edu** and log in as *Gopher*

This book, published annually by the Department of Commerce, reports on recent trends, with five-year projections for the 350 largest industries in the U.S. There's much valuable strategic information to be found in here; someone from your company should be on top of this.

## Logistics, R&D, and purchasing resources

There seem to be fewer resources on the Internet for industrial and manufacturing companies than for those that deal in information as a commodity. However, when it comes to the latest on government regulations, industry standards, patents, and news on technological breakthroughs, the Net comes into its own. Net sites can also link purchasers with suppliers, and even help you find bargains—check out the U.S. Marshal's property list in this section, and IndustryNET.

Copyright database☆☆☆☆
telnet to: locis.loc.gov

You'll find information about copyrights here, but a key attraction is that you can search a database of information about works registered in the U.S. Copyright Office since 1978.

Document Center☆☆
http://www.service.com/doccenter/home.html
Email to: info@doccenter.com

This site sells hardcopies of government and industry specifications and standards.

Federal Implementation Guidelines for EDI (Electronic Data Interchange) [NOT RATED]
ftp to: ds.internic.net/pub/ecat.library.fed.ic

Flowchart software☆☆☆
ftp to: oak.oakland.edu
Go to: SimTel/msdos/flowchrt/*

Free software to make GANTT charts, PERT charts, and organizational charts.

IndustryNET☆☆☆☆☆
http://www.industry.net

This site is a huge online mall for industrial companies: industry news, information on new products, used equipment for sale, job openings, on-line tradeshows, software for industrial companies and more are all here. IndustryNET offers free subscriptions to *Industry Report* and access to bulletin board systems. Registration is free.

Intelligent Manufacturing Systems Program☆☆☆☆
http://fuji.stanford.edu/Center/Research/IMS/ims.html

IMS is an international collaboration project of the U.S., Japan, Canada, Australia, Finland, and Norway, and was started in 1995. This site presents information on global concurrent engineering, enterprise integration for global manufacturing, and related topics. It also has links to other sites.

*Internet Patent News*☆☆☆
Email to: patents@world.std.com

Subscribe to this periodical for a complete list of U.S. patents issued that week, sent to you by email.

MediaMOO☆☆☆
http://www.media.mit.edu/Noteworthy.html
*Or* telnet to: purple-crayon.media.mit.edu:8888

This is a MUD (multi-user domain) where computer researchers hang out. If your business involves such technologies as AI, autonomous agents, speech analysis and synthesis, and image recognition, check this site out.

Patent Office Reform Panel Final Report☆☆
Gopher to: wiretap.spies.com
Choose: Government Docs

This is the report by the U.S. Patent and Trademark Office recommending that changes be made to U.S. patent procedures to match patent laws in most other countries.

*Streamlining Procurement through Electronic Commerce*☆☆☆
http://snad.ncsl.nist.gov/dartg/edi/arch.html

A free, valuable book by the Federal Electronic Commerce Acquisition Program Management Office that covers EDI, among other topics.

*Technology Review*☆☆
http://web.mit.edu/aFs/athena/org/t/techreview/www/tr.html

This MIT publication is intended to focus on the practical applications of technology, but covers policy more than how-to information. It reports on computers, space, and telecommunications technology as used in the health care, education, business, and defense industries.

U.S. Marshal's Property List☆☆☆
telnet to: fedworld.gov and go to SELLERS.TEXT

If you're bargain-hunting for business or office equipment, check the forfeited property for sale to the public listed here.

U.S. Patent and Trademark Office☆☆
http://www.uspto.gov

Includes a preliminary draft report of the Working Group on Intellectual Property Rights—which is helping the government decide, among other things, how patent and trademark law applies to cyberspace. The report is available in .html format for online browsing, or you can download it in quite a few formats. You might also want to check back here from time to time for news on the progress toward a searchable, up-to-date, online patent database.

Weekly price quotes on CPU and RAM chips☆☆
Email to: catalog@ceram.com

# Career development and employment resources

Almost everyone is either an employer or an employee, so almost everyone will find something useful among the resources described in this section. If you're in charge of your company's human resources or training programs, the Net is a particularly good place to keep up-to-date on employment law, OSHA regulations, and labor statistics.

Career Magazine ☆☆☆

http:/www.careermag.com/careermag

This online magazine, sponsored by the national recruitment firm NCS, includes lists of job openings, company profiles, articles for both job-seekers and employers, and information on executive recruiters, among other things. If you're looking to hire or be hired, you might find some possibilities here. Note that most of the postings, though, are for computer-related industries.

Daphne Jackson Memorial Fellowships Trust ☆☆

http://www.sst.ph.ic.ac.uk/trust

These fellowships enable women and men to return to science or engineering careers after a break in their employment history for family reasons.

Department of Labor News ☆☆☆☆

telnet to: fedworld.gov
Choose: Gateway System, then Connect to Gov't Systems

This site for the Department of Labor gives you statistics, daily news releases, OSHA information, summaries of *Monthly Labor Review* articles, and more.

**Employment newsgroups**

biz.jobs.offered ☆☆
80 percent of the jobs here are technical. Good listings, but many from recruiters, also called "headhunters." Many headhunters describe utopian jobs that don't exist to trick jobseekers into signing contracts with them. Watch out.

misc.jobs.contract ☆☆
Many technical jobs, but 95 percent are from headhunters.

misc.jobs.misc ☆☆
A melange of jobs offered and jobs wanted, plus information and questions about employment and the job-finding process. 5 percent irrelevant ads.

misc.jobs.offered ✩✩
U.S. jobs, 90 percent of them technical. Some from headhunters.

misc.jobs.resumes ✩✩✩✩
Hundreds of resumes are posted here. Some look impressive.

The information in these newsgroups is usually up-to-date and might be more targeted to specific business uses than the big commercial databases. Remember, though, that one of the classic, if sneaky, ways to find out about your competition is to post a blind job offer or RFP for the kind of work you do.

Job Interview Simulator ✩✩✩✩
ftp to: garbo.uwasa.fi
Go to: pc/database/yh132.zip

This free software for PCs asks you questions and times your responses, then provides advice to improve your interview skills. You can customize the questions and the interview format for specific jobs. If you're involved in hiring or retraining employees, or of course if you're in the job market yourself, check this out.

Jobs in Japan✩✩
http://www.stellar.co.jp/Wanted

Job Search and Employment Opportunities: Best Bets from the Net ✩✩✩✩✩
http://www.umich.edu/~philray/job-guide

Check here for the best sites on the Net for job postings and career information, plus descriptions and helpful evaluations. Whether you're searching for a job or looking for a candidate, this is the first place to start.

Lab Stat ✩✩✩✩
ftp to: ftp.stats.bls.gov, log in as *user anonymous* and give your email address as your password
Choose: Pub

The U.S. Bureau of Labor Statistics gives you historical and current employment data, occupational injury and illness rates, the consumer price index, the producer price index, and more from this site.

*Occupational Outlook Handbook*☆☆☆☆
Gopher to: umslvma.umsl.edu
Choose: The Libraryt, then Government Information

Consult this free book published annually by the Department of Labor for detailed information on more than 300 occupations. You'll find out what the work is like, learn about required training and education, see what the future outlook is, and be able to compare salaries, among other things.

Occupational Safety and Health Administration Regulations☆☆☆
Gopher to: stellate.health.ufl.edu
Choose: OSHA

Check the complete OSHA regulations and standards from this site.

Online Career Center [NOT RATED]
Email to: occ-info@mail.msen.com

Regional Economic Information System (REIS)☆☆☆
Gopher to: sunny.stat-usa.gov
Choose: Economic Conversion Information, then Regional Statistics

This Gopher site provides Department of Commerce statistics on employment, income, and earnings by industry, and transfer payments for states and counties.

Overseas Job Vacancies☆☆☆
Gopher to: gopher.gsfc.nasa.gov
Go to: Virtual Reference Shelf, then Economic Bulletin Board and Exchange Rates, then General Information Files, then Overseas Job Vacancies with US & FCS

Look here for a list of available jobs overseas with the Foreign Commercial Service and the U.S. Government. The FCS places businesspeople in more than 70 countries.

SkillSearch☆☆
http://www.internet-is.com/skillsearch/index.html

This recruiting company represents 700 employers and 35,000 employees. It charges $65 to put you in its database.

## Special-interest resources

This section is a catch-all for resources that are of interest to specific industries or regions of the country.

Bell Atlantic financial information☆☆
ftp to: bell-atl.com

Download 10-Q quarterlies, 10-K annual reports, and press releases.

Business and finance in Hawaii☆☆☆
telnet to: fyi.uhcc.hawaii.edu and press the Enter key twice to log in
Go to: Directory of Categories, then Business and Finance

You'll find information on Hawaii here, of course, but also on international trade, especially in the Pacific Rim.

Business process improvement mailing list☆☆
Email to: bpi@utvm.cc.utexas.edu

This discussion list deals with issues and opportunities related to business process improvement.

## Commerce Business Daily☆☆☆☆
http://www.stat-usa.gov/BEN/Services/globus.html

You'll find the indispensable U.S. government periodical for government contractors here. Just like the hardcopy version, the electronic version of *CBD* invites businesses to bid on government projects. Unlike the hardcopy version, you can quickly and easily search by keyword to find any bids for products or services you sell—and old copies won't stack up in your office. A free sample issue is available. An electronic subscription costs $25 per quarter, and is available the day before the printed version.

## Environmental Protection Agency System☆☆☆
Gopher to: gopher.rtpnc.epa.gov

Check here for proposed new regulations, access to databases, a directory of environmental resources, and more.

## Microsoft financial news☆☆
ftp to: ftp.microsoft.com

Get 10-Q quarterlies, 10-K annual reports, and press releases from the software giant. A good way to see how to display your own.

## Multimedia and Entertainment Law☆☆☆
http://www.dnai.com:80/~pzender

This site presents legal and business information about the multimedia and entertainment industries.

## *Providence Business News*☆☆☆
http://www.pbn.com

Business news from Rhode Island and Southeastern Massachusetts.

Texas Department of Commerce Bulletin Board☆☆☆☆
telnet to: texis.tdoc.texas.gov and log in as *guest*

A board by, for, and about business in Texas. You'll find Texas company directories, TEXIS (Texas Information System), the Texas Buyer/Supplier Product Matching System, Texas government procurement opportunities, a business development calendar, and information on rural commerce development. And if Texas isn't a big enough market for you, there's a section on international trade, too.

# Eleven Money-Making Businesses You Can Start Today

*"The secret in business is to know something that nobody else knows."*
Aristotle Onassis

My all-time favorite book on starting and running a business is *Growing a Business*, which was turned into a PBS television series. In this classic book, author Paul Hawken tells the story of how he ended up in the direct mail business by accident and how the process of running and growing a business changed his life for the better. What I liked most about the book was the author's philosophy of how starting and running a business can be a wonderful experience of personal growth.

When you set out to start up and run your own business on the Internet, you'll be setting in motion a course of events that could change your life drastically. If your business becomes wildly successful (and I hope it does), it'll more than likely take over your life—especially because of the fast, demanding pace of the Internet. With this in mind, make sure you select a business idea that really excites you—one that you won't get tired of when cash flow becomes a problem or you have to spend a few all-nighters handling customer support problems. And keep in mind that any business you start on the Net will probably go through a number of changes as it evolves.

To help you get started, I've come up with some business ideas that could work on the Internet. If one or more of these potential money making ideas gets your attention, try to think through the phases involved in getting the business started. Here's a list of questions you'll want to consider:

1. How much money will I need to get started?

2. How much time can I devote to starting up and running the business?

3. Should I start it up on my own or will I need additional help?

4. Do I want to start a business I can run for many years and grow it moderately or do I want to take the fast track and build it up quickly and sell it?

5. Once the business is up and running, will I have enough resources to maintain the business so that my customers will continue to return again and again?

6. If the business really takes off, am I willing to make major life changes such as quit my day job or take in a partner?

7. Are there businesses already in existence on the Internet like the one I want to start up? How much competition should I expect in the future?

8. Who are my main customers and what is the most cost-effective way of reaching them?

9. Are the customers of my business willing to buy my products and services over the Internet?

10. Would the business be easy to shut down if it is not successful enough or I have some major life changes and can't devote time to the business any longer?

With these questions in mind, take a look at the dozen great start-up ideas in the next sections. Do remember that these are *ideas*, not startup kits or roadmaps to success. Other readers will buy this book and will have the opportunity to consider these same ideas. So you'll probably want to use these 11 start-up business ideas to stimulate your imagination or trigger that entrepreneurial concept you've been contemplating for too many years now. Get creative, but most of all, get going!

## Zaggat's guide to shareware

There are more than 60,000 free or shareware software packages available on the Net. They range in quality from great to the pits. To provide an online service for computer users, you could create a review guide and model it after the famous Zaggat guidebooks to restaurants and hotels. (I love their guides because their critiques are so honest.) You could get started on the cheap by having users write reviews and pay them by giving them free access to your guides. You could make money by charging a fee for browsing or a fee per download. To sign up new customers, you might want to offer a free one-month trial.

Here's how the system could work: Users browse your site and read your reviews to locate the software they like. You could even provide a search engine to help them locate software. At the end of each description is a hotlink to the actual file to download. If your business is on a Web page, you could make the site more useful by including annotated screen shots of each software package. This would really add value because users typically can't see what a software program looks like until they download and install it on their computer.

Of course, the key to making a system like this successful is to update the reviews and add new ones often. New software pops up like mushrooms. You'll also need to make sure that the links to the software you review are always tested and updated. Files are moved around on the Internet about as fast as they first appear. If your customers are paying real money to use your service and they can't easily find and retrieve what they need, they won't remain your customers for long.

A system like this is relatively easy to set up without requiring a lot of resources. This means that if you are successful, you should expect lots of competition. You could add more value to your service by referencing important reviews in major publications and getting noted computer industry experts to contribute to your service. You could also set up an electronic newsletter for your customers that automatically gets sent to them once a week telling them all about the new releases of the best software that your reviewers have located. (Don't use the Zaggat name—that's someone else's trademark.)

## Home business shopping

One of the fastest-growing groups on the Net is home office workers. This group consists of people who work for a company and telecommute part-time or full-time, or people who actually run a business out of their home. Time is money for these people, so they are more likely to buy products electronically since they already have computers and modems. They also understand the value of being online.

When I consider a situation like this, my business instincts take over. These people who are working online probably spend a lot more time on the Internet than in shopping malls or office supply stores. To grab a piece of this large customer base, you could set up an Internet business to offer an especially-tailored range of office supplies and small-business equipment. A nice touch would be to offer local same-day delivery in major metropolitan areas. Office-supply products would be a much better product mix for these customers than the basic computer products, such as PCs, modems, and peripherals, that are offered by direct marketing companies that currently have business channels set up on the Net.

There are actually two separate business models you could apply: Either you sell over the Net and ship the products as a traditional direct merchant or you receive orders from people all over the country and farm out deliverable purchases to local businesses and ship the rest. Each time you sell a product you make money.

You could publish your full-color catalog on the Web. Your costs for distributing the catalog electronically would be lower than mailing it, and you could update it more often. The catalog could feature testimonials from some of your customers. You could also include an electronic survey that asks your customers which types of products or services they'd like to see you provide more of. The goal with a business like this is to make it as interactive as possible, which in turn will give you a major sales edge over competitors who sell their products solely through mail-order catalogs.

## Custom Medical Care News

One of the occupations that could be changed drastically by the Internet is health care. People with Internet access could go to their doctor armed with more and newer information on their condition than the doctor has. This could transform doctor-patient relationships for the better. You can help and make money from it at the same time. To pull this one off, you need to be familiar with medical terms and conditions. You'll also need access to medical resources on the Internet and probably a large University's medical library. This will take work to set up, but the payoff could be enormous.

This idea occured to me because of a kidney stone in my right kidney. This condition developed complications that sent me to the hospital several times to get rid of it. My unhelpful doctor (who shall remain nameless for obvious reasons) told me that I had a calcium oxalate stone (the most common kind)

# Financing new Internet ventures

Raising venture capital for a new Internet business is not easy. If you go to most banks and ask them for a loan, let alone a merchant account to process credit card orders for an electronic business, they'll probably show you the door very quickly. Most financial instutions and traditional investors don't quite understand the electronic business revolution that is underway around the world. One way to help your cause is to provide your banker or potential investor with practical articles from business magazines about successful Internet businesses. (You'll also want to give them a copy of this book.)

Your best bet is to ask friends or family—people who know you and would feel that you have a good chance of succeeding. But whatever approach you take, make sure you put a good business plan together and you inform any potential investor of the true risks and rewards. The best asset you'll ever have is your credibility: If you are upfront with anyone who lends you money, they'll be more likely to lend you money in the future when you need it. And if your Internet business is successful, you'll probably always be on the lookout for additional funding.

Here's one venture capital firm that could be helpful to you: In the fall of 1994, America Online bought start-up Booklink Technologies for $45 million in stock. The founders of BookLink took the money and started a venture capital firm that focuses on Internet ventures. The name of the new company is @ventures.

and that I should drink lots of water to prevent having another. He had a cartoon-like booklet displayed in his office on kidney care. I had to ask him for a copy. It had more information than the doctor's comment on water—a few diet tips and a discussion of the value of doing the right exercises. After reviewing some medical books, I found that a common symptom found in calcium oxalate stone formers is magnesium deficiency. By taking magnesium supplements you can inhibit the formation of new stones. I also have a common heart condition called mitral valve prolapse. I found an interesting thing: magnesium deficiency is common in mitral valve prolapse patients as well. I took magnesium supplements, and in two weeks my energy level—which had been down since the stone—picked up.

Why didn't my doctor tell me about magnesium? I asked him. He didn't know about it! I actually knew stuff about kidney stones that an experienced full-time urologist didn't know. Needless to say, I got another doctor. But how will all his other patients know what they have and know what to ask for?

Here's where you have a business opportunity. Every person with any kind of medical condition wants to know more: first, the basic facts, and then, the latest news. Until the Internet, there has never been a way to deliver custom-tailored information based on each person's own combination of conditions. What signs should I look for? What do I ask my doctor? What changes should I make in my diet or exercise? What new research results have been recently published? What are the side affects of a particular prescription or treatment?

I think this should be a subscription-based service. New subscribers would fill out a questionnaire about their history and conditions. (I don't know how you'd get around people who lie about their weight or age.) Your service would have an automated database that would put together a welcome message, with background on their condtions, common lifestyle changes to help improve their condition, and a list of questions to ask their doctor. Any health supplements, vitamins, prescription drugs, or new doctor visits would mean they need to send updated information to you, and you in turn can email updated info to them.

Whenever new stuff is published in medical journals about their specific disease or condition, your server would email to them an abstract with a citation, so they or their doctor could look up the full article.

There are legal conditions to watch out for. In the U.S., unless you are an M.D. you cannot diagnose a patient's symptoms, and you cannot prescribe treatments or drugs. In other countries, you may run afoul of other laws.

Although you could make money by charging a subscription fee, you could also get money from drug companies for including small discreet advertments. There is a demand for self-care health information on the Net. When the National Institute for Diabetes and Diseases of the Kidneys' Web page went online, it was jammed with 19,000 hits in six days. (It would have had more, but the server overloaded.) How many businesses do you know that have had so many potential customers walk through their doors the first week they opened? For giving you this idea, I'd like a free subscription to your health care guide and one share of your company's stock (if you ever issue any).

## E-Delivery

The Peapod company has had some success delivering groceries from orders taken online. You could use this type of delivery model to set up your own local, order/delivery system. You could offer meals, documents, sports equipment, and so on.

To do this, you'll need to tie in with local businesses and deliver their products to local customers. A good way to start is to get on the Net and contact local businesses that have Web pages. The larger the city you live in, the easier it will be to find local businesses that are Internet connected.

You'll also want to build close relationships with local Internet access providers that have local businesses as clients. You can make money by charging a delivery fee payable by the Net merchants out of their sales price. I don't think it's a good idea to make your customers pay the delivery fee because this will discourage them from using your service. But ultimately it's your call.

This is not the type of business you are likely to grow into a multi-million dollar operation, but it could be a good business if your time and resources are limited. To make it work, you'll need to devise a system so that you can constantly check the Net for orders.

## Internet Gaming and Multimedia

This field is in its infancy. Many Internet users are into electronic entertainment—games, multimedia, and so on. You could create a unique game that could be played on the Web for a fee. Or create "Internetable" puzzles that can be played online. (Crossword puzzle books are still a big business.) You could even sponsor tournaments with your best playing customers (pun intended). Of course, this type of business requires some technical knowledge, depending on what kind of games you implement. You could make money by charging subscription fees, running advertisements, and selling games and add-on products.

The entertainment field drives the computer industry. Last year more money was made by companies selling computer games and game cartridges than by the movie industry at the box office. Will this trend continue? I think so. In fact, many new technologies are being developed so that popular games, such as *Doom*, can be played across networks. Recently, I came across a hot technology that is being developed for the Internet so that Web pages can be viewed to create a virtual reality (VR) experience. You can download some of the new VR viewer software (for Windows, Mac, and Motif platforms) from **http://www.eit.com/vrml/**).

A hot ticket in this product category is Internet- and CD-ROM combinations. The advertising chapter of this book discusses one such project, the Interactive World's Fair. The Coriolis Group (**http://www.coriolis.com/coriolis**), publishers of this book, created a variation on this concept, an interactive Grand Canyon. Called *Explore the Grand Canyon*, it uses photos, video, and narration to let viewers plan and take their own journey through the hidden depths of this national park. Viewers can connect on the Internet to the Coriolis Web site and retrieve multimedia additions that automatically incorporate themselves into the product. Instead of a static CD-ROM, *Explore the Grand Canyon* becomes as changeable as the Canyon itself.

If you have a technical background and you are interested in online entertainment, now's the time to get in on the ground floor of this very promising industry. Millions will be made by both large companies and innovative start-ups.

## EDI for Small Companies

Internet EDI will boom, but small companies won't have a clue about how to implement it. If you're a technical type, there is a lot of money to be made by

implementing Internet-EDI-on-a-PC. Purchase orders are a good first implementation. You'll need familiarity with EDI and with Internet email. You can
make money by charging hourly fees or per-project fees. Your customers will
be businesses that want to implement EDI, so you can also make money from
markups on EDI software. The big marketing challenge will be to convey the
benefits of EDI simply, clearly, and dramatically to nontechnical
businesspeople.

# Online Newsletter

This is probably an obvious business to many Internet users but it's worth mentioning because it's an easy business to get going. Are you an expert on anything? There are dozens of people making a living from Internet newsletters.

David Scott Lewis publishes *HOTT (Hot Off The Tree)*, which he calls "the
Internet's first controlled-circulation publication." His monthly newsletter
has a circulation of 40,000 Internet readers. His plan is to sell advertising
space. His costs are minimal, mostly for his time. Other people charge subscription fees for their online newsletters. You have no printing costs, no typesetting bill, and no postal charges. Just a small fee from your Internet access
provider.

But creating a financially successful newsletter business takes hard work. You'll
need to select a topic where there is a great need for information. You'll also
need a good way to get subscribers. Make sure your newsletter's target demographics match those of the Internet, so you will actually have a large enough
prospect base to be viable.

# Online Index of Products

This one takes a big investment. There are all kinds of products for sale.
Several industries have catalogs of all the products available within that industry (*Books in Print* for book buyers, *Schwann's* catalog for the recording
industry, and so on). You could get really ambitious and create an omni-
catalog that lists all products from all industries, from machine tools to Ford
Aerostar vans—by name, brand name, commodity code, and so on. It should

be multilingual. Your customers would be purchasers (National Association for Purchasing Management) and buyers for stores.

You can make money by either charging a trivial, small amount per lookup (which I recommend) or a subscription fee. Look at Quote.com for a business model (**http://www.quote.com**).

## Library Lookers

This is an idea I really like. More than a hundred libraries around the world are accessible via the Internet. Well, not quite. The libraries' *catalogs* are accessible via the Internet. You can see what's in the Library of Congress, you just can't get to it. This problem frustrates researchers the world over, but if you live close to a library, you are in a position to do something about it.

I am a fan of Dashiell Hammett. His papers are at the Humanities Research Center at the University of Texas at Austin. I have looked up the Center's catalog online, but Hammett's papers are pathetically indexed, and the catalog tells me nearly nothing. I'd pay for someone to look up a couple of facts for me.

Being a looker is an ideal job for college students or retired people who love libraries. This idea requires that you make yourself known to the staff of the library you use (so they can give you referrals) and that you promote your availability on the Net. Promotion can be done using mailing lists (discreetly) and by posting on newsgroups (even more discreeetly). If you can, you should set up a looker home page where lookers all over the world could list themselves, and where people could go to find a looker.

The point of this enterprise is to specialize. Don't try to be a generalized information-hunting service. You should focus on a local library or set of libraries. Basically, you want to turn your nearby libraries into an income-producing asset for yourself. For some research fields (medicine, computer science, or law), this requires that the looker has knowledge of the subject being researched. The turfs to stake out are the biggest libraries (University of California at Berkeley is one of the ten biggest in the world), and specialized libraries (the Margaret Herrick library at the Academy of Motion Picture Arts and Sciences in Los Angeles, the geneaology library in Salt Lake City, the rare book collection of the Sutro Library in San Francisco, and the Folger Library in Washington D.C., which has the largest collection of Shakespeare material in the world). You can make money by charging a search fee based on the search(es) performed, by the document(s) returned, or by the hour.

## Set up a Talk Show

If you are a good interviewer and have access to guests, create your own read-only IRC channel (Or use Web Chat, **http://www.irsociety.com/ webchat.html**). You interview your guest, or guests, at your keyboard, typing in questions while they type in answers. After you're done with formal Q&A, if you wish, you can open the IRC channel up to questions from your audience. Online chats are a big draw. Every so often, you type in text for your sponsors' messages. This would cost little to set up, but continuing work to operate. You'd need to recruit guests, and have a great wit and strong wrist muscles.

To make a chat channel, you'd need a group of hosts with enough personality and knowledge to become celebs in their own right. Who knows? You could become the David Letterman of Internet chat. You can make money by selling commercials (which will take a lot of work). If you can't spell well or type fast, you'll need to do all the talking and have someone else work the keyboard. (If you need an author on your show to talk about Internet business, drop me a note!)

## Cato the Censor

Old Cato was a straight-laced moralist in ancient Rome, but he would have found plenty to keep him occupied on the Internet. In fact, some businesses think there is a need for someone to clean the virtual gutters of the Internet, and you can make money from them. Businesses that want to block employees from accessing sex sites, games, racist groups, humor, gambling, www.virtualvegas.com, and so on while at work. You provide an emailed list of potentially troublesome sites and why they are troublesome. The business' network administrators can program these site addresses into their router filters or firewalls to prevent employees from reaching them. You email them a list every week or so with updates, changes, additions, and deletions. This will only work with some routers and firewalls; you will probably want to rent names and addresses of customers of these devices and do a postal mailing to their buyers.

You can make money by getting businesses to subscribe to your service. and from router and firewall manufacturers/sellers who bundle your starter kit with their product. Best bet: Give the starter bundle away for free or almost free to lure in more subscribers. In any subscription business, you make money not from the initial signup but from the continuing fees.

## *Creating Your Own Business Idea*

I hope these ideas will inspire you to come up with some of your own. If you get a business up and running, I'd love to hear about it. Send me a note at **vince@emery.com.** If you've set up a Web page, send me the URL; I'd love to take a look at your site.

# The Internet, Logistics, and EDI

*"No man ever wetted clay and then left it, as if it would become bricks by chance and fortune."*
Plutarch, *Of Fortune*

Any operation involving manufacturing, purchasing, warehousing, or transportation involves moving large amounts of information back and forth as quickly as possible. As you have probably already surmised, the Internet is a useful tool for logistics operations. You are not the only one to have seen the usefulness of the Internet in this respect; Saddam Hussein and the Iraqi army figured out the same thing. They used the Internet to support their command and control system during the Gulf War, much to the annoyance of the U.S. military. Some businesses also use the Internet for these activities, often on a large scale. Several industry associations and consortia are helping to speed the adaptation of the Internet to logistics needs and to make it accessible by smaller companies.

Steven Gage, president of the Cleveland Advanced Manufacturing Program (CAMP), works on technology transfer for small and medium-sized companies. He believes the Internet can be a big help in making companies more competitive, and in providing support to these and other companies. He points to the Northeast Manufacturing Technology Center (NEMTC), which works with Tufts University to provide TECnet to small and medium-sized companies. TECnet provides government information, small business advice, and databases of used equipment for sale. Through it, manufacturers exchange information with each other and tap into technical discussion groups on the Internet. Subscribing companies pay only a small yearly fee to access TECnet.

At the forefront of the Internet and logistics is another organization, CommerceNet. A consortium of corporations, government agencies, and industry groups, CommerceNet spawned several working groups that focus on such issues as purchasing over the Internet and using the Net to integrate design and manufacturing.

AVEX Electronics (**http://www.huber.com/Avex/AVEXHome.html**) was a founding member of CommerceNet. This company has helped define strategic initiatives for shortening the time-to-market cycle for electronics manufacturers by using such techniques as concurrent product development and electronic bidding.

"Access to knowledge from anyplace at any time—that's the goal," said Paul Kozlowski, AVEX president and CEO. "Any method to improve information flow is going to dominate in the coming decades. Electronic transactions for inventory, order placement, and engineering collaboration are going to be aggressively pursued by electronics companies."

"Doing business over the Internet has the potential to significantly improve the ramp to volume production process, all the way from conceptual design to full production," explained Mike Gordon. Gordon is advanced systems manager for AVEX and a board member of EIDEX (The Electronics Industry Data Exchange Association). For example, engineers at different locations could view and edit new product designs at the same time. Engineers in quality, test, and other disciplines could collaborate in realtime. Customers of AVEX responded well to the idea of sending bills of material for competitive bidding electronically.

One company already profiting from the Internet is T.R.A.D.E., Inc., which sells Internet access to a WAIS server that lets customers look up information on all import manifests for all shipments coming into the U.S. before they arrive in port.

In the long run, putting your inventory, delivery, and order tracking on the Net makes for more inventory turns, letting your company improve planning and reduce stock levels. From your customers' viewpoint, you will have faster and more flexible delivery. But in the short term, purchasing operations realize the most benefit from the Internet.

## Purchasing and the Internet

Some applications of the Internet to purchasing are obvious. For example, consider a purchasing agent who prepares a large RFP and sends it to prospective suppliers via email or lets them retrieve an electronic copy from an FTP server. This approach saves printing costs, postage costs, and a great deal of time compared to the old hard-copy way of doing things. Electronic proposals and bidding also speed the purchasing timecycle.

Internet newsgroups can also be a big help for purchasers, from the largest companies to the smallest. There is an especially large amount of information on newsgroups about any computer-related products, including the kind of personal opinions that you can only get from someone who has used a product first-hand. For instance, this example was posted on the **biz.comp.accounting** newsgroup in response to a small business purchaser asking about the difference between two accounting software programs, Simply Accounting and QuickBooks:

```
My personal opinion is to steer clear of Simply Accounting. I've worked with
the package a few times and my experiences have always been poor. As far as
QuickBooks is concerned, I do like this package. My clients that use
QuickBooks normally are satisfied with the package. A big limitation to
QuickBooks is it is very limited in the inventory area. If you have inven-
tory for sale, as opposed to offering only services, you might consider MYOB
from TeleWare...about as easy as QuickBooks but a little more powerful.
```

Other newsgroups provide actual sources to purchase products. In these newsgroups you will find manufacturing raw ingredients and commodities and finished goods available for resale. Recent postings in the newsgroup **alt.business.import-export** offered Marlboro cigarettes in minimum lots of ten cargo containers, electrical capacitors, and 40,000 metric tons of metal-lurgical grade coke, apparently on a loading dock in China and available for quick shipment at a bargain price.

Purchasers also post condensed versions of RFPs on newsgroups, reaching a wide audience of prospective bidders. For example, I found a posting (also in the newsgroup **alt.business.import-export**) from a purchaser looking for bids to supply 1,000 PC clones.

There are many sites on the World Wide Web that can be used by purchasers. One of the best-known is IndustryNET (**http://www.industry.net**), an industrial counterpart to the consumer Internet malls. Thousands of industrial suppliers provide catalog information and specifications for all kinds of industrial equipment, parts, and supplies. The IndustryNET site is visited by more than 40,000 buyers and specifiers per month from 27 different countries. Products are viewable by product type, by manufacturer name, and by recency, so you can choose to review, for example, just the new machine tools available in the last six months.

Another valuable site, PartNet (**http://part.net**), is a project of the University of Utah under ARPA sponsorship. It lets designers specify, find, and select parts from a collection of online parts catalogs, with the purpose of encouraging companies to speed design time by purchasing existing parts rather than designing new ones.

Some industry associations have made online purchasing resources available for their members. The American Society of Landscape Architects (202-686-2752) has teamed with the Building Owners and Managers Association, the Irrigation Association, and the National Concrete Masonry Association to offer a service called Designet for landscape designers, developers, environmental designers, and related professionals. It provides online information on more than 10,000 products, including specifications and digitized CAD system drawings, so designers can copy a computerized illustration of a product and pop it into a site plan or elevation.

The National Association for Purchasing Management's branch in Silicon Valley has a site on the Net (**http://www.catalog.com/napmsv**) that provides much more information on purchasing and the Internet. It includes an Internet-based course on purchasing fundamentals, articles on purchasing and EDI (Electronic Data Interchange), and a "Purchasing Pro's Internet Directory" (but surprisingly, no links to the dozens of other Web purchasing and procurement sites).

## Electronic Data Interchange

Electronic Data Interchange (EDI) is a term used to describe the process in which the paperwork for a transaction between two organizations goes directly from the computer of one into the computer of the other, bypassing the standard paper version.

About $2 billion in sales per year is conducted electronically, with about half of that handled in the U.S. EDI is also used for many kinds of non-sales transactions. Businesses, educational institutions, and government agencies use EDI to exchange invoices, purchase orders, insurance claims, tax returns, warranty registrations, warehouse orders, inventory reports, shipping notices, vehicle inspection reports, contract proposals, inventory transfers, debit and credit memos, customs declarations, delivery schedules, and many other kinds of transactions. EDI traffic grows by 20 percent or more each year.

Most companies using EDI don't use the Internet, but are locked into proprietary vendors' systems on leased phone lines. These proprietary networks are called value-added networks, or VANs for short. Proprietary systems cost more, and make it tough for you to switch to another vendor that costs less or offers you more features. John Katsaros, president of Collaborative Marking (**katsaros@netcom.com**), surveyed VAN users and found that most are unhappy with their network provider, mentioning network downtime, lost transactions, and high expenses as reasons. Many of those companies are looking at switching to the Internet for handling their EDI transactions.

The pioneer in Internet EDI is the Lawrence Livermore National Laboratory. Since 1992, Livermore Laboratory has moved more than two million EDI transactions over the Internet, primarily for purchasing. The project has been highly successful, and has demonstrated lower costs, better reliability, and better message tracking than a VAN provides for EDI.

CommerceNet has an EDI Working Group. The group's charter is to define an architecture to link buyers, sellers, and service providers on the Net, and to enable the expansion of EDI in ways that make it affordable and practical for all types of organizations and individual people to use EDI. The group is addressing concerns about reliability, scalability, ease of use, speed, and logging and auditing. CommerceNet is conducting pilot projects that let buyers browse multimedia catalogs that can generate EDI-formatted quotations and orders, solicit EDI-formatted bids, place EDI orders without browsing, and generate EDI-formatted invoices and payments. Sellers will be able to respond to bids, schedule production, and coordinate deliveries using Internet EDI.

This is all rushing forward at breakneck speed. In the European Community, things move at a more stately pace. The EC's Commercial Electronic Data Interchange commission (called COMEDI for short—I kid you not) has an objective "to create standardized infrastructures at the European level." COMEDI is scheduled to present a report on its objective to the European

Parliament by the end of 1997. It should be an easy report. By that time, Internet EDI will be a *fait accompli* throughout the world.

Currently, about 85 percent of EDI transactions are between businesses, and 15 percent are between businesses and government agencies. The Clinton administration has done a tremendous amount to speed U.S. governmental EDI. It requires all federal agencies by January 1997 to make all purchases under $100,000 electronically (not necessarily through EDI—many are made through emailed purchase orders). This has created a bonanza for some businesses. MDT Corp. of Arnold, Maryland started making EDI sales with the federal government in 1994, and business grew so fast that in less than a year a person had to be hired just to manage MDT's email traffic.

Can your business get in on this government business? Yes, but unfortunately, not on the Internet. The government certified fifteen VANs to do business with it. You have to sign up with one of these VANs to receive requests for quotes from Uncle Sam. Right now, most quotes come from the military. Other agencies are laggards—after all, they have until the end of 1996. The Food and Drug Administration, for example, is just starting with EDI. I would hope that some Internet business group is working with the government on this issue to get acceptance of orders transacted over the Internet without an intervening VAN.

One of the biggest EDI efforts is underway from the Internal Revenue Service, the world's most successful mail-order business. It collects about $1 trillion per year. Called the Electronic Federal Tax Payment System (EFTPS), the project's goal is to eliminate paperwork from the collection of all corporate and individual tax payments. It is expected to save Uncle Sam more than $400 million through 1999.

## *Should my business do Internet EDI?*

First, EDI is not easy. You can't just drive to your local Egghead Software and buy "EDI in a Box" and pop it into your computer. Complicated technical details are involved. First, what computer systems does your company have that you would need to move data into and out of ? Even for purchasing transactions, one of the most common uses of EDI, you are looking at interacting with a lot of software programs. Your accounting software, your inventory software, and your purchasing software all have data that will need to be extracted, and other data will need to be input.

Sound like a lot of work? It gets worse. Then you need to go through the same routine for every company you do business with. Everybody uses different software. None of them format data the same way. Before we get into this deeper, you may have second thoughts, which would be wise.

EDI is not for every business. Not yet, anyway. Even with new software products that simplify EDI, it still takes a significant investment of time and technology to make EDI work. Your key to deciding whether or not to get involved should be your customers. Do you have several customers who want to conduct EDI transactions with you? Or maybe one large customer? If your customers make it worthwhile, take a closer look at EDI. If not, back off and wait for the technology to make it easier.

## *The need for EDI standards*

Since there is little chance that the makers of accounting software and other business systems will wise up and implement a standardized way of formatting business data, several organizations have developed EDI standards. With such standards in place, a company translating outbound transactions can translate all of them into one format, instead of learning new formats for everyone it does business with. And the same benefit applies in reverse. A company translating incoming transactions need only work from one format instead of many. Less variety and less work.

This idea of an EDI standard format caught on quickly. Everyone thought a standard was a great idea. In fact, organizations thought the idea was so great that they created *two* sets of standards. Incompatible, of course. The American National Standards Institute created one with the catchy name of X12. It is used in the United States. The United Nations sponsored the Electronic Data Interchange for Administration, Commerce, and Transport format (EDIFACT). It is used in the rest of the world. Fortunately, software programs are available to convert one format to the other. By 1997, the whole issue won't matter because X12 is being merged into EDIFACT, so there will be only one set of EDI standards.

## EDI mapping software

Although EDI sounds great, you still need to get the information from your software programs into EDI format, and vice versa. This has been no small challenge. In the past, companies hired huge crews of custom programmers to slog out miles of code to move information into and out of EDI transactions. A typical EDI implementation project took more than a year of solid work, and one operating in six months was considered a miracle.

To meet these needs, mapping software was created. To use most mapping software programs, you extract data from your system and feed the files to the EDI mapper. It plucks out the data and arranges it in EDI format. Then you can send the formatted data via Internet Privacy-Enhanced Mail (PEM). When you receive an incoming EDI transaction via PEM, you decrypt it and feed it to your mapper. The mapper builds a file that you can feed to your business software programs.

There are several mapping programs, ranging in price from $4,000 to $50,000: Visual EDI from EDI Able, Inc. (Malvern, Pennsylvania), WWIX-Map from Paper Free Systems, Inc. (Washington, DC), and the Unix program EDI Interface from the AI Group (Tampa, Florida). Premenos Corp. (**http://www.premenos.com**) provides software that links with Computer Associates' manufacturing and distribution products. Some of these mapping programs require your business to write a program to extract the data from, for example, your purchasing sytem, and to bring the data to your mapping software. A new product fom Coddington Software Development (415-898-0925) requires no programming, and actually can go from system to system finding the necessary data automatically, building a single EDI transaction or a relational database of several transactions when needed. This new software can decrease the technical phase of EDI implementation (which now takes 3 to18 months) to 2 or 3 weeks.

## The Internet part of EDI

For EDI, the Internet plays two roles: as a delivery mechanism and as a source of information. Lack of security on the Internet is what drives businesses to use proprietary VANs. Now that Internet security software is available, EDI users find that the Internet offers advantages of cost and, just as importantly, of reach. Using Internet email, buyers can solicit bids and place orders with thousands of EDI vendors, both the vendors on the Internet and the ones that use traditional VANs.

Most companies using the Internet for EDI use Privacy-Enchanced Mail which provides end-to-end security and message delivery notification. It works over the VAN networks as well as on the Internet. It can be used to carry both X12 and EDIFACT forms of EDI.

Premenos (mentioned previously) is at the forefront of Internet EDI. Its Templar system, available for both Unix and Windows, uses RSA public key cryptography to send secure transactions across the Internet. Any company looking at EDI should take a look at Premenos' Web site. It provides the largest collection I've found of EDI information on the Net, including links to many other organizations. (Although it is a frustrating site, making you wade through a zillion levels of single-screen data to find what you want, and leaving hundreds of links without descriptions.)

An alternative way to handle EDI over the Internet is MIME EDI. This uses MIME email and is based on CROC93A, an Internet Draft standard written by Dave Crocker of Silicon Graphics. MIME EDI can carry EDI messages in both the X12 and EDIFACT formats.

If your company is interested in EDI, you can find a good explanation of how to start at "Getting Started with EDI," available at **http://www.catalog.com/ napmsv/edi.htm**.

# Customers, Sales, and the World Wide Web

"When you lose a sale, you lose it twice: you don't get the money, and your competitor does."

Bill Gates, CEO, Microsoft Corporation

The folks who run the Yahoo server say that every day, 30 to 50 new shopping sites open on the Net. Shopping sites are only one of the ways businesses use the Net to increase sales, but they do get the highest visibility.

For example, when Paramount Pictures opened a Web site selling *Star Trek: Generations* merchandise, it received 3,600 orders in the first two weeks.

Or look at the Internet Shopping Network (**http://shop.internet.net**). 10,000 people visit it per day. About 30 percent are repeat customers. A typical first-time customer buys a low-ticket item, then comes back and makes a more expensive purchase. 30 percent of its top customers ($2,000 or more) are women.

TCI Soccer, a catalog company, mails more than 3 million printed catalogs per year. Its Web site at **http://www.tsisoccer.com/tsi** brought new customers and helped the company expand into new markets. Almost 25 percent of its visitors are from other countries, and all of its international customers are first-time buyers. Finding that Japanese and Canadians are its biggest international customers led the company to conduct large mailings of its print catalogs to those countries.

The low costs and quick turnaround time of selling on the Net make it possible for you to profit on new types of sales. A good example is the Internet-spawned phenomena called *house concerts*, a new way the music business sells tickets and CDs. Here's how house concerts work. A performer sets a date to perform in a person's private home. The performer's record label promotes the house concert by sending email notices to a mailing list of the performer's fans who live near the area where the performance will be held, and by posting notices in appropriate music fan newsgroups. Total marketing costs: nothing, thanks to the Internet. No rent is paid for a concert hall. No sales commissions are charged. From ticket sales and CD sales at the event, the performer makes as much money as from a larger venue, and generates the kind of loyal fans who build careers. Waterbug Records credits house concerts as the major force in establishing the success of folksinger Cosy Sheridan.

What makes customers buy on the Internet? Peter Drucker has written that a new technology won't be commonly used unless it offers a tenfold advantage in cost. The Internet does cost less than traditional methods, but there are two other factors at work here. First, I believe that Drucker's tenfold principle also holds true for time. The Internet saves an unbelievable amount of time. David Carlick of Poppe Tyson Advertising said the reason for sales success on the Internet is that "Buyers want instant gratification. It's an undeniable force." The Net offers instant gratification for your customer, and for you, the merchant, as well.

The second advantage is an emotional one. The Net gives your customers *direct contact* with your company. There are no middlemen. This feeds people's hunger for direct relationships. Customers want to feel as if they are in control. They want acknowledgment for what they say. The Net lets you tap your clients' demand for dialog. You can build a close relationship with your customers on the Net, closer than anything but in-person sales. This closeness rewards your Internet buyers and gives you a first-hand understanding of what your customers want and need.

So what can your business sell on the Internet? You can sell products. You can sell services—both services that you deliver electronically and services in the real world. You can sell information. You can sell subscriptions to an electronic newsletter, or to a service, or to enter your site. You can sell advertising on your Net projects. You can collect rent and sales commissions from your Net site. You can support your existing sales staff, or direct more customers to your existing distributors and dealers. Let's take a closer look at the ways you can sell on the Net.

## Types of sales on the Internet

There are almost as many ways to sell on the Internet as there are in the real world. Some are just Internetized copies of proven sales models. Some have unique twists without precise counterpoints in real life. Before you put your own sales project in motion, decide which of these Net sales models you need. You will need different Internet tools to make different types of sales, and it makes sense to know what you need before you start, rather than make a surprise change in the middle of your project.

A word of caution; don't try to launch a project based just on this book and without any hands-on experience. Book learning by itself is not enough. If you are going to sell things on the Net, first go out on the Net and *buy* things. Buy from at least three different locations. Keep your eyes open for strengths and weak spots of the places you buy. Take note of what you like and any good ideas you might see. Also remember things you don't like. As Yogi Berra said, "You can observe a lot just by watching."

## Subscription sales model

7,800 subscribers pay $100 a year to receive email from Tom Tabor. Tabor publishes *HPCWire,* a weekly newsletter delivered by email. In addition to revenue from subscribers, Tabor charges up to $4,000 per issue for advertisements. Advertisers pay based on readership; Tabor's advertising readership base is larger than just his paid subscribers because he emails all prospective subscribers who inquire about *HPCWire* the latest table of contents plus all advertisements. His second electronic magazine is *WEBster,* an ezine about the Web. Advertisers pay $10,000 a year to advertise in *WEBster.* Its subscribers pay $29 per year. *WEBster* is distributed on the World Wide Web at **http://www.tgc.com/webster.html**.

Tabor's business makes straightforward use of the subscription sales model. Many success stories have proven that this model works well on the Net. In subscription sales, you get money from subscribers. You might be paid per year, per month, per week, per hour, or per transaction, but subscribers pay you for content. In the real world, content is usually subsidized by advertising. When people pay for content—whether it is in a book or on a cable TV channel—most of the money pays for the distribution channel, not for the content. This is especially true of mass-market content. Specialized content can claim a higher per-customer price, but that is offset by the fact that specialized content usually sells in much lower quantites than mass-market content. The interesting thing about the Net is that its technology lets you inexpensively custom-tailor your content, so individual subscribers receive personalized content, highly specialized to meet an individual's precise needs. It's important to note that the final form of the content your subscribers see does not need to resemble any sort of print publication. It can be quite different. Two examples of businesses that do a good job of personalizing content for individual subscribers are InfoSeek (described on page 350), and Quote.com.

Quote.com (**http://www.quote.com**) is a classic Internet success story. Chris Cooper started the business with himself, a T1 Internet connection from BarrNet, and a Sun clone computer "because I didn't want to spend enough money to buy a real Sun." Today he has a a healthy company with employees, customers worldwide, and several real Sun computers. Cooper's idea was to receive stock and investment ticker information as it changed, to let subscribers pick exactly the companies and types of quotes they wanted, and to email their quotes to them throughout the trading day. He started programming October, 1993 and opened for business July, 1994. "I spent zero for advertising," said Cooper. "I did spend money for a PR firm to do traditional publicity for four to five months around the launch. I posted messages in newsgroups occasionally. I received a couple of flames—less than the number of fingers on one hand. When I explained to the flamers what we're doing, I never heard back from them. On newsgroups, I only posted about the free services we offer." As an appetizer, Quote.com lets prospects subscribe to quotes on a small number of stocks, delivered after business hours. To get more information on more stocks delivered during business hours, a subscriber must pay. The company reached its breakeven point seven months after its launch. By September, 1995, Quote.com had 40,000 subscribers to its free services. The number of paid subscribers averages about fifteen percent of the number of freebies. The quantity of both free and paid subscribers grows about twenty percent per month. Customers pay from ten dollars to hundreds per month to select from an ever-increasing menu of services. One imaginative offering during the week of Netscape's IPO delivered bar charts of the new stock's price action, updated every five minutes.

Cooper said that Quote.com's main problems were technical ones arising from the company's fast growth. "We had difficulties in scaling up," he reported. "As our number of customers builds, we have to keep increasing our hardware and everything else to keep up. We didn't write our software initially to scale up very well. We thought we did, but when we grew we had software problems that caused problems with customers getting their quotes for a couple of days. Our programmers put in long days and our software is more scalable now." For its Web server, Quote.com uses Netscape's Netsite Commerce Server. "It's great," said Cooper. "It's had no problems at all." Quote.com takes credit card information on its Web site, and on its 800 telephone number from customers who don't want to send their credit card numbers over the Net. Quote.com is paid with credit cards for about two-thirds of its customers and sends bills to the rest. It emails monthly bills to individuals, and sends paper invoices to institutional and corporate customers. Cooper cautions would-be Interpreneurs, "The problem is that the entry barriers are pretty low. You can get in pretty easily, but so can your next-door neighbor. Anything successful quickly creates competitors."

Quote.com uses the Web for sales and email to distribute to its subscribers, and it's good to keep in mind that the Web is not always the most effective way to distribute to your own subscribers. You can use email like *HPCWire*. Or you can use newsgroups to deliver information to paying subscribers. (If you have your own newsgroup, you can block distribution to nonsubscribing host computers.)

Remember, too, that you can generate other revenue streams in addition to subscriber fees. An Internet-delivered newspaper, *American Reporter*, generates significant revenue through sales of reprint rights to its articles. *Mercury Center* makes ten years of newspaper stories searchable online for 15 cents per minute, which "generates a heck of a lot of money" according to *Mercury Center*'s Barry Parr. And of course, there is advertising. In fact, some Internet businesses ignore sales to subscribers and prosper on advertising sales alone.

## *Advertising sales model*

According to Robert Young of ProductView, the 15 percent of consumers with home computers generate 40 percent of all consumer sales. A recent study shows that people with online services watch 25 percent less television than the national average, so TV commercials have less chance of reaching these big spenders. And consumers are only the tip of the iceberg; the real money on the Net is chasing after fat business-to-business and institutional sales prospects.

All of which makes the Net rich turf for you to sell advertising, especially if you have an electronic publication or Web site that delivers the right demographics and numbers. What kind of numbers? Net vehicles with thousands of targeted readers are common. Many have readership in the tens of thousands, some in the hundreds of thousands, and a tiny handful more than one million readers apiece. The printed magazine *Wired* is considered a hot success because it sells 145,000 printed copies per month. Its electronic counterpart on the Net, *HotWired* easily beats the print circulation, with 200,000 people registered for free subscriptions.

Numbers that size generate impressive advertising rates. The NCSA What's New page charges $7,500 to $10,000 per week to reach its hundreds of thousands of visitors. The ezine *Global Network Navigator* (**http://gnn.com**) charges $3,000 a week. You'll find every level beneath that on the Net, down to monthly fees of $25 and up for links on your Web page to other sites. These have grown so popular that a company called WebConnect, a subsidiary of Worldata, now specializes in media placement of such links. For example, if your Web page has space for links to other sites, the people at WebConnect will find advertisers willing to pay to put links on your page, sell a lease for those links, and pay the rent to you (after deducting their commission, of course).

You can sell one of two kinds of advertising: mass market or special interest. In recent years, growth in the traditional advertising industry has been in special interest advertising, and this is the area where the Internet really shines. The Net is not as good at mass market advertising. Instead of broadcasting, the Net does narrowcasting. From your point of view, that's an advantage. You don't have to invest in the heavy-duty hardware and support required by a Net site visited by millions of people. If you deliver a smaller quantity of readers who are more desirable to advertisers, the advertisers will pay you more per person. When you sell space to special interest advertisers, your revenue per reader will be higher than you'd receive from mass market advertisers.

When you charge advertisers a flat rate based on a per-reader or per-subscriber basis, you use a method of calculating prices that feels comfortable to traditional advertisers. You can also do some Internet-only variations. If your advertiser is on a Web page, you can track traffic exactly, so you can charge more precise amounts. You can charge a Web page advertiser by hits, say 5 cents every time the advertiser's file is downloaded. If your Web site uses CGI to track how many people read a page, you can charge per person. You can charge progressive fees based on how deep a visitor goes into your site and what actions your visitor takes (completing a survey, placing an order). As a form of ancillary revenue, you can sell statistical and demographic information based on your readership, although this can be a problem in some countries with strict computer privacy laws.

For a variation on this idea, you can sell *sponsorships* instead of advertisements. What's the difference between sponsorship and advertising? An advertiser pays to reach your Internet visitors or readers. A sponsor underwrites the operating costs of a site or a project. Sponsorship is better-known in the world of nonprofit organizations, but underwriting costs can be beneficial for businesses as well.

## Sales support model

The first businesses that used the Internet to increase sales applied it to support their existing sales programs. I have covered topics such as putting your sales documents and price sheets online in earlier chapters, so I will just briefly mention a couple of points here.

When planning sales support projects, remember that the Net is a two-way street. Your greatest sales leverage will come not from dumping your existing sales support materials on the Net (Pete Snell of ad agency CKS Interactive called such Web-ized print brochures "shovelware"). Your highest payoffs will come when you use the Net to reach out to your prospects and customers, and, even better, when you let them reach you.

Remember that seeing something in action is more persuasive than just reading about it. Like Digital's Alpha promotion, you can often use the Net to present remote demonstrations of product capabilities and benefits. This is especially true for software companies, which have never had such a cheap, effective, and pervasive way to show off their products' strong points.

# Targets for your Internet sales operation: benchmarks, standards and best practices

*by William J. Spaide*
*Spaide, Kuipers & Company*

Your customer who shops direct will expect the same service no matter whether the order was placed on your Web site or on your telephone. As a result, your operating and service requirements as an Internet marketer are quite similar to those of other direct marketers.

In order to better evaluate your own operating performance and to understand what separates industry leaders from also-rans, take notice of direct marketing operating benchmarks and best practices. These standards tell you what activities and costs are important for you to measure in your own business, and give you targets to meet or beat.

To this end, the following three tables present operating practices, cost standards and services standards that we have developed during our project work for more than 600 direct marketers over the past thirty years. The standards in these tables are best practices for a medium-sized direct marketing company (between $25 and $50 million).

## *Service Level Definitions (for Table A)*

### *Telephone Service*

- *% Blocked:* Percentage of calls in which the caller receives a busy signal.

- *% Abandonded:* Percentage of accepted calls during which the caller disconnects before talking to a live operator.

- *Service Level:* Percentage of calls answered within a predetermined amount of time.

## Fulfillment and Customer Service

- *Order Turnaround*

    *In-house:* The number of working days to process an order for in-stock merchandise from order receipt to shipment.

    *Total:* The number of working days to process an order for in-stock merchandise from order receipt to delivery to customer.

- *% of Customer Inquiries to Orders:* Number of customer inquiries, excluding returns, as a percentage of orders shipped.

- *Return Rate:* Percentage of returns to total shipments.

## Inventory Management (Initial Fill Rate)

Percentage of in-stock items at time of original order.

## Error Ratio (Picking)

Percentage of picking errors to items picked.

### Table A: Service Levels

| Activity | Standard |
|---|---|
| Telephone Service | |
| % Blocked  0% | |
| % Abandoned | 2-3% |
| Service Level | 80%/20 seconds |
| Fulfillment and Customer Service | |
| Order Turnaround | |
| In-house | 2 days |
| Total (including delivery) | 7 days |
| % of Customer Inquiries to Orders | |
| Toll-free customer service tel. # | 25-30% |
| Toll-paid customer service tel # | 15-20% |
| Return Rate | |
| Staples/Gifts | 5% |
| Fashion | 17-24% |
| Business-to-Business | 3% |

Inventory Management (Initial Fill Ratio)

| | |
|---|---|
| Staples/Gifts | 90-95% |
| Fashion | 75-80% |
| Business-to-Business | 95-98% |
| Error Rate (Picking) | Less than 1% |

## Operating Cost Definitions (for Table B)

### Average Wage Rate

Average pay scale for production personnel within the various departments of the fulfillment operation.

### Cost per Order

- *Direct Labor:* Direct labor costs per order, excluding fringe benefits and fulfillment management, for the following areas:

  *Order Processing:* Mail and telephone order receipt, order processing, and customer service.

  *Distribution:* Receiving, quality control, storage and replenishment, picking, packing, shipping, and returns processing.

  *Total Direct Labor:* The sum of order processing and distribution labor costs.

- *Benefits:* Employee fringe benefits

- *Shipping:* Costs associated with outbound shipments to customers, where this cost *has* not been offset by shipping and handling revenue.

- *Information Systems:* Total information systems costs, shown as a cost per order.

- *Telephone:* Communications costs (including 800 numbers) per order.

- *Banking:* Credit card discount expenses, bank fees, bad debt, and customer adjustments.

- *Supplies and Other Variable Costs:* Packing supplies, printed forms, and so on.

- *Fixed Costs:* Fulfillment management costs, occupancy, depreciation, equipment, service, and related overhead expenses.

- *Total Operating Costs:* The sum of all of the above costs.

## % of Net Sales

Total operating costs shown as a percentage of net sales.

**Table B: Operating Costs**

| Activity | Standard |
|---|---|
| Average Wage Rate | $6.50-$7.00 |
| Cost per Order | |
|    Direct Labor | |
|       Order Processing | $1.05 |
|       Distribution | $.090 |
|       Total Direct Labor | $1.95 |
|    Benefits | $0.50 |
|    Shipping | $2.50 |
|    Information Systems | $0.80 |
|    Telephone | $0.60 |
|    Banking | $0.75 |
|    Supplies and Other Variable Costs | $0.83 |
|    Fixed Costs | $0.86 |
| Total Operating Costs | $8.79 |
| % of Net Sales | 15% |

# Operating Practices Definitions

## 50%+ part-time workers (at peak)

Percentage of production workers during peak processing who are part-time.

### Toll-free telephone service
Provided for the following:
- Order-taking
- Customer service/support

### Work measurement
The company has a formal work measurement system in place.

### Bar-coding/scanning
The company uses bar-coding technology in its distribution function.

### Materials handling automation
The company has an extensive automated materials handling system.

### Inbound freight consolidation
The company has a program to consolidate shipments from its vendors.

### Expedited delivery
The company provides next day and/or second day delivery service to customers.

### Labor scheduling process
The company employs a system to project workload and staffing needs on a daily basis.

*William J. Spaide is a partner in the firm of Spaide, Kuipers & Company, which provides operations management and information technology solutions to direct marketing companies in the United States, Europe, and the Far East. He can be reached by phone at 610-668-8296.*

Sales support on the Net is not only for businesses that sell to consumers or end-users. If your company sells to wholesalers or distributors, you can develop Net projects to support your own sales staff, plus programs to direct consumers to your resellers. For instance, you can use the Net to ask for your end-buyers' ZIP codes, and then display a page or send email telling where to find the closest dealers, or how to contact the distributor for their area. One Net site even displays maps showing how to find nearby retail outlets.

Remember that although the World Wide Web gets the lion's share of the publicity, it may not always be your best option. For instance, if your staff sells to government accounts, your buyers may not have access to the Web. Email is much more common among government buyers. Your staff may generate lots of sales from frequent use of email to keep in close contact with government prospects and clients.

## *Direct sales model*

It must be the dream of every retailer and catalog merchant to set up a Web site and watch sales roll in. Real life is not as effort-free as the dream—direct sales on the Net requires sustained work—but there are plenty of success stories.

One is a retail shop and cataloger, which created a Web site that generated worldwide media coverage and sales. Hot Hot Hot sells nothing but bottled hot sauce. A manager with Internet access provider Presence was a regular customer of the Hot Hot Hot retail store. The Presence manager persuaded the couple who owns the store to set up shop on the Presence Web server in return for a percentage of sales. "My husband and I wrote all the text. We made it cartoony and fun and light. With our kind of product, you want it to stay fun," explained Hot Hot Hot's Monica Lopez. "You can't just say, 'Hey, buy from me!' For a Web site to attract people and get them to buy, there has to be information and/or entertainment." The Presence staff helped shape the site and handled technical matters, and an artist was hired to create graphics. It took a couple of months of part-time work to create the Web site. Lopez learned as she went along: "We didn't read any books about how to do the Internet until we were already on it." (Words to make an author quake with fear!)

Hot Hot Hot's Web site went online Sept. 29, 1994. "We were surprised at the international orders, that people would actually do that," commented Lopez. It shipped a bottle of "Satan's Revenge" to Tel Aviv, and ten bottles of sauce to Australia for a wedding. "We had to learn more about international shipping very quickly." Lopez quickly noticed differences between its Internet customers and its catalog customers. "Customers from our catalog order multiple bottles. Internet customers are more likely to order one sauce. They order lots of gift packs at Christmas." Internet orders generated 17 percent of Hot Hot Hot holiday sales. "You get more information from Internet customers," said Lopez. "They send you information and comments, or they email you information on what they want to see."

Hot Hot Hot received coverage in consumer magazines around the world for the fun design of its site. It also drew attention from the Internet community for its technical astuteness. Hot Hot Hot was one of the first sites to include an *electronic shopping cart*. As you go through its site and click on sauces you'd like to buy, Hot Hot Hot keeps track of what you choose. When you go to its order page, your items and their costs are automatically popped into the order form. Hop over to **http://www.presence.com/hot** and try it yourself. You can change your selections or cancel them at any time. An electronic shopping cart is so helpful in the Net order process that it has become widespread. Hot Hot Hot accepts credit cards (unencrypted). Its Web pages email the orders and card numbers to Presence, which then faxes the orders to Hot Hot Hot's warehouse.

In spite of its fiery products, Hot Hot Hot has never been flamed, and its sales from the Internet grow every month. Lopez notes that weather does not impact her Net sales the way it affects her retail store business: "When it's pouring rain, nobody comes to your store. You have no weather on the Internet." Lopez continually changes and adds to the Hot Hot Hot site. She compares it to catalog sales: "You keep sending catalogs to the same people; otherwise they forget you exist. But you don't send them the same catalog twice, you move products around and add things and change the art. The Web store is the same. You're constantly looking to improve it, so customers see something new. It really is a work in progress. I don't think it's the type of medium that would support a stagnant thing."

While Hot Hot Hot makes sales like a retail store or catalog business, there are other models for making direct sales on the Net. Since accessing a database is easy on the Net, some companies charge per lookup for you to use their database. Other companies look at commission-based sales and other transaction fees. The *New York Times* is working on a way for readers of an online *Times'* movie or theater review to buy tickets after reading the review. The *Times* will pocket a fee for each ticket sold. Newspaper publisher Knight-Ridder plans to add a section to its online travel articles so readers can book tickets to destinations mentioned in the articles. Knight-Ridder will receive the travel agent's commission.

# Cybermalls

At first glance, if retail stores work well on the Net, the shopping mall model should be even better. That hasn't proven to be true.

The Internet has not been kind to cybermalls. A project by MecklerMedia to create a mall of advertisers died after spending more than a quarter of a million dollars and attracting only one tenant. Slickly-designed Marketplace.com opened January 1994 and closed 16 months later. CyberMall closed in May 1995. NetMall may be another casualty; I haven't been able to reach its site for days.

The reason these cybermalls died is because they offered nothing to their tenants that their tenants couldn't get on their own for a far lower cost. Some people say that to sell on the Net you need to have a "storefront" on a mall. Rubbish. There is no such thing as a "prestigious" location on the Net. There are places with more visibility than others, but that is because they have higher amounts of traffic, or good volumes of *appropriate* traffic. On the Internet, customers don't walk through an entry passageway to go to a retail site. They look up a URL on a search engine like Yahoo and go straight to the store. No one knows or cares what institution hosts a site as long as the site has the product or information they want.

In a real-world shopping mall, the landlord has two revenue streams: rent and a percentage of gross sales. The rent covers fixed expenses. The percentage of the action is an incentive for the landlord to do everything in its power to pull customers into the mall. Retail stores become tenants because the mall brings traffic to their stores. Malls with a high quantity and a high quality of customers can charge a premium for retail space. With a cybermall, the "landlord" collects fees that are fixed (like rent), or possibly per transaction, or on a percentage of sales, or per hit. There may also be additional charges for disk space used and services performed.

What does the cyber-retailer get in exchange for these fees?

- *A listing and hot link on the cybermall's homepage.* This is worthless; Internet shoppers will bypass it.

- *Space on the cybermall's computer and technical assistance.* This is better, but Internet service bureaus offer the same service at a far lower price. It costs so little to open a Web site that it makes no sense to pay a cybermall $10,000 a year just to be a passive host.

- *Secure credit card processing and an electronic shopping cart.* This is better. This price of secure Web servers are falling, and virtual Web servers like I-Site also offer secure card processing, but this is of some value—though not as much as some cybermalls charge.

- *Access to customer traffic.* Bingo! On the Internet, this is the only reason that will hold up over time for a merchant to join a cybermall. Cybermalls that bring customers to their tenants' virtual doors are the only ones that will succeed.

With the cost of setting up shop on your own going down steadily and more than a thousand new Internet merchants opening every month, it becomes more and more difficult for retailers to make themselves heard above the roar. If you are considering signing a lease with a cybermall, look for one that draws customers, especially if it brings in exactly your kind of customers. If you are thinking of opening a cybermall, drawing traffic should be your number-one goal.

Keeping that in mind, let's check out some cybermalls:.

IndustryNet (**http://industry.net**) is a solid example of a mall that focuses on a target market and offers an overwhelming number of reasons for its market to visit. It targets purchasers of equipment and machinery for factories. Besides offering the latest equipment and prices, IndustryNet provides industry news, free classified ads, a job bank, and even a place to buy and sell used equipment. IndustryNet offers so much valuable information that industrial purchasers would be foolish to ignore it.

I wouldn't normally call the Internet Shopping Network (**http:// shop.internet.net**) a cybermall, but it does include other merchants on its site. It charges no up-front fee and no monthly rent, but between 10 and 15 percent of sales. Merchants on the site include Lillian Vernon, FTD Florists, Hammacher Schlemmer, Celestial Seasonings teas, Minolta cameras and Radio Shack. The guest merchants are all there to take advantage of the flow of customers to the ISN site, and ISN promotes them heavily throughout its site. Getting paid only by commission certainly would motivate it to do so.

The Electronic Newsstand (**http://www.enews.com**) was started in July 1993 as a joint venture of *The New Republic* and the Internet Company. It sells only magazine subscriptions, and its tenants are all publishers. It charges publishers between $1,000 and $5,000 per year plus a commission of about 10 percent. It has been so successful offering one-stop shopping for hundreds of magazines that it now has a couple of Internet competitors.

The Internet Underground Music Archives (IUMA) at **http://www.iuma.com** is another kind of specialized mall. IUMA features music from more than 1,000 bands, which it gives away for free. How can IUMA make any money by giving everything away for free? Easy as pie. To enter IUMA, you register. IUMA adds your registration data to a database. It tells potential sponsors how many tens of thousands of registrants it has and what their demographics are. Sponsors such as Intel, Volvo, and Coca Cola pay IUMA for advertising space. Bands and record labels give recordings for free to IUMA because people who wouldn't otherwise hear about the bands discover them and buy their CDs. So IUMA has few expenses and a steady cash flow, which grows as it gets more visitors.

For businesses with international customers, MarketNet (**http://mkn.co.uk**) offers a couple of advantages. This U.K.-based cybermall not only takes secure credit card payments for its retailers, it also makes Web pages available in eleven languages and computes and displays prices in eight currencies.

Branch Information Services (**http://branch.com:1080**) tries to compete by offering its tenants more services: secure credit card processing, email autoresponders, and more.

MarketplaceMCI (**http://www.internetmci.com**) charges customers an arm and a leg to provide the same services as other, lower-priced cybermalls, plus detailed activity reports.

Interactive Super Mall (**http://supermall.com**) draws customer traffic by offering free Web pages for visitors. The mall's own home page is a useless waste of electrons.

## Setting up shop on the World Wide Web

Most businesses new to the Internet—according to some estimates, as many as 70 percent—are small businesses putting up a Web site. Once the decision has been made to "do something" on the Web, it seems like they ask more questions than can possibly be answered. Do I need to buy a separate computer for a Web server? Should I lease space on a cybermall? How long will it take? How much will it cost?

The early part of this book deals with these questions in more detail, but here is an outline of your choices strictly from the point of view of sales on the World Wide Web.

1. You need a *Web site*, which will probably consist of multiple *Web pages*. Your "front door" is called your *home page*. These are made of computer files. The simplest ones are just text files. Most commercial Web sites also have graphics files. Some have sound files, video files, databases, or software programs. They range from simple and cheap to elaborate and expensive.

2. You need someone to write and design your Web pages, or you may do this yourself, depending on your available time and marketing and technical knowledge. Creating your initial Web pages is the easy part. Maintaining and updating your site after it opens will take the most time and work.

3.  You need space on a computer to put all the files that make up your Web site. You can:

    • *Rent computer space on a service bureau's computer* for your Web site. This service bureau may either be your Internet access provider or another company. To receive sales orders from your service bureau, you will need either email or a fax machine. If you want to correspond with your customers, you will need Internet email. This is your least expensive option, but has disadvantages discussed below.

    • *Rent space on a cybermall.* To receive sales orders, you will need either email or a fax machine. If you want to correspond with your customers, you will need Internet email. Depending on the rates charged by the cybermall, this may be your most expensive option.

    • *Rent space on a virtual server.* Virtual servers are discussed later. To receive sales orders, you will need email.

    • *Buy or lease a server computer and place it at your access provider's site,* where your access provider will run it for you. To receive sales orders, you will need email. With this option, you will need to buy or build all the software needed to run your site. You also need a 56 Kbps ISDN, Frame Relay, or faster phone line to go to your computer.

    • *Buy or lease a server computer and place it on your own premises.* This is your second most expensive option. This is definitely your most time-consuming option, because out of all the alternatives. this is the only one in which you have to worry about running the hardware. You will need at least a 56 Kbps ISDN or Frame Relay phone line to your server. If you want to link this server computer with any computer you use for your business, you will need a firewall.

4.  Sometimes small businesses can get a service bureau or mall to fax sales orders to them. (For an example of this, see the Hot Hot Hot story earlier in the chapter.) But email is easier for order processing

than faxed orders and has many other uses, so get email if at all possible. Email requires you to run email software on at least one computer. It also requires you to have an Internet account, which you will get from an Internet access provider. If you want to route your email over a LAN to more than one person in your company, talk to your access provider before you sign anything. That can be tricky.

5. If your business wants to accept credit cards and does not yet have a credit card merchant account, you will need to open one. You will also need an account with a clearinghouse to authorize each credit card purchase. These are usually done over the phone, and may require you to add hardware and a phone line. If you intend to accept credit card orders on your Web page, check with your Internet access provider before you open your account.

6. You will need the support staff and systems to receive orders, process them, and forward the needed information to your inventory and accounting systems. These order fulfillment processes are important, but complex enough that they would require a complete chapter. To give you an idea of the operations and costs involved, read the sidebar panel by fulfillment expert William Spaide. Someone will also need to read and process email messages from your customers, and to read activity reports profiling the choices made by your Web site visitors.

## Secure server software

If you decide to run your own Web server on your own computer, you will need to buy Web server software. There are dozens of Web server software packages, but not many can handle encryption. You need encryption to process credit card orders securely. Your customers who cruise the Web using Netscape's browser software are already making secure credit card purchases. Since Netscape has about 70 percent of the Web browser market, other software companies are scurrying to comply with Netscape's encryption scheme. All this boils down to the fact that if you plan to make credit card sales, you need secure server software to do so. Here's a list of the leading secure server software packages.

**One key tip:** When buying a server, ask how many concurrent users the software (and the hardware's operating system) will accept. The quantity ranges from 1,200 simultaneous connections to less than 100. I have not indicated that on this list because server software companies are increasing capacity right now, so you can get the most up-to-date information by asking.

- Netscape (**http://www.netscape.com**) is undoubtedly the king of the secure server heap. It offers an entire line of secure servers, with more functions than its competitors, but often at higher prices:

    *Netscape Commerce Server* - The foundation of Netscape's secure server family, with versions for Windows NT and Unix. $5,000.

    *Netscape Istore* - Equips a standalone store for Internet commerce with credit card processing, reports, billing, order processing, end-of-day sales journals (including customer order fulfillment information), and audit trails. This Unix system includes the Netscape Commerce Server. $20,000.

    *Netscape Publishing System* - This electronic publishing system creates custom Web pages on the fly based on reader requests. It handles subscription-based online publications, billing, access authorization, and user demographics. It tracks response rates to ads and articles, archives past issues and provides multiple billing options and subscription info. A Unix system, it includes the Netscape Commerce Server. $50,000.

    *Netscape Merchant System* - Creates cybermalls. It handles multiple stores, builds invoices as customers make purchases (electronic shopping cart), provides payment and billing options, and handles order processing. MCI uses this Unix system (which includes the Netscape Commerce Server) for MarketplaceMCI. $50,000.

- O'Reilly and Associates is releasing a secure version of its Windows NT product *WebSite*. At press time, no price was announced, but you can find out more at **http://www.ora.com**.

- *Internet Office Server* from CompuServe Seattle (formerly Spry Inc.) costs $3,000, and lets you set security for individual pages. It runs on Unix and Windows NT. You can find out more at **http://www.compuserve.com/prod_services/corp_solutions/corp_solutions.html.** Who thinks up these ridiculously long URLs?

- *Purveyor*, from Process Software Corp (**http://www.process.com**) is available for for Windows 95, Windows NT, and Open VMS for $2,000 and up.

- Open Market's *Secure WebServer* costs $5,000, which includes card authentication services and buyer payment processing. The Unix system supports 1,000 simultaneous connections. For more, visit **http://www.openmarket.com**.

- *Secure OneServer* from Connect, Inc. (**http://www.connectinc.com**) handles billing, credit card processing, order entry, email, chat, and newsgroups, and provides electronic shopping carts. It runs on Unix.

- *WebSTAR* (formerly MacHTTP) for the Mac (**http://www.starnine.com/webstar/webstar.html**) is not secure, but its manufacturer, Star Nine Technologies, plans to add a Security Toolkit and a Commerce Toolkit that will make it so. The base price is $600, but add-ons cost more.

## *Renting Web space vs. virtual Web servers*

Running a Web server on your own computer (whether you locate your computer on your own premises or in a service bureau's building) is the most expensive and time-consuming way to build your Web site, but it does offer more control than other options. This can be essential if you plan to link your Web page to an existing internal database, such as your product catalog or inventory. Most businesses don't need that much control, and opt for one of two other alternatives: renting space from a Web service bureau or renting a virtual Web server. The demand is so huge that now more than 500 companies lease Web space.

Tens of thousands of businesses rent Web space on computers owned by their Internet access providers or by service bureaus. Every computer magazine published today carries ads for leasing Web space for between $10 and $100 per month. One site on the Web provides a long list of companies that lease Web server space: **http://union.ncsa.uiuc.edu/HyperNews/get/www/leasing.shtml**. This is a good list. If you check it out, be sure to read the helpful FAQ at the end about Web space leases. (Note: This list may move to another URL soon. I'll post the new address on **http://www.emery.com/cx.htm**.)

If you rent a Web site for sales, the crucial question for you is: How will you receive your sales orders? You can put instructions on your page for visitors to submit all orders via fax or phone. This is more secure than sending credit cards over the Internet, but not nearly as convenient for your customers. Some service bureaus have mechanisms in place to accept encrypted credit card numbers for you. The bureau receives the information and forwards it to you via fax or encrypted email. This is your best bet, and is worth paying extra for. Some service bureaus receive unencrypted orders and will pass them to you by email or fax. If the credit card number is stolen along the way, you, the merchant, are usually liable. That reduces the attractiveness of having orders forwarded by open email.

There are potential problems with renting Web space. Many service bureaus will not let you use your own domain name. This may force you to use a URL such as **www.servicebureau.net/~yourco** when you would rather use **www.yourco.com**. Some will only let you use your domain name with a file name added to the end: **www.yourco.com/yourco**. Some will force you to have a tilde (~) in your URL. Tildes are hard to type, hard to remember, and impossible to explain to someone over the phone. Some service bureaus limit the number of files you can use, the amount of disk space you can fill, the number of changes you can make to your site, or the number of hits you can have without an extra charge. Ask how easy it is for you to delete old files and add new ones to your Web site. Good services bureaus put good security on file changes but still make it fast and simple for you to update them. The biggest problem with a service bureau may not happen until you leave it. For technical reasons, many bureaus cannot let you take your old domain name with you. You will lose the traffic you've built at your old Web address, will break all the links on other Web pages that point to your site, and will have to change the URL on all your marketing material. Check to make sure that this won't be the case with any bureau you consider.

You can skip these problems by using a new wrinkle called a virtual Web server. A virtual server costs more than leasing space, but has none of the drawbacks and provides nearly as much control as if you went to all the trouble of running your Web server on your own computer. A virtual server runs on a service bureau's computer, but while the bureau runs the hardware, you have remote control over the software.

The virtual Web server I'm most familiar with is I-Site from Internet Direct (**http://www.direct.net**). Businesses using I-Site range from large (Motorola, Phoenix Suns) all the way down to mom and pop startups. What makes I-Site special is a site administration software package that is included with it. Called EZ-Admin, and available in Mac and Windows versions, it gives you the tools to install and maintain your virtual server, which in addition to a Web server includes an FTP server, an email POP server (so you can create email accounts), and a simple email autoresponder. (If you need a full-scale Major-domo mailing list server, that costs extra.) I-Site uses the Netscape Commerce Server, which supports HotJava and the newest Netscape enhancements, and lets you accept encrypted credit cards. If you don't have your own credit card merchant account, Internet Direct helps you open one. I-Site can run CGI scripts. Internet Direct provides a template script, which you will probably need to change or replace with your own. I-Site includes activity audit logs and reports and your own domain name and IP address. It includes 24-hour tech support via phone and email at no extra charge. Your site is completely portable and can be moved to another service bureau. The only limitation I found on I-Site was disk space; if you use more than 25 megabytes of storage space, you are charged extra. The base rate for I-Site is a $150 setup fee plus $150 per month for a one-year contract, or $600 setup plus $150 per month otherwise. There are no per-transaction charges.

I've gone into detail on I-Site because it is one of the first of a new breed of Web server. It offers more than current competitors, and gives you a checklist of features to compare others against.

That covers the places to keep the files which make up your Web site. The next step is to review what you can do with your Web pages.

# How to build an order form

When you use the Web for sales, the most important page of your entire Web site is your order form. It should be the culmination of your visitors' experience on your site. Everything else on your site should subtly direct your prospect to your order page. Your order page itself needs to be understandable at a glance, and your prospect should feel that completing your form will be simple.

Of course, one man's "Simple!" is another man's "Huh?" To make your order form work, you will need to invest more thought and do more testing of this page than anything else on your site.

If you do not accept credit cards online, design options for your order form are limited. You can list your phone, fax, and snail mail addresses and ask prospects to order by those methods. A step up is to provide text that customers can copy, print on their computer's printer, fill out in pen or pencil and mail or fax to you. This is secure and can be simple for your customer to fill out after it's printed, but many nontechnical people have an extremely difficult time printing a Web text file. In my experience, such "download-and-print" forms are mostly used by programmers and other technical folks. If your customers are among the technically-impaired, you might provide other options for them.

Fortunately, the World Wide Web makes interactive order forms easy to create. If you are using the Netsite Commerce Server or similar software (or if your service bureau or virtual Web server provider supplies it), it is even relatively easy to receive encrypted credit card orders. The key is that you must have software programs that run under CGI, the Common Gateway

Interface. (Note that many rent-a-space Web service bureaus will *not* let you use CGI programs, so you cannot create Web pages with interactive forms.)

CGI lets you do a lot of things on your order page. Your customer can look things up in your database, use an electronic shopping cart to build a list of purchases that includes a running total of costs, have shipping and taxes calculated automatically, check your inventory levels, have shipping information verified ("UZ is not a valid state name."), and have credit card information verified while the customer waits online. Behind the scenes, CGI programs can interface your order entry system to decrement your inventory quantities, authorize credit, enter the order, and pass information to your accounting department. Not bad for a little ol' order form.

Your business may not want to do all that stuff. But take a look at what a full-blown Web order form can do, and then you can scale it down for your own needs.

## *Steps in an order form*

1. *Build a shopping list* - This optional step requires a CGI electronic shopping cart program. It runs not just on your order form, but is part of all your Web pages that list products to purchase.

2. *Calculate charges* - including prices, currency conversion, taxes, shipping, and/or customs duties.

3. *Check stock levels* - An optional step if you want to sell only what you have in stock, or if you want to notify your customer when a product is out of stock and may take longer to ship.

4. *Accept credit and shipping information* - The most important step.

5. *Verify credit information* - Whether you accept credit cards or debit a corporate account.

6. *Return acknowledgment to customer* - The second most important step. If your customer does not immediately receive some kind of acknowledgment that you received the order, the customer will assume that

something went wrong and will get angry, will send you the same order again, or both.

7. *Pass information to fulfillment department* - The third most important step. Get the order to your fulfillment people as quickly as you can so they can act on it.

8. *Pass information to accounting department* - Don't re-enter the data when you can move it electronically.

9. *Make information available for order status inquiries* - Sounds boring, but isn't when you've got an angry customer yelling in your ear.

## Portfolio of order form ideas

Before delving into detail on some of these steps, take a gander at what other businesses have done with Web order forms. Every order form out there (especially your competitors') can serve either as inspiration or as a bad example.

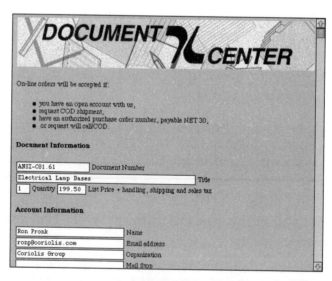

**Figure 16.1** *Document Center at* **http://www.service.com/doccenter/dcorder.html? doc=+&desc=+&price=+** *provides this clear order form. This is the top half of Document Center's order page.*

| 7309 E. Acoma Ste. 7 | Address |
| Scottsdale, AZ 85260 | City, State Zip Code |
| 602-555-1908 | Telephone |

**Payment Information**

| 455-597773-8355 | Document Center Account Number |
| 0542 | Purchase Order Number |

**Delivery options (check one)**

○ [              ]  Your FedEx Account No. ○ Overnight ○ 2nd day
⦿ [ 1-602-555-0192 ]  Your FAX number ( FAX delivery is $1.00 per page )
○ [              ]  Other
○ WILL CALL

Clicking the button below, obligates you to pay for the documents ordered. If you are "just looking", please do not click the button.

[ **Order Document** ]  [ **Clear Form** ]

***Figure 16.2*** *This is the bottom half of Document Center's order page. This site also provides its customers with clear explanation of order terms and the ordering process.*

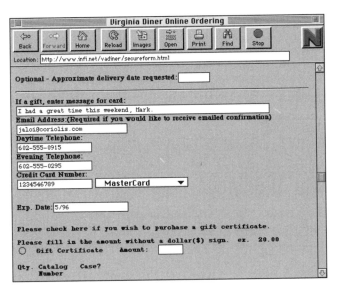

***Figure 16.3*** *Virginia Diner at **http://www.infi.net/vadiner/secureform.html** includes in its order form a place for customers to type a message, which Virginia Diner will imprint on a gift card enclosed with the order.*

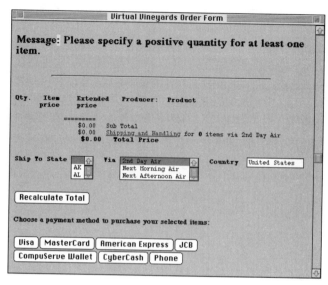

**Figure 16.4** *Virtual Vineyards at **http://www.virtualvin.com/vvplaceorder** accepts more familiar credit cards as well as JCB (Japan Credit Bureau, Japan's most popular credit card) and CyberCash digital money. It also gives a customer the option to send an order over the Internet and still give credit card information by phone. A previous page gives new Virtual Vineyards customers extremely clear instructions on how to shop and order.*

We discussed HotHotHot in previous pages. Its order form uses an electronic shopping cart to create an online invoice for you as you shop. It also gives clear error messages. If you leave a required line blank in the order form and try to submit your order, a message pops up saying "Please fill in the critical information you have left blank." Then the message lists what blank or blanks you need to fill, so you don't have to guess about it or use trial and error. Error messages are an important part of your Web order form design. Customers only encounter error messages when something has gone wrong, so put extra effort into giving complete and clear explanations. Nothing is so simple it cannot be misunderstood.

Like many businesses that sell on the Net, Racquet Workshop (**http://arganet.tenagra.com/Racquet.Workshop/Workshop.html**), a tennis equipment store in Houston, now has Internet customers from all over the world. To encourage international orders, its order form includes international shipping rates, plus a link to the Koblas Currency Converter (**http://www.ora.com/cgi-bin/ora/currency**) "to help you convert our prices to your currency." This may be helpful to international buyers, but it does take them out of the Racquet Workshop Web site right in the middle of a purchase, and is not as self-contained as another solution to the same problem. Some other sites let you select your currency and automatically give you prices in that currency. This does require entering updated currency prices daily.

Cisco (**http://www.cisco.com**) gives customers a dandy feature it calls Status Agent. It's a Web page that lets customers see all outstanding orders they've placed with Cisco, inspect line-item detail, check expected shipment dates, and track shipments to them via Fed Ex or UPS. Cisco restricts entry to its Status Agent page to people who have a registered user name and password, protecting the privacy of its customers' orders. Restricting your customer base to only members or registered customers has some additional advantages. You can collect background information on registered customers. You can track frequent buyers easily, and find out who buys less than normal amounts, so you can market to them to increase their purchases. You can send marketing announcements and other communications to registered customers as well.

For an example of what *not* to do on an order form, visit Stolichnaya Vodka at **http://www.stoli.com.** When you click on the link to its order form, you are passed to a merchant that dumps Stoli on a page with all its competitors!

## *Making your form work*

All this is great, but how does all this order information get to you? By email. Any form your customer fills in on your Web page is emailed to you. Or actually, to your Web server. The order form you send to your customer is a standard HTML document like any other Web page, but with one difference: It contains the name and address of a CGI script on your Web server. When your customer completes your order form, your customer's Web browser sends the information to your CGI script. Your CGI script reads the returned information, decides what to do with it and what response is required, and then passes the information wherever it needs to go while sending your customer an order acknowledgment, an error message, freshly calculated shipping charges, or whatever else you think your customer should see.

This leads to an important point. Make sure your Web server sends your orders to an email address set up just for orders and nothing else. Make sure you send an emailed order confirmation before you ship an order. Send confirmations from an email address used for confirmations and nothing else. If an order confirmation returns to you as bounced mail, you may have received a fraudulent order. Of course, the cause may also just be a typo. But when an order confirmation bounces back to you, give it a high priority. You need to determine why it returned before you ship your product.

The ideal time for your customer to receive a confirmation is while the customer is still online with your Web server. This requires your software to forward the purchase amount and credit card information to your credit card clearinghouse and receive approval from the clearinghouse while your customer is still online. This is only possible with an automated transaction processing system, but is the safest method for you as the merchant. If you can't do this and your customer is offline before you get approval, email a confirmation to your customer saying that the transaction was approved.

What payment method should your form use? As many as you can. A good Web order form lets your customer choose which way to pay. Accept encrypted credit card orders. Provide your fax and phone numbers for people who don't want to send credit card data over the Net. For business-to-business customers, you'll profit by opening corporate accounts that are billed monthly. Give your customers as many ways as possible to buy from you.

Your order form should include your snail mail address. Even in this paperless age, you'll be surprised how many people send you checks and money orders. Specify what currency checks and money orders should use: "In U.S. dollars drawn on a U.S. bank." Most American banks are babies at currency exchange. They can take weeks to clear a foreign check, and will hit you with a painful service charge. This is another reason credit cards are popular for international purchases. Cards convert currencies for you.

When you write and design your order form, make sure your design team includes someone who has daily *hands-on* experience with your current operation: customer service, order taking, fulfillment. "Hands-on" is the key phrase here. With all due deference to your highly-paid managers, who I am sure are very intelligent, you want feedback here from your grunts under fire in the trenches. If possible, run your order page design by *everyone* in your customer service department, especially order clerks. Sometimes adding a single question to your form can dramatically reduce your fulfillment error rate, or can save you hundreds of dollars in long-distance troubleshooting phone calls.

And before you create your Web order form, remember author Douglas Hofstadter's Law: "It always takes longer than you expect, even when you take Hofstadter's Law into account."

## Getting paid

Say your customers send you orders with encrypted card numbers (via a Web order form, Privacy-Enhanced Mail, or whatever). You receive their encrypted card numbers and move them to a computer not connected with the Net. There you safely decrypt them. Now what? How do you turn those card numbers into money?

To collect money from credit cards, your company must first open a credit card *merchant account*. It is hard for any business—especially a new business—to open a credit card merchant account. It is even harder for a direct merchant. Bankers assume that all direct merchants steal from the oppressed, such as widows, orphans, and bankers. But they're even more afraid of Internet merchants. We scare bankers so much their jowls quiver. Heathens who want to accept credit cards over the Internet can expect interrogation by their bank's version of the Spanish Inquisition.

If your bank refuses to open a merchant account for your Internet business, you have another option. Banks' antiquated attitudes have created a major marketing opportunity for middlemen who act as matchmakers between banks and the merchants who deal in *non-swiped transactions,* the kind of sales when credit card numbers are key-entered instead of pulled off physical cards (also called *card-not-present transaction).*

One such matchmaker for Internet merchants is Cardservice International (phone 206-623-7802 or 800-488-3559). It serves hundreds of merchants that accept credit cards online. It charges a non-refundable $155 application fee. Most individuals and businesses that complete its application receive an account, because Cardservice does extensive prequalification before you pay its $155 fee. It charges merchant accounts $49 monthly, plus a per-transaction rate of between 3 and 3.5 percent, depending on your creditworthiness. Applications take about three weeks to process.

A second company that acts as matchmaker for Internet merchants is Northwest Bank Service (phone 602-948-3102). Northwest charges an application fee of $125 to $195, depending on the size of your business. After you have your account, it charges no monthly fee as long as your transaction volume remains above a monthly minimum. The per-transaction discount Northwest charges varies depending on your business volume.

Once you have your merchant account, you will need to select a firm for payment processing, which is also called *payment enabling*. One of the largest payment processing companies, First Data Card Services Group's Electronics Funds Services (EFS) actively pursues Internet merchants. Enroll in First Data service through your bank. First Data processes all major U.S. and international cards, and has secure software that works with Netscape's Web servers and others. Its software runs on Unix, Windows NT, and Novell IPX. InternetMCI and MarketplaceMCI use First Data. For information, send email to **banking@mcom.com.**

With your payment enabler and your merchant account in place, here is how a credit card sale currently takes place on the Internet: You receive your customer's card number and other information. You pass that information (including the card number) to your payment enabler. The enabler passes the transaction information to the bank with which you have your merchant account. Call it Bank1 for easy reference. Bank1 makes an authorization request, forwarding your transaction data to whichever bank or other institution anywhere in the world issued your customer's credit card. We'll call it Bank2. Bank2 checks your customer's account and sends an "okay" to Bank1, which passes the "okay" to your enabler, which passes the "okay" to you, so you can tell your customer (who is still online) that the credit card transaction was authorized and the purchase is completed. This entire process usually takes less than 30 seconds. At the same time, after Bank1 receives the "okay," it also transfers the purchase amount into your checking account (which may be with Bank1 or with another bank, Bank3).

When something goes wrong, and the card number does not go through or there are any other problems with the order, you will save yourself time and keep your customers happier if your order page requires your customer to provide a telephone number for contact, not just an email address. Some people don't like to give out their phone number because they hate telephone solicitors, so to reassure them that you won't do that, your order page can say "Only used if we have questions about your order" or something similar. You need this *and* an email address because most Internet people check email only once a day. If you have a problem, you can respond to impatient customers faster with a phone number.

In any case, the above description is how Internet credit card sales happen now. This will change over the next 12 months. The Microsoft/Visa standard for handling credit card transactions securely (mentioned on page 192) gained steam when MasterCard and Netscape came aboard to support it. Called Secure Transaction Technology (or STT for short), it passes credit card information to credit card issuers (Bank2) in secure form, bypassing the merchant. As a merchant using STT, you never actually receive the credit card data yourself. Instead, you receive approval for your transaction from Visa, MasterCard, or another authorized company. This eliminates card number theft by hackers using packet sniffer software (since the card number never goes across the Net) and card number theft by hackers breaking into your computer (since the card number never goes into your computer). It also eliminates the number-one source of card number theft: merchant employees. Your employees never see your customer's credit card number, so they can't steal it.

Visa's dominance of the credit card business means that any changes in Visa's procedures drag all other credit cards and merchants in its wake. (Its motto "One world, one currency, Visa" is the most dominating corporate slogan I've

# Possibly the most profitable
# e-store on the Internet

Digital Equipment Corporation uses the Internet more than most other companies, especially for customer service and sales. Digital's online sales operation, Electric Connection, sells well over $1 million on the Internet each month. In 1994, the "e-store" (as employees call it) sold more than $20 million on the Net.

The Internet is only one part of Electric Connection, which in total has an annual sales volume of "lots of hundreds of millions," according to Steve Painter, Digital's electronic commerce marketing manager. Electric Connection started in mid-1984 as a modem-in way to sell software. Prospects dialed in to see software demos, and Digital provided answers to technical questions. Next it expanded Electric Connection to calculate prices and actually take sales orders via modem. Then, Digital moved to the Internet, at first just to make product information available. It found that more and more customers used the Net to get sales information. The company surveyed its customers. Forty percent wanted pricing information via the Net, and another 35 percent wanted to place orders over the Internet. In response, Digital began accepting orders over the Internet in February 1994.

Before the Electronic Connection, Digital had not provided a price list because its prices change often, so a printed list would quickly grow out-of-date. On the Internet, Digital's prices are always up-to-date, and they are automatically calculated individually for each customer—and for some exclusive customers, Digital even provides special prices that it doesn't want others to know. Now customers have all the information they need to make a purchasing decision. Before, customers had to call sales reps, answer questions, and then wait for the reps to go through many complicated steps to calculate prices.

To use Digital's Internet ordering service, customers enter a customer ID number. They fill in a form that considers the customer status of the company placing the order, the order's size, and special discounts to create a price quote good for sixty days. Customers can confirm an order based on a quote or create a new order from scratch. For each order placed, the customer receives online acknowledgment and a projected delivery date. Human assistance can be provided from Digital if an order grows complicated or if a customer has questions, but customers complete and send most orders entirely online. Instead of going to a sales rep, Internet-generated orders go directly to Digital's manufacturing departments, triggering an immediate build order. Customers can track the status of their orders on the Net whenever they wish. Deliveries are faster and more predictable. And since sales reps don't waste time on small, everyday orders, they can focus on building customer relationships, winning new customers and planning complex sales—all situations where face-to-face salesmanship is still essential.

"It's a traditional catalog, only online," explained Painter. "We will download as much information as we can to help them get through the purchasing process. A customer can even call up an existing price quote, change it, and use it to make an order. Resellers can place stocking orders, like 1,200 PCs, delivering 100 per month for one year. We try very, very hard to make it as easy and as fast for people to use as we can." The key to generating repeat business, said Painter, is to make your Web order pages as fast as you can. "Time seems to be the best measurement for people trying to do business online. Use only the graphics you need. Some sites get carried away with pictures, which make it take longer to place an order. Those art files go against you."

Digital's Web site practices what Painter preaches. Most pages at **http://www.digital.com** display flashy art files, but to speed order-taking, Electric Connection's pages at **http://www.digital.com/info/misc/electronic-connection.txt.html** have almost no art.

To move its high volume of transactions quickly, Electric Connection runs on a 4-node VAXcluster with smaller machines hanging off as gateways, all outside a firewall and separated from Digital's internal network. Its Internet connection is carried on three T1 lines from Tymnet. Six hundred phone lines handle modem, fax, and voice calls, and leased lines directly connect with Digital's largest customers. A staff of thirty includes ten technical people.

According to Electronic Connection manager Ethel Hughey, the completeness of the information available on the Net site delighted Digital's customers. "They said, 'Oh, wow! We finally can see what Digital has!" she related. This was especially the case for customers in remote locations, who were excited to get information that was *current*.

Internet customers differ from others, said Hughey. "Internet people are a bit more technical and know how to move around more than the modem dial-in customers we have. And Internet people expect a faster response. Between comments and email, I get seventy to eighty pieces of email a day. If there is a problem (replying quickly to email), the phones start ringing." The Internet brings customers from other countries, who also have different expectations. "Somebody has come in from just about every place in the world and opened an account," said Hughey. Customers from overseas "are more formal. They usually always identify themselves and try to explain a problem in-depth: 'I did this and this and this, and this happened.' Customers from the U.S., on the other hand, assume that I know them and say, 'I can't find this server. What's wrong?'" Digital's Web site is now in English only, but to increase international sales, the e-store may add other languages.

"Price Lookups is the busiest module," Hughey said, because so many Internet prospects do price checks. "Order Status is used even more than the order process itself. They just keep checking on how their order is doing until it's delivered."

One of Digital's most creative Internet promotions is its "Test drive an Alpha" campaign. Visitors to Digital's Internet site can use super-fast Alpha AXP computers to run their own software programs, or to run programs that Digital makes available. This promotion is enormously successful, but only because Digital triumphed over unexpected obstacles. When the company first put two of the high-speed computers online, a federal security agency warned Digital that opening its Alphas to the public was a national security risk. It threatened to fine the company up to $80 million. Digital yanked its Alphas offline. The agency wanted Digital to block entry by known computer criminals and by people from nuclear proliferation countries. Engineering and legal experts created screening software, which the government approved. Three months after the aborted first launch, the Alphas went back online. Then Digital discovered a competitor logging on and running software that devoured memory and slowed the machines. Digital modified its screening software to block competitors, too. In the next 5 months, 3,000 people registered to use the computers. 100 new accounts registered each week. The computers average one prospect logging on every 4 minutes. In a survey, DEC found that 26 percent of people who tried Alpha bought one, generating more than $20 million in sales. (Note that it took a survey to discover this; Digital didn't track sales leads generated by its Test Drive promotion.)

Digital does a lot on the Net. It provides more than 9,000 documents and company software programs through FTP, plus another 300,000 public domain software programs. 20,000 documents a month are downloaded from its FTP archive of sales documents. Digital also uses the Internet to reduce customer support costs. On newsgroups, its customers solve the problems of other customers. Sixteen of Digital's newsgroups rank among the top ten percent in readership out of all 13,000 newsgroups. Its best-read group, **comp.sys.dec**, has 95,000 readers. Digital also uses mailing lists to distribute email press releases and a monthly electronic newsletter of product information.

Internet sales grow weekly for Digital. More and more customers prefer ordering online, even though the company offers no incentive to do so. "No extra discounts, coffee cups, pens, or bonus premiums," said Painter. Digital is improving its Net activities both to increase sales and to reduce costs. It implemented Activity-Based Cost Management (ABC), "tracking expenses and tying them to work with the idea of driving costs down," explained Painter, looking at, for example, "the cost of keying orders into a system, not the number of orders, not the number of line items. We home in on high-volume transactions and high-cost transactions." For companies starting out on the Net, Painter recommends that you "Start small. Start simple. Take your easiest product first, and your easiest customer set. Make that work extremely well. Then expand. That really works for us. It's a lot like any other business I've ever been in. The same things still apply. If you don't know who your customers are, you're not going to get much attention."

ever seen.) Visa lumps Internet merchants with mail order merchants. If your business has no retail storefront and accepts non-swipe transactions, Visa will want you to participate in its program called PCS2000 Customer Payment Service. When Visa announced PCS2000 in 1994, it promised to keep rates stable for PCS2000 participants at least through March 1997. It may soon implement a rate increase for Internet merchants who don't participate—the old carrot-and-stick approach. For many merchants, implementing Visa's requirements will mean major modifications to credit card processing systems. Check with the company that processes your Visa transactions to see what changes will affect your business.

If your company is in the software business, you might like to know about a special credit card company for your industry. SoftLock Services of Rochester, New York sells automatic processing of credit cards to software developers. It lets prospects try your software free, but some parts are locked. To use your entire program, your customer must pay first. For more information, email to **introlong@softlock.com**.

Payment on the Net is evolving rapidly. We have workable methods to handle it now, but we aren't even close to the final resolution. For the latest information on credit cards and payments over the Net, every month or so take a look at AT&T's Web site on electronic commerce: **http://www.research.att.com/ www-buyinfo/index.html**. AT&T's site includes searchable archives of a mailing list on electronic commerce and pointers to most important Web sites on the subject.

# Free Long-Distance Phone Calls on the Internet

"Watching the phone company look at the Internet
is like watching a dinosaur look at mice."
William Gibson

The Internet doesn't care what kind of data you send—as long as it's digitized. You can send text. You can send pictures. You can send software programs. And you can send *sound*.

Sending sound over the Net can save your business hundreds or thousands of dollars, because software is available now that lets you make long-distance telephone calls anywhere in the world for free—or at least for no extra cost beyond what you already pay your Internet access provider. Note that you aren't actually calling someone's *telephone*. Instead, your audio-equipped computer reaches out across the Internet to someone else's audio-equipped computer and your voices travel between the two computers.

Using the Internet for free phone calls is especially valuable if your business makes frequent long-distance calls to the same parties over and over again—to a branch office, for instance, or an important supplier or a frequent customer. In fact, some businesses buy the necessary software and give it free of charge to their frequent callees, because the money the businesses will save on long-distance fees dwarfs the small cost of the software ($30 to $100 per computer).

In addition to the inexpensive software, some hardware is required for making free phone calls over the Internet. The specific hardware you need depends on your computer. It is easier by far to set up a Macintosh computer for Internet phone calls. A second Macintosh advantage is that it delivers the best sound quality. As Charles Kline of the University of Illinois observed, "A Mac has better audio processing ability than a Sun." (This is true!) With a Windows PC, you will need a sound card and either a telephone headset (to listen and talk) or a loudspeaker (to listen) and a microphone (to talk). The type of PC sound card you need will vary, depending on which software program you use. Some programs require either an expensive duplex sound card or *two* 16-bit SoundBlaster-type cards. Some PC programs only need one SoundBlaster-type card. Macs have built-in duplex sound cards and built-in loudspeakers. Some Macs (specifically, the AV Macs) have built-in microphones, and others have a built-in socket where you can plug in a mike. Nothing else to add, nothing to configure.

Of course, no matter what brand of computer you use, you also need an Internet connection and a modem (for faster connections, the equivalent of a modem). In spite of manufacturers' claims to the contrary, you need at least a 14.4 Kbps connection and modem to get decent sound quality and response time. A 28.8 Kbps connection is more realistic, and a 56 Kbps ISDN connection is even better. If you access the Net through a shell account, stick to email. Phone calls are not practical over Internet shell accounts, no matter what manufacturers say.

# What to watch out for

When you evaluate Internet phone software, watch out for three problems:

## *1. Poor sound quality.*

One manufacturer used to claim its software sounded *better* than regular telephone calls. Nonsense. I have not heard an Internet phone call product that sounds as good as a regular phone call. Sound quality ranges from the equivalent of a hissy satellite call to listening to Marlon Brando on acid through a cardboard mailing tube. But, hey, the call's free, so it's worth the minor quality distractions. Regular two-way voice transmission generates a huge amount of data when digitized, more than even a fast ISDN connection can move and more than most computers can process. To avoid waiting a week for each sentence, Internet phone software compresses the digitized voices, sends them through the Net, and decompresses them at the other end. All sound compression routines lose some data, resulting in lower-quality sound. Quality varies tremendously depending on the software manufacturer. Some Internet phone software sounds far better than its competitors, and software companies improve compression quality almost every month.

When you consider Internet phone software, evaluate 1) the understandability of speech, 2) the amount of background noise and hiss, and 3) the amount of *dropouts*—quick, short silent patches in the middle of words and sentences, caused by the software losing data.

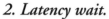

### 2. Latency wait.

When you make a regular long-distance phone call and your phone company routes your call through a satellite, you may have noticed that your conversation does not happen in real time. There is a short delay between when you speak and when the other party hears you, and an equal delay between when the other party talks and when you hear what was said. This delay is called *latency.*

For Internet phone software, the length of time you have to wait for latency is a factor of three things: the software you use, how fast the sending and receiving computers can process sound (Macs have an advantage here), and how fast the Internet is (including connection speeds—both yours and the other party's, as well as the speed of all the Net connections made between the two of you). Some software regularly produces latency waits of more than a second for each sentence. Other software reduces the delay to that of satellite phone calls.

### 3. Incompatibility.

Most phone software programs cannot talk with other manufacturers' phone software. This means that for right now, at least, if you want to call your best customer and you use DigiPhone software, your customer has to use DigiPhone, too. If your customer uses Internet VoiceChat, you are both out of luck. (Assured compatibility is another reason some businesses give software to their frequent callees.)

At present, incompatibility is the single biggest issue slowing the growth of Internet phone calls. (Even so, the growth rate is enormous. Slowing that growth may be a blessing in disguise, allowing more time for some much-needed infrastructure to evolve.) This will probably all be past us by mid-1996. I predict one of three possibilities. Maybe one of the Internet phone software products will achieve a dominant market share, forcing other manufacturers to be compatible with its format. Maybe a cross-industry standard will evolve. (There are steps in this direction with RTP, the Real-Time Protocol. RTP will be a big step forward when it is completed, but it still won't resolve all compatibility issues.) Or maybe Netscape will build phone call capabilities into its browser software, and everyone else will adopt its format or be left in the dust.

When you buy Internet phone software, always ask to see if the manufacturer plans to support any standard that evolves. For example, DigiPhone has publicly pledged to support RTP.

Note that I said "buy." There are free software programs that you can download from the Net to make phone calls, but using one for the heavier demands of your business would be like throwing Woody Allen into the ring against Mike Tyson. You'll be laughed at and beaten up. Don't be tempted to "save" money with software that won't do the job. Like everything else on the Net, this is subject to change, especially if a company of the caliber of Netscape starts giving away a more solid Internet phone program.

Use the list below to start your shopping. Prices are changing rapidly, so I haven't listed them. Manufacturers are adding new features and functions almost every month, so check with each manufacturer to find out what's new.

Also, look for phone software that is *full duplex*. Full duplex lets both parties talk. With *half duplex*, you must take turns, as you would do when using walkie-talkies: "Can you attend a meeting next Tuesday? Over."

## Commercial phone software

**DigiPhone.** As I write, DigiPhone has the best feature set for businesses. It is a Windows product, with Mac and OS/2 versions due shortly. In addition to full duplex telephone calls, DigiPhone supports caller ID, call screening, a personal phone book, voice mail (but only to other DigiPhone users), and multiple voicemail boxes. Some businesses may find it important that DigiPhone supports encrypted calls. It lets you plug in any encryption routine you want. DigiPhone has adjustable compression, so you can trade off for better sound quality versus shorter latency delays to suit your own taste. In addition to Internet phone calls, the product also runs on LANtastic and Novell NetWare local area networks, so you can use it to make phone calls within your LAN. It even runs on wide area networks, so it can act as a secure phone system for everyone on your WAN. Placing a call is simpler with

DigiPhone than with most other products. You just type in a person's email address. If your party is online, he or she receives a notice that your call has come in and your party can take it. If your party is not online, you can leave a text or voicemail message at your party's regular email address. A DigiPhone advantage over some other Windows products is that it can work with a standard SoundBlaster 16 sound card or its equivalent. DigiPhone does not require a more expensive full-duplex sound card. The product comes in two versions: DigiPhone and DigiPhone Deluxe. The Deluxe version includes call recording and playback (so you can save and replay your calls), conference calling, tools for programmers to add custom functions, plus a Web browser. I have not used this Web browser, but I have heard that it is simple and not useful. The hooks and tools for programmers, however, are a major advantage. For more information, email to **tdn@ordata.com** or Web-browse to **http://www.ikon.com/digiphone**.

**Internet Phone.** Manufactured by VocalTec Inc., this Windows product makes it as easy to answer an incoming call as DigiPhone does. Internet Phone runs in the background while other Windows programs are being used. When a call comes in for you, you hear a bell and a window pops up so you can answer it. Making outgoing calls is more cumbersome. If your party is not online, you can't leave a message, so many users schedule Internet Phone calls in advance. Internet Phone uses Internet Relay Chat (IRC) servers as phone directories. To make a call, you must go to a special IRC server, scroll down a list of people logged into that server, and choose one. Note that IRC does not carry your voice. It just acts as a telephone book. Your voice never goes to any IRC server, but the nuisance of going to an IRC server is not as easy as typing in someone's email address. Internet Phone works on LANs and on any TCP/IP network. It requires a duplex sound card or two regular 16-bit SoundBlaster-type cards. VocalTec aggressively pursues market share: Cirrus Logic Inc. has agreed to include this software with sound and modem chips it manufactures, Motorola will include it with its Power Class modems, and Netcom will build Internet Phone into its NetCruiser browser. This means that there should be a substantial number of users within a short time. A free demo version of Internet Phone lets you call and talk for one minute. For information, email to **info@vocaltec.com** or browse **http://www.vocaltec.com**.

**NetPhone.** This full-duplex product runs on Macs, with a Windows version due soon. It includes caller ID and call screening, and has a Call Alert feature that tells you when you have an incoming call. It handles multiple active calls (no busy signals). NetPhone uses GSM, the same format used for digital cellular phone calls in Europe. This lets NetPhone users call people who use other manufacturers' products that support GSM or VAT, including Maven, Vat, and CU-SeeMe. NetPhone's manufacturer, Electric Magic Company, sponsors *Netpubs*, where NetPhone users from around the world call in to chat. Netpubs are like floating conference calls, and can be useful in business for holding technical discussions and marketing meetings on the phone. Electric Magic makes its Netpub server software available for free. To make an outgoing call with NetPhone, you need to know the name or IP address of the computer you want to reach. This can be tricky for some people whose Internet connection is a SLIP or PPP account, because providers may assign them a different IP address each time they log on. A future release of NetPhone will take care of this by giving users a permanent address so they can be reached at one address, no matter what computer in the world they use. NetPhone runs native on Power Macs and plans to support RTP when RTP stabilizes. A free demo version of NetPhone limits calls to 1.5 minutes. For information, email **netphone-orders@emagic.com** or browse **http://www.emagic.com**. For a list of Netpubs, try **http://www.emagic.com/netphone/netpublist.html**.

**Internet VoiceChat.** Formerly a shareware product for Windows, this software was purchased by a telephone company and will shortly emerge in an enhanced form. One announced enhancement is to use built-in PC speakers, so no sound card will be required. VoiceChat includes caller screening, a caller history log, a built-in answering machine, and pop-up announcements that tell you when you receive an incoming call. The old version used IP addresses as phone numbers, making it easy to call out, but tricky for people to call you if you have a SLIP or PPP connection. The new version may fix this. The old version did not support conference calls. I have no email or Web address for Internet VoiceChat, but it does have its own newsgroup: **alt.winsock.ivc.**

# Free phone software

**Maven.** This full duplex Mac software allows understandable but noisy calls. It works best with a 28.8 Kbps or faster connection. For information , browse **http://pipkin.lut.ac.uk/~ben/video/maven.html** or send email to **listserv@cnidr.org** with the body of your message: **subscribe maven Yourfirstname Yourlastname**

**Voice Chat/2.** No relation to *Internet VoiceChat*, this OS/2 software is available from **http://cjb.ico.net/~dan/voicechat.html**.

**Powwow.** This Windows software uses URLs to make calls from Web pages. You would type **powwow:vince@emery.com** to reach me if both you and I were running Powwow. Email **feedback@tribal.com** or browse **http://www.tribal.com** for information.

**Internet Global Phone.** Not yet in release, this full duplex Windows product uses the same GSM compression scheme as DigiPhone, and may be compatible with it. Contact **ftp://ftp.cica.indiana/edu/pub/pc/win3** or **ftp://ftp.cica.indiana.edu:/win3/demos/IGP\*** for unfinished software and information.

**Vat.** This full-duplex Unix program was the very first software for making phone calls on the Net. Vat supports conference calls and runs on high-end workstations such as Sun Sparcstations, Silicon Graphics boxes and DECstation 5000. You can download software and documentation from **ftp://cs.ucl.ac.uk/mice/videoconference/vat**.

**NEVOT (Network Voice Terminal).** This Unix software is a joint project of AT&T Bell Labs and the GMD-Fokus of Germany. It uses several different compression routines so it can (theoretically) communicate with users of software by different manufacturers. NEVOT requires high-end workstations running SunOS 4.1, Solaris 2, Irix, or HP/UX. For information, browse **http://www.fokus.gmd.de/hgs/nevot**.

**Mtalk.** This experimental Linux program requires only a very slow Internet connection. Mtalk runs on PCs that run Linux and have a SoundBlaster-compatible sound card. For information, email **misch@elara.gsag.de** or **ftp://sunsite.unc.edu/pub/Linux/apps/sound/talk.**

**Ztalk.** This experimental Linux software includes voice mail capabilities. Email **feinmann@cs.mcgill.ca** or FTP **ftp://sunsite.unc.edu/pub/Linux/apps/sound/talk** for information.

## Q

## R

## S

*Usenet Book*, 81, 282
Usenet, 62, 81, 90, 101, 103. See also newsgroups
  creating your own Usenet newsgroup, 281-282
  defined, 21
  FAQ archive, 282
Usenet Marketplace FAQs, 305
U.S. West, 54
UUCP. *See* Unix-to-Unix Copy Protocol
Uuencode, 228

## V

Valjean, Jean (miserable kind of guy), 352-353, 354
Value-added network, 78, 410, 411, 413-414
VAN. *See* value-added network
Van de Moer, Solange (marketing expert), 252
VAX/VMS, Internet guide for, 100
Verifone, 193
Veronica (to find Gopher sites), 108, 297
ViaCrypt Products and PGP, 177
Videoconferencing, 36, 39, 57-58, 62. See also conferencing
*Videoconferencing, the Whole Picture*, 94
video newsletters, 224
Vincent, Patrick (author), 80-81, 89
Virtual cash. *See* digital money
Virtual money. *See* digital money
Virtual Private Data Networks, 173
Virtual reality software, 399
Virtual Web servers, 439-440
Viruses, 150, 182
  emergency response to, 195-197
  Internet Worm, 125, 151
  Trojan horse, 159
Virtual Library, 109, 299
Visa. *See also* credit cards
  NetBill, 193
  Web server software, 192
Voice/View, 39
VPDN. *See* Virtual Private Data Networks

## W

W3 Catalog of Web sites, 108, 299
WAIS. *See* Wide Area Information Server
WAIS Inc.
  design of DowVision Web site, 315, 316
*Wall Street Journal*, xix-xx, 182, 202, 330, 351
WAN. See wide area network
Washington & Lee Law Library, 364
Waterbug Records and net marketing, 308, 416
Watterson, Karen, 111
WaveRunner Digital Modem, 29
Web. *See* World Wide Web
WebChat, 40, 328, 402
Web Communications Corp., 317
WebConnect, 421
Webmaster, defined, 326
Web page,
  copyright notices for, 132-133
  design of 80-81, 313, 314
  storyboarding, 315, 316
  home page, defined, 313

how to license copyrighted material, 134-135
interactive forms, 315, 316
need to update often, 256-257
writing for, 312-313, 314, 325-326
popularity of different types of content, 314
Web server, 27, 39, 62, 65, 80, 260. *See also.* credit cards
  chat software for, 328
  compared to mail archive server, 287
  compared to print media, 311, 314
  compared to FTP server, 293
  compared to Gopher server, 309-310
  computers for, 52
  connection speed needed, 28-29, 45-46, 57
  converting documents to HTML, 327
  credit cards and, 151-152, 163, 191-192, 319
  Datapro analysis of successful, 315
  defined, 19
  design tips, 320-324
  distributing your FAQ on, 271
  flash crowds, 256
  free art for, 324
  hits yield misleading statistics, 352-354
  internal corporate servers, 312
  most browsers are Netscape, 191, 319
  most sites fail to generate desired response, 260
  need for multitasking, 28
  need to promote, 120-121, 260, 266, 296
  promote with a mailing list, 296
  example letter for new subscriber, 286
  promote by providing newsgroup archive, 281
  where to publicize, 296, 299
  Netsite Communications Server, 319
  Netsite Commerce Server, 191, 319-320
  order forms, 187, 315
  example, 316
  search tools for. *See* Harvest, WAIS
  security of, 151-152, 162-163, 166, 171
    list of secure server software, 191-192
    Secure HTTP, 191-192
    Secure Sockets Layer (SSL), 177, 191
  storyboarding, 315-317
  surveys, conducting via, 344-347
  ten steps to successful project, 139-142
  time required to manage, 122, 124
  value of statistics generated, 114-115
  writing tips, 314, 325-326
Web service bureaus, 315, 317-319, 438-440. See *also* Aspen Media, Web Communications Corp.
  can be located anywhere in the world, 317
  credit card processing and, 319-320
  evaluating, 318-319
  negotiating with, 318-319
  typical fees, 319
Web site, defined, 313-314. See also Web server.
*Webster* (magazine), 418
Welsh, Carol, 213
*West Coast Online*, 87
What's New page, 6, 107, 299
What's New in Japan, 108, 299
What's on the Internet, 90